JUDICIAL REVIEW AND ELECTORAL LAW IN A GLOBAL PERSPECTIVE

This book fills a gap in the literature on constitutional law by examining the global trend towards the substantive constitutional adjudication of electoral legislation. It explores the premises on which this judicial scrutiny is grounded, seeks to explain the trend, and examines its consequences for representative democracy.

The book offers a comparative analysis of the issue, investigating how the exchange of models and arguments among judges has catalysed the progressive departure from a traditionally deferential approach to electoral norms – an approach that still persists in a few jurisdictions.

To accomplish this, the book delves into the democratic foundations of electoral systems and their evolution. It also explores the methodological choices that constitutional judges face when dealing with electoral legislation. This groundwork sets the stage for an in-depth review of case law in more than 15 legal systems spanning North and South America, Africa, Asia, Oceania and Europe. The objective is to identify the underlying concept of democracy that courts aim to promote. The authors critically discuss the varying ideas of democracy evident in each jurisdiction, including the use of constitutional borrowing, and they analyse the effects of judgments on the relationship between courts, representative institutions and voters.

Given its global scope, the combination of theoretical and practical approaches, and the comprehensive comparative assessment it provides, this work is of interest to academics in the fields of law, political science and philosophy. It is also relevant for policymakers and judges in constitutional democracies across the continents.

Volume 31 in the series Hart Studies in Comparative Public Law

Hart Studies in Comparative Public Law

Recent titles in this series:

Soft Law and Public Authorities
Remedies and Reform
Greg Weeks

Legitimate Expectations in the Common Law World
Edited by Matthew Groves and Greg Weeks

The Dynamics of Exclusionary Constitutionalism
Mazen Masri

Constitutional Courts, Gay Rights and Sexual Orientation Equality
Angioletta Sperti

Australian Constitutional Values
Edited by Rosalind Dixon

Human Rights in the UK and the Influence of Foreign Jurisprudence
Hélène Tyrrell

The Nordic Constitutions
Edited by Helle Krunke and Björg Thorarensen

Regulation in India
Design, Capacity, Performance
Edited by Devesh Kapur and Madhav Khosla

New Media and Freedom of Expression
Rethinking the Constitutional Foundations of the Public Sphere
András Koltay

Why Religious Freedom Matters for Democracy
Comparative Reflections from Britain and France for a
Democratic 'Vivre Ensemble'
Myriam Hunter-Henin

The Role of Monarchy in the Modern Democracy:
European Monarchies Compared
Edited by Robert Hazell and Bob Morris

Responsible Government and the Australian Constitution:
A Government for a Sovereign People
Benjamin B Saunders

Federalism and the Rights of Persons with Disabilities:
The Implementation of the CRPD in Federal Systems and its Implications
Edited by Delia Ferri, Francesco Palermo and Giuseppe Martinico

Constitutional Courts, Media and Public Opinion
Angioletta Sperti

Judicial Review and Electoral Law in a Global Perspective

Edited by
Cristina Fasone
Edmondo Mostacci
and
Graziella Romeo

•HART•
OXFORD • LONDON • NEW YORK • NEW DELHI • SYDNEY

HART PUBLISHING

Bloomsbury Publishing Plc

Kemp House, Chawley Park, Cumnor Hill, Oxford, OX2 9PH, UK

1385 Broadway, New York, NY 10018, USA

29 Earlsfort Terrace, Dublin 2, Ireland

HART PUBLISHING, the Hart/Stag logo, BLOOMSBURY and the Diana logo are trademarks of Bloomsbury Publishing Plc

First published in Great Britain 2024

A catalogue record for this book is available from the British Library.

Library of Congress Cataloging-in-Publication data

Names: Fasone, Cristina, editor. | Mostacci, Edmondo, editor. | Romeo, Graziella, editor.

Title: Judicial review and electoral law in a global perspective / edited by Cristina Fasone, Edmondo Mostacci, and Graziella Romeo.

Description: Oxford ; New York : Hart Publishing, 2024. | Series: Hart studies in comparative public law ; volume 31 | Includes bibliographical references and index. | Summary: "This book fills a gap in constitutional law by investigating the global trend towards substantive constitutional adjudication of electoral legislation. On what premises is this judicial scrutiny grounded, what can explain the trend, and with what consequences for representative democracy? Given the global reach, the combination of theoretical and practical approaches, and the comparative assessment provided, this work is of interest for academics in the field of law, political science and philosophy, and for policy-makers and judges in constitutional democracies across the continents"—Provided by publisher.

Identifiers: LCCN 2023048575 (print) | LCCN 2023048576 (ebook) | ISBN 9781509957880 (hardback) | ISBN 9781509957927 (paperback) | ISBN 9781509957897 (Epub) | ISBN 9781509957903 (ebook)

Subjects: LCSH: Election law. | Judicial review. | Constitutional courts. | Courts of last resort. | Representative government and representation. | Democracy.

Classification: LCC K3293 .J83 2024 (print) | LCC K3293 (ebook) | DDC 342/.07—dc23/eng/20231018

LC record available at https://lccn.loc.gov/2023048575

LC ebook record available at https://lccn.loc.gov/2023048576

ISBN: HB: 978-1-50995-788-0
ePDF: 978-1-50995-790-3
ePub: 978-1-50995-789-7

Typeset by Compuscript Ltd, Shannon

Foreword

Back in 2004, I published a lengthy article, entitled *The Constitutionalization of Democratic Politics*,[1] as the *Harvard Law Review's* major reflection on the United States Supreme Court's most recent Term. A major aim was to bring wider attention to a fundamental transformation in the nature of judicial review and the role of constitutional courts that had begun in the US in the 1960s, a role that by the 2000s was becoming more and more prominent – not just in the US, but in courts around the world.

Before the 1960s, at least in the US, much of our Supreme Court's role in the area of constitutionalism centred on defining the boundaries of political authority between the various institutions of government: state v. national government, state v. state, Congress v. the President. Beginning in the twentieth century, the Court also began to protect individual constitutional rights and, eventually, ensure equal protection of the laws. Similarly, with the rise of post-World War II constitutionalism, constitutional courts in many countries also took on the role of protecting fundamental rights and ensuring equality under the law.

But before the 1960s, constitutional courts did not define as a major aspect of their role the oversight of the structures and processes of democratic politics itself. Indeed, to the contrary: in the US, the courts dismissed such efforts by holding that claims about 'political rights' were off-limits to the courts – not the appropriate subject of judicial review. To be sure, in countries in which post-World War II constitutions explicitly banned anti-democratic practices or political parties, such as in Germany, constitutional courts enforced these specific bans. But absent such specific textual guidance, courts did not generally understand it to be their role to determine the normatively appropriate principles and foundations for democratic politics.

In the US, that conception changed dramatically in the 1960s. As the Supreme Court became more aware of the tendency of those temporarily in power to try to leverage that power to insulate themselves from the forces of legitimate democratic competition, the Court concluded it could no longer refrain from addressing claims concerning 'political rights'. In broad constitutional provisions, the Court began to find constraints on the ability of legislatures to manipulate democratic institutions and processes, such as the design of election districts or voting rules. By the time of John Hart Ely's highly influential book,

[1] RH Pildes, *The Constitutionalization of Democratic Politics The Supreme Court 2003 Term – Foreword* (2004) 118 *Harvard Law Review* 29.

Democracy and Distrust,[2] in 1981, a profound conceptual shift had taken place: now, for many judges, academics, and advocates, ensuring that democratic institutions and processes remained sufficiently open and free from illegitimate manipulation had become one of the principal justifications for the institution of judicial review itself. And by 2000, that conception had expanded to the point that the Supreme Court played a major role in resolving our 2000 presidential election – a role unimaginable 40 years earlier.

Part of my aim in 2004 was also to suggest that the US Supreme Court's new conception of the judicial role was becoming influential among other constitutional courts. At the time, I noted actions from courts in Ireland, Australia, Spain, Turkey, India, Israel, Canada, Germany, and the European Court of Human Rights, all of which had issued major decisions taking on the role of judging the normative foundations of their democratic systems. This volume now shows how much farther that judicial project has developed over the last generation. It presents the most comprehensive exploration of how courts around the world now address a broad range of issues concerning the legitimate framework within which democratic politics occurs.

Yet the challenges facing courts and democracies today are far greater than they were a generation ago. When I wrote in 2004, I called it 'The Age of Democracy', with the number of democracies having doubled since 1985, all of which were structured as constitutional democracies. Ironically, though, that turned out to be democracy's high point. Starting in 2006, the number of countries classified as democracies began to decline, according to various measures. By 2021, the number of liberal democracies had regressed to the number that existed in 1989, on the eve of the break-up of the former Soviet Union. In several countries, the independence of constitutional courts has come under attack or been effectively neutered.

The question of the relationship of constitutional courts to democracy now has a strikingly different tenor. The stakes have become much higher. We know that courts in some post-1989 democracies have not been able to fend off government attacks on their independence. In a populist age of impatience with institutional barriers to pure majoritarian control, how well will courts in more established democracies be able to fend off such attacks, should they occur? The authority of courts, like that of political elites more generally, is under greater challenge today. Where will public opinion side in such confrontations? In addition to more aggressive efforts to undermine judicial independence, some democratically-elected governments have become more aggressive in their efforts to manipulate or change the rules of the game to tilt elections in their favour. How far can courts go in striking down such measures without provoking a major political backlash?

[2] JH Ely, *Democracy and Distrust: A Theory of Judicial Review* (1981) , www.hup.harvard.edu/catalog.php?isbn=9780674196377 (last accessed 4 April 2020).

For several decades after courts re-defined their role to include policing of the democratic process itself, the risk of constitutional crisis between the political branches and the courts seemed a more theoretical concern. That risk has become more concrete. The future of judicial review over the foundations of democracy has become more uncertain.

Richard H Pildes
Sudler Family Professor of Constitutional Law
NYU School of Law

Contents

Contributors

Erika Arban is Senior Research Associate (Honorary) at Melbourne Law School, and Adjunct Professor at the University of Milan Statale. Her research interests include comparative constitutional law and theory, with a focus on federalism and legal methodology. Erika is the co-convenor of the IACL research group *New Frontiers of Federalism*, and comments editor of *Comparative Constitutional Studies.* Her most recent publications include *Italian Regionalism and the Federal Challenge: Reconciling Economic Regionalism and Solidarity* (Palgrave, 2023) and *Cities in Federal Constitutional Theory* (OUP, 2022).

Elisa Bertolini is Associate Professor of Comparative Public Law at Bocconi University, Milan. Her fields of research include Japanese constitutional law, constitutional systems of microstates, freedom of expression and Internet governance. She is the author of monographs, essays, and articles in Italian, French, Spanish, and English.

Eleonora Bottini is Full Professor of Public Law at University of Caen Normandy and Associate Director of the Caen Institute of Legal Research. She is also Martin-Flynn Global Professor of Law at University of Connecticut (2023–25 appointment). Her research interests include Comparative Constitutional Law and methodology, Legal Theory, French Public Law, Jurisprudence and Legal Reasoning, and Human Rights Law. The author of a monograph on constitutional sanctions (Dalloz, 2016), she is currently leading a project on constitutional 'landmark' judgments.

Robert Bray is a former head of secretariat of the European Parliament's Legal Affairs Committee and a member of the Council of the European Law Institute. As a lawyer and a linguist, he also worked in private industry and for the Court of Justice of the European Communities, the European Economic and Social Committee and the Bank for International Settlements. He has a particular interest in legislative drafting, quality of legislation, private international law, comparative law and parliamentary immunity.

Sarah Burton is PhD candidate, Faculty of Law, at the University of Ottawa.

Giacomo Delledonne is Assistant Professor of Constitutional Law, Dirpolis, Sant'Anna School of Advanced Studies, Pisa, and since 2022 is the holder of the Jean Monnet Module 'ENACTING – European Values in Context: Challenges and Comparative Insights'. He has published extensively in French, English,

German, Italian and Spanish and has authored two monographs, on constitutional homogeneity in composite legal systems (Editoriale Scientifica, 2017) and on constitutions and electoral legislation in comparative perspective (Editoriale Scientifica, 2019).

Rekha Diwakar is Senior Lecturer in Politics at the University of Sussex. Before joining Sussex, she was Lecturer in Politics and Research Methods at Goldsmiths College, University of London. Her research interests include Indian politics and public policy, comparative politics, especially electoral competition and voting behaviour, size of the party systems and research methods in political science. On those topics she has published extensively, including a monograph on *Party System in India* (OUP, 2017).

Cristina Fasone is Associate Professor of Comparative Public Law at Luiss University (Italy), where she is also the Director of the BA in 'Politics, Philosophy, and Economics', and Visiting Professor at Nicolaus Copernicus University of Toruń. Co-coordinator of the IACL Research Group on 'Judicial Review and Electoral Law', she has recently published 'The Constitutional Role of Independent Fiscal Institutions in the Eurozone', *German Law Journal* (2022) and 'Fighting back? The Role of the European Parliament in the Adoption of Next Generation EU', *The Journal of Legislative Studies* (2022).

Berihun Adugna Gebeye is Lecturer in Law, Faculty of Laws, at University College London and a Visiting Professor at the Department of Legal Studies of Central European University in Vienna. His research interests focus on comparative constitutional law, constitutional theory, human rights, and international law. He has published on several top-ranked international legal journals and is the author of the book *A Theory of African Constitutionalism* (OUP, 2021).

Bastian Michel is a PhD Candidate in Constitutional Law, Faculty of Law, at the University of Amsterdam, and the managing editor of the European Constitutional Law Review. His research focuses on the remuneration of members of Parliament, electoral law and other aspects of the constitution of politics.

Edmondo Mostacci is Associate Professor of Comparative Law at University of Genova (Italy). His research interests focus on the intertwining of institutions, democratic processes and economic and social dynamics. His most recent publications include 'Il diritto pigro. Appunti per una metodologia di analisi del testo giuridico quale macchina presupposizionale corale', *Diritto pubblico comparato ed europeo* (2021), on the use of semiotics in the comparative analysis of legal systems.

Julian R Murphy holds a PhD from the University of Melbourne, School of Law, and an LLM from Columbia Law School. He is a barrister at the Victorian Bar.

Lucas H Muniz Conceição is a PhD student in Legal Studies (International and European Law curriculum) at Bocconi University. He holds an LLM/MA degree in Constitutional Politics, Law & Theory (summa cum laude) from Birkbeck College, University of London and an LL.B from the Federal University of Parana. His research interests lie in comparative public law, constitutional theory and the constitutional implications of the regulation of new technologies.

Michael Pal is Associate Professor, Faculty of Law, University of Ottawa. He has advised all levels of government in Canada on matters relating to election law and constitutional law. In 2017 he served as a Commissioner with the Far North Electoral Boundaries Commission for the Province of Ontario. His research focuses primarily on the law of democracy, comparative constitutional law, and election law. He publishes regularly in law, political science, and public policy in top-ranked international journals and he is the co-editor of *Cyber-Threats to Canadian Democracy* (McGill-Queen's, 2022).

Pasquale Pasquino has been Senior Fellow at the CNRS in Paris and is Global Distinguished Professor at New York University and Professor at Luiss School of Government. Before joining the CNRS and NYU he worked at the Max-Planck-Institut für Geschichte – Göttingen, at the Collège de France, Paris, and at King's College – Cambridge. He published notably a book on Emmanuel Sieyès and the invention of modern constitutionalism in France and numerous articles on the history and theory of state, on constitutionalism, constitutional adjudication and the political systems in Germany, France, England and Italy.

Paolo Passaglia is Full Professor of Comparative Law, University of Pisa and is *Pro-tempore* scientific coordinator of the Comparative Law Area of the Research Department, Constitutional Court of the Italian Republic. His work focuses on constitutional adjudication, sources of law and fundamental rights' protection, the French constitutional system, on which he has published extensively in Italian, French, and English. His latest book deals with the abolition of the death penalty (Leo S. Olschki, 2021).

Richard H Pildes is Sudler Family Professor of Constitutional Law, NYU Law School. He has been elected into the American Academy of Arts and Sciences and the American Law Institute. President Biden appointed him to the President's Commission on the Supreme Court of the United States. His acclaimed casebook, *The Law of Democracy* (6th edn, 2022), created an entirely new field of study in the law schools. Most recently, he has written about the challenges facing democracies across the West, the neglect in legal and political theory of the value of effective government, the role of the Supreme Court in overseeing American democracy, and the dysfunctions of the American political process. His work has been translated into Chinese, French, Spanish, and Portuguese.

Graziella Romeo is Associate Professor of Comparative Constitutional Law at Bocconi University in Milan (Italy), where she is also stream lead of the Lab for European Studies. She co-coordinates the IACL Research Group on 'Judicial Review and Electoral Law'. Her research interests lie in constitutional theory and comparative law. Her most recent publications include 'The Conceptualization of Constitutional Supremacy: Global Discourse and Legal Tradition', *German Law Journal* (2020) and *A Material Understanding of Constitutional Changes: Revisiting 'Constitutional Maintenance' Doctrines*, in the Cambridge handbook of the material constitution (CUP, 2023).

Jan Sawicki holds a PhD in Theory of the State and Comparative Political Institutions, from the University of Rome 'La Sapienza'. He has taught Public Law and Comparative Public Law at the University of Milan, at Università Cattolica del Sacro Cuore, and at the University of Rome La Sapienza. His research focuses on the constitutional systems of central and eastern Europe, on the law-making function, and on 'illiberal democracies', to which he has devoted hist latest book (Franco Angeli, 2020).

Irene Spigno is General Director of the Inter-American Academy of Human Rights of the Autonomous University of Coahuila (Mexico). She works, under a comparative constitutional perspective, on freedom of expression, cultural rights and minority rights, women' rights, multiculturalism. On those topics, she has published extensively in Italian, Spanish, and English. In 2018, she published a monograph on the regulation of hate speech in comparative perspective (Giuffrè) and, in 2023, she co-authored a textbook on comparative constitutional law for Latin America (Tirant lo Blanch, in Spanish).

Emmanuel Voyakis is Professor of Law at LSE Law School. His main areas of research are private law (contract and tort) doctrines, how they should be understood and applied, and public international law especially the role of normative propositions in determining what international law requires or allows. He has published widely on those topics, including a monograph on *Private Law and the Value of Choice* (Hart Publishing, 2017).

Bob Watt is a retired Professor of Law, University of Buckingham; sometime Head of School of Law, University of Essex. He has been Visiting Fellow of the Bonavero Institute of Human Rights, University of Oxford (2017–18). An international expert in electoral law and reforms; he has published extensively, including *UK Election Law: A Critical Examination* (Routledge, 2006). More recently he has written for the UK Electoral Commission, submitted evidence to the UK Government, the Fawcett Society, and *Senedd Cymru*.

Davide Zecca is post-doctoral research fellow in Comparative Public Law at the University of Milan (Italy). He has published articles in Italian and English about the role of judges and lawmakers in the regulation of political processes and the limitation of the access to suffrage, especially in the US. He recently published 'Tutela costituzionale della segretezza delle comunicazioni ed evoluzione tecnologica. Uno studio comparato' (Editoriale Scientifica, 2023) about the development of prophylactic rules for criminal proceedings by constitutional courts.

1

Introduction

CRISTINA FASONE, EDMONDO MOSTACCI AND GRAZIELLA ROMEO

I. THE CONTEXT

Electoral legislation is characterised by a deep political nature, both creating and shaping the representative bond linking voters and elected representatives. It lies at the heart of the model of representation embodied by political institutions. Yet, over the last few years we have witnessed the increasing engagement of constitutional judges with electoral matters; a phenomenon that raises important constitutional questions ranging from the place of electoral rules in constitutional adjudication to the ability of courts to manage electoral norms and even the desirability of such a trend.

Indeed, from a historical perspective, the relationship between electoral processes and courts has been anything but easy. Both ordinary and administrative judges had been traditionally deprived of the power to review electoral laws particularly in relation to the national Parliament's election. Furthermore, some courts embraced the theory of the speciality of electoral litigation (the so-called theory of the *Act politique* developed by the French administrative jurisdiction). Even within systems generally keen on the idea of judicial review of legislation, courts for many years tended neither to scrutinise electoral legislation nor to rule on the electoral formula or other technical features. For example, the US Supreme Court was proved, until 1962, to have a deferent attitude towards the Congress when coming to electoral legislation. Likewise, in *Baker v Carr*, in his vibrant dissenting opinion, Justice Frankfurter harshly criticised the new activism of the court in malapportionment cases.[1]

Against this backdrop, the deferential approach to electoral legislation and political choices progressively faded away in the great majority of the systems of the western legal tradition, even though that happened in different moments in time from country to country.[2]

[1] 369 U.S. 186.

[2] See, eg, Bundesverfassungsgericht, ruling no 3/11 of 25 July 2017; the Italian Constitutional Court's judgments nos 1/2014 and 35/2017; French Conseil Constitutionnel's decisions no 2008-573 DC of 8 January 2009 and 2010-602 DC of 18 February 2010.

This development led comparative constitutional scholars to explore novel research questions or to reflect on them from a new perspective. The aim of the present volume is, thus, to engage with the following paths of investigation bringing to the fore the idea(s) of democracy that constitutional adjudication on electoral matters embraces: 1) On which conditions and on which premises may (and do) constitutional judges scrutinise electoral laws? 2) What is the 'idea of democracy' that the electoral case law seeks to advance? 3) Is such an intrusive constitutional scrutiny needed and desirable to better safeguard the representative model or does it amount to an overreach of the courts' remit?

The volume has been developed within the Research group on Judicial Review and Electoral Law that the editors have established under the aegis of the International Association of Constitutional Law (IACL). This volume brings together research findings that have undergone extensive deliberation among contributors on various occasions. The journey commenced with a workshop at Bocconi University in 2018. Over the course of two years, the research group expanded its comparative scope, culminating in discussions about its advancements at the Global Summit hosted by the International Forum on the Future of Constitutionalism and sponsored by the Constitutional Studies Program at the University of Texas at Austin in 2021. Eventually, in December 2022, the forthcoming chapters were unveiled during the IACL's annual conference at University of Johannesburg Faculty of Law.

The volume represents the first comprehensive comparative study engaging with the progressive rise of a more pervasive judicial constitutional scrutiny towards electoral legislation and it reflects on its causes and consequences. It explores the ideas of democracy, focusing extensively on the fundamental elements of electoral legislation as shaping the relation between representative institutions and political community.

Electoral systems are not extensively studied by constitutional lawyers and when constitutional analyses are carried out, they typically focus on a national experience or on a specific region of the world.[3]

Remarkable is the activity of the European Commission for Democracy through Law in this field in compiling a list of good practices on electoral issues,[4] drawing on national experts from 61 countries. However, its elaboration remains at the level of official documents and recommendations, without entailing an in-depth reflection on the cross-country variations of the same mechanism and the domestic constitutional implications of allowing a great discretion to the political decision-makers or to constitutional judges. There are a few exceptions to this assessment on the lack of comparative constitutional studies,[5] but even

[3] See, eg, JA Douglas and E Mazo (eds), *Election Law Stories* (Saint Paul, MN, Foundation Press, 2016); G Delledonne, *Costituzione e legge elettorale. Un percorso comparatistico nello Stato costituzionale europeo* (Napoli, Editoriale Scientifica, 2019).

[4] European Commission for Democracy through Law (Venice Commission), Code of Good Practice in Electoral Matters, Opinion no 190/2002, CDL-AD(2002)023rev2-cor, as revised on 25 October 2018.

[5] See, eg, R Pildes, S Issacharoff and PS Karlan, *The Law of Democracy: Legal Structure of the Political Process*, 5th edn (Saint Paul, MN, Foundation Press, 2016) (1st edn, 1998); R Albert and

in these cases the focus is not eminently on constitutional adjudication and on the (new in this field) problematic interplay between courts and legislatures on the electoral rules.

Indeed, studies on electoral law tend to be focused on regulatory and technical aspects of the electoral formulas and systems,[6] while this volume distinguishes itself for being essentially devoted to the role of the constitutional adjudication on electoral laws and on the 'ideas of democracy' underpinning this judicial scrutiny.

All in all, this book aims to contribute to the literature on electoral law and on comparative constitutional adjudication from three perspectives, at least. First, it will trace and critically assess the rise of a more intruding approach of constitutional review on electoral legislation through classical instruments of constitutional theory, notably constitutional interpretation and models of constitutional adjudication in both the institutional and the argumentative perspective. Second, it will shed light on the conditions under which this form of judicial activism is put in place, ie, how it is justified, for instance by resorting to foreign models and case law and/or benefitting from alternative 'ideas of democracy'. Third, it will elaborate on the consequences of the new activist trend in the electoral case law on the relationship between citizens and representatives and the role of courts in constitutional democracies, when they are called to decide on the ultimate rules for the democratic participation in the political life. With this regard the contributions are also instrumental to foster a reflection on the suitability of courts to replace or supplement the activity of policymakers in electoral matters and to better understand the risks of such a practice for the courts' legitimacy and for the development of a balanced relationship between judicial and political actors in a stage of global democratic retrenchment and constitutional retrogression.

II. CONCEPTUAL FRAMEWORK AND METHODOLOGY

The conceptual frame of analysis relies on the 'ideas of democracy' stemming from constitutional adjudication of electoral law, that is on the fundamental elements of electoral legislation as the basic junction in the relationship between representative institutions and political community.

Courts can engage with a variety of ideas of democracy across space and time, for example connected to procedural[7] or substantive[8] views of democracy

M Pal (eds), 'Symposium on Electoral Reform in Constitutional Democracies' (2017) 16 *Election Law Journal* 263–71.

[6] See, recently, D Schulz and J Toplak (eds), *Routledge Handbook of Election Law*, 1st edn (London, Routledge, 2022).

[7] From different angles, see JA Schumpeter, *Capitalism, Socialism and Democracy* (New York, Harper & Row, 1942) and H Kelsen, 'Foundations of Democracy' (1955) 66 *Ethics* 1–101.

[8] A Pitkin, *The Concept of Representation* (Berkeley, University of California Press, 1967) and LR Jacobs and RY Shapiro, 'Studying Substantive Democracy' (1994) 27 *Political Science and Politics*, 9–17.

and linked, but not limited to, democracies and polyarchies,[9] electoral democracies, 'illiberal' regimes v constitutional democracies, and majoritarian and consensus democracies.[10] In a constitutional system, such an idea of democracy can change or can remain consistent over time, sometimes even when the electoral rules are amended.

The fact that courts on a global scale carry out an increasingly 'intrusive' judicial scrutiny of electoral laws and the reasoning used in terms of idea(s) of democracy inevitably trigger important consequences on constitutional democracies, fragile democracies and on those systems experiencing a democratic backsliding. The consequences of this development affect the entrenchment and legitimacy of democratic institutions, the role of courts and case law, the people's attachment and confidence in institutions and, ultimately, voters' turnout. Moreover, wider socio-economic implications are at stake. As it is well known, indeed, not only the choices of representative institutions on electoral law and the outputs of elections, but also the attitude and activism of the courts has an effect on the evaluations of economic operators and élites (courts that, in turn, are influenced by them).[11] For example, the level of electoral stability, which can be affected by too far-reaching interventions of courts in the electoral realm, can also impact on the level of foreign investments collected in a country.[12]

In order to identify the concept of democracy, which inspires constitutional judges' approach at domestic and supranational level, the focus of the analysis will be both on disputes linked to allegations of fundamental rights' violations as well as on the mechanic and dynamic of the electoral system and of the electoral formula in particular. The level of detail of the constitutional provisions regulating electoral matters appear of the utmost importance here. Indeed, the moving away from the traditional courts' restraint in electoral matters seems more likely to occur where the court is able to draw from the constitutional yardstick precise indications on the expected relationship between voters and representatives and on the nature of the political representation envisaged by the Constitution. It cannot be denied, however, that judicial activism is often triggered by several concurring factors, not originating just from within the courts, but linked to the 'constitutional environment' in which courts operate.

[9] RA Dahl, *A Preface to Democratic Theory* (Chicago, The University of Chicago Press, 1956) and RA Dahl, *Democracy and its Critics* (New Haven, Yale University Press, 1989).

[10] A Lijphart, *Patterns of Democracy: Government Forms and Performance in Thirty-Six Countries* (New Haven, CT, Yale University Press, 1999).

[11] See, notably, R Hirschl, *Towards Juristocracy. The Origins and Consequences of the New Constitutionalism* (Cambridge, MA, Harvard University Press, 2007).

[12] On the weight of political stability on foreign investments see MD Amore and M Corina, 'Political elections and corporate investment: International evidence' (2021) 52 *Journal of International Business Studies* 1775–96.

The patent poor quality and internal inconsistency of the electoral legislation, a highly fragmented and conflictual political system that makes the legislature unable to decide and to amend the electoral legislation, the serious threat of a rule of law and democratic backsliding pursued by the government through the electoral law are all factors that may explain the new course of action by so many courts.

Relatedly, the progressive overcoming of traditionally deferent approaches as a global trend now has also been the result of a fruitful circulation of models and arguments between constitutional judges: substantial similarities in the criteria used by different jurisdictions when scrutinising domestic electoral law can be detected and constitutional judges are increasingly resorting to explicit and/or implicit references to previous decisions of foreign courts. For example, the principle of equality has been widely used by the US Supreme Court, the German and Italian Constitutional Courts.

At the same time, there are outliers to this global trend, for example Japan (with some caveats), not by chance where constitutional provisions remain vague on electoral matters and where courts are not willing to cite foreign precedents and foreign law in general.

Differences in domestic electoral legislation and the peculiarities of each constitutional and political system make things problematic for a comparative inquiry. Indeed, an analysis aimed at outlining similarities and differences in the courts' case law requires an appropriate methodology meant to identify the level of the comparative analysis. Otherwise, any similarity, which may be found, would be a mere insight, not helpful at tracing a global path going beyond the mere juxtaposition of national experiences.

The proposed volume embraces an innovative research methodology by limiting differences that emanate from specific circumstances of each national experience. To do so, the methodology, common to all contributions, will require each legal system under investigation to explore the following main issues: a) the 'ideas of democracy' embraced by the electoral legislation and by the constitutional interpreters. To this end it will be important to consider the 'original intent' of the legislatures when the electoral legislation was designed and if any clear direction is provided under the Constitution with this regard; b) the substantial yardsticks and the standards of review developed by those Courts when they adjudicate matters on electoral laws; c) the detailed analysis of the judicial reasonings of domestic (and supranational) courts, highlighting the arguments they advance and their consistency over time; d) considering if any 'cross-judicial fertilisation' can be detected and, in case, whether it provides a further justification for a more intrusive constitutional scrutiny of electoral law; and e) the reception of the electoral case law in the political system, both on the relations between voters and representatives and on the role of courts vis-à-vis representative institutions.

III. OBJECT(S) OF INVESTIGATION

The book speaks to the copious literature on judicial activism, constitutional interpretation and their limits,[13] on the judicialisation of politics,[14] and on the complex relationship between constitutional judges, parliamentary democracy and representative institutions.[15] It adds to this scholarship by bringing into such a debate the challenging perspective of electoral law. Indeed, while the role of constitutional adjudicators tends, by definition, to be problematic from a democratic standpoint (as for the composition, appointment and source of legitimacy of the courts), this is even more the case for the electoral field under investigation – by definition in the realm of politics – which is the basis of the ordered legitimate functioning of a democratic community.

At the same time, addressing the validity and entrenchment of the ultimate rules governing representative democracy, the volume will also engage with the important strand of scholarship dealing with the crisis of constitutional democracies and the rule of law backsliding.[16] Much has been written on the crucial role of courts, as guarantor of constitutional democracies,[17] but also as targets of 'illiberal constitutionalism' and of populist attacks against their independence.[18] This book highlights the inherent tension in the work of constitutional judges by using electoral law as an illustrative case study: on the one hand, courts are asked to 'save' constitutional democracies, when in danger or under pressure, and, at least, to protect their liminal functioning as electoral democracies, which is a necessary, yet not sufficient condition to ensure the enforcement of liberal constitutional values; on the other hand, courts may be accused of overstepping their powers if they enter into the 'political realm' of the electoral rules and of parliamentary procedures in general.[19]

[13] See the seminal works by A Bickel, *The Least Dangerous Branch: The Supreme Court at the Bar of Politics* (Indianapolis, The Bobbs-Merrill Co Inc, 1962), JH Ely, *Democracy and Distrust. A Theory of Judicial Review* (Cambridge, MA, Harvard University Press, 1980) and by Hirschl (n 11).

[14] M Shapiro and A Stone Sweet, *On Law, Politics, and Judicialization* (Oxford, Oxford University Press, 2002).

[15] See, for different angles, A Stone Sweet, 'Constitutional Courts and Parliamentary Democracy' (2002) 25(1) *West European Politics* 77–100; S Gardbaum, *The New Commonwealth Model of Constitutionalism. Theory and Practice* (Cambridge, Cambridge University Press, 2013); G Webber et al, *Legislated Rights. Securing Human Rights through Legislation* (Cambridge, Cambridge University Press, 2018).

[16] See, amongst many, MA Graber, S Levinson and M Tushnet (eds), *Constitutional Democracy in Crisis?* (New York, Oxford University Press, 2018); T Ginsburg and AZ Huq, *How to Save a Constitutional Democracy* (Chicago, The University of Chicago Press, 2019); M Loughlin, 'The Contemporary Crisis of Constitutional Democracy' (2019) 39 *OJLS* 435–54.

[17] See, eg, S Issacharoff, *Fragile Democracies. Contested Power in the Era of Constitutional Courts* (New York, Cambridge University Press, 2015).

[18] See W Sadurski, *Poland's Constitutional Breakdown* (Oxford, Oxford University Press, 2019) and G Halmai, 'Rights Revolution and Counter-Revolution: Democratic Backsliding and Human Rights in Hungary' (2020) 14 *Law & Ethics of Human Rights* 97–123.

[19] Y Roznai, 'Constitutional Paternalism: The Israeli Supreme Court as Guardian of the Knesset' (2018) 51 *Verfassung und Recht in Übersee* 415–36.

The collection aims to improve the knowledge of how the ultimate rules of a democratic regime, ie, the electoral rules, are set and work, more and more often with the involvement of constitutional judges, at state and at supranational level. At the same time, the in-depth comparative analysis offered may foster the predictability of judicial decision-making concerning electoral legislation by advancing knowledge of the conditions under which courts tend to be more active on electoral matters, on which grounds and arguments.

To ensure that these objectives are reached the book offers insights from the five continents, paying specific attention to western and constitutional democracies and especially to European democracies (both at domestic and at supranational level), where the trend towards an increasing judicialisation of electoral rules is more evident. It also includes case studies from Asia, South America and Africa, where either the courts have kept a traditionally deferent approach (Japan), have actively supported their visions of democracy (India), or where there is a 'combination of courts' likely to intervene in the field, from ad hoc electoral tribunals to the Supreme Court (Mexico).

IV. STRUCTURE OF THE VOLUME

The book is divided into three parts. The first part addresses the conceptual hurdles of constitutional reasoning concerning electoral matters. The second and third parts consist of chapters devoted to national and supranational case studies illustrating, with due attention to the differences, the trend toward judicial activism in electoral matters.

The first chapter, authored by Pasquale Pasquino, tackles the foundational aspects of democratic legitimation to show how political and constitutional thought places central importance to the right to vote. Yet, the 'double-edged incompleteness'[20] of the relationship between constitutionalism and democracy is magnified by the varieties of electoral formulas deemed to offer the best democratic output. According to Pasquino this leaves Constitutional/Supreme courts without guidance or solid standards to perform their adjudicatory tasks on the matter.

The second chapter, authored by Emmanuel Voyakis, challenges the rationales of gerrymandering, the types of gerrymandering techniques in place and their constitutional pitfalls. Also resorting to national case law, especially in the US, it will use philosophical and moral arguments to advance the thesis that gerrymandering is fundamentally at odds with the idea of constitutional democracy.

[20] See N Walker, 'Constitutionalism and the Incompleteness of Democracy: An Iterative Relationship' (2010) 39 *Rechtsphilosophie und Rechtstheorie* 207. In his words: 'modern constitutionalism has become dependent upon, even parasitic upon the political forms and imperatives of democracy'.

The second part of the book is devoted to European case studies. Bob Watt illustrates the UK's constitutional experience where the Westminster Parliament has held its proceedings not subjected to judicial scrutiny. The chapter argues that, on one side, the Parliament later gave up its prerogative in 1868 and, on the other, after certain judicial developments, a return to the previous status quo would be impossible. The author further discusses the possibility to challenge the procedure in light of the Strasbourg Court's judgments on Article 3, First Protocol of the European Convention on Human Rights.

In the following chapter, Eleonora Bottini explores the French constitutional system. In particular, Macron's constitutional reform, aimed at shaping a more efficient, transparent and participatory-oriented representative government, is expected to have consequences on the size and shape of French electoral districts. Bottini then addresses the necessity to comply with the Conseil constitutionnel's case law, which has played a crucial role in the electoral field. Indeed, judicial scrutiny has had a significant impact on shaping a demographic electoral representation.

Giacomo Delledonne and Bastian Michel focus on the German Constitutional Court's review of the electoral law, underlying its main features and arguing how they have contributed to shaping the concept of political representation, influencing other national Constitutional Tribunals in Europe.

The Italian constitutional experience is addressed by Paolo Passaglia, who explores the path of the Italian Constitutional Court's attitude towards the adjudication of the national electoral legislation, highlighting its recent activism in outlining the margin of discretion the legislative power enjoys while regulating elections.

Remaining in the European context, the following chapter by Jan Sawicki examines the Polish and Hungarian judicial intervention towards the voting rights of citizens living abroad as well as other relevant aspects for the democratic life of the country, in the presence of a visible shift from liberal to 'illiberal' constitutionalism.

The second part is closed by Cristina Fasone and Robert Bray who study the role played by the Court of Justice of the EU and the European Court of Human Rights. As outlined, electoral laws fall within a sensitive field, in which the confines between political and legal aspects may be blurred, putting constitutional judges in a difficult position. The situation seems to be intensified for the above-mentioned supranational judges. The authors explain that these Courts tend to adopt a deferential approach in the electoral field where both Courts develop few essential standards to which democratic representation has to abide while resorting, for the rest, to a 'parasitic' understanding of democracy modelled on national constitutional systems.

The third part of the book moves away from Europe to address case studies from Africa, America, Asia and the Pacific region.

Berihun Gebeye describes African courts' activism in the context of presidential elections. The author delves into the arguments and the doctrines elaborated to justify courts' intervention into political disputes aimed at annulling elections. In particular, he addresses the 'substantive impact' and 'process outcome' doctrines to clarify that the African courts may need to move beyond these theories to a more dynamic judicial doctrine to ensure judicial legitimacy and institutional stability.

Irene Spigno opens the line-up concerned with the American region by exploring the role of courts in Mexican electoral disputes. In this area of the world, the Supreme Courts have tried to push towards the inclusive model of political participation. Following the political alternation, the Court has emphasised the importance of the principle of proportional representation. The author argues that the Court's attitude may help to limit the excesses inherent in the idea of representation and contribute to the democratisation of the country. The role of this Court, however, needs to be assessed in light of the peculiar role played by electoral tribunals, culturally perceived as tools to protect democracy, especially in times of crisis. Lucas H. Muniz da Conceição brings about the same argument with reference to the Brazilian case where electoral adjudication has been crucial in transitional circumstances where power is contested and there is room for democratic backslidings.

Sarah Burton and Michael Pal introduce the Canadian case by stressing the role played by the Supreme Court's (and courts in general) driving role in developing the content of electoral law along with the legislators. According to the authors, however, the trend towards judicial activism is likely to continue in the future because of the lack of comprehensive constitutional principles as well as of reasonable prospect of constitutional amendment in electoral matters.

Graziella Romeo and Davide Zecca explore the US Supreme Court's attitude towards electoral litigation by addressing the problem of political equality as emerging from recent case law. The authors contend that rather than embracing a distinctive understanding of democracy, the US Supreme Court exercises the judicial review of electoral legislation irrespective of a predetermined theory of politics. In such a context, activism in electoral disputes seem now to depend on the intention to progressively restore state sovereignty over elections rather than on the existence of an underlying strong theory of political equality.

Rekha Diwakar analyses the Indian experience by emphasising the different souls that animate its constitutional text: while, on one side, it aims at finding an equilibrium between different instances and thus it seems to adhere to the Kelsenian model of democracy, and on the other, it promotes a majoritarian and competitive democracy. In this context, the author contends that the Supreme Court's attitude seems to uphold a Kelsenian view of democracy.

Elisa Bertolini brings our attention to the careful activism of the Japanese Supreme Court in electoral matters. She highlights that the Court's abandonment of its initial deferential approach coexists with calls for Diet's intervention in redressing imbalances in the political representation.

Julian R Murphy and Erika Arban analyse the increasing willingness of the High Court to intervene in electoral matters and to invalidate statutes regulating elections. The authors however maintain that the Australian Court oscillates between legal and political constitutionalism in electoral law, an attitude that they explain as a consequence of its genealogical indebtedness to the US and the UK respectively.

The last chapter conveys the concluding remarks providing a comparative assessment of the case studies analysed, with a view to further developing the theoretical framework set up in the introductory part. Largely based on the analysis of national cases, it also highlights the potential and actual implications of judicial activism in electoral matters, on both the link between representative institutions and voters and the courts themselves. Finally, it challenges the idea that voting rights can be ascribed only to individuals. Escaping the methodological individualism implies understanding democracy as the result of societal participation in political decisions.

Part I

Theoretical and Methodological Issues

2

Democracy and Elections

PASQUALE PASQUINO

I. INTRODUCTION

ELECTIONS – free, repeated, and competitive – are one of the building blocks of any contemporary constitutional democracy. They were an essential character of the representative government/republic, as was established in the late eighteenth century by the US Constitution.

James Madison gave the classical definition of this form of government in Section 39 of the *Federalist Papers*:

> What, then, are the distinctive characters of the republican form? [...] If we resort for a criterion to the different principles on which different forms of government are established, we may define a republic to be, or at least may bestow that name on, a government which derives all its powers directly or indirectly from the great body of the people and is administered by persons holding their offices during pleasure, for a limited period, or during good behavior [here Madison is referring to the exception as to federal judges, who in the US are indirectly elected but not electorally accountable]. It is *essential* to such a government that it be derived from the great body of the society, not from an inconsiderable proportion, or a favored class of it; otherwise a handful of tyrannical nobles, exercising their oppressions by a delegation of their powers, might aspire to the rank of republicans, and claim for their government the honorable title of republic. It is *sufficient* for such a government that the persons administering it be appointed, either directly or indirectly, by the people; and that they hold their appointments by either of the tenures just specified; otherwise every government in the United States, as well as every other popular government that has been or can be well organized or well executed, would be degraded from the republican character (emphasis added).[1]

Sieyès, speaking in the National Constituent Assembly against the royal veto, made the same argument, arguing that the King could not be representative

[1] J Madison [1788] *The Conformity of the Plan to Republican Principles* – Federalist Paper no 39, in *The Federalist Papers* (New York, Palgrave Macmillan, 2009).

of the nation – that is, exercise a legitimate legislative authority – because his power to legislate through the veto did not derive from popular election.[2]

II. THE ORIGINAL LINK BETWEEN ELECTIONS AND LEGITIMATE POLITICAL AUTHORITY

To begin with I want to draw attention to the origin of elections as a necessary procedure for establishing the legitimacy of political authority. Traditionally, in the early days of representative government, the core was considered the sovereign legislature, the executive and its head being accountable to Parliament, or directly – in the American presidential version – elected and accountable to the voters.

The original foundation of electoral authorisation are the doctrines of natural rights that emerged in Europe from the seventeenth century, particularly in England.

Thomas Hobbes was the crucial figure in a conceptual revolution that introduced into political theory the idea that public authority has no *natural* basis, but is an artifact produced by popular authorisation.[3] Authorisation was regarded by Hobbes as the only foundation of legitimate public authority, the only one which creates a rational political obligation for citizens. In Hobbes, authorisation – that is, the social contract – takes the form of the rational obedience to an agency that can guarantee the fundamental *equal* rights of all members of the political community: life and limbs.

Indeed, it took more than a century to transform the idea of popular authorisation into the legal practice of elections and even longer to expand active citizenship (the franchise) into what we now call universal suffrage. But the starting point was the revolution of legal equality of citizens as members of the body politic. And the dismantling of doctrines of a natural hierarchy as the foundation and legitimacy of government – we can think of Robert Filmer's *Patriarcha*.[4] For Hobbes and natural rights theorists, only authorised members of the community can exercise public authority. The government is an artifact and the artifex are the politically equal members of the community: the citizens.

[2] Speech given on 7 September 1789 at the National Constituent Assembly *Sur l'organisation du pouvoir législatif et la sanction royale*: 'Les citoyens qui se nomment des représentants renoncent et doivent renoncer à faire eux-mêmes la loi ; ils n'ont pas de volonté particulière à imposer. S'ils dictaient des volontés, la France ne serait plus cet état représentatif ; ce serait un état démocratique. Le peuple, je le répète, dans un pays qui n'est pas une démocratie (et la France ne saurait l'être), ne peut parler, ne peut agir que par ses représentants'.

[3] T Hobbes [1651] *Leviathan*, JCA Gaskin (ed) (Oxford, Oxford University Press, 2008).

[4] See R Filmer [1680] *Patriarcha and other Writings*, JP Sommerville (ed) (Cambridge, Cambridge University Press, 1991).

III. THE DISTINCTNESS OF ELECTING POLITICAL REPRESENTATIVES

The function of elections by the way is not limited to establishing the legitimacy of authority, since through elections voters also select, from among the candidates, those we call representatives – members of the parliaments and sometimes heads of state. In reality, this is possible only because of an algorithm capable of transforming a large number – often millions – of individual preferences (mostly, since the twentieth century, secret) into a small number of seats (occasionally, in the case of the popular election of the head of the state, only one). The name of this algorithm is *stricto sensu* the electoral law. I will return to this topic. For now, it seems important to me to point out that the vote cast by citizens in political elections is a distinctly different act from others that we also call voting.

Here is why. Todays the vote of a citizen member of the electoral body who selects representatives is, as I said, secret. Which implies that not only she is unaccountable for her decision, but she does not even need to give a reason or present an argument of her choice. Voting, in the case of contemporary political elections, is a *sovereign* act. Each voter in a representative government is a microscopic fragment of the Baroque sovereign. She could therefore say, as the absolute King: *sic volo, sic jubeo, stat pro ratione voluntas.*

On the other hand, when a member of a supreme or constitutional court votes, she must present an argument or, if she disagrees with an argument presented by one of the members, she must explain the reasons of her disagreement (which in some courts may be published). Thus, we could say that the representative government explodes the baroque sovereign by creating a *dissentiens multitudo* of private individual preferences. Whereas the absolute King has a will, the popular will does not exist, it is in turn an artifact, shaped by the mechanism of aggregation: the electoral law. Crucially, changing the mechanism or the algorithm for aggregating individual preferences changes what we call, with a conceptual shortcut, the *popular will.*

IV. VARIETIES OF ELECTORAL SYSTEMS AND THE PUZZLE OF THE DEMOCRATIC COMMITMENT

As it is well known, different countries with different histories have different electoral systems. Italy, for instance, has repeatedly changed the mechanism for aggregating individual voters' preferences since 1994 for reasons related to the absence of a stable systemic equilibrium, resulting from the collapse of the parties' system that ruled the country for more than 40 years after World War II.

Before considering the electoral systems limited to European representative governments that I am familiar with, I want to dispel a question which seems impossible to answer in a nonpartisan way: which electoral rule is more democratic. Clearly, the answer to that question depends on normative theories of a just society (rather than on a descriptive theory of the representative government), which are controversial and may give greater weight to the inclusiveness of the diverse views in the society or to the stability and governability of the political system. Certainly, extreme rules such as a parliamentary access threshold of ten per cent (as in Turkey) or more can be considered excessive,[5] even more so by small/medium parties.

In general, different major versions of electoral laws try, with greater or lesser success, to combine the principle of representativeness of the political pluralism present in a given society with the stability of executive and Parliament and their ability to govern the country.

The two main families of electoral law are majoritarian and proportional, of which exist subspecies, including mixed versions. The proportional formula tries to reproduce inside the legislative assembly the variety of organised political opinion present in a given society. The first consequence of such a mechanism of aggregation of individual preferences (votes) in parliamentary regimes is that, with very rare exceptions, executive power is the result of a coalition that emerges through negotiations in the Parliament *after* the popular vote. Voters choose a party (or even a candidate within the party) rather than the cabinet, which will be formed by the parties, once their members elected, in the representative assembly.

The oddly named majoritarian system allows a minority of votes, allocated to a party or to a pre-electoral coalition, to translate into a majority of the seats. The minority in question must be the largest (sometimes the term plurality is used as the equivalent of relative majority).

A. The UK

In the old and still working English system of uninominal districts, if there are more than two candidates in a district the one with the most votes will get the seat in the House of Commons, even if he gets less than 50 per cent plus one of the votes. Thus, in general, the largest minority of a popular vote will produce a majority of seats in the representative assembly. Given the UK's essential two-parties system, *hung parliaments* (those in which no single party controls an absolute majority of the seats) are rare.[6]

[5] In its Resolution no 1547/2007 the Parliamentary Assembly of the Council of Europe recommended a 3% electoral threshold limit for 'well established democracies'. In 2008, however, in *Yuman and Sadak v Turkey* (application no 10226/03), the Grand Chamber of European Court of Human Rights considered the 10% threshold for the election of the Turkish Grand Assembly legitimate on the ground that it avoided excessive parliamentary fragmentation while foreseeing the possibility of independent candidatures. See also R Bray and C Fasone, ch 9 in this volume.

[6] Since the elections of 1929, there have been three general elections in the UK that have resulted in hung parliaments: 1974, 2010 and 2017.

Figure 1 UK general election vote share and resultant governments (1950–2017)[7]

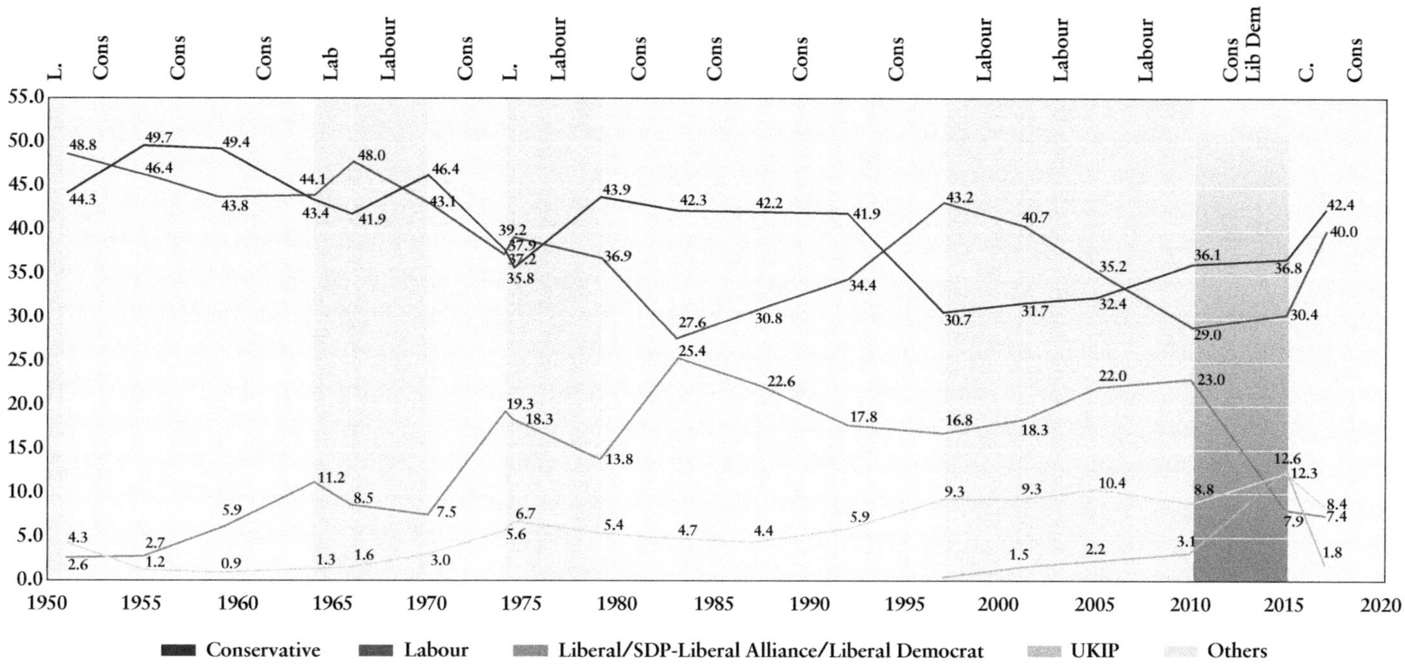

[7]Source: 'UK parliamentary election results 1950–2017', in Elections in the United Kingdom — Wikipedia, available at https://en.wikipedia.org/wiki/Elections_in_the_United_Kingdom – 4 June 2023.

It is worth noticing that in 2005 alone, the winner (Blair's Labour Party) won a majority of seats in the Commons 355 (55.2 per cent) with less than 40 per cent of the popular vote (35.2 per cent). This shows that the English and then British electoral system has not only been characterised by a quite regular alternation of government, but that the disproportionality induced by the majoritarian formula also works because of limited disproportionality.

B. Germany

Post-World War II Germany adopted a mechanism for electing the *Bundestag* (the federal Parliament)[8] based on a proportional formula with five per cent threshold for a party to enter the representative assembly.[9] For a long time, the political system was dominated by three political actors: the Cristian Democratic Party (CDU plus the Bavarian variant CSU), the Social Democratic Party (SPD) and the Liberal Party (FPD).

From 1949 to 1969 the Christian Democrats were able to govern the country mostly in coalition with the FDP. Only once, in 1957, did the CDU alone win just over 50 per cent of the popular vote. In the context of proportional representation this is a quite exceptional event, and cabinets are usually (unlike in the UK) composed of a coalition. From 1969 to 1982 the SPD in coalition with the FDP controlled the chancellery, first with Willy Brand then with Helmut Schmidt. After 1982 and until 2005, alternating coalitions in power dominated by the CDU and the SPD characterised the German political life. Then a new type of coalition controlled the government in Berlin under Angela Merkel, notably from 2005 to 2009 and again from 2013 through to 2021, the so-called *große Koalition* between the CDU and the SPD. In the meantime, and partly because of German reunification and of the grand coalition, after the growth of the ecologist party, the left and the right split and two new radical parties emerged: *Die Linke*, on the left of the political spectrum, and *Alternative für Deutschland*, on the right.

Under Merkel, Germany was ruled from the centre by the alliance between the two liberal-democratic parties at the origin of the 1949 Constitution. This centrist option was maintained by the new Chancellor, social democrat Olaf Scholz, who replaced the grand coalition with a coalition government including the Green Party and the moderate conservative FDP.

[8] The *Bundesrat*, the federal Senate, is not directly elected by the voters, but made up by delegates of the *Laender* (states) of the German federal regime.

[9] See G Delledonne and B Michel, ch 6 in this volume.

Figure 2 German parliamentary elections and formed coalition governments[10]

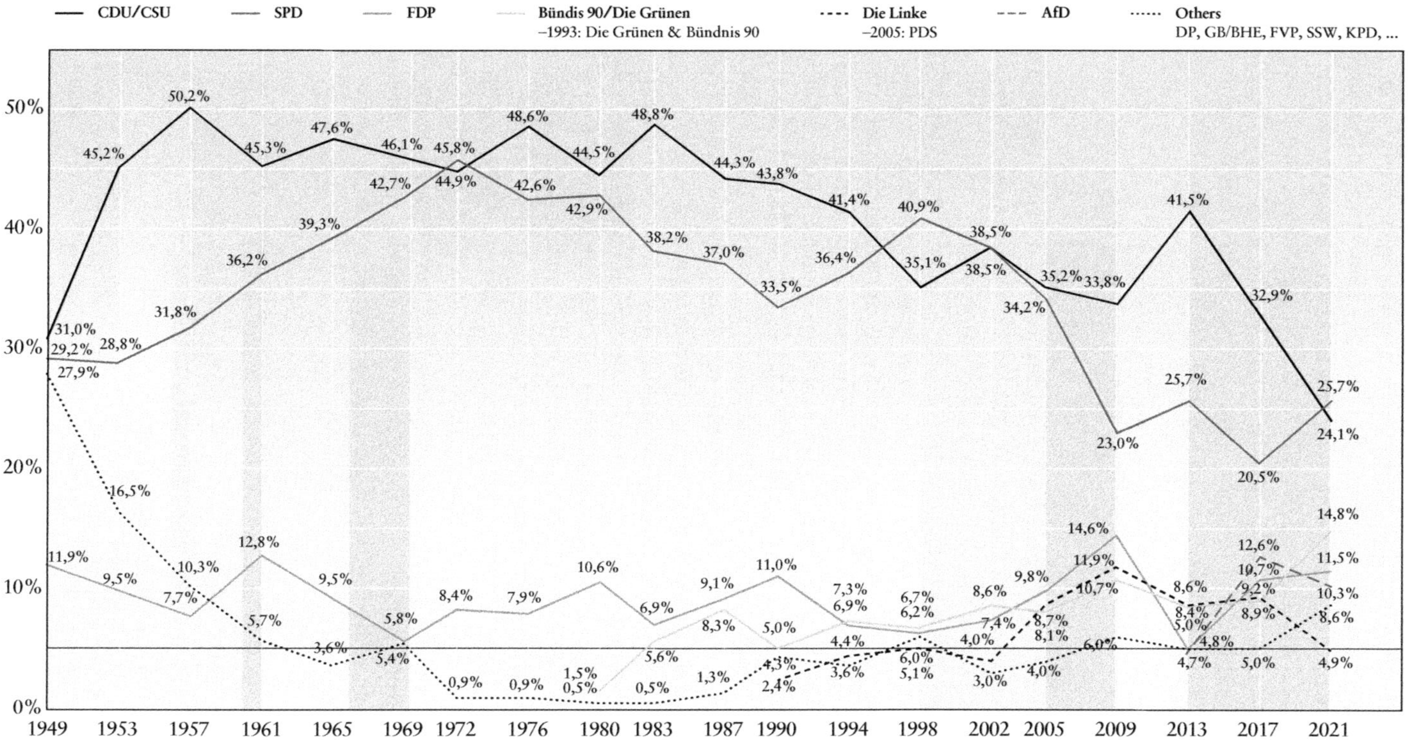

[10] Source: 'German parliamentary elections results', in Elections in Germany – Wikipedia, available at https://en.wikipedia.org/wiki/Elections_in_Germany – 4 June 2023.

One pattern seems to characterise German government for most of the past 20 years: the exclusion of extremes from the government through centrist coalitions. An alternative pattern to that typical of the Anglo-American politics, where electoral law has organised competition around the two major parties, which, in the absence of a possible coalition, need to keep the radical segments of the electoral body within them – think of the radical left component of the Democratic Party and the Trumpists within the Republicans.

C. France

The French Fifth Republic has been characterised by a different electoral formula, both for the presidential and for the election of the *Assemblée nationale*,[11] that involve two rounds.[12] If no candidate for the presidency or in the uninominal constituencies for the legislative assembly reaches 50 per cent plus one of the votes, a second round must be held. Here begins a difference between the rules of the two elections. For the President of the Republic only the two candidates with the best score at the first round can enter the runoff. Since 1962, when due to a popular referendum the election of the head of state was introduced into the Constitution, De Gaulle has also never been elected at the first round. As to the election of the legislative assembly, on the other hand, access is possible for any candidate who has obtained 12.5 per cent of the popular vote – actually now around 20 per cent due to the significant percentage of abstention in legislative elections.

For a long time, the 'consequence of the two-ballot system [was] that not only has it encouraged binary competition in general terms, it has also encouraged binary competition specifically between the left and the right'.[13] Indeed, after the 2017 presidential and legislative elections and, again, in 2022 the French electoral rule did not have the same effect.

The presidential election held in April 2022, presented a France divided into three rather than two parts. The legislative elections confirmed the same results Rather than pitting left and right, it showed a France divided on the one hand between a centre composed of moderate pro-European voters and the radical anti-European *souverainistes*, divided in turn between components of the radical left and the radical right.

[11] As in Germany the French *Sénat* is not directly elected by the citizens, its members are elected by the elected officials of the country.

[12] On its origin see: J Huber, *Rationalizing Parliament. Legislative Institutions and Party Politics in France* (Cambridge, Cambridge University Press, 1996) 48–51, who mentions the arguments that led to the choice of the double-round electoral law based on uninominal constituencies. For more detail: JM Denquin, *1958. La genèse de la Ve République* (Paris, Presses Universitaires de France, 1988) 378–85. See also E Bottini, ch 5 in this volume.

[13] This is what R Elgie wrote in the chapter on the French electoral system in his contribution to M Gallagher and P Mitchell (eds), *The Politics of Electoral System* (New York, Oxford University Press, 2005) 127.

While the electoral formula ensures the stability of the chief executive, because of the constitutional structure that does not make the president accountable to Parliament, it does not ensure that the president controls the parliamentary majority. The last one expresses a Prime Minister, who is accountable to the *Assemblée nationale*, which has its majority. Three times between 1962 and 2000 the president had to compromise with a parliamentary majority of a different colour. Twice the socialist Mitterrand was forced to live with a conservative Prime Minister: Chirac (1986–88) and Balladur (1993–95). And Chirac, elected president, had to live with a socialist Prime Minister, Jospin, for five years (1997–2002). It was to avoid the *cohabitation* – somehow the equivalent of the American *divided government* – that in 2000 Chirac succeeded in amending the Constitution by changing the presidential term from seven to five years. This had the effect that the members of the legislative assembly are chosen by the voters a couple of weeks after the president, with a twofold consequence: the *cohabitation* had been ruled out, so far, and the turnout of the legislative election rapidly and quite dramatically declined.

Table 1 Electoral turnout

Year	Presidential election (5 year-term since 2000)	Parliamentary election	Difference
1995	80%	71%	−9%
2002	80%	60%	−20%
2007	84%	60%	−24%
2012	80%	55%	−25%
2017	75%	42%	−33%
2022	72%	46%	−26%

It should also be noted that the French electoral formula is characterised by a high rate of disproportionality in term of the number of inhabitants per constituency: 'in metropolitan France ranged from a high of 188,200 in the second constituency of the Val d'Oise department in the Paris suburbs to a low of 34,374 in the second constituency of the Lozère department'.[14]

[14] ibid 121. As of 1 January 2011, excluding overseas collectivities and foreign countries, the smallest constituency is the second constituency of Hautes-Alpes with 63,148 inhabitants and the most populous is the sixth constituency of Seine-Maritime with 146,866 inhabitants. fr.wikipedia.org/wiki/Circonscriptions_l%C3%A9gislatives_fran%C3%A7aises [4 June 2023].

Table 2 Deviations from proportionality in National Assembly elections 1958–97 (least square index)[15]

Election	Disproportionality
1958	21.2
1962	15.0
1967	10.0
1968	19.2
1973	11.0
1978	6.6
1981	16.0
1986 (PR)	7.2
1988	11.8
1993	25.0
1997	17.8
2002	21.9

D. The Difficulty in Ranking the Democratic Credentials of Electoral Systems

As I said, it would be pointless to ask which one of these electoral systems is more democratic. It is well known that two major theorist of contemporary democracy, Hans Kelsen and Joseph A Schumpeter, considered the former proportional representation and the latter the English *majoritarian* system typical of democracy – perhaps because the UK represented for the economist the model of a good government, based on competition in a two-party system that guaranteed easy accountability and alternation in power, while the legal theorist had in mind the electoral law of Austria, which favoured compromise and the decisive role of the political parties.

Be that as it may, opinions differ on this issue. And some political systems like Italy, since the early 1990s, have chosen mixed systems.

V. CONCLUSION

For the reasons alluded to at the beginning, electoral law, whatever it may be, plays a fundamental role in the composition of representative bodies – Parliament, presidential systems also the head of the executive. Together with

[15] Source: Communications from Arendt Lijphart and Michael Gallagher (n 13) 132. I could not find more recent data.

the constitution, the legal mechanism for choosing members of the government in a modern liberal democracy is an essential norm without which representative democracy is not possible. Often, however, electoral law is embedded into ordinary legislation – so among many other countries Italy, Germany, Japan, etc – therefore under the control of the body that can decide, if required, on its conformity with the constitution.

But since today's liberal democratic constitutions do not include, with some exceptions, precise canons regarding the structure and the content of electoral law,[16] if we exclude the criterion of universal and equal[17] vote, it is not always easy for the constitutional judges to decide on the constitutionality of electoral norms, and, first of all, on whether it is appropriate to decide or not, being the question inadmissible or involving a political question.

This volume aims to make a broad and original contribution to the issue of constitutional adjudication of electoral law and to the way it impacts representative democracy, both conceptually and practically.

[16] A clear exception is the Austrian Constitution, which writes:

> Art 26.1 'The National Council is elected by the Federal people in accordance with the principles of proportional representation on the basis of equal, direct, personal, free and secret suffrage by men and women who have completed their sixteenth year of life on the day of election.'

[17] The term *equal* in regard to voting is ambiguous. In fact, it cannot mean anything other than that the electoral law must assign each citizen one vote and one vote only. The impact of the single vote on the aggregate of votes, which transforms these into seats, with the exception of proportional systems without thresholds, is always unequal. Consider the case of the electoral system in the United Kingdom, where the votes allocated to the losing candidate or candidates have no impact on the composition of the elected chamber.

3

The Moral Wrong in Partisan Gerrymandering – A Review of Some Arguments

EMMANUEL VOYIAKIS*

WHAT IS WRONG about gerrymandering? Maybe nothing, but the name does not flatter the practice. It suggests that one tinkers with the rules of an electoral contest so that one gets the result that one wants, and that looks morally suspect. However, that intuition only takes us so far. An intention to favour a particular candidate through the choice of a particular electoral design does not suffice to make that design wrong. Suppose that the designer has a choice between an electoral map that packs people of one race into a single distinct, and a map that does not. The designer chooses the latter map only because it favours their preferred candidate, who has better cross-racial appeal than their opponent. The designer may have the wrong intention, and may be blameworthy on that ground, but it does not follow that their choice of map is morally problematic. After all, sometimes people have the wrong reasons for doing something that is morally permissible.

Asking whether gerrymandering is morally permissible is not the same as asking whether that practice is constitutional.[1] Perhaps gerrymandering is a moral but not a legal or constitutional wrong. Or perhaps, as the

* I am grateful to participants in the Panel on Judicial Review and Electoral Law (Global Summit on Constitutionalism, January 2021), out of which this chapter grew, and to Jacco Bomhoff, Jo Braithwaite, Neil Duxbury, David Kershaw, Nicola Lacey, Martin Loughlin, Tom Poole, Graziella Romeo, and Gerry Simpson for their most helpful comments on previous versions.

[1] From a large literature on the latter question, see R Pildes, 'Principled Limitations on Racial and Partisan Redistricting' (1997) 106 *Yale Law Journal* 2505; P Schuck, 'The Thickest Thicket: Partisan Gerrymandering and Judicial Regulation of Politics' (1987) 87 *Columbia Law Review* 1325; M Berman, 'Managing Gerrymandering' (2005) 83 *Texas Law Review* 781; B Ross, 'Partisan Gerrymandering, the First Amendment, and the Political Outsider' (2018) 118 *Columbia Law Review* 2187; M McDonald, 'Redistricting and Competitive Districts' in M McDonald and J Samples (eds), *The Marketplace of Democracy: Electoral Competition and American Politics* (Washington, DC, Cato Institute, 2006) 222; L Alexander and S Prakash, 'Tempest in an Empty Teapot: Why the Constitution Does not Regulate Gerrymandering' (2008) 50 *William & Mary Law Review* 1.

US Supreme Court held in *Rucho v Common Cause*, it is justiciable and potentially unconstitutional when done on racial grounds and non-justiciable when done on party-political or partisan grounds.[2] I want to discuss gerrymandering as a matter of morality rather than constitutional law or political science, because I want to understand better certain complaints of those who oppose it. The people I have in mind believe that, absent some special justification, gerrymandering is morally impermissible and that if the constitution does not recognise this, we ought to change the constitution or interpret some of its more abstract clauses in a way that identifies, discourages, and corrects the relevant moral wrong. I find these complaints intuitive but hard to evaluate. To narrow the challenge, I will focus on partisan gerrymandering and discuss only incidentally more egregious types, eg, those that seek to protect incumbents, or to restrict the political representation of racial minorities.

I will consider five arguments on the moral permissibility of partisan gerrymandering. Some have been framed in constitutional terms but also have clear moral analogues, so I propose to address them in the latter guise. One claims that partisan gerrymandering causes 'expressive' harm to society through the meaning it conveys about the character of government action. The others claim that partisan gerrymandering harms individuals by diminishing their voting power; by impairing their freedom of assembly and association; by imposing on them an unfair proportion of the costs of the electoral system; or by misleading them about the electoral stakes. I will argue that each argument illuminates important aspects of the moral problem, but none succeeds in defending the intuition that partisan gerrymandering is generally impermissible. The case for that intuition therefore remains to be made. I conclude with a tentative sketch of an alternative, which focuses on the permissibility of the use by public institutions of information about voter allegiance.

I. GERRYMANDERING: THE PRACTICE AND SOME BASIC LIMITS TO IT

Charles Beitz defines gerrymandering as 'an effort to influence the outcomes of elections to representative bodies by manipulating the boundaries of electoral districts'.[3] Different definitions are available, and perhaps less contentious (eg, 'effort to influence' seems to require intention, the significance of which is an open issue), but I will take this as an initial guide. So defined, gerrymandering can occur in any context where electoral districts are to be drawn, though its practical impact tends to be much higher in systems with single-member or 'first-past-the-post' districts than in systems of proportional representation.[4]

[2] *Rucho v Common Cause*, 588 U.S. __ (2019).

[3] C Beitz, 'How is Partisan Gerrymandering Unfair?' (2019) 46 *Philosophy & Public Affairs* 323, 326.

[4] See the statistical analysis in F Martínez i Coma and I Lago, 'Gerrymandering in Comparative Perspective' (2018) 24 *Party Politics* 99.

The US has been a high-profile and fertile testing ground of gerrymandering techniques, so my discussion will use mainly US-based examples.

Gerrymandering relies on information about voter allegiance. The content of one's vote may be confidential, but in some countries, including the US, whether a person voted in an election is a matter of public record. Combined with circumstantial evidence about party affiliation and political sympathies (and other information that political science treats as a reliable proxy, eg, one's social media network), that pool of data can help generate astonishingly granular reports of likely voting behaviour. Modern statistical techniques allow neighbourhood-by-neighbourhood and household-by-household reports of who votes for whom. Several 'see how your neighbours vote' tools are freely available online.[5] Large political campaigns tend to rely on even more sophisticated, and often custom-made, tools.

Information about voter allegiance gives officials with the authority to draw electoral maps the opportunity to influence the outcome of the election in two ways: by 'packing' electoral districts and by 'cracking' them. In a single-member district system, winning by one vote and winning by several thousand delivers the same electoral result, so packing draws district boundaries in ways that turn a likely majority into an overwhelming one. This restricts the number of that party's voters in neighbouring districts and therefore makes those districts more easily winnable for the party of the packer's preference. Cracking is the mirror image of packing: maps that draw boundaries so that a likely majority for a party falls into different districts reduce that party's chances of obtaining a majority in any of them. Every gerrymander is an instance of packing or cracking, occasionally both. The description of a particular instance as one or the other can be tricky (not least because intentions and effects can diverge), but the distinction between them is not particularly important for our present discussion, as it seems obvious that both techniques are subject to the same moral standards. It would be astonishing if packing were morally OK and cracking were not.

Some limits on districting are widely accepted, both as a matter of law and of political morality, that it makes sense to take them as given and build them into more interesting versions of the moral problem. One is that gerrymandering is wrong when it discriminates between people on account of their race.[6]

[5] See eg, the *New York Times* 'Extremely Detailed Map of the 2020 Election' at www.nytimes.com/interactive/2021/upshot/2020-election-map.html.

[6] See *Thornburg v Gingles*, 478 U.S. 30 (1982) and *Shaw v Reno*, 509 U.S. 630 (1993), applying strict scrutiny to 'racial gerrymanders', and *Miller v Johnson*, 515 U.S. 900 (1995) and *Allen v Milligan*, 599 U.S. ___ (2023), confirming the constitutionality of 'affirmative' racial gerrymanders, the aim of which is to ensure the representation of racial communities that have faced historical disenfranchisement and discrimination. *Shelby County v Holder*, 570 U.S. 529 (2013) did not disturb those lines of precedent, though it declared unconstitutional the requirement that some states obtain federal clearance before making changes to their electoral maps. For the view that racial gerrymandering is not unconstitutional, see Alexander and Prakash, (n 1) 47 ff.

A second is that officials may not draw electoral maps in ways that create significant inequalities in the population of individual districts, eg, make it so that one district includes 20,000 people, and the other 1,000. While the drawing of electoral boundaries is primarily a matter of state law, the US Constitution requires that congressional seats be apportioned according to population, and the requirement has been understood to require reconsideration of electoral district lines with every census, ie, every ten years.[7] A third limit is that each district must have a closed shape or be 'contiguous', so that one can travel from any point in the district to any other without having to cross the district's boundary. It is not clear whether contiguity is a constitutional requirement, but state laws tend to follow it closely.[8]

Within those limits, the main bone of legal and political contention has been *partisan* or party-political gerrymandering. Such gerrymandering has been the topic of several decisions by the US Supreme Court. In *Rucho v Common Cause*, the Court held that such gerrymandering is not justiciable because, unlike racial gerrymandering, there are no clear standards that courts can apply to its review.[9] For the majority, striking down a partisan gerrymander requires some benchmark of what a non-gerrymandered electoral map should look like, but that benchmark is the very topic of political contention surrounding districting, so there is no neutral or natural way to fix it.[10] The minority found that partisan gerrymandering violates the equal protection clause, as it dilutes the voting power of those who support the party targeted by the gerrymander, and also the freedom of speech and association.[11]

The most widely used metric to measure the practical impact of gerrymandering on electoral results is the 'partisan symmetry' test, which asks how seats would have been distributed between parties if their shares of the vote were reversed.[12] On that basis, the Princeton Election Consortium estimated that, as a result of Republican-friendly gerrymandering, Democrats needed to win the popular vote by +six per cent in order to obtain control of Congress in the 2018 election cycle. That margin fell to about +three per cent in the

[7] *Reynolds v Sims*, 377 U.S. 533, 568 (1964). The requirement concerns equality of population, not voting population. Very small deviations from equality are allowed, though the applicable standard tends to be phrased differently depending on whether the districts are congressional or state/local.

[8] Exceptions are rare, eg, when intra-district travel requires water transit, as in Hawaii.

[9] *Rucho v Common Cause* (n 2). The holding in *Rucho* continues a longer trend in the Supreme Court's treatment of partisan gerrymandering, see also *Gill v Whitford*, 585 U.S. ___ (2018); *LULAC v Perry*, 548 U.S. 399 (2006); *Vieth v Jubelirer*, 541 U.S. 267 (2004); *Davis v Bandemer*, 478 U.S. 109 (1986).

[10] *Rucho v Common Cause* (n 2) V (30): 'Federal judges have no license to reallocate political power between the two major political parties, with no plausible grant of authority in the Constitution, and no legal standards to limit and direct their decisions'.

[11] ibid, per Kagan J (dissenting) at C (11-3).

[12] For more detail see, SSH Wang, 'Three Tests for Practical Evaluation of Partisan Gerrymandering' (2016) 68 *Stanford Law Review* 1263.

2020 elections.[13] The exact metric and measurements do not matter much for my present discussion. I will simply take it as given that, even under the constraints of racial equality, equal population and contiguity, gerrymandering can have a noticeable impact on electoral results. Of course, the *net* effect of gerrymanders is a complex matter. Political action begets political reaction. For example, there is some evidence that the passage of state laws requiring voters to carry an ID, a standing item in the Republican political agenda, has resulted in a very small net benefit for Democrats, who have pointed to the disenfranchising effect of those laws in order to energise their political base.[14] However, given that the possibility of such reaction cannot serve to justify otherwise morally impermissible practices, I believe that we can set them aside for the purposes of our discussion.

II. A SIMPLE EXPLANATION AND ITS LIMITATIONS

To my knowledge, no-one claims that partisan gerrymandering is a valuable practice, or one that ought to be encouraged. For that matter, no-one has called Rep. David Lewis, erstwhile member of the districting commission for North Carolina, a moral beacon for having gone on record as saying, with disarming candour:

> I think electing Republicans is better than electing Democrats. So I drew this map to help foster what I think is better for the country.[15]

There is a simple explanation of what might be wrong with this attitude. The institutional powers of the office Mr Lewis occupied are not supposed to be used in the way he used them. In particular, if there are good reasons why electoral district boundaries should be malleable rather than fixed in perpetuity, the exercise of the power to redraw them falls to be assessed in the light of those reasons, and the desire to see a certain candidate or party elected is not one of them. I believe that this simple explanation captures reasonably well the intuition that gerrymandering constitutes an abuse of power. On that explanation, the moral wrongness of gerrymandering is relatively unmysterious, on broad par with the wrongness of supporting or opposing legislation for reasons of personal gain, or of appointing patently unqualified friends in official posts. In all these cases a person occupies an office invested with certain powers and proceeds to use them in ways or for ends that are at odds with the reasons that

[13] Princeton Election Consortium, 'Election Tracking 2020: U.S. House of Representatives' at election.princeton.edu/election-tracking-2020-part-1-the-u-s-house/. See also the PEC's handy gerrymandering tracking tool at https://gerrymander.princeton.edu/.

[14] For a cautious view of the research, see J Grimmer et al, 'Obstacles to Estimating Voter ID Laws' Effect on Turnout' (2018) 80 *Journal of Politics* 1045.

[15] *Rucho v Common Cause* (n 2) A (4).

justify that investment. Explaining why a particular use of that power is wrong is therefore largely a matter of identifying the relevant reasons and asking how far officials have conformed to their requirements. In the case of gerrymandering, this involves explaining how the power to change electoral boundaries should be exercised, eg in order to maintain equality of population across districts, to observe certain principles of contiguity and compactness, to be appropriately sensitive to territorially identifiable communities of interest, to maintain existing district boundaries unless there is sufficient reason to change them, etc.[16] It seems clear that Mr Lewis's credo does not fare well under that standard. In fact, despite their substantive disagreement, majority and minority in *Rucho* agreed that partisan gerrymandering is 'incompatible with democratic principles',[17] and that state and federal law may limit or outlaw it completely.

This simple explanation has no dramatic implications. For a start, it presents partisan gerrymandering as a plain-vanilla political misdeed, rather than a special wrong that calls for a strong institutional remedy. It does not settle, for example, whether courts ought to have the power to control partisan gerrymanders. Perhaps such gerrymanders are abuses of official power but the significance of that fact should be left to the judgment of the voters. Moreover, the explanation does not impugn all partisan gerrymanders. For example, it is consistent with allowing officials to use partisan preference as a tie-breaker when more than one electoral map designs conform to the reasons that govern good districting.

The real problem with the simple explanation is that it comes under severe stress when we ask *how much* weight officials may legitimately attribute to partisan preferences. Consider a strong version of the explanation, according to which Mr Lewis's attitude is wrong because partisan preference ought to play *no role* in the administration of public powers. It is not clear how this strong claim could be defended. Partisanship may carry a bad name, but partisan preference is a political preference like any other. Say that a party announces that it intends to gerrymander for maximum partisan advantage, wins a majority in the polls, and delivers on its promise. If acting on its announced policy is morally wrong because it satisfies partisan preferences, should we say the same of decisions that satisfy the preferences of that party's voters for more public parks or better pre-school services? Perhaps districting preferences should be treated differently, but an argument to that effect would need to reach well beyond the simple explanation. For example, the fact that districting preferences affect electoral outcomes over multiple election cycles only takes us so far. Many political choices, from public investment plans to the adoption of a single-member district system over proportional representation, have similarly long-lasting political impact. We could, alternatively, adopt a more modest

[16] R Pildes (n 1) 2549, noting that such factors are 'neutral' as they are based 'on the objective circumstances of districting' rather than on value-judgements about representativeness.

[17] *Rucho v Common Cause* (n 2) V (30) per Roberts CJ and B(8) per Kagan J.

reading of the explanation and say that partisan gerrymandering is wrong not because it satisfies partisan preferences but because it accords *undue weight* to them, or allows them to dominate other appliable reasons or values. That reading is much more plausible, but it is not in any sense simple, as it must rely on some account of how much weight partisan preferences are due and why. After all, the gerrymandered maps Mr Lewis's favoured were consistent with equality of population and contiguity. They only offended, if they did, the less categorical principles of compactness, sensitivity to communities of interest, respect for long-existing boundaries etc. Perhaps those principles enjoy normative priority over the satisfaction of partisan preference, but the simple explanation does not tell us why and how far that is the case.

III. PARTISAN GERRYMANDERING AS EXPRESSIVE HARM

It is therefore no surprise that arguments about the moral wrongness of partisan gerrymandering have tended to follow more complex paths. Such arguments generally come in two types: arguments that point to the social impact of partisan gerrymandering on public life and the political culture more broadly (eg, that it undermines an electoral system's responsiveness to shifts in the popular vote, the principled and fair-minded administration of public affairs, or respect for the efforts of grassroots political networks), and arguments that point to its impact on individuals (eg, that it dilutes the voting power of some persons, or saddles them with an unfair share of the costs of a particular voting system).

Making an argument of the first type, Richard Pildes and Richard Niemi have claimed that partisan gerrymandering involves a kind of social harm they call 'expressive':

> An expressive harm is one that results from the ideas or attitudes expressed through a governmental action, rather than from the more tangible or material consequences the action brings about. On this view, the *meaning* of a governmental action is just as important as what that action *does*. Public policies can violate the Constitution not only because they bring about concrete costs, but because the very meaning they convey demonstrates inappropriate respect for relevant public values … Expressive harms are therefore, in general, social rather than individual. Their primary effect is not as much the tangible burdens they impose on particular individuals, but the way in which they undermine collective understandings.[18]

[18] R Pildes and R Niemi, 'Expressive Harms, "Bizarre Districts", and Voting Rights: Evaluating Election-District Appearances after *Shaw v Reno*' (1992) 92 *Michigan Law Review* 483, 506–07 ff. The account was endorsed in *Bush v Vera*, 517 U.S. 952 (1996) at 984 per O'Connor J: 'we also know that the nature of the expressive harms with which we are dealing, and the complexity of the districting process, are such that bright line rules are not available'. See also S. Issacharoff and R Pildes, 'Politics as Markets: Partisan Lockups of the Democratic Process' (1998) 50 *Stanford Law Review* 643; Berman (n 1) 826.

Pildes and Niemi put forward the idea of expressive harm as part of the best interpretation of the Supreme Court's case-law on partisan gerrymandering, rather than as a purely moral argument.[19] However, the moral aspect of their claim is similar to the modest version of the simple explanation: partisan gerrymandering causes expressive harm when it gives partisan preference undue weight amongst the plurality of reasons that good districting ought to take into account.[20]

Like the simple explanation, the appeal to the expressive harm does not tell us how much weight partisan preference is due as a moral matter. But the argument also faces a more general normative challenge. While government actions or practices can sometimes display contempt for public values and undermine social understandings that support a democratic culture, the significance of those effects for the *moral permissibility* of those actions is unclear, at least on accounts that see moral justification as being owed to individuals rather than to societies. For example, TM Scanlon's version of moral contractualism holds that the permissibility of an action depends on whether any person affected by that action could reasonably reject a principle that permits it, and that the grounds of such rejection are the person's individual interests, rather than collective or social ones.[21] On such accounts, sometimes an action will have adverse effects on public life or convey lack of respect for civic values (eg, fuel anti-democratic sentiment, or erode norms of civility and good faith in public debate) and still be morally permissible. Another implication of such accounts is that while the intention of the acting agent can sometimes affect the permissibility of their act, this connection is not morally fundamental, as an agent can have the purest of intentions and still act impermissibly, and vice versa. Pildes and Niemi are right to say that the reasons for which an agent acts affect the meaning of their act,[22] and that the permissibility of an action can sometimes depend on its meaning.[23] For example, when an employer turns down a job applicant because of the applicant's race, the impermissibility of the employer's action turns partly on the fact that their decision conveys a particular meaning, namely a judgment that people of that race are of lesser worth. However, the meaning of that action affects its permissibility *not* because of the social effects of the action, but because persons in the position of the unsuccessful applicant could object to the control that

[19] Pildes and Niemi (n 18) 506–16.

[20] ibid 500, describing the problem in terms of value-reductionism: 'When decisions reflect value reductionism, policymakers have transformed a decision process that ought to involve multiple values -as a matter of constitutional law- and reduced it to a one-dimensional problem. They have permitted one value to subordinate all other relevant values.'

[21] TM Scanlon, *What We Owe to Each Other* (Cambridge, MA, Belknap, 1998) 229.

[22] See TM Scanlon, *Moral Dimensions: Permissibility, Meaning, Blame* (Cambridge, MA, Belknap, 2008) 4, defining the meaning of an action as 'the significance, for the agent and others, of the agent's willingness to perform that action for the reasons he or she does'. Calling my sick relative because I care for them has a different meaning to calling them because I hope to inherit their fortune, as each reason casts my relationship with them in a different light.

[23] ibid 62 ff.

persons on the position of the employer would have over them, if the latter were permitted to act on their racist reasons.[24]

Perhaps contractualists like Scanlon are mistaken to insist that only appeals to individual interests can block the permissibility of an action,[25] or that meaning matters for permissibility only when it grounds individual objections. My point is that we can agree with Pildes and Niemi that the meaning conveyed by partisan gerrymandering may sometimes affect its permissibility, and still doubt that cases of expressive harm are fundamentally different to those involving individual harm. In both cases, the challenge is to identify the personal interests at stake and to ask how far those interests ground objections to a principle that allows government officials to act on partisan preferences when they design electoral maps.

IV. FOUR PERSONAL OBJECTIONS TO PARTISAN GERRYMANDERING

I now turn to arguments that account for the wrongness of partisan gerrymandering by appealing to the individual rather than the social harms that it causes, or by identifying objections that particular individuals could have to its permissibility.[26] I discuss four objections. One says that partisan gerrymandering treats some persons unequally by diluting their voting power. A second says that it inhibits some voters' freedom of expression and association. A third says that partisan gerrymandering brings about an unfair distribution of the costs of single-member district systems. The fourth says that partisan gerrymandering is wrong insofar as it is surreptitious.

A. Equality

One of the most intuitive complaints against partisan gerrymandering is that it impairs the voting power of some persons. As Kagan J put it in her dissent in *Rucho*:

> this Court in its one-person-one-vote decisions prohibited creating districts with significantly different populations. A State could not, we explained, thus 'dilut[e] the weight of votes because of place of residence.'… The constitutional injury in a partisan gerrymandering case is much the same, except that the dilution is based on party affiliation. In such a case, too, the districters have set out to reduce the weight

[24] ibid 73.

[25] For a critique of this 'individualist restriction' as making insufficient allowance for the aggregation of individual interests, see D Parfit, 'Justifiability to Each Person' (2003) XVI *Ratio* 368, 373–78.

[26] Constraints of space do not allow me to discuss whether such objections support a moral *right* against partisan gerrymandering, a question that I take to lie downstream of the discussion in the text.

of certain citizens' votes, and thereby deprive them of their capacity to 'full[y] and effective[ly] participat[e] in the political process'.[27]

'Weight dilution' may be a mixed metaphor, but the claim it supports is reasonably clear: partisan gerrymandering makes some votes count for less, either because it inflates existing majorities by packing them with additional like-minded voters, or because it reduces materially the possibility of achieving such majorities by cracking existing voting blocks amongst different districts. On this argument, partisan gerrymandering is impermissible because it creates inequalities in voting power in much the same way that violations of the equal population rule do.

The argument draws on an attractive conception of equality as a fundamental political and constitutional value in democratic societies. The question is whether partisan gerrymandering offends that conception. For a start, unlike laws that make the exercise of the right to vote more burdensome (eg, by requiring voters to carry ID), partisan gerrymanders do not offend the one-person-one-vote principle. They simply affect which of several ballot boxes of equal size a person's vote goes into. As Beitz describes the difference, as long as the districts are of equal size, gerrymanders do not affect a person's a priori voting power, but only their ex ante voting power, ie, the chance that their vote will be decisive in determining the result of the election, given how other people in the district are likely to vote.[28] The problem for the equality argument is that there is no clear reason for thinking that people are entitled to equal ex ante voting power. Suppose that my preferred candidate in the election is likely to be heavily outvoted, so my vote has a negligible chance of being decisive. Any principle that would require the electoral system to design districts so as to boost my chances of ex ante decisiveness, and make the district more competitive than it is, would be guilty of the same charge as a partisan gerrymander, and therefore objectionable to voters of the majority party. The same applies if we change the metric of equality from ex ante voting power to likelihood of satisfaction of political preference.

The deeper problem is that the appeal to equality of voting power relies on a premise that is not open to it. Suppose that the Blue Party gains 60 per cent of the vote in a given state but, due to the way district boundaries are drawn, wins only two of the five seats in play, ie, 40 per cent of the seats. Does this impair the equal voting power of Blue Party voters? As the majority in *Rucho* pointed out, this framing is questionable. The intuition that 60 per cent of the vote should correspond to 60 per cent (or something near enough) of the seats in play appeals an electoral model that the US has chosen *not* to adopt: proportional

[27] *Rucho* per Kagan J at 11-2, quoting *Reynolds v Sims*, 377 U.S. 533 (1964) at 555, 565–66.
[28] Beitz (n 3) 338–40.

representation.[29] For a country organised in single-member or first-past-the-post electoral districts, the potential for divergence between votes obtained and seats won is a not a bug but a feature. This suggests that complaints against partisan gerrymandering must be *internal* to the single-member district system. Within such a system, it is not clear why support at the level of the jurisdiction should set the baseline for assessing voting power at the level of districts. Even if one could give a plausible story about this, eg, show that voters identify more with their jurisdiction and therefore that jurisdiction-level support confers greater political legitimacy on the result, those facts are contingent and have no fixed moral weight. The point carries over to ex ante voting power: the risk that large groups of voters will have no representation in the legislature is inherent in the single-member district system. Gerrymandering aggravates that risk for voters of one party, but it does not create an inequality of ex ante voting power where there would otherwise be none.

This conclusion holds even if we shift focus to the meaning of the gerrymanderer's attitude towards voters of the targeted party. It is arguable that the gerrymanderer treats those voters as beans to be moved from one bag to another in order to satisfy the gerrymanderer's political aims and, in that way, fails to accord them appropriate respect. That is a plausible charge when we consider how this practice affects our political culture and our role as democratic citizens. However, it is weak as a charge of unequal treatment. For the gerrymanderer, *all* voters are beans.

B. Free Expression and Association

Perhaps partisan gerrymandering impedes the freedom of expression and association because, in the words of Kagan J, it subjects certain voters

> to 'disfavored treatment' – again, counting their votes for less – precisely because of 'their voting history [and] their expression of political views.' And added to that strictly personal harm is an associational one. Representative democracy is 'unimaginable without the ability of citizens to band together in [support of] candidates who espouse their political views.' By diluting the votes of certain citizens, the State frustrates their efforts to translate those affiliations into political effectiveness.[30]

This argument does not apply symmetrically to packed and cracked voting blocks. While a cracked block does indeed make it more difficult for like-minded voters to turn their shared affiliations into political effectiveness, a packed block

[29] *Rucho* per Roberts CJ at III(B); S Levinson, 'Gerrymandering and the Brooding Omnipresence of Proportional Representation: Why Won't It Go Away?' (1985) 33 *UCLA Law Review* 257, 281.

[30] *Rucho* per Kagan J at 12, citing *Vieth* at 314 and *California Democratic Party v Jones*, 530 U.S. 567, 574 (2000).

makes it easier. This would seem to suggest that the argument applies against only one of those gerrymandering methods. That impression is mistaken, for two reasons. First, there is no way of packing a voting block without cracking another, so it could be said that the injury in question is inflicted on voters of the latter block. Second, if we read the argument's reference to political effectiveness as effectiveness within a single-member district system, it becomes clear that voters in the packed block do not make a gain that mirrors the loss of voters in the cracked one, at least not in a way that might require a pairwise comparison of their relative positions. Given that voters have no control over which of the two blocks they will fall into, I think we should accept Kagan J's conclusion that partisan gerrymandering leaves a voter of the targeted party worse off in terms of their ability to translate their political affiliations into political effectiveness.

The question is how that setback should be described for the purpose of discussing the permissibility of actions that inflict it. A tempting answer is to describe that setback, as Kagan J does, in terms of its consequences for voters of the targeted party. The appeal to consequences could be construed in at least two ways. On a 'positive' reading, the presence of such political affiliations in a community counts in favour of a district design that allows them to flourish and achieve their full political effectiveness. Suppose that the east side of Westville and the west side of Eastville are heavily Democratic enclaves within otherwise solidly Republican districts, and let the fact that their political affiliation straddles the district boundary count in favour of joining them into a single district that would be Democrat by a bare majority. That would be nothing short of partisan gerrymandering which, in the terms of the argument itself, would impair the interests of Republicans in original districts. The claim looks more plausible on a 'negative' reading. When a person spends a lot of time and effort building a grassroots political network and cultivating relationships in their local community as defined by existing district limits, perhaps our institutions have reason, other things being equal, *not* to act in ways that cause this expenditure of personal and political capital to go to waste. The problem with the negative reading is that similar consequences can sometimes come about without any gerrymandering, eg, as a result of population change. If gerrymandering is wrong because it impairs a voter's ability to band together effectively with like-minded others, such wrongness should extend to non-gerrymandered impairments too, and that claim looks much too strong. A more nuanced alternative is that voters have a moral objection to revisions of an electoral map not simply when those revisions undercut the voters' effort to cultivate local political networks, but when the reasons for those revisions are not important enough to justify bringing about that consequence. Kagan J's argument assumes that the answer is no when the revisions are motivated by the districting official's partisan preferences.

It is not clear that this is the case. Suppose that the official in question is disinterested, that they see no compelling reason to adopt one or the other map, and that they hold a public consultation as to what should be done. Aliyah, a community organiser who has been cultivating a grassroots political network in the district for the last three years, points out that one of the proposed designs would split that network into three different districts and thus frustrate her efforts. Marsha, a pensioner, says that the same design would put her neighbourhood in a district with a majority of senior citizens, a prospect she welcomes because it can help generate political momentum in favour of making local public buildings more accessible. Suppose, finally, that it is not practically possible to heed both Aliyah and Marsha's preferences. It seems to me that the official would not be wronging Aliyah if, in choosing a map, they attached greater weight to Marsha's preferences, and that this conclusion would not change if we specified that both the official and Marsha are Republicans, whereas Aliyah is a Democrat. Aliyah's preferences are no less partisan than Marsha's, and it is not clear that frustrating Aliyah's organising efforts is a weightier or more important setback than frustrating Marsha's desire to join a district where, by her lights, her concerns have a higher chance of being acted upon.

A further question is whether this choice of map would become impermissible if Marsha's interests are not involved, and the official simply intends to choose whichever map makes it less likely that Democrats will win. The problem here is that this intention does not seem to have a tight enough connection with Aliyah's interest that her community network remain in one district, as the official would presumably have had the same intention even if we removed Aliyah from the picture. That problem will not arise if the official specifically intends to frustrate Aliyah's efforts (say, out of personal animus), or when they have misled the electorate about their policy or intentions regarding districting, eg, they have claimed that their choice of electoral map would not rely on partisan considerations. However, in those cases too, the wrong involved would not be based on the freedom of assembly and association, but on the relevant principles of honesty and fidelity to political commitments – I return to this point in D. below.

C. Fairness

A third argument, defended by Charles Beitz, says that partisan gerrymandering is impermissible not because it creates inequalities between voters, but because it distributes unfairly the costs of single-member district electoral systems. This complaint against gerrymandering is internal to that electoral system, and to that extent is immune to the objection of the *Rucho* majority against the arguments from inequality of voting power. As Beitz notes, single-member districts are, by definition, also winner-takes-all. The single-member aspect creates costs for all voters, because it funnels every potential candidacy through a primary contest that delivers a single candidate for each party, and that winner may not be a given voter's preferred candidate. The winner-takes-all aspect creates high costs for voters who find themselves on the losing side of the election, as their vote does not succeed in affecting the representation of the district. Taken together, the overall costs of the system are considerable for all voters, insofar as the distance between a voter's preferences and the preferences of the winning candidate is likely to be larger in single-member districts systems than in systems of proportional representation. Of course, we could regard these costs as the price voters must pay for having a single-member district system rather than one of proportional representation. But this way of thinking should also lead us to ask whether that price is a *fair match* for whichever benefits the single-member district system is supposed to deliver (eg, more stable legislative majorities, empowerment of geographically defined communities of interest, facilitation of a personal attachment between representative and electorate etc).[31] If there are several ways of producing those benefits, and some of them involve higher costs for some or all voters, those voters can reasonably object that they are being charged too much for the political goods they are receiving. Beitz believes that this idea has important implications for the permissibility of partisan gerrymandering:

> If we think of a shortfall in the correspondence of a voter's priorities and the legislature's agenda as a cost that should be allocated fairly among voters, then we might say that gerrymandering's impact is to induce inequalities in the distribution of this cost that cannot be justified as necessary to achieve the benefits of SMD. On this view, the effect of partisan gerrymandering is to impose an unjustifiably large share of the costs of SMD on those whom it disadvantages … The unfairness would lie in imposing an electoral disability on some citizens that cannot be justified in terms of the aims of the system. It is important to see that on this interpretation of the objection, it is not claimed that gerrymandering introduces an inequality where otherwise there would be equality. It introduces an avoidable disability, but avoidance of the disability would not normally eliminate all inequality in the value of the vote.[32]

As Beitz notes, the argument has a very dramatic implication: the wrong of unfairness in the distribution of the costs of single-member district systems can occur even in districts that have not been gerrymandered at all:

> If the differences produced by gerrymandering in *ex ante* voting power are objectionable because they represent an unfair allocation of the costs of SMD, then it is no longer clear why we should think that 'naturally' occurring differences *arising from the geography of partisanship* are innocuous.[33]

On this view, stable district boundaries can become morally objectionable simply because of shifts in party allegiance in the district, whether these are due to gerrymandering, population change, or successful political organising.

[31] Beitz (n 3) 344.
[32] ibid 345.
[33] ibid (emphasis added). Later in the paper (at 350 ff), Beitz argues that partisan gerrymanders also lead to the 'cartelization' of districts and a loss of responsiveness to changes in the popular vote.

The presence of an effort to manipulate district boundaries is merely an aggravating circumstance. In effect, as Niko Kolodny has noted, what begins like a case against partisan gerrymandering becomes a case in favour of continual, if in Beitz's view benign, gerrymandering for the benefit of electoral minorities.[34]

Beitz's account faces two difficulties. First, it is not clear why the cost of the likely distance between one's voting preferences and the legislative agenda ought to be distributed fairly. Second, the link between that cost and single-member district systems is not as tight as Beitz makes out. Under plausible assumptions, similar costs may be incurred under systems of proportional representation too.

To continue with a previous example, let it be true that, unless the electoral map is redrawn in a certain way, there will be a considerable distance between the legislative agenda and Marsha's preference for more accessible public buildings in her area. The question is whether leaving that cost with Marsha is something that can be justified to her, given that a similar justification must be given to everyone else too, including Aliyah, whose efforts in community organising would suffer were the map to be so redrawn. The answer may be negative when the cost to Marsha is *so much higher* than the cost to Aliyah, that this difference becomes a reason for Aliyah and others to accept the more moderate cost to themselves. For example, if Marsha has mobility problems, she has particularly high stakes in whether the community should pay for making public spaces more accessible. Given that persons in Marsha's position can easily be outvoted when the matter comes up for decision, other people have moral reason to agree to a system that gives the interests of persons with mobility problems a degree of protection regardless of the outcome of the vote (eg, by making accessibility a matter of legal right, giving the votes of persons with mobility problems a different weighting, and so on). Note, however, that what gives others such a reason is not Marsha's *preference* that the community pay for improved accessibility of public spaces but the *importance of her substantive interest* in being able to access and use those spaces. That is why preferences regarding public funding for luxury items have different moral weight compared to preferences regarding public funding for improved accessibility of public spaces, even when the distance between them and the legislative agenda is similarly high. This is not to say that the representation of preferences is morally irrelevant. The point is that, priority of need aside, it is not clear why people owe each other anything more than a *fair opportunity* to have their preferences represented in the legislative agenda. This opportunity may perhaps be smaller in absolute terms in a single-member district system than in a proportional one, but the distribution of that opportunity will not be unfair for that reason.

[34] N Kolodny, 'What, If Anything, Is Wrong with Gerrymandering?' (2019) 56 *San Diego Law Review* 1013, 1028. The reach of Beitz's account extends beyond typical partisan gerrymanders in another way: it includes situations where the gerrymander aims to make it more likely that certain candidates are elected, rather than to change the split of seats between the parties.

Kolodny notes a second difficulty. The claim that single-member district systems create the risk of a greater distance between a voter's preferences and the legislative agenda trades on the following set of assumptions about the profile of a district in which people vote for one of two parties, *A* and *B*:

> (i) that no *A* representative is closer to any *B* voter than some *B* representative – and vice versa; (ii) that the greater number of *B* representatives, the greater the range of *B* voter preferences represented by someone in the legislature – and vice versa, and (iii) the spread of *B* voter preferences is just as wide as the spread of *A* voter preferences.[35]

Whether these assumptions hold true in a district or jurisdiction is a contingent matter. The problem is that their truth-value is independent of the choice between single-member district and proportional systems. Say that, in a proportional system, there are 100 seats in play and that A has 60 per cent of the vote while B has 40 per cent. If the aim is to minimise the maximum distance between a voter's preferences and the legislative agenda, there will still be a case for splitting the seats 51-49 rather than 60-40. Proportional systems will be less costly, or (in Beitz's terms) less 'disabling', than single-member district systems on that score, but that seems an unavoidable aspect of the difference between the two systems. One cannot get the benefits of a single-member district system (whatever these may be) and expect no loss of opportunity to have one's preferences reflected in the legislative agenda.

D. Surreption[36]

Kolodny has pointed to a fourth possibility. In his view, what makes partisan gerrymandering wrong is that the party that starts using that practice first, without advance notice of its intention to do so, obtains an unfair advantage in future elections. The wrongness of such gerrymandering lies not in its partisanship but in the surreptitious character of its first use.

Starting from the premise that citizens in a democratic society are owed an equal opportunity to be informed about the applicable decision-making procedure, Kolodny looks at Republican strategy from around 2010 onwards, and concludes:

> Republicans … systematically targeted elections of state governments in 2010, in order to gerrymander to an unprecedented extent. Democrats falsely believed that

[35] ibid 1026.

[36] The adjective 'surreptitious' dominates modern usage, but the original noun is both true to the substance of Kolodny's argument and more elegant than the bloated 'surrepticiousness'. *Cf* Ben Jonson's 'Fame by surreption got / may stead us for the time but lasteth not' in *The Speeches at Prince Henry's Barriers* (1610).

> both sides were competing in the traditional contest, and this was a reasonable belief – or at any rate cheap and easy for Republicans to correct … It was as though Republicans knew but withheld from Democrats when the 'real' election - that is, the one that would determine partisan composition of state's congressional delegation-would take place.[37]

Kolodny acknowledges that this narrative might not be an accurate reflection of recent US political history, but since he uses it chiefly to fix moral ideas, sceptical readers could treat it as a hypothetical. Moreover, the substantive argument could be extended, as the requirement of honesty and fair dealing applies both to parties and individual candidates. If a candidate undertakes not to appeal to partisan preference in districting, they may not permissibly do so if elected, nor could they plausibly claim that their voters have given them a mandate to that effect (as the candidate was never told about it). Even in its extended form, though, the argument is exceedingly modest. It takes partisan gerrymandering to be permissible as long as the intent to use it is duly advertised, much more so if the policy gains voter approval, and it suggests that surreptitious gerrymandering ceases to be wrongful from the moment people come to expect its use as part of the normal political game (though existing gerrymanders remain wrongful as long as their effects persist).

I suspect that Kolodny may also be a little too gentle on the opposition. In ordinary democratic politics, the stakes of an election are not determined by any single party. Each side gives its own story about those stakes and hopes to shape voters' perceptions accordingly. In fact, one of the main strategies in political campaigning involves trying to uncover the 'real' agenda of the opposition, so as to make its policies less palatable to the electorate.[38] That effort focuses not only on what a party will do if it acquires power, but also its record in government. The surreptitious character of gerrymandering over an electoral cycle can become one of the central issues in the next, and so on.[39] While this does not undermine Kolodny's substantive point, it suggests that the responsibility for the failure to identify the possibility of partisan gerrymandering as part of the stakes of an election may not be as one-sided as he makes out.

[37] Kolodny (n 34) 1035.

[38] As a solid amount of research suggests that voting behaviour is primarily driven by *dislike* of policies. On the distinction between 'cheering' and 'booing' voting behaviour, see G Brennan and L Lomaskys, *Democracy and Decision: The Pure Theory of Electoral Preference* (Cambridge, Cambridge University Press, 1993) ch 2; A Hamlin and C Jennings, 'Expressive Voting' in R Congleton et al (eds), *Oxford Handbook of Public Choice – Vol. 1* (New York, NY, Oxford University Press, 2019) 333; J Rivas and J Rockey, 'Expressing voting with booing and cheering: Evidence from Britain' (2021) 67 *European Journal of Political Economy* 101956.

[39] Apparently, Democrats have had some success on that front, see, eg, *How Democrats Turned the Tables in the Gerrymandering Wars*, New Republic, 8 February 2022. A priceless resource in that regard is Doug Spencer's *All About Redistricting* at redistricting.lls.edu.

V. PRELIMINARY CONCLUSIONS AND A TENTATIVE SUGGESTION

In the main, debates about the moral permissibility of partisan gerrymandering are not concerned with devious officials rubbing their hands in glee as they feed data about voter allegiance into a supercomputer. Rather, they are concerned with explaining which, if any, of the less dramatic examples where districting can affect election outcomes are morally problematic. Producing such an explanation is harder than it might seem. Partisanship carries a bad name, but partisan preference is a political preference like any other. Subject to constraints of equal population, partisan gerrymandering does not obviously undermine equality of voting power. When advertised in advance, it does not mislead voters and the opposition. And while it may cause a setback to a person's interest in maintaining and cultivating existing political associations, and make it harder for some voters to have their preferences reflected in the political agenda, neither interest seems compelling enough to justify banning officials from appealing to partisan preference in choosing electoral maps.

Accounts that focus on the 'expressive' harms of partisan gerrymandering, ie, its adverse impact on public life, have very strong appeal, but their claims about the meaning that gerrymandering conveys are not easy to translate into claims about the moral permissibility of the practice, especially on accounts that see moral justification as being owed to individuals rather than to societies. On such accounts, we should allow that sometimes a political practice can demean our institutions or corrupt our democratic culture and nevertheless be permissible, unless particular individuals could object to the principle that permits it. Those accounts are, of course, controversial. Moral consequentialists, amongst others, hold that if partisan gerrymandering makes things go socially worse, we have reason to regard the practice as impermissible. Those attracted to that view have a clear way of accounting for the wrongness of partisan (and any other kind of) gerrymandering. This remains an open challenge for deontologists, or so I have argued.

I would like to close with a tentative suggestion of an alternative way to meet it. Perhaps partisan gerrymandering is morally impermissible not because it treats people unequally or because it is unfair, but because voters may object to the use by public institutions of data regarding their political allegiance. One way to make the case for this would be to draw a parallel between partisan and racial gerrymandering. Generally speaking, I can reasonably object to a principle that allowed the state to collect information about my race in making decisions that affect me, eg, in deciding how much tax I pay or which schools I can attend.[40] Of course, that principle will still allow appeals to race in special

[40] I am assuming that government action is special in that regard. For an account of occasions in which one may rationally act on racially or sexually prejudiced views that one does not share, eg, because one cannot afford to antagonise those who hold them, see J Gardner, 'On the Ground of Her Sex(uality)' (1998) 18 *OJLS* 167, 169 ff.

circumstances, eg, when people of my race are a historic or present victim of systematic discrimination, when my race affects my chances of developing some serious disease etc. Moreover, such special justifications may extend over large parts of state activity. The moral wrong of racism leaves a stain on every aspect of social and institutional life, so information about a person's race can, under certain conditions, be part of a very large suite of measures of redress. This does not change the fact that, in the absence of such special justification, my objection to government decision-making that relies on my race retains its force, whether or not the state goes on to discriminate against me. It is enough that the collection and use of such information is not needed for the discharge of the state functions or powers in question, and that it subjects me to a non-negligible risk of bias or differential treatment. In the context of gerrymandering, such a 'risk of bias' account provides a straightforward explanation of both why racial gerrymanders are impermissible and why the creation of 'majority-minority' districts is sometimes morally required.

Perhaps there is a case for extending this account to information about a person's voting record and party allegiance. If I have reasonable grounds to believe that allowing the state to use data about my voting record would expose me to a risk of differential treatment, and the state can discharge the function of drawing district boundaries without access to such data, I can object to a principle that allowed the state to do this, whether or not such differential treatment ends up having an adverse effect on me. Here too, some cases will be special. If I allege that the state has prevented me from voting, the state may legitimately appeal to my voting record in rebutting the charge. If I allege that the polling stations in my district had no ballot papers for the party of my choice, the state may appeal to voting results in those stations to prove me wrong, and so on. Moreover, a 'risk of bias' account does not prohibit every partisan gerrymander, only those that rely on individualised voting data. Of course, establishing that a decision has been based on a certain kind of information will be a difficult task, but it is not an impossible one. For example, we could follow Sam Wang's 'zone of chance' method and regard a map that is highly favourable to one party as impermissible only when it is exceedingly unlikely that officials blind to information about voting allegiance would have selected that map.[41]

[41] Wang (n 12) 1287–89. For a broadly similar method see Berman (n 1) 838 ff.

Part II

The European Context

4

Electoral Challenges and the Doctrine of Parliamentary Sovereignty

BOB WATT*

I. INTRODUCTION

THIS CHAPTER ADDRESSES the question as to the reality of challenges to elections to the Westminster Parliament in the context of the doctrine of 'parliamentary sovereignty'. If a parliament – the Westminster Parliament – is sovereign how can the people who are subordinate to Parliament challenge its sovereign will? To avoid the repeated use of 'Westminster Parliament', the abbreviation WP will be used throughout this chapter where the sovereign Westminster Parliament is being discussed. The reason for insisting upon the term 'Westminster Parliament' (or WP) is that there are a number of other Parliaments in the UK – the Scottish Parliament and the Welsh Parliament (and the Northern Ireland Assembly). None of these bodies is fully sovereign; they derive their powers from the WP, which could (if it considered it expedient and politically possible) remove their powers and abolish them. The WP is the only fully sovereign Parliament in the UK. If the WP is 'in charge' of the country, how are the people empowered to remove it? First, it should be noted that this is a concept fundamentally alien to, eg, the French or the German Constitutions, both of which place sovereignty in the hands of the people. Article 3 of the French Constitution and Article 20(2) of the German Constitution are explicit in this effect.

That having been said there does remain an obvious answer – a 'General Election' – an election in every constituency of the WP to elect (or re-elect) a Member of the House of Commons. The House of Commons, which is the effective elected part of WP has a finite lifespan. The Dissolution and Calling

* I would like to express my gratitude to the organisers and participants in the Workshop on Judicial Review and Electoral Law (Bocconi University, 29–30 November 2018), which served as the foundation for this chapter. Additionally, I appreciate the invaluable feedback provided by the participants and the editors on earlier versions.

of Parliament Act 2022[1] provides that the maximum life of a parliament – the assembly of people which make up the effective, elected WP – can only be five years. The absolute discretion of the Prime Minister to advise the monarch (the head of state) to call a General Election to the WP must be exercised within five years of the date of the last General Election. This Act encapsulates the doctrine of parliamentary sovereignty – a majority in the WP can alter the frequency of elections and reverse one of the commitments made by the Conservative leader, David Cameron, in 2001 to secure the support of the Liberal Democrat party in forming a Coalition Government. This neatly shows parliamentary sovereignty has both a legal and a political wing; this will be further discussed below. However, the neglect of this fundamental point demonstrates that the doctrine of parliamentary sovereignty is not properly understood by observers. This is because it is rarely, if ever, properly stated – it is usually overstated. Second, even if the doctrine is properly stated, and is thus comprehensible, the control of electoral law has been expressly assumed by successive Parliaments since, at the latest 1430,[2] and thus, unless it is somehow entrenched in a written Constitution (as in, for example, France, Germany, South Africa, and the US) it will remain under the control of successive WPs. It should be noted that the electoral laws of Wales and Scotland are under the partial control of their own governments, where control has not been retained by the WP. So, what is parliamentary sovereignty?

A summary answer – which will be explored, fleshed-out and explained in the succeeding sections of this chapter – is that it is a mixed doctrine of law and politics. It has both legal and political components and the consideration of one and the neglect of the other will lead to misunderstanding and an erroneous result. It is to be regretted that 'parliamentary sovereignty' is an invariable component of university undergraduate courses in constitutional law, which is, of course, taught by lawyers; but it is a much less frequent component of courses in British politics – taught by political theorists or political scientists. The subject is best understood by looking at it both as a lawyer and as a scholar of politics – because it has two dimensions, and it is the interplay of these dimensions which determines its nature. This chapter contains an attempt to examine electoral law through the medium of challenges to elections – in the light of parliamentary sovereignty. It is hoped that parliamentary sovereignty is thus illuminated.

This chapter considers election law in the context of 'parliamentary sovereignty' and accordingly it is advisable to have, from the outset, a definition of such sovereignty. As we will soon see, the concept is simple in form, but is more complex because it is not legally defined in one place; it requires a certain amount of 'gap-filling' and explanation. Parliament in an extra-legal and

[1] Dissolution and Calling of Parliament Act 2022: www.legislation.gov.uk/ukpga/2022/11/section/2/enacted (accessed 30 May 2022).

[2] What sort of men shall be choosers and who shall be chosen Knights of the Parliament, see, Act 8 Henry VI. cap. VII.

rather informal way has offered the following definition, which is expanded and elucidated in this chapter:

> Parliamentary sovereignty is a principle of the UK constitution. It makes Parliament the supreme legal authority in the UK, which can create or end any law. Generally, the courts cannot overrule its legislation and no Parliament can pass laws that future Parliaments cannot change. Parliamentary sovereignty is the most important part of the UK constitution.
>
> People often refer to the UK having an 'unwritten constitution' but that's not strictly true. It may not exist in a single text, like in the USA or Germany, but large parts of it are written down, much of it in the laws passed in Parliament – known as statute law. Therefore, the UK constitution is often described as 'partly written and wholly uncodified'. (Uncodified means that the UK does not have a single, written constitution.) Over the years, Parliament has passed laws that limit the application of parliamentary sovereignty. These laws reflect political developments both within and outside the UK.
>
> They include:
>
> - The devolution of power to bodies like the Scottish Parliament (Pàrlamaid na h-Alba) and Senedd Cymru. (Welsh Senate).
> - The Human Rights Act 1998.
> - The UK's entry to the European Union in 1973 – and subsequent exit in 2020.
> - The decision to establish a UK Supreme Court in 2009, which ends the House of Lords function as the UK's final court of appeal.
>
> These developments do not fundamentally undermine the principle of parliamentary sovereignty, since, in theory at least, Parliament could repeal any of the laws implementing these changes.[3]

II. PARLIAMENTARY SOVEREIGNTY

The first limb of the traditional doctrine of parliamentary sovereignty, which originates in the British constitutional settlement of 1689 following our Civil Wars, is that the WP can make or unmake any law it chooses. The most obvious and let me make it clear from the outset – highly regrettable, modern example is the repeal of the European Communities Act 1972 by the European Union (Withdrawal) Act 2018. This explains the comment made above about the abolition of, for example, the Scottish Parliament; no-one thought that withdrawal from the EU was politically possible, but it happened. This exposes the second limb – which will become important towards the end of this chapter – that one Parliament cannot bind its successors. 'Parliamentary sovereignty' is, of course, formally a legal doctrine. However, law does not wholly define the

[3] UK Parliament 'Parliament's authority': www.parliament.uk/about/how/role/sovereignty/ (accessed 5 June 2023).

relationship between the people and Parliament – the doctrine has a political dimension which restricts its application. The example often given in introductory lectures to undergraduates reflects both the true extent of the doctrine, and something, it is feared, of the British popular psyche, comes from the extended examination and development of Albert Venn Dicey's work by Sir Ivor Jennings: the Westminster Parliament could as a matter of law 'ban smoking on the streets of Paris', but it lacks the political power so to do. During the extended and ongoing discussions of the Northern Ireland Protocol, which sets out special customs arrangements for Northern Ireland, which is part of the UK, there have been ill-informed calls in the popular newspaper press for the UK Government to reincorporate the Republic of Ireland by ignoring the subsequent legislation and restoring the Act of Union of 1800. This is pure fantasy.

Moving away from fancy, we do have the well-known example of the Aviation Security Act 1982 which extends the jurisdiction of the domestic courts to try those who (allegedly) attempt or succeed in hijacking aircraft wherever in the world the (alleged) offence took place and whatever the nationality of the hijackers. Whether any such trial would ever take place in circumstances where the alleged hijackers are protected by another (hostile?) sovereign state is doubted. One recalls the lengthy negotiations between the bombing of Pan-Am flight 103 over Lockerbie Scotland in 1988 and the handing over for trial of Abdelbaset al-Megrahi in1999. One can only speculate about the treatment of any request to try the Russian military intelligence suspects in the Wiltshire nerve gas poisonings.

These are obviously international examples and seem to hint at an unrealistic world view rooted in Empire and British exceptionalism. In order to make a convincing case that there is a political dimension to the doctrine, we need to look at two domestic examples drawn from controversial areas of employment law in the 1970s. The reason employment law has been chosen is that there has been little real political controversy over election law since 1918 and so it is impossible to give election law examples. The first is the doomed Industrial Relations Act 1971. This Act was passed following a bitter parliamentary battle between the Conservative Government led by Edward Heath and the Labour opposition. The Bill was debated clause by clause on the floor of the House and eventually passed into law. Its intention was to provide a more effective than hitherto system for resolving labour disputes; its effect was to stimulate and exacerbate labour unrest. The trade unions resolutely defied the law and employers declined to use it and, in one famous incident, an anonymous employer paid the fine levied on a union. In another, yet more surprising turn, workers who flagrantly and explicitly breached the law on picketing and were imprisoned were freed after the intervention of one of the Crown's Law Officers because the government feared a general strike. The Act was a complete dead-letter by 1972 and was repealed by the incoming Labour

Government in 1974.[4] The second example which might be seen – to adopt a slogan from 'Star Wars' – as the 'Empire Striking Back' is to be found in the Grunwick Processing Laboratories dispute in the late 1970s where the Labour Government's 1974 Employment Protection Act – a replacement for the Industrial Relations Act – which provided for workers to be consulted on the recognition of their trade union by the employer was defied by the employer encouraged by a member of the (Conservative) Shadow Cabinet and the free-market, libertarian Freedom Association.[5]

Whilst the legal doctrines explored in the cases attached to these events are complex, they are matters of (largely superseded) employment law and do not need to detain us. However, we do need to examine the third limb of the doctrine which provides that primary legislation may not be challenged in a court. The clearest statement of this doctrine can be seen in Lord Diplock's speech in (another employment case) *Duport Steels Ltd v Sirs*.[6] This is directly contrary to the doctrine of fundamental (or constitutional) judicial review established in many jurisdictions.[7] In this case Denning MR in the Court of Appeal sought to disapply a number of statutory protections of trade unions because he saw them as being in restraint of trade. The House of Lords was short in reversing the decision, saying that Parliament, not the judges was sovereign, and the courts could not simply rewrite the law.

It would be wrong to characterise the Declaration of Incompatibility (with the provisions of European Convention of Human Rights/Human Rights Act 1998) provision included in section 4 of the Human Rights Act 1998 as an example of fundamental judicial review because the section 4(6) provision explicitly states that the issue of such a Declaration: (a) does not affect the validity, continuing operation or enforcement of the provision in respect of which it is given; and (b) is not binding on the parties to the proceedings in which it is made.

The ultimate legal effect of a Declaration of Incompatibility is thus nugatory because, as we have seen in the discussion of the Industrial Relations Act 1971 above, a law which is simply ignored by citizens is barely a law, and one which is ignored by the officials of the state to whom it is addressed is no law at all.[8] If a

[4] For a brief, highly partisan, but largely accurate, illuminating, and useful account see the newspaper article published by the *Communist Party of Britain Marxist-Leninist* 'Engineers Demolish Industrial Relations Act 1971–1974' (2015) www.cpbml.org.uk/news/engineers-demolish-industrial-relations-act-1971–1974 (accessed 30 May 2022). This hyperbolic account is to be preferred over more sober assessments because it demonstrates what happens in the last instance – when 'push comes to shove'.

[5] For litigation on this matter which also provides a useful account of the events, see *Grunwick Processing Laboratories v Advisory, Conciliatory and Arbitration Service* [1978] ICR 231; [1978] AC 655.

[6] *Duport Steels Ltd v Sirs* [1980] ICR 161.

[7] See, eg, Art 61 of the French Constitution, Art 93 of the German Basic Law, or for a court's establishment of such an action, *Marbury v Madison* 5 U.S. 137 (1803).

[8] See TA Cowan, 'Law without Force' (1971) 59(3) *California Law Review*: www.jstor.org/stable/3479597 (accessed 31 May 2022).

formal law has, on its face, a statement that it has no coercive force whatsoever one does not have to be a full-blown Kelsenian positivist to regard it as not a law at all. It is a mere political wish and thus it would seem to require some political impetus to make it effective. Whether or not the WP has amended legislation in all incompatibility cases, or will continue so to do, is irrelevant because one can well conceive of circumstances where political considerations have led the government to continue for some time to ignore judicial findings.[9]

This introduction has established a general claim – that the doctrine of parliamentary sovereignty is legally absolute but politically constrained. The people exercise ultimate political sovereignty, but – from time to time or, at least, from General Election to General Election the WP gets away with whatever it can. It will be seen below that, in the circumstances of the 'Partygate' affair – where the Prime Minister appeared to be ignoring the law, that this, rather cynical view may require revision.

Let us now consider the validity of this claim when applied to election petitions – challenging elections under the laws of the UK.

III. THE ELECTION PETITION

The procedure for challenging an election is known as an 'election petition'. Here we are going, in the main, to deal with parliamentary election petitions since we want to explore whether the doctrine of parliamentary sovereignty affects the hearing of election petitions. Much of the case law – the interpretation of the grounds of challenge – is common between parliamentary and local government petitions and this accounts for the reason we must look at some local government petitions. It is called an 'election petition' for historical reasons which need not concern us. After the Civil Wars of the seventeenth century, especially following the important case of *Ashby v White*[10] at the beginning of the eighteenth century and the reforms of 1770, the petition was addressed directly to Parliament. As we shall see, from 1868 petitions have been heard by the ordinary courts, albeit by members with special expertise.

Now a parliamentary election challenge must be brought under section 120 of the Representation of the People Act 1983 (RPA 1983), whilst a local government challenge must be brought under section 127 RPA 1983. These challenges are presented to the courts. The terms of the two sections are identical in substance, but the wording differs to accommodate the differences between the legislature and subordinate administrations.

[9] See, eg, *Hirst v UK (no.2)* (2005) ECHR 681 – the blanket ban on prisoner voting case.
[10] *Ashby v White* (1703) Ld Raym 938, (1703) 92 ER 126; but see also (1703) 1 Brown 62.

Section 120 RPA 1983 states:

(1) No parliamentary election and no return to Parliament shall be questioned except by a petition complaining of an undue election or undue return ("a parliamentary election petition") presented in accordance with this Part of this Act.
(2) A petition complaining of no return shall be deemed to be a parliamentary election petition and the High Court.[11]

(a) … or
(b) …

Put simply – No election shall be challenged save by an Election Petition made in accordance with the provisions of the Act.

IV. PETITIONS FROM 1689 TO THE PRESENT DAY

For the purposes of our analysis, we can safely discount cases decided before 1689 when the Constitution was fundamentally reshaped. Following the Civil Wars which led to the execution of King Charles I and the period of the Commonwealth where England did not have a King; Charles II was restored to the throne. On his death James II came to the throne and it appeared that he was going to try to reign in a similar fashion to Charles I, being a Roman Catholic and a defender of the divine right of kings to rule autocratically. There was civil unrest, James II vacated the throne and fled, and William of Orange and his wife Mary were invited to take the thrones as joint constitutional monarchs – the supreme power being stated to reside with 'the Crown in Parliament'.

The Bill of Rights 1689[12] contains the following provisions:[13]

> That Election of Members of Parlyament ought to be free.
>
> That the Freedome of Speech and Debates or Proceedings in Parlyament ought not to be impeached or questioned in any Court or Place out of Parlyament.

It is these provisions which give rise to the difficulty with sovereignty. If an election to Parliament is a 'proceeding in Parliament' there is some tension between these two provisions. That was indeed the issue at trial in *Ashby v White*. Here

[11] A complaint of 'no return' would be made in circumstances where the Returning Officer – a locally based official failed, or refused, to complete the necessary documents after an election. Documents setting out the election result and naming the person elected have to be sent to a parliamentary official immediately after an election. The author is unable to find any complaints of 'no return'; for that reason, the procedure for dealing with such complaints is omitted from this statement of the statute.

[12] Royal Assent was given to the Act on 16 December 1689. The Act is The Bill of Rights [1688] 1 Will & Mary session 2, c. 2.

[13] I have retained the original spelling in this first recitation – it is copied from the Legislation website www.legislation.gov.uk/ (accessed 27 May 2022).

a person claiming to have the right to vote in Aylesbury was prevented from so doing by a public official. The disenfranchised man challenged the election result in the common law courts. The (lowest in the appropriate hierarchy) Court of King's Bench held that no action would lie at common law, because the matter was reserved to Parliament under the provisions of the Bill of Rights. The matter was appealed to the Court of Common Pleas where, by a majority of eight to one, the judgment was upheld. The powerful dissent was delivered by Sir John Holt CJ who held that there was an action at common law to vindicate the right to vote which, at that time, was intimately linked to the right to property because those rights were 'precedaneous to parliament'. This seems to indicate that they were some form of 'natural right' and were thus within the province of the courts. The matter was further appealed to the House of Lords – which at that time did not have a Judicial Committee but heard cases on the floor of the entire House – which upheld Holt CJ's position as a valid statement of the law. This proved unacceptable to the House of Commons; the eponymous reporter of Brown's Cases saying that: 'Scarce any judicial determination ever occasioned such a disturbance in both Houses of Parliament as the present.'[14]

The House of Commons on 25 and 26 January 1703 passed five Resolutions (which did not and could not become Statute because they were not passed through the law-making process) which reserved the hearing of election petitions to itself. Election petitions were heard as part of the political process on the floor of the House of Commons until 1848. The most infamous of the cases of expulsion from Parliament and its refusal to seat a person duly elected concerned John Wilkes over the period 1764–74.[15] Whilst it must be remembered that few were enfranchised in the eighteenth and nineteenth centuries and voting was conducted by an open poll until 1872, the business of the House of Commons was so disrupted by multiple challenges over the period 1832 to 1848, that the hearing of Election Petitions was passed to a Parliamentary Committee. The situation worsened (so far as the government/Parliament were concerned) and in the 1865 General Election some 35 Petitions were raised. The government initially intended to put the resolution into the hands of specialist Commissioners rather than block up parliamentary time and resources but were persuaded to direct the matter to the courts. Whether this was a matter of principle – that of legality and separation of powers – or of pragmatism in the face of mutterings that disputed elections were decided by political expediency and party loyalty, or of a simple desire to give the problem to someone else to solve is not clear. In any event the 1868 Act was

[14] See (1703) 1 Brown 62 at 64.

[15] For summary see: R Cavendish, 'John Wilkes Expelled from the House of Commons' (January 2014) 64(1) *History Today*: www.historytoday.com/richard-cavendish/john-wilkes-expelled-house-commons (accessed 31 May 2022).

passed and provided a form of election petition which I observed in 2006 (and the Electoral Commission endorses this view) survives almost unchanged until this day.[16]

The '1868 procedure' (ie, that now set out in Part 3 of the Representation of the People Act 1983 and which follows on from section 120 of the 1983 Act providing the procedural steps) is seriously defective. The Electoral Commission's Report *Challenging Elections in the UK* is utterly damning (see Appendix). Here we need only note the introductory sentence:

> 206. This report has shown that in many respects, the UK's petition system fails to comply with internationally recognised principles.

The content of chapter 13 of the Law Commissions' Interim Report on reforming electoral law is scarcely less damning.[17] Whilst there is a later Final Report which contains proposals for the reform of electoral law, this is not considered here because the provisions require far greater analysis than space permits and, given that the next General Election must take place in 2024, and progress on the implementation of them has not been timetabled for the next session of the WP, it is unlikely that they will be seriously considered in their present form. It must be remembered that the basic format of the UK's electoral laws was set in the late nineteenth century. As the present author wrote in 2006: '... the basic legislation governing modern election procedures was firmly in place by 1900'.[18] Whilst there have been changes since then, an election lawyer transported from 1900 to 2022 would recognise the basic format, although they may marvel at the parliamentary enfranchisement of women started in 1918.

Given that Article 3 of the First Protocol to the European Convention of Human Rights[19] applies to elections to the legislature (although not referenda)[20] it is a little surprising that no challenge has been made in the ECHR to the UK's election petition system. It is clear that the general principles of legality contained in the Convention – 'it should be interpreted in order to maintain the ideals and values of a democratic society'[21] have been held to require that a High Contracting Party provide an effective means for investigating and determining

[16] See, Electoral Commission, *Challenging Elections in the UK* (September 2012).

[17] *Electoral Law: A Joint Interim Report* (4 February 2016). This Report was prepared jointly by the Law Commissions of England & Wales, Scotland, and Northern Ireland.

[18] B Watt, *UK Election Law: A Critical Examination* (London, Glasshouse, 2006) 7.

[19] The High Contracting Parties shall hold free elections at reasonable intervals by secret ballot, under conditions which will ensure the free expression of the opinion of the people in the choice of the legislature.

[20] See, most recently, *Moohan & Gillon v UK* 22962/15 and 23345/15, especially para 40 which puts the matter beyond reasonable doubt: www.hudoc.echr.coe.int/eng?i=001-175572 (accessed 26 May 2022).

[21] See the Preamble to the Convention, *Kjeldson & Others v Denmark* (1976) Eur Ct HR Series A vol 23 at para 23; *Matthews v UK application* 24833 ECHR (GC) at para 34.

electoral disputes.[22] The most likely reason that no such challenge has been made is because of the paucity of parliamentary election petitions; one of which would be needed to provide the peg upon which a potential breach of Article 3 of the First Protocol could hang. The substantial reason for that might have been suggested by Joseph Heller – 'it is so difficult to bring an election petition that no-one brings one to show how difficult it is!!' It is clear that there are allegations of electoral malpractice in parliamentary elections for, at the time of delivery of the original Conference paper, Craig Mackinlay MP was facing criminal charges relating to an alleged false declaration of expenses in the 2015 General Election. Mackinlay was subsequently acquitted in the Crown Court, so the matter is closed. This matter was clearly one which was ideally suited for resolution by means of an Election Petition, but the matter was not discovered until any such Petition was time-barred.

We will return to the question of what should be done to reform the Election Petition procedure after we have considered whether the House of Commons would ever try to reclaim the petition procedure for itself.

Before we consider any such reclamation, we will briefly examine the use of the Election Petition procedure. Whilst the Election Petition procedure is cumbersome, it is effective. There have been two parliamentary Election Petitions in recent years, one of which was successful.

V. THE USE OF THE PETITION

The defeated Liberal Democrat candidate Elwyn Watkins successfully challenged by Petition the election of Phil Woolas in Oldham East and Saddleworth in the 2010 General Election.[23] This decision was subsequently upheld in a Judicial Review of the decision which is itself of interest on two points.[24] The first issue was whether the decision of an Election Court could be challenged other than by means of an appeal to the higher courts. It was held that it could be challenged by means of Judicial Review rather than by Appeal because the Election Court is a temporary tribunal convened simply for the purpose of trying an Election Petition rather than a full court in its own right. This strikes the present author as puzzling because one might reasonably think that in a matter as serious as a challenge to an election a full court ought to be convened. It somehow suggests that the matter in question is not sufficiently serious to merit the attention of a 'proper court'. The second issue was rather more prosaic in comparison. In the original Petition, Woolas was held personally liable for the little-used electoral

[22] See para 87 of *Uspaskich v Lithuania* 14737/08: www.hudoc.echr.coe.int/eng?i=001-169844 (accessed 25 May 2022) and especially para 81 of *Namat Aliyev v Azerbaijan* 18705/06: www.hudoc.echr.coe.int/eng?i=001-98187 (accessed 26 May 2022).

[23] *Watkins v Woolas* [2010] EWHC 2702.

[24] *R (Woolas) v The Parliamentary Election Court* [2010] EWHC 3169.

offence of making false statements about the personal character of his opponent contrary to section 106 RPA 1983. Woolas published a leaflet falsely claiming that Watkins was personally sympathetic to convicted Islamic terrorists and members of proscribed organisations. In the Judicial Review the point was raised that the Election Court should have considered whether Woolas was protected by the freedom of speech provision of Article 10 ECHR. The Court hearing the Judicial Review, rather unsurprisingly, held that deliberately and knowingly lying does not attract the protection of Article 10 ECHR.

Woolas was unseated, but in a subsequent criminal trial, was found not to deserve further punishment – his unseating and his consequent inability to stand for election or hold office for five years – being sufficient deemed penalty. A fresh election was held, but Watkins again lost; his Labour opponent greatly increasing the unseated Woolas' majority. One might think that this was due – at least in part – to the subsequent electoral pact between the Conservatives and the Liberal Democrats disillusioning Liberal Democrat voters who are substantially anti-Conservative.

In a later case *Carmichael*[25] which was held in Scotland, which has its own legal and judicial system but decided on the same law as applies in England and Wales – the Representation of the People Act 1983 – the Inner House of the Court of Session heard allegations that Alistair Carmichael MP made the false statement that he was an honest person in political matters. The rather elaborate argument derived from shady allegations concerning the leaking of memoranda regarding the desirability by parties of a particular result in the Scottish Independence Referendum. Carmichael had claimed that he did not leak these memoranda, but all the available (but inconclusive) evidence was that he was the source of the leak. By claiming that it was not him, the Petitioners claimed that Carmichael represented himself as honest. The (alleged) unlawfulness of claiming that one is honest when the opposite is the case, is, in electoral law terms, determined by some remarks made by the judges in *Woolas*. These remarks did not strictly contribute to the finding in *Woolas*, but the Court of Session was persuaded by the legal argument, however it declined to find Carmichael personally liable. One is left with the impression from the judgment that the Inner House would have loved to deliver the singularly Scottish verdict 'Not Proven' – which is taken to mean – 'yes, you are guilty, but it has not been proved beyond reasonable doubt'. This issue of the 'Burden of Proof' which must be satisfied in a trial is one which is particular to Common Law jurisdictions. In civil matters the plaintiff simply needs to show that their allegations were more likely to be true than untrue – the so-called 'balance of probabilities' test. In a criminal matter, the prosecution has to show 'beyond reasonable doubt' that the allegations were true. As to the precise difference between these terms as a matter of psychology – and the interpellation of 'not proven' can only complicate matters – it is

[25] *Morrison v Carmichael* [2015] ECIH 90.

clear to the courts. The 1983 Act and its predecessors make it absolutely clear that whilst the Election Petition procedure itself is civil in form, the burden of proof which must be satisfied in order to overturn an election is the criminal standard – beyond reasonable doubt. This was established in the local government Election Petition of *R v Rowe ex parte Mainwaring and Others*.[26] This was confirmed by the Judicial Committee of the Privy Council hearing a case on appeal from the Supreme Court of Mauritius where the Privy Council was careful to draw a distinction between the Mauritian law (civil standard of proof) and the English law (criminal standard of proof).[27] This point provides an important technical reason why the WP – or, at least the elected portion of it – the House of Commons – should not attempt to reclaim the procedure for the challenging of elections. It is to this question which we must now turn.

VI. COULD THE HOUSE OF COMMONS RECLAIM THE ELECTION PETITION? THE INTERPLAY BETWEEN LAW AND POLITICS

In the abstract this question seems absurd. As a matter of legal doctrine, the answer is 'Yes, of course'. If the WP decided to make a law returning the determination of Parliamentary Election Petitions to itself, it could simply do so. It was able to produce a Fixed Term Parliaments Act in 2011 as a matter of political expediency to secure the Coalition Agreement which made David Cameron Prime Minister; when the constraints of coalition were removed and Boris Johnson found the position politically inconvenient and the Conservatives with an 80-seat majority, a simple Act – the Dissolution and Calling of Parliament Act 2022 was passed in order to remove the inconvenience. Unlike the majority of countries, the UK has neither a written Constitution (or Basic Law) or a Supreme Court armed with powers of fundamental constitutional review able to set aside whatever laws it found to be inimical to the Constitution.

Having said that a government would face a number of legal difficulties in reclaiming the power of determining Election Petitions. As we have seen the use of the criminal standard of proof – beyond reasonable doubt – which is established in the law of Election Petitions – would be very difficult to operate in front of 650 Members of Parliament. If MPs were expected to act as members of some gigantic jury it would be legally impossible to mandate a vote to condemn or acquit, because the essence of a jury system is that its members cannot be compelled and must use their own independent judgment.

The most fundamental legal difficulty would come in the following way. As a matter of theory, Parliament could provide that election petitions be once again

[26] *R v Rowe ex parte Mainwaring & Others* [1992] 1 WLR 1059.
[27] See *Jugnauth v Ringadoo* [2008] UKPC 50.

heard on the floor of the House, but it would provoke a constitutional crisis. The Constitutional Reform Act 2005 substantially revised the duties of the Lord Chancellor and established the Supreme Court in place of the old Judicial Committee of the House of Lords in order to avoid challenges under the independent and impartial tribunal provision of Article 6 ECHR. If the Westminster Parliament did try to hear election petitions on its floor it is beyond doubt that a challenge under Article 3 of the First Protocol ECHR would be brought. One might think that the obvious challenge to a Parliamentary reclamation of the Petition would be under Article 6 ECHR – the right to an independent judicial resolution of one's civil rights and liabilities – but in *Pierre-Bloch v France*[28] the ECtHR held that electoral matters involved 'political rights' rather than 'civil rights' and, accordingly, the determination of electoral disputes was held to be outside the ambit of Article 6. This matter may benefit from further consideration by the Court because *Pierre-Bloch* was determined on its own particular facts and the case is now 20 years old. A wider challenge may produce a different result. In any event *Namat Aliyev v Azerbaijan* makes it explicitly clear that High Contracting Parties must provide an effective means of resolving electoral disputes:[29]

> 81. In this connection, having regard to the principles developed by its case-law on Article 3 of Protocol No. 1 (see paragraphs 70–73 above), the Court considers that the existence of a domestic system for effective examination of individual complaints and appeals in matters concerning electoral rights is one of the essential guarantees of free and fair elections. Such a system ensures an effective exercise of individual rights to vote and to stand for election, maintains general confidence in the State's administration of the electoral process and constitutes an important device at the State's disposal in achieving the fulfilment of its positive duty under Article 3 of Protocol No. 1 to hold democratic elections. Indeed, the State's solemn undertaking under Article 3 of Protocol No. 1 and the individual rights guaranteed by that provision would be illusory if, throughout the electoral process, specific instances indicative of failure to ensure democratic elections are not open to challenge by individuals before a competent domestic body capable of effectively dealing with the matter.

This would seem to ensure that an attempt to restore the resolution of Election Petitions to the WP would fail. However, Lord Phillips in *Chayto*r did leave a loophole in that he said that the previous law could be overcome by the use of primary legislation. If primary legislation was passed expressly invoking section 19(1)(b) of the Human Rights Act 1998 which recognises that the proposed measure is incompatible with the ECHR but, nevertheless, the government wishes to proceed. This may provoke a constitutional crisis of a different sort – a political constitutional crisis.

[28] *Pierre-Bloch v France* 120/1996/732/938 Decision of 21 October 1997. See, in particular, para 50.
[29] *Namat Aliyev v Azerbaijan* 18705/06: www.hudoc.echr.coe.int/eng?i=001-98187 (accessed 27 May 2022).

A government with a large majority – and the present government has a majority of about 80 – may be able to force legislation through just by weight of numbers. Such a government would need to rely on the goodwill or compliance of members of the governing party. This may simply amount to persuasion or may involve compulsion. Furthermore, if an attempt was made to compel (or, as the usage goes, to 'impose the whip'), this may become politically unacceptable both inside and outside the WP.

An example of this 'use of the whip' – to mandate MPs of a particular political party to vote in a particular way has recently arisen in the case of the former Conservative MP Owen Patterson. It was alleged that Mr Patterson had accepted money in order to promote the business of a firm for which he was a paid consultant. The allegation was that he tried to obtain government contracts for the firm. The matter was investigated by the Commissioner for Parliamentary Standards, who concluded that Mr Patterson had breached those standards and recommended that he should be suspended from the WP for 30 sitting days. This would expose Mr Patterson to the possibility of a 'recall petition' under the Recall of MPs Act 2015.[30] The Conservative Party attempted to whip its MPs to vote against the recommendation to suspend Mr Patterson. In the face of threatened rebellions by Conservative MPs, the derision of the Opposition parties and the press, the Conservative Party was on the point of backing down when Mr Patterson resigned.[31] This prompted the obvious question about the voluntariness of his resignation. Mr Patterson held the North Shropshire seat in the WP, which was one of the safest Conservative seats, but it was lost to the Liberal Democrats.

There are cases where MPs have been accused or convicted of criminal offences, and in the context of the knowledge that an election offence is a criminal or quasi-criminal matter we need to consider some of these cases. The reason for this is that, until very recently, the WP has been very censorious of criminal offences committed by its members and has not sought to defend them but has allowed the criminal law to take its course.

To recap, Mr Patterson was accused of a breach of Parliamentary Standards. Beyond such a breach there are, of course, criminal offences of making false claims of expenses. The most important of these is the case of *R v Chaytor and Others*.[32] An attempt was made during a prosecution of a number of former MPs (and a sitting Member of the House of Lords) to move a prosecution for fraud in submitting a parliamentary expenses claim from the ordinary criminal court to the appropriate House of Parliament. The defendants sought to avoid

[30] Recall of MPs Act 2015: www legislation.gov.uk/ukpga/2015/25/contents/enacted (accessed 30 May 2022).

[31] J Scott, 'Owen Paterson quits as MP over lobbying row 'nightmare'' BBC News (4 November 2021) www.bbc.co.uk/news/uk-politics-59167783 (accessed 29 May 2022).

[32] *R v Chaytor & Others* [2010] UKSC 52.

criminal prosecution for fiddling their parliamentary expenses by claiming that rather than it being an ordinary crime, it was a Proceeding in Parliament and thus protected by Article 9 of the Bill of Rights and should therefore be dealt with by the Committee on Privileges in the Commons or its equivalent in the Lords. Lord Phillips in delivering a decision with which all nine members of the Supreme Court hearing the case agreed said: (at paragraph 61)

> There are good reasons of policy for giving Article 9 a narrow ambit that restricts it to the important purpose for which it was enacted – freedom for Parliament to conduct its legislative and deliberative business without interference from the Crown or the Crown's judges. The protection of Article 9 is absolute. It is capable of variation by primary legislation, but not capable of waiver, even by Parliamentary resolution.

The Bill of Rights only protects members of the legislature doing their work as deliberators or legislators not any other function. There is an important contemporaneous example. Lord Hain named, in the course of the business of the House of Lords, a prominent businessman who was able to protect his identity from disclosure by means of an injunction when he was accused of serious, sexist, and racist bullying.[33] For an ordinary person, or a Member outside of Parliament, to name the businessman would have been in breach of an injunction and thus the law. Hain was freed from liability. Furthermore, from *Chaytor* it is clear that the activities of a person seeking election to Parliament could never be covered by privilege. This affirms the view of Sir John Holt CJ in *Ashby v White* that such a matter is 'precedaneous' to (ie, comes before or precedes election to) Parliament. It is no part of Parliament and is therefore not subject to its internal or legal sovereignty.

The Patterson story, as recounted above, recalls to a considerable extent the progress of election petitions being heard on the floor of the House of Commons between *Ashby v White* in 1706 and 1848; political expediency seeming more important than justice. However, the most egregious example of bad behaviour in the WP remains on-going. It is, of course, the breach of the laws introduced during the 2020–22 COVID-19 pandemic designed to prevent spread of the virus. The laws themselves are complex but do not need recitation or examination. The fundamental scheme was that indoor gatherings of people from different households were made unlawful in most circumstances and the police were charged with issuing fixed penalty notices (fines) for breaches. As a result of a number of reported breaches the Prime Minister, Boris Johnson, was fined by the Metropolitan Police. Furthermore, as a result of political pressure, Johnson was obliged to instruct a senior civil servant to conduct an Inquiry into a number of potentially illegal gatherings in a number of government buildings

[33] BBC News, 'Sir Philip Green named over harassment claims' BBC News (25 October 2018) www.bbc.co.uk/news/business-45981436 (accessed 30 May 2022).

including 10 Downing Street which is the Prime Minister's residence and workplace.[34] The Report of the Inquiry was very damaging to the reputation of the Prime Minister, but he has hitherto refused to resign. This is in accordance with the law; his position as an MP and as Leader of the largest party in the House of Commons is unaffected. However, this behaviour and the Report has provoked intense public anger, not least amongst those prevented by the law from visiting sick or elderly relatives or attending their funerals. Conservative MPs grew dissatisfied with his leadership and pressured to remove him from their leadership, either because they viewed him as an electoral liability, or because they considered his behaviour as intolerable.[35] This may seem a very long way from the issue of the potential return of the Election Petition to the forum of the House of Commons or the WP. However, it is not, because first it shows how MPs are sensitive to the public mood – and second, if the Commons were to control elections and Election Petitions, MPs would have to bear the consequences, moral, political, and electoral, of their decisions. Here is a stark and distressing example. The late Fiona Jones was elected as a Labour MP in the 1997 General Election which the Labour Party won. Her local Labour Party was annoyed about the way she was selected as a candidate and refused to work for her election and some members of it presented a complaint to the police about the calculation of her election expenses which are legally capped. Without doubt Ms Jones had only followed the normal practices in the constituency, but she was found guilty at first instance. She then appealed and was acquitted. She took her seat in the WP but was ostracised by her fellow Labour MPs and was one of the few Labour members to lose their seat in the following General Election. She then descended into depression, alcoholism, and family estrangement before dying in a wretched condition.[36]

VII. CONCLUSIONS

It has been shown that the doctrine of parliamentary sovereignty has both legal and political dimensions. At least in the case of challenges to elections to Parliament it has been shown to be something of a sham because, whilst the legal form of a challenge could be reduced to that of a WP parliamentary procedure, the political dimension would either prevent that from happening

[34] Findings of Second Permanent Secretary's Investigation into Alleged Gatherings on Government Premises During COVID: Restrictions www.assets.publishing.service.gov.uk/government/uploads/system/uploads/attachment_data/file/1078404/2022-05-25_FINAL_FINDINGS_OF_SECOND_PERMANENT_SECRETARY_INTO_ALLEGED_GATHERINGS.pdf (accessed 26 May 2022).

[35] BBC News 'Pressure grows on Boris Johnson after Partygate report' *BBC News* (31 May 2022) www.bbc.co.uk/news/uk-politics-61645661 (accessed 31 May 2022). Johnson subsequently resigned.

[36] For a full account, see B Watt, *UK Election Law: a critical examination* (London, Glasshouse, 2006) 129–51.

or would ensure that the procedure was very much like that which currently occurs in the courts, notwithstanding the grave procedural difficulties. One might therefore helpfully characterise 'parliamentary sovereignty' as 'legal totipotency' (the ability to pass whatever laws one chooses) subject to popular political sovereignty. The word 'subject' in this sentence is far more weighty than its seven letters tends to suggest. If the WP were to interfere in a way which the populace found particularly oppressive, it seems likely – following the examples drawn from employment law in the first part of this chapter, and the successful campaigns to reform the franchise in 1832, the introduction of the secret ballot in 1872, and the granting of the parliamentary franchise to women starting in 1918[37] – that there would be a political movement to force a change.

[37] See B Watt, *UK Election Law: A Critical Examination* (London, Glasshouse, 2006).

5

Judicial Review of Representative Democracy: The French Demographic Perspective

ELEONORA BOTTINI

I. INTRODUCTION

A SPEECH DELIVERED in 2010 by former South African President Jacob Zuma brought attention to the inherent tension between the political nature of electoral rules and their justiciability in courts:

> The powers conferred on the courts could not be regarded as superior to the powers resulting from a mandate given by the people in a popular vote. To provide support to the judiciary and free the courts to do their work, it would help if political disputes were resolved politically.[1]

The main message of the speech shows a political actor's endeavour to keep disputes concerning democratic participation outside the realm of courts, raising the necessity of a political question doctrine in South Africa.[2] It is interesting that such a message would be delivered at a time when, in African countries and elsewhere, courts seem to be more and more involved in elections, as election law as an area of study becomes more structured.[3]

It is increasingly important today to shed light on the complex relationship between apex courts and the electoral sphere in democracies. The latter, which is eminently political, has been increasingly invested in recent years by constitutional and supreme courts, whereas the political question doctrine[4] initially

[1] M Mhango, 'Is It Time For a Coherent Political Question Doctrine in South Africa? Lessons from the United States' (2014) 7 *African Journal of Legal Studies* 457–93, 458.

[2] ibid 459, where the author states that 'The underlying theme is that such questions must find resolution in the political process.'

[3] D Schultz and J Toplak (eds), *Routledge Handbook of Election Law* (London, Routledge, 2023) 2, arguing that in the last 30 years, election law has become an independent body of law and the study of it is critical in promoting democracy around the world.

[4] M Tushnet, 'Law and Prudence in the Law of Justiciability: The Transformation and Disappearance of the Political Question Doctrine' (2002) 80 *North Carolina Law Review* 1203–236

developed by the United States Supreme Court, which had advocated deference to other elected powers, is losing its momentum. The 1962 judgment *Baker v Carr*[5] started the reversal of that doctrine, which continued with *Bush v Gore*[6] in 2000. Today the Supreme Court has full jurisdiction on redistricting, especially after the *Voting Rights Act* of 1965, as the most recent judgment of the Court *Allen v Milligan*[7] shows. Analysing the impact of judicial review on representative democracy elucidates the significant influence of legal processes towards the realisation of 'democracy through law'.[8] From a comparative perspective, it is possible to identify a trend in the judicialisation of elections and electoral politics through the increased intervention of courts in the definition of electoral rules, which raises the question of the legitimacy of non-elected bodies when confronted to such deeply political issues.

The story of judicialisation of elections is not straightforward and encounters both openings and resistance. Famously, Justice Brennan wrote in the majority opinion of *Baker v Carr* that the political character of a fundamental right does not mean that it necessarily belongs to a political question.[9] This decision altered the perspective of the US Supreme Court regarding its role in relation to electoral rules, particularly by opening the door to judicial review of malapportionment and gerrymandering cases, especially when allegations of racial gerrymandering are raised.[10]

In western Europe, such a trend has been demonstrated in many countries such as Germany[11] and Italy,[12] where constitutional courts have recently started to apply strict judicial review to electoral laws.[13] Electoral laws are

(explaining the decline of the political question doctrine in the case-law of the US Supreme Court and the impossibility of retrieving a prudent practice of judicial review).

[5] Supreme Court of the United States, *Baker v Carr*, 369 U.S. (1962).

[6] Supreme Court of the United States, *Bush v Gore*, 531 U.S. (2000).

[7] Supreme Court of the United States, *Allen v Milligan*, 599 U.S. (2023).

[8] Famously, the Venice Commission of the Council of Europe, founded in 1990, is formally called 'European Commission for democracy through law'. The Commission is in favor of the idea that electoral disputes should be subject to judicial review either by an independent commission or by a court, as it is clearly stated in its Code of Good Practice in Electoral Matters of 2002 (rm.coe.int/090000168092af01).

[9] 'Of course the mere fact that the suit seeks protection of a *political right* does *not* mean it presents a *political question*', *Baker v Carr*, para 41.

[10] RE Barkow, 'More Supreme than Court? The Fall of the Political Question Doctrine and the Rise of Judicial Supremacy' (2002) 102 *Columbia Law Review* 237, arguing that the demise of the political question doctrine in the US Supreme Court is both evident and worrisome.

[11] BVerfGE, 2 BvC 1/07 of 3 July 2008, available at www.bverfg.de/entscheidungen/cs20080703_2bvc000107.html, where the German Federal Constitutional Court ruled that the 'negative vote weight' allowed by the electoral law was unconstitutional and violated the principles of equality and directness of vote.

[12] Italian Constitutional Court, judgment no 1/2014 (available in English: www.cortecostituzionale.it/documenti/download/doc/recent_judgments/1-2014_en.pdf) and judgment no 35/2017 (available in English: www.cortecostituzionale.it/documenti/download/doc/recent_judgments/2017_35_EN.pdf), where the Italian Court first declared the 2005 electoral law unconstitutional and then modified substantially the new version adopted by parliament.

[13] For a comparative analysis of electoral justice in France, Germany, Italy and Spain, see G Milani, *Sistemi comparati di giustizia elettorale in Europa* (Padova, CEDAM & Wolters Kluwer, 2023).

inherently intertwined with democracy, as they operationalise the majoritarian principle – one of the fundamental pillars of 'lawful governments', as emphasised by Locke.[14] As a result, the way members of the assembly that will be in charge of expressing such a majority are chosen is arguably the most important question in every democratic system. That is why the relation between courts and elections is structured around democratic legitimacy: are courts legitimate enough to decide on electoral matters?

While the growing influence of constitutionalism seems to grant courts increasing powers to adjudicate on broad areas of public life, including democratic participation, other state powers may resist this trend of judicialisation of elections. In France, a compromise solution was found in 1958 with the creation, by the Constitution of the Fifth Republic, of the Constitutional Council, the first organ in charge of constitutional review of legislation and at the same time of electoral disputes, which is not a court nor part of the judiciary power. The French case is of particular interest because of its history of distrust towards judges and constitutional review if compared to the rest of post-war Europe.

Similar to many other constitutions in Europe, the French Constitution does not explicitly prescribe a particular 'electoral system'[15] in terms of the precise formula for converting votes into seats, despite the constitutional significance of the issue. Even though one of the founders of the Fifth Republic, Michel Debré, wished to do so, the choice of the electoral system was delegated to the legislator to be included in an ordinary law because of Charles de Gaulle's (the other founding father of the Constitution) opposition.

From a comparative perspective, this choice is far from unique. The electoral system is absent from the Italian Constitution as well, even though the election of the Constituent Assembly through proportional representation may have influenced the electoral system subsequently chosen by the ordinary legislator.[16] Finally, the same choice can be observed in Germany, where the federal law sets up the mixed proportional and majority voting system, whereas in 1949 'the

[14] 'Whosoever, therefore, out of a state of Nature unite into a community, must be understood to give up all the power necessary to the ends for which they unite into society to the majority of the community, unless they expressly agreed in any number greater than the majority. And this is done by barely agreeing to unite into one political society, which is all the compact that is, or needs be, between the individuals that enter into or make up a commonwealth. And thus, that which begins and actually constitutes any political society is nothing but the consent of any number of freemen capable of majority, to unite and incorporate into such a society. And this is that, and that only, which did or could give beginning to any lawful government in the world.' J Locke, *The Second Treatise of Civil Government*, JW Gough (ed) (Oxford, Basil Blackwell, 1946).

[15] M Luciani et al, 'Cours constitutionnelles et systèmes électoraux' (1996) 12 *Annuaire international de justice constitutionnelle* 416.

[16] For example, Art 138 provides for an absolute and not a reinforced majority for the second vote of the laws of constitutional revision, from which it could be deduced that the Constituent power had considered that in a proportional system, it would have been very difficult to obtain the reinforced two-thirds majority for a single party or coalition.

constitutionalisation of the electoral system was not pursued. Article 38 of the Basic Law merely lays down some fundamental principles'.[17]

The clear choice of the French legislator of 1958 was one of a majoritarian uninominal electoral system with two rounds of elections for the National Assembly, the only one of the two chambers directly elected by the people.[18] Majoritarian systems always amplify results, as seats are never proportional to the number of expressed votes. Even though the second round of election mitigates the brutality of a 'first pass the post' system as it exists in the UK, the principle of voters' equality does not apply in France to the choice of the electoral system. It resurfaces however in constitutional case-law applied to redistricting. The interpretation of a such principle that seems to be straightforward is in fact very different depending on the political context and the electoral culture. In France, voters' equality (or equality of suffrage) has been established as a democratic requirement by the *Conseil constitutionnel*. While being the guardian of voters' equality, the Constitutional Council has pushed forward a demographic perspective of democracy, partially violating its usual self-restraint.

This book wonders about the idea of democratic representation that is envisaged by courts, and whether this idea is explicit or implicit in the courts' case-law. To answer this question about France, I will first explain why the French case is interesting to study in that regard and what its specificities are (II); I will then discuss in detail the Constitutional Council's case-law on redistricting through three main series of judgments during its history, presenting the demographic idea of representation pushed forward by the Council (III); finally, I will conclude by arguing that the French Council's interpretation of electoral rules and redistricting shows a form of partial self-restraint that is more ambitious that its regular judicial attitude (IV).

II. SPECIFICITIES AND INTEREST OF THE FRENCH CASE

With regard to judicial review of electoral rules, the French case presents several interesting features. First, the composition of the organ responsible for such litigation, the Constitutional Council, sets it apart as it is not a constitutional court in the traditional sense. Unlike other courts, the Council consists primarily of former political actors appointed by the highest political personalities in the state (President of the Republic, President of the National Assembly, President of the Senate) without any requirement of legal background or any experience in legal professions. Additionally, former presidents can serve as members for life. This is a unique feature in comparative law, discussed and criticised regularly in

[17] M Robin, 'Le système électoral de la République fédérale allemande' (1957) 4 *Revue française de science politique* 825. See also, on the latest reform of the German electoral law, A Fourmont, 'La nouvelle loi électorale fédérale allemande' (2013) 11 *Jus Politicum*.

[18] The French Senate is elected through indirect suffrage by big electors who are themselves elected officials, both nationally and locally.

France but still existing today, even though currently there are no member for life seats on the Council. These factors contribute to the Council's relative lack of legitimacy[19] when compared to other European constitutional courts.

The second notable aspect of the French case is the dual role of the Constitutional Council. It functions both as a constitutional judge responsible for judicial review of legislation and as a court for resolving national election disputes, including presidential and legislative elections, as well as national referendums. In contrast to the Italian and German constitutional courts, which do not have an electoral role, the French Council was established in 1958 mainly to address electoral disputes. Prior to that, the verification of the legality of national elections was one of the roles of Parliament; that had been the case since the French Revolution in order to prevent any form of interference by other branches of power, especially the Crown, in legislative matters.[20] Members of the National Assembly and the Senate had to pronounce the validity of the election of their future colleagues. This system was known as 'verification of powers' ('*verification des pouvoirs*') and came from the revolutionary desire to give independence to the legislative power but often resulted in partial and politically motivated assessments.

The 'verification of powers' was based on the idea that a Chamber of Parliament, since it had to assess the regularity of a political act that was the election of one of its members, was not subject in its assessment to any rule except laws adopted by Parliament itself (like the law on ineligibility). This point was regularly discussed, particularly during the debate in June 1879 on the invalidation of Auguste Blanqui's election,[21] who was convicted of crimes that rendered him ineligible by law. Still, in the decision about his ineligibility, Clémenceau supported the thesis of the 'discretionary and sovereign power of the Chambers to rule sovereignly [...] on each of the cases of ineligibility established by the Assemblies that preceded them'.[22] Even if the election of Blanqui was invalidated in the end, in an even more extreme comment Eugène Pierre concluded that an essential principle emerged from this controversy: 'The Chamber deciding on the verification of powers is not bound by the text of the laws or by the decisions of universal suffrage. It is sovereign and of absolute and unreserved sovereignty.'[23] A judicial review of electoral rules and results was then completely out of the question.

[19] For a discussion of the legitimacy deficit of the Council after the three latest appointments, see T Perroud, 'A Male, White and Conservative Constitutional Judge: The Composition of the French Constitutional Council After the New Appointments' (2022) *VerfBlog*, 2022/5/03, verfassungsblog.de/a-male-white-and-conservative-constitutional-judge/.

[20] See M Leloup, 'Post-election Disputes in Europe', in Schultz and Toplak (n 3) 222.

[21] B Daugeron, 'Le contrôle des élections parlementaires avant le Conseil constitutionnel: la 'vérification des pouvoirs', histoire et théorie' (2013) 41 *Nouveaux Cahiers du Conseil constitutionnel*.

[22] E Pierre, *Traité de droit politique électoral et parlementaire*, 2nd edn (Paris, Librairie imprimeries réunies, 1902) 411.

[23] ibid 412.

On an opposite direction, since 1958, electoral acts (preparation of elections, campaigns, votes, results, …) can be referred to the external scrutiny by the Constitutional Council. Unlike the US, where it was the Supreme Court which had to revert itself on judicial review of electoral matters, in France, it was the constituent power – chaired by the very popular General De Gaulle – that discarded the political question doctrine. It did so without encountering significant debate, while in the US Justice Whittaker would never recover from the tension around *Baker v Carr*.[24]

The newly created Constitutional Council was the demonstration that a new era was to begin: 1958 marked the end of the absolute sovereignty of Parliament by the creation of a strong executive power (with a powerful President) and of an impartial supervisor of elections (and a supervisor of Parliament altogether). As part of the 'rationalisation of parliamentarism', this shift allowed a non-elected body to oversee the electoral process and invalidate elections when necessary.

The relationship between electoral disputes and judicial review of electoral laws in France is not straightforward. Although both fall within the purview of the Constitutional Council, they are based on separate constitutional provisions (Article 61 for the former, Articles 58 and 59 for the latter). The Council itself ensures the separation of these roles and does not rely on case law from one area to decide the other. However, I argue that the Council's legitimacy in shaping its own notion of demographic representation stems from its role as an electoral judge. While there is ongoing debate about the Council's status as a court, particularly regarding its constitutional review function, there has never been doubt about its judicial role in electoral disputes.

France serves as an important case study for analysing the relation between elections and judicial review, not only due to its historical context but also considering more recent developments. The current political landscape anticipates a constitutional reform proposed by President Emmanuel Macron during his first term (2017–22), aiming for a more efficient, representative, and responsible democracy.[25] Amongst other aspects, the reform aims to reduce the number of representatives in Parliament and to introduce a part of proportionality in the electoral system. The number of members of Parliament would be reduced by 30 per cent: the number of MPs from 577 to 404; the number of senators from 348 to 244. This would dramatically change the shape and size of French electoral districts, while having to abide to the Constitutional Council's case-law. For example, the French electors living abroad would vote in a unique district with a proportional system with only one turn instead of the 11 districts that now divide the various continents where French living abroad are established. The constitutional reform had been initially stuck in Parliament because of a

[24] Justice Whittaker is known to have sunk into a fatal depression right after (and possibly because of) the ruling in *Baker v Carr*.

[25] For an analysis of this attempted reform, see E Bottini, 'France', in LR Barroso and R Albert (eds), *The International Review of Constitutional Reform – 2020* (SSRN 2021) 112–16.

political scandal surrounding the presidency called the 'Benalla affaire'[26] and resumed in 2019, when it was again slowed down by the Gilets Jaunes protests and then by the COVID-19 pandemic. The constitutional reform was ultimately abandoned for the rest of the term, and it has not resumed for Macron's second term (2022–27) at the time this chapter was written.

Since its creation, the role of the Constitutional Council has gradually evolved, resembling more a constitutional court, albeit lacking an elaborate decision-making method and the legitimacy associated with more interventionist courts. The Council is known for its self-restraint and deference to legislative decisions, typically aligning with the government's position. The idea of representation that the Council puts forward in its case-law is not very specific and does not influence the choice of the electoral system (majoritarian or proportional), but it is quite straightforward and has remained consistently the same in the last 30 years.

The main constitutional principle involved in electoral rules is the principle of equality, whether it is equality between citizens, voters, or constituencies. It is the foundation of the revolutionary Declaration of 1789 which is still at the core of the French constitutional regime. Kelsen had already linked democracy to equality of suffrage in the *General Theory of Law and State* in terms of weight: all voters should exercise an equal weight on the results of elections[27] for representative democracy to be realised.

The Council consistently interprets this principle, which lies between the realms of politics and legal rules, as preserving the freedom of action for the legislator and the government in these delicate political matters. The main application of the principle of equality in elections is the design of the electoral map, on which a significant case-law of the Constitutional Council has developed in the last three decades.

III. THE CONSTITUTIONAL COUNCIL'S CASE-LAW ON REDISTRICTING

The Constitutional Council has fulfilled its role as an electoral judge since the establishment of the Fifth Republic. However, it was only in the 1980s that the Council began to actively scrutinise the principle of equality in the allocation of electoral districts, known as '*égalité devant le suffrage*', in its constitutional review of legislation. The Council's first attempt of such scrutiny occurred in 1985,

[26] 'France's Benalla affair: Timeline of an Élysée Palace scandal', *France 24*, 24 July 2018, www.france24.com/en/20180724-france-macron-benalla-affair-timeline-elysee-palace-scandal-politics-parliament-inquiry.

[27] 'Democracy requires that the right of suffrage should be not only as nearly universal but also as nearly equal as possible. That means that the influence which each voter exercises on the result of the election should be the same, in other terms, the weight of vote of every voter should be equal to that of every other voter.' H Kelsen, *General Theory of Law and State*, translated by A Wedberg (Harvard, Harvard University Press, 1949) 294.

in a decision regarding members of congress in New Caledonia.[28] The Council primarily focused on redistricting in 1986 for the election of members of the National Assembly. Since then, there have been limited instances where the Council has assessed the constitutionality of redistricting in relation to the principle of equality. Redistricting has taken place only three times during the Fifth Republic: in 1958 with the initial district plan of the new Republic, in 1986 based on the 1982 census, and finally in 2009 based on the 1999 census.

It is worth noting that the few redistricting operations have consistently been implemented by right-wing governments. This has led to accusations of partisan bias and malapportionment by the left, resulting in referrals to the Constitutional Council. Concurrently, the Council has continued to verify compliance with the principle of voters' equality in local elections, such as municipal councils (including a notable case in Marseille in 1987)[29] and the assembly of French Polynesia (in 2001).[30] These instances demonstrate the Council's broad understanding of democratic elections, extending beyond national sovereignty.

However, the most significant constitutional case law relates to national legislative elections and consists of three distinct periods: the foundational moment of 1986 (A), the consolidation in 2009 (B), and the disappointment of 2010 (C).

A. The Foundation of the Demographic Rule: The 1986 Decisions

The context of 1985 is crucial in explaining the evolution of legislative elections in France. For the first and only time during the Fifth Republic, a socialist majority modified the electoral law, replacing the majoritarian system established by General De Gaulle in 1958 for the elections of the *Assemblée nationale* (lower chamber of Parliament) with a proportional system. This change aimed to ensure the stability of strong majorities in Parliament, as well as reduce the number of political parties in France. Unlike Italy and Germany after World War II, France sought stability after the Third and Fourth French Republics, prioritising a majoritarian electoral reform over ensuring multipartyism.

The socialist majority's decision to switch from a majoritarian to a proportional system was partly motivated by a 'divide and conquer' strategy. The government, lacking a strong majority at the time, aimed to prevent the far-right party from entering Parliament.[31]

However, the sole election held under the new proportional system resulted in an absolute majority for the right-wing party. Subsequently, the new

[28] Constitutional council, decision no 85-196 DC of 8 August 1985.
[29] Constitutional council, decision no 87-227 DC of 7 July 1987.
[30] Constitutional council, decision no 2000-438 DC of 10 January 2001.
[31] Le Pen father-and-daughter's political party, at the time called *Front National* and now known as *Rassemblement National*. This maneuver did not work, since the Front National gained 35 seats in the March 1986 elections.

government swiftly reverted to the majoritarian system, which remains in place to this day. Although the one-year change had limited political significance, the reintroduction of the majoritarian system in the 1986 electoral law provided the Constitutional Council with an opportunity to apply its ex ante constitutional review to electoral rules based on the principle of equality. The Council's interpretation of this principle was prompted by its inherent ambiguity. The most important case-law concerns the elections of the members of the National Assembly, the only chamber in Parliament that is elected by direct universal suffrage thus the only one in the view of the Constitutional council that really represents the French people.

The principle of equality in elections translates to the concept of 'one person, one vote',[32] which appears straightforward in the context of universal suffrage. It entails that every voter should possess one vote, with no individual holding more than one vote.[33] As applied to apportionment, the Constitutional Council interprets it as the obligation to distribute seats in electoral districts on 'an essentially demographic basis', based on the population of each district. In fact, the 'one person one vote' principle prohibits discriminatory differentiations based on factors such as birth, wealth, race, occupation, or gender. It also suggests that the place of residence should not affect the weight of a vote. However, due to the unequal distribution of electoral districts, the weight of a vote, or the chance of a voter's preference influencing the results, depended on their place of residence. The Council began examining whether these discrepancies in weight were disproportionately affecting districts.

It is important to note that equality of suffrage in France implies accepting the inherent discrepancy between votes and results in the majoritarian electoral system. Nevertheless, the Constitutional Council applies a form of strict scrutiny to redistricting. In order to ensure that voters have equal electoral weight, districts must be roughly equal in population, although exact parity is not required. This demographic rule represents a fundamental aspect of the French electoral system, with the Council allowing for exceptions and discrepancies based on different circumstances or the goal of the law. In comparison to other courts, such as the US Supreme Court, the Constitutional Council exercises a less stringent level of control.

The Constitutional Council's significant case-law on redistricting is primarily composed of two decisions from 1986.[34] The decisions, published on 2 July and 18 November, respectively dealt with the reinstatement of the majoritarian electoral system, the authorisation of Parliament to Government for redistricting, and

[32] For an analysis of the principle and its inconsistencies in French law, see P Avril, 'Un homme, une voix?' (2007) 120 *Pouvoirs* 123.

[33] The Constitutional council applied this principle for the first time in its decision no 78-101 DC of 17 January 1979.

[34] Constitutional council, decision no 86-208 DC of 2 July 1986 and decision no 86-218 DC of 18 November 1986.

the implementation of the redistricting itself. Given that France adopts a majoritarian uninominal system with only one seat per district, the size of electoral districts holds particular importance, necessitating adherence to the principle of vote equality during redistricting. The Council derives this principle from various constitutional sources: Article 2 of the Constitution on equality before the law and the prohibition of discrimination; Article 3, paragraph 1 of the Constitution on popular sovereignty; Article 3, paragraph 3 of the Constitution on universality and secrecy of suffrage; Article 24 of the Constitution on the election of members of Parliament through universal and direct suffrage; Article 6 of the Declaration of rights of man and citizen of 1789, which has constitutional value, on equality before the law. As a result, the National Assembly must be elected 'on essentially demographic basis':[35] two districts cannot have the same number of representatives (one) and at the same time bear a large difference in their population. The demographic rule also applied to departments, the intermediate level of administrative division between the region and the communes.

One key issue addressed by the Council was the reference used for counting the demographic aspect. Instead of the number of registered voters, the Council opted to consider the population living in the district. This approach is grounded in the theory that every elected member of Parliament represents the entire nation, not just their specific voters. Although this theory of representation exists in the US and the EU, it has drawn some criticism for potentially contradicting the principle of fair representation, particularly in districts with a significant presence of non-voters (non-nationals). Nonetheless, the Council decided to adhere to this theory and did not question the method of calculation.

The term 'essentially' used in the Council's decision indicates that the proportion between population and representatives does not need to be exact, and districts should have roughly equal populations, though not necessarily identical. In contrast to the US, where minimal or no discrepancies are tolerated, the demographic rule in France allows for exceptions based on differing circumstances or justified goals. One such exception arises from the parliamentary tradition that each department must elect a minimum of two members of the National Assembly. However, this exception reveals an inconsistency in the Council's argumentation, as it contradicts the general theory that elected representatives have a general relationship with the entire nation, regardless of their specific voters.[36]

[35] Constitutional council, decision no 86-208 DC, para 21: '(...) it follows from these provisions that the National Assembly, designated by direct universal suffrage, must be elected on an essentially demographic basis; (...) if the legislator can take into account imperatives of general interest likely to attenuate the scope of this fundamental rule, he can do so only to a limited extent'.

[36] 'The legislator's intention in reserving at least two deputies for each department is to ensure a close link between the elected representatives of a constituency and the electorate. Such a choice is not contrary to the Constitution, having regard, on the one hand, to the distribution of the population over the national territory and, on the other hand, to the very limited number of departments for which the choice thus made entails a difference in representation in their favor', Constitutional Council, decision no 86-208 DC, para 22.

To be considered 'essentially demographic', the population of districts within a department should not deviate from the average district population of the department by more than 20 per cent. The Constitutional Council interprets this difference as a maximum threshold, allowing exceptions only in extraordinary and duly justified circumstances that serve the general interest. Such exceptions are examined on a case-by-case basis and are only allowed in a limited number of instances.[37] One justification for these exceptions is the principle of territorial continuity and solidarity between territories, especially relevant to overseas territories that may be overrepresented due to their small populations. However, if these exceptions accumulate, they can lead to an unconstitutional situation. The Council adopts a pragmatic approach to its constitutional review, leaving room for examining specific situations realistically. Ultimately, in this 1986 decisions, the laws are upheld and considered compatible with the 'fundamental rule' of demographic representation, with the aforementioned caveats.

Additionally, in the same 1986 decisions, the Constitutional council issues a warning against gerrymandering. It argues that the design of electoral districts must not stem from arbitrary government decisions.[38] One example of an arbitrary decision would be the creation of discontinuous districts, which is why the 1986 law specifies that districts must consist of continuous territory. Although the potential consequences of constitutional review in cases of arbitrary district design are not explicitly stated in the 'political equilibrium clause', the Council's scrutiny could lead to intervention in a political decision. However, the Council believes that the procedural demographic rule is sufficient to avoid such issues, reducing the risk of judicial intervention.

Despite the Constitutional council's rigorous scrutiny of redistricting rules, which is considered strict by French standards, it is essential to remember that, unlike in Italy, there is no principle of legitimate expectation for voters to have equal voting weight in France (ie, the ability to influence, by the expression of one's preference, on the actual election of the chosen candidate).[39] The Council generally exercises self-restraint, characterised by the French variant of the political question doctrine, where the Council explicitly acknowledges that it does not possess the same power of appreciation and decision-making as the legislator. Consequently, the Council refrains from making suggestions or influencing the legislator, in contrast to the Italian and German courts. Instead, the Council's role

[37] 'The implementation of the maximum deviation mentioned in paragraph 4 of article 5 must be reserved for exceptional and duly justified cases; the use of this option may only be made to a limited extent and must be based, case by case, on precise imperatives of general interest', Constitutional Council, decision no 86-208 DC, para 24.

[38] '(…) finally, the delimitation of constituencies must not be arbitrary in any way; that any other interpretation would be contrary to the Constitution', Constitutional Council, decision no 86-208 DC, para 24.

[39] M Nardini, 'L'omogeneità delle leggi elettorali e la 'legittima aspettativa' dell'elettore (nota alla sentenza della Corte costituzionale del 9 febbraio 2017, no 35)' (2017) *Amministrazione in cammino* (www.amministrazioneincammino.luiss.it/wp-content/uploads/2017/03/Nardini.pdf).

remains limited to a negative one, and the second 1986 decision (November 18) explicitly says so, while reminding the differences with the Council of State, which has advisory functions and may be required to make suggestions.[40] This approach has led to disappointment among the opposition, as the Council refused to impose the best possible apportionment on the government and only verified that the apportionment was not manifestly disproportionate.

B. An Appearance of Strict Scrutiny: The 2009 Case-law

The foundation of the demographic rule by the Constitutional Council underwent further developments in 2009 when the Council took the opportunity, during the last redistricting operation, to clarify its rulings. Although two general censuses of the French population had been conducted in 1990 and 1999,[41] they did not lead to a redistricting, despite political demands to do so. In 2007, legislative elections still relied on the 1982 census, sparking protests due to the resulting discrepancy in the demographic principle. The population had increased by at least seven million by then.[42] The issue was that there was no constitutional mechanism to enforce changes in electoral districts or compel the legislator to adopt new electoral laws.[43] Until 2010, only ex ante constitutional review existed in France, and the Constitutional Council lacked the power to censure executive or legislative inaction. To address this issue, the Council used its role as an electoral judge to encourage the government, through non-binding press releases called 'Observations on legislative elections',[44] to undertake redistricting. However, as an observer of electoral procedures, the Council's advisory power held no mandatory power.

[40] 'Considering that the Constitution does not confer on the Constitutional Council a general power of assessment and decision identical to that of Parliament; that it is therefore not for it to determine whether the constituencies have been delimited as fairly as possible; nor is it for it to make proposals in this respect, as the Conseil d'État may be called upon to do in the exercise of its administrative functions', Constitutional council, decision no 86-218 DC, para 10.

[41] Since 2004, a new method of census has been implemented with a partial annual survey with a rotating technique, so there will not be any more general census operations after the one in 1999.

[42] The Council referred to population variations, by constituency, ranging from 75,131 to 125,393 in the 3rd and 21st constituencies of Paris, from 82,974 to 151,565 in the 3rd and 12th constituencies of Bouches-du-Rhône, from 86,690 to 158,193 in the 6th and 1st constituencies of Yvelines.

[43] N Susani, 'Une aporie de la justice constitutionnelle française: l'impuissance du Conseil constitutionnel face à l'inconstitutionnalité de l'actuel découpage électoral pour les élections législatives de 2007' (2007) 69 *Revue française de droit constitutionnel* 145–59.

[44] Two press releases in particular were outspoken about the growing necessity for the government to act with redistricting operations: see Constitutional council, decision no 2005-22 ELEC of 7 July 2005 and decision no 2008-24 ELEC of 29 May 2008, where it is affirmed that 'It is therefore the legislator's responsibility to modify this electoral distribution. In its observations of July 7, 2005, the Conseil had argued that if the redistricting was not carried out before the next legislative elections, which it considered regrettable, it should be undertaken the day after. This reasoning led to a reservation of interpretation in paragraph 7 of decision no 2007-547 DC of February 15, 2007. *It is now imperative to proceed with this redistricting operation.*'(emphasis added).

Following the Council's initial intervention on redistricting rules, debates continued in France regarding the political implications of creating electoral districts that favoured the ruling majority. Suspicions grew, both among opposition politicians and civil society, due to the government's authority over redistricting through parliamentary ordinances (following Article 38 of the Constitution). However, granting the government competence through executive orders was an established principle. To address concerns, a compromise was reached with the 2008 constitutional reform, which added a new paragraph to Article 25 of the Constitution[45] establishing an independent commission responsible for overseeing redistricting projects and advising the government on proposed electoral districts. The Law of 13 January 2009 formalised the commission's composition, consisting of three judges representing each of the supreme courts, elected by their peers (Cour des Comptes, Cour de Cassation, and Conseil d'État), and three qualified individuals designated by the presidents of the two chambers of Parliament and the President of the Republic. Although the commission has only functioned once, in 2009, immediately after its establishment, its advisory role carries weight. Governments find it difficult to ignore the commission's advice since it is made public. Consequently, the commission's 2009 report influenced the government's work on redistricting. Additionally, given the commission's attentiveness to the Constitutional Council's case-law, it can be said that the Council's interpretation of the principle of equality applied to elections indirectly influenced the latest redistricting in France.[46] This influence supplemented the Council's existing practice of issuing non-normative press releases to encourage new apportionment and insist on governments taking action to align electoral districts more accurately with demographic factors.

In the two decisions of 2009 rendered on the same day,[47] the Constitutional Council reaffirmed the principles previously announced in 1986. The Council reviewed the organic law implementing the new Article 25 of the Constitution and the ordinary law authorising the government to proceed with redistricting and organise the independent redistricting commission. While the first decision has limited relevance to the subject of this article,[48] the second decision

[45] Article 25, para 3 of the French Constitution: 'An independent commission, whose composition and rules of organization and operation shall be set down by statute, shall publicly express an opinion on the Government and Private Members' Bills defining the constituencies for the election of Members of the National Assembly, or modifying the distribution of the seats of Members of the National Assembly or of Senators.'

[46] Nonetheless, the commission remains today a mysterious object of French constitutional law: since it has never served since 2009, and there is no redistricting in sight, its members have not been renewed since 2015 and all of them have finished their term by now.

[47] Constitutional Council, decisions no 2008-572 DC and 2008-573 DC of 8 January 2009.

[48] Decision no 2008-572 DC on the organic law of 13 January 2009 focused on the mechanism for replacing members of Parliament who have been appointed to a ministerial function in government. The two functions are incompatible under the French Constitution, so the debate on this topic is important in France. However, this point is unrelated to elections per se and falls outside the scope of this chapter.

is crucial for understanding the Council's influence on elections. This decision demonstrates a more rigorous scrutiny than the 1986 rulings, particularly as parts of the law were deemed unconstitutional by the Council. Furthermore, the Council provides detailed explanations of its previous case-law on voters' equality while analysing the changes introduced by the new legislation concerning electoral districts.

First, the 2009 law aimed to consider the prospective evolution of the population and the number of voters enrolled in certain districts, leading to the recognition of exceptions to the demographic principle. It was an amendment inscribed in the statute by Réné Dosière, a member of the National Assembly who wanted to correct the demographic principle for those districts where the non-nationals are an important part of the population. It was essentially intended for Guyana and Mayotte where the difference between the population and the voters is very important (as most of the population is non-French nationals). For the Council, this provision was unconstitutional as it is contrary to the demographic principle as stated in 1986 and as such violates the principle of voters' equality.

Second, the law repeated the existing principle of minimum two representatives per department: this rule, which had been validated by the Council in 1986, was found to be no longer compatible with the demographic principle in 2009, given the changed circumstances that the Council decided to take into consideration. Since 2008 in fact, with the constitutional reform, the number of members of the National Assembly is constitutionally limited to 577; at the same time, the population had increased by 7.6 million people since the last redistricting. As a result, it was no longer considered as an imperative of general interest to maintain a minimum of two members of the Assembly per department. This provision is struck down from the statute and shows the will of the Council to strongly reaffirm the demographic rule and its tendency of limiting possible exceptions to the rule.

On the other hand, it is possible to retain that the Constitutional council accepts the general idea that every department must have at least one representative, which responds to a pragmatic political vision related to the general idea that the basis for representation in Parliament are the departments themselves. No department can remain without any representative at all, while having two is no longer justifiable for smaller departments in light of the growth of the French population in urban departments and of the reduction of the overall number of representatives in the lower chamber. For that reason, applying the Constitutional council's case-law, the independent commission had considered in its advice of 27 June 2009[49] that it was constitutional for the islands of Saint Pierre and Miquelon and Wallis and Futuna to have one deputy, because of their geographical isolation and despite the low numbers of their population (respectively 6,000 and 11,500 people), but that it was also in conformity with

[49] *Journal officiel de la République française*, 27 June 2009, annexe 1, 51–61.

the demographic principle that the two small islands of Saint Martin and Saint Barthélemy (two separate '*collectivités d'Outre Mer*', the most recent denomination for some of the French overseas territories) elect a single deputy for both.

In 1986 the Council had already announced the possible exceptions to the general rule: specifically, the Council permitted discrepancies of up to 20 per cent between the populations of districts and the departmental average. To clarify this point, the Council explained that certain smaller areas, such as cities with fewer than 5,000 inhabitants or cantons with fewer than 40,000 inhabitants (excluding Paris, Lyon, and Marseille), should not be divided between constituencies. This decision aligns with the Council's earlier case-law, emphasising the importance of territorial coherence in electoral representation.

Third, the intensity of scrutiny increased compared to the 1986 case-law. The Council moved from minimal scrutiny to normal scrutiny, meaning that it scrutinised the redistricting operation in greater detail and with higher requirements. In fact, the tolerated discrepancies must be justified not only in exceptional and justified cases and in a limited number of cases for general interest reasons (which was already the case before), but a proportionality review is introduced by the Council for those derogations to the rule. The Constitutional council explains the introduction of proportionality – a stricter type of scrutiny – by saying that that 'the national assembly must be elected on essentially demographic basis by a distribution of seats and an apportionment that *better respect* the principle of equality of the vote'. This expression – 'better respect' – appears for the first time in the 2009 case-law and signifies that 'it is not sufficient that districting be more or less equal; it must be *as equal as possible*' [emphasis added].[50]

This evolution is important to assess the intensity of the scrutiny by the Council[51] of electoral redistricting: on one hand, it seems a step up from the minimal scrutiny of 1986, when only the largest and more visible mistakes in apportionment were to be sanctioned by the Council. At the time, the council had referred to the 'manifest error of assessment' ('*erreur manifeste d'appréciation*') which is the usual reference for self-restraint towards the more legitimate assessment by the legislator. In 2009, the adjective 'manifest' cannot be found in the decision, signalling the choice of the Council to apply a normal scrutiny instead of a minimal one.

However, the Council's control over redistricting remained limited in certain aspects. First, there is no specific timeframe provided for redistricting, which could lead to prolonged periods of outdated electoral districts. Second, the Council cannot enforce adjustments based on population movements, as it has no prerogative to make such adjustments. Third, the tolerance of exceptions

[50] G Carcassonne, 'Découpage électoral : pas de démocratie sans égalité des citoyens devant le suffrage' (2009) 36 *La Semaine Juridique Générale* 202.

[51] For a discussion of the intensity of the control of constitutionality on electoral matters, see R Ghevontian and S Lamouroux, 'Jurisprudence du Conseil constitutionnel. Le contrôle des lois d'application de l'article 25 de la Constitution' (2009) 79 *Revue française de droit constitutionnel* 575.

leaves the government quite free to violate the principle of equality and even if the Council admits that an accumulation of exceptions can create unconstitutional situations,[52] those do not seem to be easy for the Council to recognise without interfering with the political sphere. Finally, the Council acknowledges the need for political considerations, especially in territories such as overseas territories or islands, where it is not feasible to have no representation at all. In such cases, the Council tempers its strict scrutiny with political pragmatism.

Overall, the Constitutional Council's role in redistricting operations in France, especially through its advisory power and case-law, has influenced the development of the demographic rule and the principle of equality in elections. While the Council's influence is significant, there are still limitations to its control, and the redistricting process remains a complex and politically influenced operation.

Equality and democracy are intrinsically linked. The principle of equality of suffrage, as interpreted by the Constitutional Council, serves as an embodiment of formal equality and affirms the right of every individual to participate in national sovereignty. By intensifying its scrutiny of electoral districts and their organisation, the French Council initially showed potential for advancing the democratic model. However, subsequent case-law demonstrated a partial retreat from this potential, as the Council reverted to self-restraint and deference towards the legislator.

C. The Disappointment about Constitutional Review of Redistricting: The Case-law of 2010

The characteristic of executive orders ('*ordonnances*') under Article 38 of the Constitution is that, after a certain period, the ordonnance must be ratified by Parliament to become permanent legislation; otherwise, it becomes null and void. Redistricting in 2009 was conducted under 'Ordonnance' n° 2009-935 of 29 July 2009 and ratified with the Law of 23 February 2010. The ratification Law of 2010 provided an opportunity for the Council to examine the constitutionality of the previous redistricting following its implementation. The Council was asked to apply constitutional review to the Law before its enactment, which led to its decision of 18 February 2010, the last to date on electoral redistricting. In light of the 2009 case-law, the opposition took the expression 'to better respect' seriously in the context of redistricting and challenged the law, urging the Constitutional Council to compel the government to implement the most equitable apportionment possible. However, the outcome was disappointing as the Council deemed the newly divided constituencies compatible with the Constitution.[53] To reach this

[52] The Council affirms about the exceptions to the demographic principle 'that they could, however, by their combination or by the conditions of their application, give rise to arbitrary delimitations of constituencies or result in situations where the principle of equality would be disregarded' (Constitutional Council, decision no 2008-573 DC, para 26).

[53] Constitutional Council, decision no 2010-602 DC of 18 February 2010.

conclusion, the Council employed a minimal form of judicial review and adhered to its customary self-restraint. Consequently, the Council's oversight ensures not the best possible apportionment (as stated in the 2009 decision), but rather the least incorrect one.

When the complainants attempted to demonstrate that an alternative apportionment method would have 'better respected' the demographic principle of suffrage equality, the Council reiterated its distinctiveness and difference from the Council of State and the independent commission established by the 2009 law. While those institutions possess the authority to advise the government on optimal apportionment, it is not the role of the Constitutional Council to do so. The Council stated,

> Considering that the Constitution does not confer on the Constitutional Council a general power of assessment and decision similar to that of Parliament; (…) it is therefore not within its purview to determine whether the constituencies have been delimited as fairly as possible. Unlike the commission outlined in Article 25 of the Constitution and, as it may do in the exercise of its administrative functions, the Conseil d'État, the Council is not tasked with making proposals in this regard.[54]

As a result, the executive branch possesses considerable discretion in determining apportionment, while the Council's role is limited to rectifying glaring disparities, rather than actively safeguarding elections.[55]

Once again, the Council acknowledges that the principle of an 'essentially demographic basis' can be breached in cases of general interest and specific legal and factual circumstances. Ultimately, these exceptions enable the Council to validate the distribution of electoral constituencies that still significantly differ from one another in terms of population, striking a compromise between a mathematical rule (demographic equality) and the recognition of historical, human, and political considerations. This decision appears to establish the final interpretation of the term 'essentially demographic' as a compromise between mathematical equality and other imperatives.[56] The disappointment provoked by such a compromise shows in the reaction by some representatives: a proposal for a constitutional amendment was initiated in 2023 by a senator suggesting that the obligation of judicial review of redistricting should be added to the Constitution.[57] Such proposal never passed the very first stage of the constitutional reform procedure.

[54] ibid at para 20.

[55] The idea of courts as guardians of elections comes from the famous discussion between Carl Schmitt and Hans Kelsen on who's to be the guardian of the Constitution, during the Weimar Republic. See L Vinx (ed), *The Guardian of the Constitution: Hans Kelsen and Carl Schmitt on the Limits of Constitutional Law* (Cambridge, Cambridge University Press, 2015).

[56] C Castor, 'L'égalité devant le suffrage' (2012) 90 *Revue française de droit constitutionnel* 1.

[57] Text no 364, deposed at the Senate on 17 February 2023 by Senator Jean Louis Masson and available at: www.senat.fr/leg/ppl22-364.html.

IV. A RELATIVE FORM OF SELF-RESTRAINT FOR ELECTORAL RULES

The evolution of judicial review on redistricting in France over three decades highlights the significant importance of this case-law for the French Council. The 2009 decision had raised hopes for a robust scrutiny by the constitutional and electoral judge over political decisions regarding apportionment. It aimed to impose constitutional constraints on state powers and establish safeguards to ensure fair and equal elections. The relative boldness displayed by the Constitutional Council in this matter seems to stem from its well-established role as an electoral judge. Although the two roles are kept separate, the Council has positioned itself as an authority on elections, as evidenced by its use of press releases and observations on elections to encourage redistricting, which is subsequently subjected to judicial review.

However, this initial hope is subsequently diminished by the Council's reluctance to apply the same stringent scrutiny once redistricting has taken place.

While it may be challenging to criticise the Constitutional Council for an attitude that has characterised its existence from the outset, and is largely motivated by the distinctions from an actual constitutional or supreme court in terms of legitimacy, it is possible to highlight one of the main inconsistencies in its reasoning. This inconsistency lies in the frequent reference to the 'legislator' as the reason why the Council cannot substitute its judgment for that of democratically elected representatives. Considering the significant role of the executive power, specifically the government, in redistricting, with the legislative power merely ratifying the decision afterward, the electoral system of the parliamentary chambers largely escapes the Council's purview and the oversight of the Chambers themselves.[58]

The real question of constitutionality, therefore, appears to be not about the mathematical method of calculation – for which the Council is right to defer to an independent commission of experts – but rather about the possibility for governments to bypass parliamentary approval for a decision that has such a profound impact on the elections of both chambers of Parliament, especially the lower chamber, the National Assembly, which directly represents the French people. In this regard, the control of the Constitutional Council is indeed minimal, as it is sufficient for the delegation of powers to the government to be authorised by Parliament through a 'legislative habilitation' ('loi d'habilitation') for the entire procedure to be considered compliant with constitutional requirements. This holds true even if Article 34 of the Constitution explicitly reserves to Parliament the power to determine the rules concerning the electoral system of its two chambers. This formal interpretation of Articles 34 and 38 combined (where even matters reserved for the legislator can be delegated to the government

[58] T Ehrhard, 'Le découpage électoral des circonscriptions législatives: le parlement hors jeu?' (2013) 146 *Pouvoirs* 117.

if the proper procedure is followed) is consistent across all three instances of case-law on redistricting.

In the end, when compared to other courts examined in this volume, the French Constitutional Council is not an activist court and does not possess a specific vision of representation (such as majoritarian or proportional, for example). However, when compared to its own French standards, the Council's actions as an electoral judge validate a slightly more active role in interpreting a vague principle like the equality of suffrage, transforming it into a fundamental rule regularly applied since the 1980s. The Council has effectively transformed a potentially ambiguous principle – the principle of equality as applied to democratic voting – into a normative constitutional rule through its interpretation. The Council's judgments on redistricting seem to rely on the legitimacy derived from its other role as an electoral court. Nonetheless, this interpretation remains cautious and guided by self-restraint, which is a consequence of the unique nature of the French Constitutional Council.

6

Proportional Representation and Electoral Equality in German Constitutional Thinking and Case Law

GIACOMO DELLEDONNE AND BASTIAN MICHEL*

I. INTRODUCTION

IN THIS CHAPTER we take a look at how electoral laws have been addressed in the case law of the German Federal Constitutional Court, with occasional focus on the constitutional courts in the Länder. Due to the fact that no specific voting system was entrenched in the Basic Law of 1949, the main constitutional yardstick that surfaces in the case law is the principle of voting equality. Article 38(1) Grundgesetz (GG): 'Members of the German Bundestag shall be elected in general, direct, free, equal and secret elections.' However, the reading of the principle of voting equality by the Bundesverfassungsgericht is influenced by a deeply rooted legislative tradition that has favoured proportional representation. Since the very beginning of its activity, the Bundesverfassungsgericht has rendered a number of judgments concerning federal and municipal electoral laws, as well as the law on the election of the members of the European Parliament allocated to Germany. In many of these decisions, the interplay between voting equality and proportional representation was central. Limitations on strict equality and deviations from it, for instance the well-known five-per cent threshold, have been assessed in the light of long-standing assumptions on how the prevalence of proportional representation defines the meaning of equal suffrage in the German constitutional order. This principle has played a key role, also due to the fact that the Court has generally looked at it as a right, protected by means of individual complaints raised under Article 93(1)(4a) GG.[1]

* Although this chapter is the result of joint reflections, Giacomo Delledonne wrote II.A, III.A, and IV.A; Bastian Michel wrote II.B, III, B, and IV.B. I and V were elaborated on jointly.

[1] See H Meyer, 'Wahlgrundsätze, Wahlverfahren, Wahlprüfung' in J Isensee and P Kirchhof (eds), *Handbuch des Staatsrechts der Bundesrepublik Deutschland*, vol 3, 3rd edn (Heidelberg, CF Müller, 2005) 543, 561.

The German approach to analysing equality in the light of proportionality sits in a rich comparative context. Electoral equality is a fundamental principle of the representative democratic system and, in this sense, has something universalist about it. During the transitions to constitutional democracy in central and eastern Europe over the last three decades, comparison with long-established constitutional democracies in western Europe played a crucial role.[2] With most European countries now being Member States of the European Union, the European Parliament provides a nucleus case in which the separate electoral regimes come together and show a similarity of problems and a range of possible roles for supreme and constitutional courts, often with interesting differences in approach and outcome.[3] A broader politico-constitutional context is that of a perceived crisis of representative democracy and the growing 'judicialisation of politics'.[4]

The aim of this chapter is to shed some light, through the prism of electoral equality and proportional representation, on the German thinking about representative democracy and to point to some comparative contrasts.

Equality and proportionality have a complicated history of intertwinement from the Weimar Republic into the post-war period, which forms a peculiar historical backdrop of conceptual thinking in Germany today (II). Two areas of application of equality and proportionality bring out the contrast with other jurisdictions more concretely: the case law on thresholds and the judgments on the problems caused by the mixed-member electoral system (III). The European context, and specifically the German case law on European elections, ultimately reveals a certain view of the democratic polity and its organisation within the organs of the state (IV).

II. EQUALITY AND PROPORTIONALITY

Before looking into the case law in greater detail, some clarifications are needed with regard to the status of proportional representation in the German constitutional order. Unlike a majority of constitutions in the Member States of the EU – including, among others, Austria and Spain – no voting system is entrenched in the Basic Law of 1949. When the Parliamentary Council was called on to draft both a Basic Law for the still to be established Federal Republic of Germany and an electoral law for its federal legislature, it discussed electoral matters extensively. Therefore, although the Basic Law is silent on voting systems, this should

[2] See W Sadurski, *Rights Before Courts: A Study of Constitutional Courts in Postcommunist States of Central and Eastern Europe*, 2nd edn (Dordrecht, Springer, 2014) ch 6.

[3] See G Delledonne, '"A Goal That Applies to the European Parliament No Differently From How It Applies to National Parliaments": The Italian Constitutional Court Vindicates the 4% Threshold for European Elections' (2019) 15 *European Constitutional Law Review* 376.

[4] See R Hirschl, 'The Judicialization of Mega-Politics and the Rise of Political Courts' (2008) 11 *Annual Review of Political Science* 93.

not be mistaken for indifference.[5] The members of the Parliamentary Council sought to establish a well-functioning parliamentary form of government; therefore, they critically engaged with the legacy of the Weimar years. According to influential analyses, one of the shared assumptions of the drafters of the Basic Law was that the Constitution of 1919 carried responsibility for the collapse of the Weimar Republic.[6] When discussing the reasons for the rise to power of National Socialism, they made reference, among other factors, to the nefarious effects of the proportional voting system, which, incidentally, had enjoyed constitutional status in the Weimar Republic.[7] Apparently, the drafters of the Basic Law were guided by the dominant feeling that 'Bonn is not Weimar'.

However, a more nuanced appreciation is also possible. Within the Parliamentary Council, no majority emerged for a majoritarian system based on single-member constituencies. In an early version, the Federal Electoral Law did not even provide for a threshold to access the federal legislature. Overall, an unspoken but clear preference for proportional preference seems to pervade the German constitutional order, so much so that an influential scholar used the label 'eloquent silence' to describe the attitude of the Basic Law in this domain.[8] As an Italian Germanist put it, 'Bonn is also Weimar'.[9] In the light of the ambiguous relations between the Basic Law and its antecedent enacted in 1919, a closer look at the legacy of Weimar is needed (II.A), before turning to the current doctrine as it emerges from the Bundesverfassungsgericht's case law (II.B).

A. Systematics and the Legacy of Weimar

The aim of this paragraph is not to retrace the debates about the entrenchment of proportional representation at the Weimar Constituent Assembly;[10] rather, it aims to highlight some points that contributed to shaping the 'credo' of the Federal Constitutional Court in the post-war decades.

First, an idea that seemed to inspire the supporters of the entrenchment of the 'principles of proportional representation' (*Grundsätze der Verhältniswahl*) in Article 22 of the Weimar Constitution was that this move was the culminating

[5] See, in general terms, M Foley, *The Silence of Constitutions* (Abingdon, Routledge, 1989).

[6] See, among others, FK Fromme, *Von der Weimarer Verfassung zum Bonner Grundgesetz. Die verfassungspolitischen Folgerungen des Parlamentarischen Rates aus Weimarer Republik und nationalsozialistischer Diktatur* (Tübingen, Mohr Siebeck, 1960); W Weber, *Spannungen und Kräfte im westdeutschen Verfassungssystem*, 3rd edn (Berlin, Duncker & Humblot, 1970).

[7] Among Ferdinand Hermens' highly influential works, see FA Hermens, *The Representative Republic* (Notre Dame IN, University of Notre Dame Press, 1958).

[8] H Meyer, 'Demokratische Wahl und Wahlsystem' in J Isensee and P Kirchhof (eds), *Handbuch des Staatsrechts der Bundesrepublik Deutschland*, vol 3, 3rd edn (Heidelberg, CF Müller, 2005) 521, 537.

[9] A Bolaffi, 'Lo spettro di Weimar e la coscienza politica d'Europa', preface in A Wirsching, *Weimar, cent'anni dopo. La storia e l'eredità: bilancio di un'esperienza controversa* (Roma, Donzelli, 2019) 10.

[10] On this, see C Gusy, *Die Weimarer Reichsverfassung* (Tübingen, Mohr Siebeck, 1997) 116 ff.

point of a decade-long struggle for political equality. Proportional representation seemed to go hand in hand with universal, equal and secret suffrage. Sceptics of proportional representation like Friedrich Naumann argued that the latter were political rights, while the adoption of proportional representation was one of the possible solutions to the question of how to determine the political leadership. Hugo Preuß championed the opposite view and assumed that the recognition of (male and female) universal and equal suffrage, with the ensuing demise of elitist mechanisms like Prussia's three-class franchise, had to be complemented by the adoption of proportional representation. Not only were voters equal when they cast their votes, but the effects of this equality had to be extended to the composition of the legislature. In this vein, the constitutional recognition of political rights was tightly connected to the decisions on the voting system, and embracing the 'principles of proportional representation' was seen as a direct consequence of the affirmation of equal suffrage.[11] By contrast, the Weimar constituents were not particularly interested in the interplay between proportional representation and the relations between the legislature and the executive under the new Constitution.

The subsequent interpretation and implementation of the principles enshrined in the Weimar Constitution, most notably proportional representation *and* equal suffrage, deserve careful consideration. First, the Constitution mentioned the principles of proportional representation but did not define the contents and technical features of the federal voting system in greater detail. The electoral law, the Reichswahlgesetz of 1920, opted for the strictest possible reading of proportional representation. Within multi-seat constituencies, each party list would receive a seat for every 60,000 votes, and unused votes would be allocated to national party lists. Accordingly, the overall size of the Reichstag was not predetermined in advance.

Second, the inspiration of the Reichswahlgesetz was paralleled by a 'maximalist' approach in the case law of the State Court (Staatsgerichtshof) for the German Reich.[12] In three judgments rendered on 17 December 1927, the Staatsgerichtshof struck down the state electoral laws of Hamburg, Hesse, and Mecklenburg-Strelitz.[13] On 22 March 1929, it annulled the election that had been held in the Free State of Saxony three years before.[14] In its reasoning,

[11] In fact, this component of the Weimar legacy has rapidly gone out of fashion; nowadays, there is no consensus on the fact that proportional representation should be preferred over other voting systems in the same way that universal and equal suffrage finally prevailed over, respectively, limited franchise and plural voting (H Meyer, *Wahlsystem und Verfassungsordnung: Bedeutung und Grenzen wahlsystematischer Gestaltung nach dem Grundgesetz* (Frankfurt am Main, Metzner, 1973) 20 f).

[12] Under Art 19 of the Constitution of 1919, the Staatsgerichtshof decided constitutional controversies arising within a state 'for the decision of which there is no competent court', and public-law controversies arising between different states or between the Reich and a single state, 'if no other court of the Reich is competent'.

[13] StGH 6/27.

[14] StGH 13/28.

the Staatsgerichtshof moved from a strong reading of the principle of equal suffrage, which could not simply be seen as a mere prohibition to revert to plurality voting; rather, equal suffrage entailed that the votes cast should be treated equally when seats were allocated and should have equal influence (*Erfolgswert*) on the outcome. Therefore, a proportional voting system had to be compatible with equal suffrage requirements at all stages, from the casting of votes to the allocation of seats. This strand of case law was met with mixed reviews; more particularly, Hermann Heller analysed the proportional electoral laws that were in force in many European states at that time and argued that 'discriminations with regard to the equal *Erfolgswert* of the votes cast [...] are not incompatible with the postulate of equal suffrage in a proportional electoral system if they are not exclusively directed against individual political parties but against all small parties'.[15]

Although the entrenchment of proportional representation in the Constitution of 1919 was later described as an ominous decision – also because of an apparently cumbersome amending procedure – it is correct that ordinary legislation and the case law of the Staatsgerichtshof went further than the Constitution in imposing strict electoral equality. The legacy of the Weimar years can be traced back not only to a certain preference for proportional representation but also to the emergence of a tight link between proportional representation and a strict understanding of electoral equality, including both the one person, one vote principle and equal *Erfolgswert* of the votes cast.

B. Current Situation and Case Law of the Bundesverfassungsgericht

As already mentioned, the new Grundgesetz for West-Germany of 1949 did not fix the electoral system for the Bundestag and left that decision to the ordinary legislature. The choice in fact made, on the level of ordinary legislation, was for proportional representation based on party lists, combined with plurality voting in single-member constituencies to fill part of the seats won through proportionality. The Parliamentary Council's own draft for an electoral law for the first Bundestag elections already contained that system of 'personalised proportional representation' and this system has continued in place, unchanged in its fundamentals, ever since. After a failed attempt to introduce first-past-the-post voting at the time of the first Grand Coalition in the late 1960s, the decision for proportional representation has generally not been challenged any longer, if not in the aftermath of the federal election of 2005 and the ensuing stalemate.[16]

[15] H Heller, 'Die Gleichheit in der Verhältniswahl nach der Weimarer Verfassung. Ein Rechtsgutachten' in *Gesammelte Schriften*, vol 2 (Leiden, AW Sijthoff, 1971) 319, 344 (this author's translation).

[16] See L Helms, 'The Grand Coalition: Precedent and Prospects' (2006) 24 *German Politics and Society* 47, 59.

All German Länder use proportional representation for elections to their Land Parliament, most of them through a similar system of personalised proportionality,[17] as well as for municipal elections.[18] European elections in Germany have always been based on proportionality even before that became a requirement under the Direct Elections Act.[19] The overall impression one gets, looking back at 70 years of constitutional life in the Federal Republic, is that proportional representation is very much entrenched in Germany, certainly as a matter of politico-constitutional culture. It remains true, though, that proportional representation is not entrenched in the text of the Grundgesetz.

It is in this context, and against the background of Weimar, that the Bundesverfassungsgericht's case law can best be understood. With a constitutional text silent on the choice of electoral system, but equality being there as a core element of elections, there are two potential views on the situation that are simple and straightforward: one view would hold that equality implies proportional representation, in other words that a majoritarian system (say the British simple plurality vote in single-member constituencies) is so unequal that it would be unconstitutional in Germany; the other view would be that equality can go no further than it would in the least equal but still permissible electoral system, providing a uniform minimum standard that any electoral system would have to respect but no more than that.

The Bundesverfassungsgericht has always rejected both views. Continuing its predecessor's case law of the 1920s, it has held, from as early as 1956 onwards, that the meaning of equality depends on the system chosen. Under the Grundgesetz, the legislature is free to opt for a majoritarian system, in which electoral equality means each vote had to be counted equal (*Zählwertgleichheit*); or it can opt for proportional representation, in which case not only have votes to be counted equal but must have equal influence on the outcome, more precisely the same potential for success in contributing to one more seat for the party chosen (*Zählwertgleichheit* plus *Erfolgswertgleichheit*).[20]

The Bundesverfassungsgericht arrived at this position by using the doctrinal construction variously know as 'correctness of consequence' (*Folgerichtigkeit*) or 'self-binding of the legislature' (*Selbstbindung des Gesetzgebers*). This doctrine says, as these terms suggest, that the legislature, once having made a principal choice of overall legislative approach to an area of life to be regulated,

[17] The majority of the Länder have proportional representation entrenched in their constitution, those constitutions that do not mention the system often implicitly assume proportionality where they set a threshold; see 'Zur Regelungsdichte des Wahlrechts in den Verfassungen der deutschen Bundesländer und der Mitgliedstaaten der EU' (Bundestag, Wissenschaftliche Dienste, WD 3-3000-136/14, 2016) 8–12; also W Zicht, 'Übersicht über die Wahlsysteme bei Landtagswahlen' (2009, last update 25 March 2020), www.wahlrecht.de/landtage/index.htm.

[18] Mostly with an open list system; see W Zicht 'Übersicht über die Wahlsysteme bei Kommunalwahlen' (1999, last update 21 May 2018), www.wahlrecht.de/kommunal/index.htm.

[19] § 2 Europawahlgesetz (as originally enacted 16 June 1978) BGBl I 709.

[20] BVerfGE 1, 208, 244 ff with reference to the case law of the Staatsgerichtshof and to Heller (n 15).

is bound by its own principal decision and has to fill in the detailed rules in a way consistent with it. Or, as the Bundesverfassungsgericht put it with regard to the electoral system in 1952:

> The advantage associated specifically with proportional representation is that it provides for fractions of all parliamentary seats that correspond, as best as possible, to the fractions of votes gained by the several political streams in the country. It is therefore regarded as a requirement of equity, here, that each vote have the same success value in principle. A legislature that chooses this system, even if merely in addition to election by majority, thereby accepts this requirement of equity and subjects its law to that standard.[21]

In later decades, specifically in its judgment of 2012, the Bundesverfassungsgericht seemed slightly to edge away from this language of a self-binding legislature and instead focussed on electoral equality and the substance of what elections are. Electoral equality meant votes had to be treated strictly equally, having the same counting value and the 'same chance of success legally' (*gleiche rechtliche Erfolgschance*). This was, in the words of the Court, a uniform standard, it just meant different things under different electoral laws. In a majority or plurality single-seat constituency system it would mean constituencies had to be of roughly equal size and votes had to be counted equally. In a list-based proportional system it meant that, after counting votes equally, they also had to have the same degree of influence in each step of the necessary calculations that would ensue.[22] So this reasoning leads, in the end, to the very same test of equal counting value plus equal success value.

In the next part of this chapter, we look at two areas of application of this approach by the Bundesverfassungsgericht to see how very powerful and far-reaching it can be. Before doing so, it is worth briefly to put the approach into its broader electoral-law context as represented in the German case law, including the standard of review the Court says it uses, and to flag up a few strands of critique on it.

According to the Bundesverfassungsgericht's stable case law, seen that the Grundgesetz itself leaves open the question of which electoral system is to be used, the legislature is free to choose one system or another and to modify it. In doing so, it must have regard to the functions that elections have in the representative democratic system and the constitutional requirements connected with these: elections create a relationship between voter and elected, and are an expression of the sovereign people's will in legitimising the organs of the state.[23] The elected assembly must be able to fulfil its functions, especially legislating

[21] BVerfGE 1, 208, 248.

[22] BVerfGE 131, 316, 337 f.

[23] On the 'chain of legitimation' (*Legitimationskette*) from voters to Parliament to the government and the administration, see, critically and with further references, U Schliesky, *Souveränität und Legitimität von Herrschaftsgewalt* (Tübingen, Mohr Siebeck, 2004) 276 ff.

and installing an executive. Elections must be designed in such a way that the integration of different political forces can take place and so that significant desires, concerns and interests do not remain unrepresented. Some of these aims are in tension with each other and meeting them at the same time can only be successful if the legislature enjoys wide discretion.[24] The bottom line that the Bundesverfassungsgericht draws, and which the legislature may not transgress, is each citizen's right to free and equal participation in the process of democratic self-determination. In addition, the strictly formal character of electoral equality means that there is very little room of manoeuvre to differentiate between votes. It is for the legislature to identify the constitutional aims that might require some degree of differentiation in voting equality and to lay down a balanced solution. It is not for the Court to say whether such solutions are adequate or desirable as a matter of constitutional policy; scrutiny by the Court is restricted to asking, by way of proportionality test, whether the aims behind a differentiation are legitimate, whether the means to reach them are suitable, and whether they go no further than required. Lastly, the legitimacy of a differentiation in voting equality can depend on real-world circumstances that may change. The legislature is therefore under an obligation to monitor developments and intervene if needed.[25]

Despite the Bundesverfassungsgericht's rhetoric of restricted scrutiny, a proportionality test in particular is, of course, a strong means. The critique on the Court's overall approach, moreover, highlights the potentially too broad view on permissible electoral systems and the too deep-reaching test once a system is chosen.

As pointed out by Hans Meyer in his 1973 book, one cannot conclude from the Grundgesetz's silence on which electoral system is to be used that all known systems are permissible or that any specific system will be. Whether introduction of a British-style simple plurality system would be permissible in Germany depends on whether such a system meets the requirements that the Grundgesetz *does* contain.[26] Fifty years later, that critique still stands. With the broad use of proportionality in Germany, now deeply entrenched as a matter of politico-constitutional culture, it is less likely that this question will be tested in the near future, but perhaps more likely that a majoritarian system would have to be seen as unconstitutional in Germany if it ever came to such a test. Meyer also criticises the Court's view that there are essentially two archetypes of electoral system, majoritarian and proportional, with modifications. Despite his strong appeal to take a more realistic view about a range of systems, possibly to be ordered along a scale from restrictive to more open, this classic view is still prevalent in the Bundesverfassungsgericht's case law.

[24] BVerfGE 131, 316, 335f with references to preceding case law.
[25] BVerfGE 131, 316, 336–39.
[26] Meyer (n 11) 193. On this, see also G Delledonne, *Costituzione e Legge Elettorale* (Napoli, Editoriale Scientifica, 2019) 53.

Critique on the Court's deep scrutiny goes in a similar direction. A doctrine of a self-binding legislature is problematic in that the Court takes it upon itself to determine which choices by the legislature are the principal ones and what the legislature's aim was in enacting them. Countervailing choices can then be presented as questions of detail, which may be held to be impermissible. The forms of law in Germany do not, in themselves, have any structure of hierarchy within the class of ordinary legislation that would justify this technique. Departing from the presumption that there are essentially two electoral systems to choose from, albeit with modifications, further enhances the Court's grip on the legislative design. In particular, in a situation that a detailed rule encroaches upon an individual right like electoral equality and fits ill with the principal choice of system, it is then no defence for the legislature to say that under a different principal choice, also open to the legislature, the encroachment of right would be even worse but permissible.[27] In other words, the Court seems to compartmentalise constitutional review into pillars, then to require that rules within each pillar are in harmony whilst disallowing any sideway comparison between pillars. This becomes more clear in the concrete application of the Court's approach to the questions of thresholds and the problems around the mixed system, to which we turn now.

III. TWO AREAS OF APPLICATION

When addressing the Federal Election Law (Bundeswahlgesetz) or other electoral laws (for instance, the Europawahlgesetz), a recurring point in the case law of the Bundesverfassungsgericht is resort to thresholds (III.A). These judgments are of great relevance also in comparative terms. Thresholds are a typical, although not a necessary, component of proportional voting systems, which allows to explain the great influence of the Bundesverfassungsgericht in this area. Other issues that have been addressed in the case law, most notably the much-discussed 'excess seats', are more directly related to the technicalities of the German mixed-member system (III.B).

A. Limiting Equality by Thresholds

A five-per cent threshold is generally described a distinctive feature of the German system of personalised proportional representation. However, a closer look at the discussion within the Parliamentary Council shows that the introduction

[27] See M Payandeh, 'Das Gebot der Folgerichtigkeit: Rationalitätsgewinn oder Irrweg der Grundrechtsdogmatik?' (2011) 136 *Archiv des öffentlichen Rechts* 578 with a critique on the doctrine, at 600ff specifically in the context of electoral law.

of a five-per cent threshold at Land level was the result of last-minute pressure from the occupying powers. Initially, the threshold for federal elections applied for each Land separately. Since 1953, with the sole exception of the first federal election after the reunification in 1990, the threshold has applied nationally.

The first significant judgment was issued by the Bundesverfassungsgericht in 1952.[28] The Court held that proportional representation may favour smaller parties 'that would not stand the slightest chance of success under a single-seat constituency system', possibly resulting in 'perturbations of constitutional life'.[29] A representative assembly fragmented into several small groups might not be able to perform its functions, first and foremost 'to create a politically active government'.[30] To prevent political instability, political parties could be treated differently when seats are allocated; because of the proportional inspiration that pervades the system, such exceptions to the general rule of equality can only be admitted on compelling grounds. The issue of which differential rules are admissible cannot be settled once and for all; however, and in spite of the silence of the Basic Law, a comparative analysis of the constitutions then in force in several West German Länder suggested that a five-per cent threshold, barring exceptional circumstances, was not an unjustified measure.

The reasoning of the Court may be saluted for its cautious, realistic approach or, conversely, criticised as unsatisfactory. To assess the constitutionality of thresholds, constitutional provisions have to be read with an eye to empirical evidence:

> An electoral law provision may be justified in one state at a given point in time and not in another state or at another point in time; when it is issued, the circumstances of the country to which it is supposed to apply must be taken into account.[31]

In 1990, this led the Court to invite the federal legislature to adapt the Bundeswahlgesetz to the exceptional circumstances arising from the reunification of Germany.

What the need for a functioning representative body requires is not completely clear in the case law of the Bundesverfassungsgericht. In 1952, the judges in Karlsruhe hinted at the formation of a politically active government. In subsequent judgments, the Court has resorted to a slightly different wording: smaller groups may make it difficult or impossible 'to form a stable majority' and undermine 'the Parliament's ability to act and to make decisions'.[32] Therefore, one may argue, a functioning Parliament is needed per se, independently from its relations with the executive (which, of course, are no less important); this, in turn, may represent a compelling reason to justify the introduction of thresholds.

[28] See also above II.B (text at n 20).
[29] BVerfGE 1, 208, 248.
[30] ibid.
[31] BVerfGE 82, 322, 338.
[32] ibid.

As mentioned above, these arguments are not inherently related to the distinctive features of the German model of personalised proportional representation; rather, they reflect memories of the Weimar legacy and a systematic reading of the electoral law and the constitutional provisions. The Federal Republic of Germany having a parliamentary form of government, the relations between the Bundestag and the Federal Government cannot be ignored when addressing the constitutionality of electoral thresholds. From an entirely different viewpoint, the arguments used by the Bundesverfassungsgericht have been criticised as 'weak and contradictory'.[33] On the one hand, the silence of the Grundgesetz may have been overinterpreted by courts and scholars; on the other hand, an unbiased consideration of the very stable German party system in the 1970s may have suggested that thresholds were no longer necessary. Fifty years on, it might be argued that the ever-greater fragmentation of the party system – and the composition of the Bundestag – in the last two decades shows that the five-per cent threshold is no longer fit for purpose.

The case law of the Court developed as a result of challenges brought against the Bundeswahlgesetz and the electoral laws of the Länder; indeed, the judgment released in 1952, which represents a leading case in this respect, focused on a threshold clause in the electoral law of Schleswig-Holstein that was deemed to penalise the Danish-speaking minority party.

The case law of the Court looks less consistent if the electoral laws for the European Parliament and municipal councils are also taken into account. In 1957, the Bundesverfassungsgericht held that the municipal councils, for all their differences from the Federal and Land parliaments, were dominated by political parties and, consequently, their functioning could be 'perturbed by the existence of small parties, just like the normal operation of a parliament'.[34] The decline of mass political parties at the local level and, even more importantly, the introduction of the direct election of mayors in several Länder led both the Bundesverfassungsgericht and constitutional courts in the Länder to change their approach. The significant differences between municipal councils and parliaments and the option for a new form of government at the local level, with the mayor not depending on the support of a majority within the council, weakened the compelling grounds for providing for thresholds in the electoral laws for the municipal assemblies.

In the run-up to the first election of the European Parliament by direct universal suffrage, the Europawahlgesetz of 1978 provided for a national five-per cent threshold. Soon after the European elections of 1979, the Bundesverfassungsgericht adjudicated constitutional complaints based on the alleged violation of the principle of equal suffrage. To reject these claims, the Court built on the similarities between the European Parliament and the Bundestag: due to its tasks and its role as defined by the Treaties,

[33] Meyer (n 1) 564.
[34] BVerfGE 6, 104, 118.

> [t]he European Parliament can only effectively deal with the tasks assigned to it if it provides all its members with the necessary expertise and is able to form a convincing majority. Both [preconditions] can be jeopardized if the division of Parliament into many groups, which is unavoidable in any case due to the large number of member states, takes on such proportions that its ability to function is seriously called into question.[35]

This line of reasoning was further strengthened by comparison with the other Member States of the European Communities, whose electoral laws for the European Parliament contained, more often than not, explicit or implicit thresholds. Three decades later, in a significant overruling of its previous judgment, the Federal Constitutional Court declared the five-per cent threshold unconstitutional. In spite of the constitutional evolution of the Communities and later the EU, the Court firmly rejected any analogy between the European Parliament and the Bundestag. With regard to the latter, the Court said, the five-per cent threshold is justified because a stable majority is needed to form a functioning government and to support it over time. In the supranational scenario, in turn,

> [t]he European Parliament does not elect a Union government depending on its continued support. Nor is the Union's legislation dependent on a stable majority in the European Parliament [...] [T]here are no compelling reasons to affect equal suffrage and equal opportunities through threshold clauses.[36]

Echoes of the much-discussed case law of the Bundesverfassungsgericht on the relations between the domestic and the European legal and constitutional orders resonate in this judgment, which was confirmed after the federal legislature tried to reintroduce a three-per cent threshold ahead of the 2014 European election.[37] In spite of major transformations in the institutional architecture of the EU, the Bundesverfassungsgericht could no longer seen any 'compelling reasons' to justify resort to a threshold for the European elections in Germany.

B. Deviating from Equality through Mixity of the System

Germany is well known for its mixed-member electoral system of 'personalised proportional representation'. It also has not gone unnoticed that the problems around 'excess seats' (*Überhangmandate*) and 'negative voting effect' (*negatives Stimmgewicht*) have made the system, as it was until 2011, untenable. A brief discussion is warranted here, as the complexity of the federal electoral system

[35] BVerfGE 51, 222, 246 f.

[36] BVerfGE 129, 300, 336.

[37] BVerfGE 135, 259. See also B Michel, 'Thresholds for the European Parliament Elections in Germany Declared Unconstitutional Twice' (2016) 12 *European Constitutional Law Review* 133; G Taylor, 'The Constitutionality of Election Thresholds in Germany' (2017) 15 *International Journal of Constitutional Law* 734.

puts constitutional review by the Bundesverfassungsgericht into a problematic position between the norms of the constitution and their established interpretation, the general understanding of the system amongst the broad public, the interests of party politics, and the hard limits of simple mathematics.

It is globally correct to say that the two main elements in the German federal electoral system – plurality vote in the single-member constituencies and proportionality based on a list vote overall – cannot always be brought together in harmony and that this clash causes the problems: too many constituency seats won can 'exceed' a party's seat allotment under proportionality. But the problems partly come from, and are partly exacerbated by, a third ingredient: party lists are drawn up for each Land separately and an intra-party contest between each party's several Land subsections takes place. This third element, although having little traction with voters and not prominently present in public debate, is essential for political career paths. Overloading the electoral system with not one, or even two, but three first principles, puts it against the limits of what is mathematically possible. In the old Bonn republic, with its two large parties plus a small third kingmaker, this did not lead to significant problems. But with four or more parties going beyond the five-per cent threshold and the larger parties losing in the proportional vote but remaining dominant in the constituencies, the numbers simply do not pan out any longer. In this situation, the Court has steadily become stricter towards the legislature over the past decades.

The line of case law goes from acceptance of excess seats as a small and legitimate deviation from overall proportionality, lastly confirmed in a 1997 judgment, through to the 2008 judgment finding negative voting effects a reason for unconstitutionality of the system, up to 2012 when the Court mooted a concrete upper limit to the number of excess seats.

The judgment of 3 July 1997 continued the long-standing case law of the Bundesverfassungsgericht.[38] The general nature of the electoral system was proportionality. But the absolute rule that constituency seats won by plurality were to be maintained, even where exceeding proportion, was legitimate in view of the aim to create a narrow bond between each constituency and its elected member.[39] The Court did recognise, however, that there would be a quantitative limit beyond which the intrusion into proportionality could no longer be tolerated, which the legislature had to keep an eye on and act if necessary. Such a limit might, the Court added tentatively, lie around five per cent of the standard seat number, as that was a limit on proportionality that the legislature itself had recognised in setting the five-per cent threshold.[40] The Court's judgment was adopted on a knife's edge, with four judges in favour of the reasoning just summarised and four against. The dissenting reasoning of the other four judges

[38] BVerfGE 95, 335, *Überhangmandate II*.
[39] ibid 357 ff, with references to standing case law that goes back to 1957.
[40] ibid 366.

gave a preview of what was to come later. In their view, excess seats meant that some voters had more influence on the Bundestag's composition than others and, therefore, excess seats were a breach of electoral equality.[41]

The mixed system with its excess seats remained in place until the Bundesverfassungsgericht's judgment of 2008 finally declared it unconstitutional in some respects and ordered the legislature to reform it by mid-2011.[42] The case was, in a sense, easier than the preceding one: it focussed on the negative voting effect, which is an obvious violation of electoral equality. The effect was an indirect consequence of excess seats combined with each party's separate lists per Land: more votes for party X in Land A might not win the party overall any additional seat but could lead, in the intra-party competition, to X losing a seat in Land B in favour of its list in Land A; but if X already had excess seats in Land A, then no additional seat would accrue; still, X lost a seat in Land B. The upshot was that an elector's vote could actively damage the party of choice. The Court pointedly remarked that the effect made the electoral system illogical and contrary to the very nature of an election; moreover, it discriminated against voters for larger parties as only those were potentially affected. It was clear the effect did occur regularly and would continue to do so. Having a third element of proportionality between the Länder was, in principle, a legitimate choice, as the federal structure of Germany was something the legislature could take in consideration; but that aim was not of such an importance that it could outweigh the absurdity of a negative voting effect.[43] A solution could lie in severing the intra-party competition by making each Land a more closed electoral area, or in wholesale reform of the system, for instance by switching to a 50-50 hard split between constituency seats and proportionality list seats.[44]

The Bundestag was deadlocked on the question of how to reform the system. Exceeding the deadline of mid-2011 by several months, the legislature ultimately introduced a system that maintained excess seats without correction. In following on the hint by the Bundesverfassungsgericht that severing intra-party competition might be a solution, the legislature, through its conservative-liberal government majority, attempted to make the Länder more closed electoral subareas. But it took the wrong path for that, introducing a first allocation of seats over the Länder by valid votes cast, followed by distribution over parties within each Land separately. Consequently, negative voting effect could no longer occur in the exact form it had before, but was to occur in a different and even worse form: additional votes on the elector's party of choice could win over seats from another Land which might not merely be of no effect for the party chosen, they could actually fall to a competing party in the same Land that the elector had not voted on, potentially damaging their own party elsewhere and actively helping

[41] ibid 375 ff.
[42] BVerfGE 121, 266.
[43] ibid 299 ff.
[44] ibid 306 ff.

another party in their own area. The new law was declared unconstitutional in the Court's 2012 judgment.[45] But not only did the Court point to the negative voting effect in its new form, it also found excess seats in too large a number a self-standing violation of the constitution's principle of equal elections. In principle, it was for the legislature to decide which number of excess seats would be too large; but as error or inaction by the legislature on this point could put into doubt the future elections to the Bundestag and might lead to elections being declared invalid, the Court decided itself to point to a limit: excess seats going beyond half the size of a parliamentary *Fraktion*, hence 2.5 per cent of all seats, would be unconstitutional.[46]

In its reaction to the 2012 judgment, the Bundestag could not agree on deeper reforms of the electoral system. Instead, it decided to revert to the pre-2011 system in principle and repair the defect of excess seats by introducing top-up seats to restore proportionality. This solution comes at the cost of a significant increase in the overall size of the Bundestag. The standard size of the Bundestag is 598 seats. The 2013 election, with excess seats and newly introduced top-up seats, resulted in an overall size of 631; the election in 2017 resulted in 706 seats; in 2021 this increased further to 736. Under the current rules it is perfectly plausible, based on reasonable assumptions about future voting behaviour, to expect a size of more than 1,000 seats. There is broad political consensus that this is undesirable. Changes adopted in 2020 sought a partial solution in allowing for a limited number of excess seats to remain uncorrected and there was an intention to reduce the number of constituencies in the longer term.[47] The most recent reform goes further than this and makes a radical choice in favour of the proportionality element: excess seats are no longer allocated, leaving single-member constituencies unrepresented where simple-majority winners are not covered by their party's seat allotment under proportionality.[48]

The developments since 1998 suggest that the Bundesverfassungsgericht has steadily become stricter towards the legislature, partly due to changing realities and partly in developing its case law and arriving at higher standards. But there are more concrete observations to be made: one on the problematic nature of the Court's doctrinal approach, one on its institutional position.

The case law on the problems of the mixed-member system provide a stark example of the Bundesverfassungsgericht's doctrine that the principal choices by the legislature are binding on the legislature itself: where constituency seats cannot be counted against allotments under proportionality, one solution

[45] BVerfGE 131, 316.

[46] ibid 363 ff.

[47] Fünfundzwanzigstes Gesetz zur Änderung des Bundeswahlgesetzes (14 November 2020) BGBl I 2395; this law is currently object of an *abstrakte Normenkontrolle* brought by Bundestag members of the Greens, Linke and FDP, BVerfG pending case 2 BvF 1/21.

[48] Amending law BGBl I 2023, no 147, commenced 14 June 2023; parliamentary record under dip.bundestag.de/vorgang/gesetz-zur-%C3%A4nderung-des-bundeswahlgesetzes-und-des-f%C3%BCnfundzwanzigsten-gesetzes-zur/295762.

mooted by the Court is to change to a 50-50 hard split system in which no constituency seats are ever counted against proportionality; of course this is much worse, but if overall proportionality is not the starting position then it is unproblematic in the Court's view. Or to put it more bluntly: if *all* constituency seats are always in excess, but this is by design rather than by accident, then there is no problem. One can see, here, how the doctrine developed by the Bundesverfassungsgericht goes very deep into consequences of the legislature's principal choice and, deep in there, forbids looking sideways and compare to a different system. Logically neat on the one hand, but somehow detached from the broader picture and almost anti-holistic on the other, we suggest that this approach is intellectually and doctrinally problematic.

On the institutional level, it is striking how clearly the German Federal Constitutional Court differs from a classic Kelsenian, pure negative-legislator model. The Bundesverfassungsgericht suggests solutions to the problems found, in one case leading the Bundestag to adopt an incorrect strategy that it erroneously believed had received the Court's approval beforehand. And the Bundesverfassungsgericht points out concrete quantitative limits, intended to assist the legislature in designing an acceptable system. But these limits are not based on anything, in fact they are plucked out of thin air, and, in the latest case, are understood by the legislature not as a margin of tolerance for unforeseen deviations but as an invitation actively to wire these deviations into the system. This is not a typical relationship between a legislature and a constitutional court.[49]

The years since 2008 have shown German politics unwilling to confront wholesale reform of the electoral system; in designing reforms along the lines suggested by the Court, the legislature has aimed at a necessary minimum, but has more than once transgressed that line and ended up with equally unconstitutional solutions or worse ones. In the meantime, it is doubtful whether the basic idea of the German mixed-member system – proportionality as an expression of equality along party lines, plus a close local connection with a constituency candidate – can really be fulfilled; in reality, the two votes that electors cast do something quite different from what voters are told. But such profound critique of the system only comes from academic quarters[50] and has not, as far as can be seen, reached the broader public discourse or triggered a movement fundamentally to re-think within politics. The current reform proposals, although keeping a mixed system, do go a bit further than previous ones in giving clear priority to proportionality between parties over all other aims. The negative consequences for some constituency candidates are set to be a main consideration in a likely constitutional review case against these reforms. In that context, it is worth mentioning that voters'

[49] For contrast, consider CZ Constitutional Court 2 February 2021, Pl. ÚS 44/17, on which M Antoš and F Horák, 'Proportionality Means Proportionality: Czech Constitutional Court, 2 February 2021, Pl. ÚS 44/17' (2021) 17 *European Constitutional Law Review* 538.

[50] S Schönberger, 'Die personalisierte Verhältniswahl – eine Dekonstruktion' (2019) 67(1) *Jahrbuch des öffentlichen Rechts der Gegenwart* 1.

influence on the personal element, as an aspect of direct elections, has attracted much less constitutional scrutiny and closed lists seem to be much less a worry to constitutional thinking in Germany compared to other countries.[51]

IV. EQUAL REPRESENTATION AND THE FUNCTIONS OF THE PARLIAMENT

Electoral equality is central to the notion of democracy as a political system of equal free citizens. But the precise purport and reach of the principle of electoral equality can be perceived differently in different jurisdictions. The preceding paragraphs have concentrated on some of the aspects of constitutional thinking and case law that are specific to Germany: the peculiar background of the Weimar Republic (II.A), the current approach by the Bundesverfassungsgericht to equality and its dependence on the electoral system chosen (II.B), and its decisions on two concrete problems, namely thresholds (III.A) and the mixed electoral system (III.B). Several points in which the German case law differs from that of the courts in neighbouring countries have already been highlighted. Here, we want to bring that contrast a bit more to the fore, by turning to the Bundesverfassungsgericht's view of the European electoral context. Our hypothesis is that German case law on Europe reflects, in a kind of mirror effect, some peculiarities of how the Bundesverfassungsgericht qualifies the German representative system and, to some degree, how it sees representative democracy in general. This can be demonstrated by looking at two functions of parliament: the creation of an executive (IV.A), and lawmaking (IV.B).

A. Electing and Sustaining a Government

Governmental stability is a recurring concern in the case law of the Bundesverfassungsgericht. A functioning (*funktionsfähig*) legislature is one that is able to create and support a functioning government. This, in turn, can be seen as a compelling ground to justify derogations from a strict understanding of voting equality, for instance, by introducing thresholds. According to the Bundesverfassungsgericht, the access of 'a myriad of smaller groups' to federal representation may decisively hamper the formation of a stable government.[52] Conversely, those compelling grounds do not apply to municipal assemblies or the European Parliament due to the lack of comparable conditions (see above at III.A). These lines of argument, that have become even more evident in the last two decades, highlight the peculiar role of the Bundestag within the German constitutional order and are based on a peculiar reading of the constitutional provisions.

[51] Only few cases, eg BVerfGE 7, 63, 68 ff. Contrast this with the Italian case law, on which see the contribution by P Passaglia ch 7, IV.C in this volume.

[52] BVerfGE 1, 208 (248).

In other European systems, for instance Italy, representative democracy coexists with some elements of direct democracy, and the representative component of democracy 'circulates, in multiple forms and to different extents, throughout the whole state machinery, although this is most evident when it comes to the [national] Parliament'.[53] In Germany, in turn, there is a tight link between popular sovereignty, representative democracy,[54] and the constitutional role of the Bundestag. As the Bundesverfassungsgericht put it in the Lisbon judgment, the right to vote under Article 38 Grundgesetz is, first and foremost, a right to elect the members of the Bundestag by universal, direct, free, equal and secret suffrage; this allows all German citizens to express directly their political will. The representative legislature implements popular self-government, and 'the Chancellor – and, consequently, the Federal Government – is determined from it'.[55] In the Court's words, a 'will of majority' has to be articulated in the federal election.[56] Although the Bundesverfassungsgericht in its case law has addressed the electoral laws for the Bundestag, the European Parliament, and municipal assemblies, the federal legislature has clearly been at the forefront of the concerns of the Court. On the one hand, the Bundestag is the prime seat of political representation because of its link with the *Staatsvolk* in its capacity as electoral body. On the other hand, the Bundestag's power to elect the Federal Chancellor by a majority of its members (Article 63(2) Grundgesetz) lies at the heart of the line of argument used by the Court, and the need for a functioning Parliament, a stable working majority and a functioning executive are a recurring theme in its judgments. Still, the obsession for political stability seems to loom large in the case law of the Bundesverfassungsgericht as well as in German political culture, and may lead to underestimate the significance of other constitutional provisions which, for instance, consider the possibility of forming a minority government (Article 63(4) Grundgesetz).

B. Legislating, the Legislature and the Representative Assembly

How the Bundesverfassungsgericht sees the German democratic system, and representative democracy more generally, is reflected in its analysis of the European system also in the context of legislating. This is first a question of majority formation, again, and the tensions it can create with equality; indeed,

[53] V Crisafulli, 'La sovranità popolare nella Costituzione italiana (note preliminari)' in *Stato popolo governo. Illusioni e delusioni costituzionali* (Milano, Giuffrè, 1985) 89, 92.

[54] See, among others, EW Böckenförde, 'Mittelbare/repräsentative Demokratie als eigentliche Form der Demokratie' in G Müller, RA Rhinow, G Schmid and L Wildhaber (eds), *Staatsorganisation und Staatsfunktionen im Wandel. Festschrift für Kurt Eichenberger zum 60. Geburtstag* (Basel, Verlag Helbing & Lichtenhahn, 1982) 301.

[55] BVerfGE 123, 267, 340 f.

[56] ibid 342.

the Court mentions government creation and legislating in the same breath.[57] But there is a second aspect to the Court's case law on Europe which is interesting as well, one that leads from considerations on electoral equality to a strange difference between the representative assembly or 'Parliament' and the legislature. Briefly looking at this, we want to suggest that the difference is not just terminological but conceptual as well, and one that sets German constitutional thinking about representative democracy apart from that in comparable countries.

This aspect comes to the fore where, in its judgment on the Lisbon Treaty, the Court turns to the distortion of electoral equality as between voters throughout the EU. This distortion is caused by the fact that seat contingents in the European Parliament are assigned to the Member States in degressive proportionality. The inequality this introduces – much more influence on the composition of the European Parliament for each voter in smaller Member States than in the larger ones – was not a reason for the Court to declare accession to the Treaty unconstitutional: the EU was still an association of states and peoples, not of equal citizens forming one European people in a Union analogous to a state. The Treaties therefore needed not to provide for a 'political decision organ, created through equal elections by all Union citizens, that is capable of unitary representation of the will of the people'.[58] Such an organ would be required if the Union were a federal state and the Court turns to a short comparative exercise, holding unequal representation occurs at most for a 'second chamber next to the parliament'.[59]

There is something subtly wrong about this nomenclature. For instance the Australian Parliament, mentioned by the Bundesverfassungsgericht in this passage, consists of a first chamber, the House, and a second chamber, the Senate (plus the Crown). The Australian Parliament is the legislature. A similar terminology of both chambers together forming 'the Parliament' would hold for Italy, France, Belgium etc. Not so in Germany: the doctrinal position is that the Bundestag is the unicameral federal Parliament; the Bundesrat only co-operates in legislation. This doctrinal position has the consequence that the term 'legislature' remains undefined in Germany. Indeed, the informal expression 'der Gesetzgeber' points to an abstractum that can be concretised into the institutions mentioned in the Grundgesetz only through a complex exercise that is strongly dependent on subject matter.

More than mere terminology, there is something striking conceptually as well about the 'organ of unitary representation of the will of the people', supposedly positioned at the centre of every democratic system, like the Bundestag is for Germany. Very far-reaching requirements of equality hold for it, as equality

[57] See above III.A (quote at n 36).
[58] BVerfGE 123, 267, at 280.
[59] ibid 283 ff, especially 286.

within the people is a cornerstone of democracy. But co-legislative organs, based on territorial subdivisions of the people into unequal parts with resulting unequal influence, hardly enter the picture. In this perspective, condemning inequality in elections to the European Parliament can never be countered by saying that in Germany, too, voters' influence on legislation through the Bundesrat is highly unequal – for the Bundesrat is not at the centre of the legislative process. Even within Germany itself, the Bundesverfassungsgericht has taken this approach very far, limiting the functions of the inter-institutional Bundestag-Bundesrat conciliatory committee (Vermittlungsausschuss) in view of the pre-eminence of the Bundestag as the directly elected representative assembly.[60] It is on such points, ironically where the Bundesverfassungsgericht claims universality of its conception of representative democracy, that its concepts become very specifically German.

V. CONCLUSION

In this chapter, we focused on specific aspects of electoral law that, by now, look quite stabilised in the case law of the Bundesverfassungsgericht. On 17 March 2023, the Bundestag passed an electoral reform bill that had been strongly supported by the ruling traffic light coalition. On 8 June, after some speculation, the electoral reform law was countersigned by the Federal President and subsequently promulgated in the Federal Law Gazette.[61] As the reform aims to eliminate the Basic Mandate Clause (Grundmandatsklausel), which allows for limited derogation from the national five-per cent threshold, it will likely lead to new constitutional litigation before the Bundesverfassungsgericht and provide the judges with an occasion to revisit the cornerstones of their approach to electoral laws and voting systems. Regardless of the final outcome, this will probably confirm one of the key observations in this chapter: the Bundesverfassungsgericht has never refrained from playing a strong, assertive role in this area of the constitutional order. Other constitutional courts, like the Italian one, were long seen as very cautious, also due to objective reasons that contributed to hindering the effective scrutiny of electoral laws and to the possible impact of a declaration of unconstitutionality.[62] By contrast, the German Federal Constitutional Court has always actively engaged – more often than not through the demanding lens of voting equality – with election-related issues. This testifies to the high level of

[60] See U Schliesky, '§ 5 Parlamentsfunktionen' in M Morlok, U Schliesky and D Wiefelspütz (eds), *Parlamentsrecht* (Baden-Baden, Nomos, 2016) marginal no 48, with reference to BVerfGE 120, 56 and BVerfGE 125, 104.

[61] See above n 48.

[62] See P Faraguna, '"Do You Ever Have One of Those Days When Everything Seems Unconstitutional?": The Italian Constitutional Court Strikes Down the Electoral Law Once Again' (2017) 13 *European Constitutional Law Review* 778, 781 f.

juridification of political life in post-war Germany. This attitude of the Court may have even intensified in the last few decades, as the increasing fragmentation of the party system has led to a closer scrutiny of legislative decisions. Moreover, the idea that a legislature may be acting 'in its own case' (*in eigener Sache*) when it modifies electoral laws has surfaced in several judgments of the Court in the last two decades.[63] In practice, the legislature has often struggled to amend the Bundeswahlgesetz or the Europawahlgesetz to the principles laid down in the judgments of the Bundesverfassungsgericht. On a different note, the case law of the Bundesverfassungsgericht proved to be very influential outside Germany, including in western Europe.[64] However, comparative references to judgments of the German Court have contributed to highlighting some idiosyncratic traits of the latter's approach to electoral matters. These peculiar features have particularly emerged in the judgments that addressed the constitutionality of thresholds in electoral laws for the European Parliament.[65]

[63] BVerfGE 120, 82, 105; BVerfGE 129, 300, 322; BVerfGE 135, 259, 289; BVerfGE 146, 327, 352.

[64] See inter alia judgment no 1/2014 of the Corte costituzionale (para 3.1) and the official commentary attached to decision no 2019-811 QPC of the Conseil constitutionnel.

[65] See A Antonuzzo and N Lupo, 'The thresholds for the EP elections: the EU Electoral Act, national legislation and the case-law of Constitutional Courts' in T Marguery, S Platon and H van Eijken (eds), *Les élections européennes 40 ans après. Bilan, enjeux et perspectives/The European Elections, 40 years after: Assessment, Issues and Prospects* (Bruxelles, Bruylant, 2020) 119.

7

The Italian Constitutional Court and Electoral Law: After the Landmark Judgments no 1 of 2014 and no 35 of 2017

PAOLO PASSAGLIA

I. INTRODUCTION

CONSTITUTIONAL COURTS IN Europe are often endowed with powers related to the review of electoral processes.[1] It is not the case of the Italian Constitutional Court, that has no special jurisdiction on the subject:[2] in Italy, the courts that have jurisdiction are the ordinary ones, except for the parliamentary elections, for which Article 66 of the Constitution gives the Chambers themselves the power to verify the lawfulness of the election of their members.[3]

The lack of direct appeals to the Constitutional Court by individuals and political bodies make the review of electoral laws quite difficult to activate, so

[1] For comparative analysis, see F Delpérée, *Le contentieux électoral* (Paris, Presses universitaires de France, 1998); F Delpérée, 'Le contentieux électoral en Europe' (2002) 13 *Cahiers du Conseil constitutionnel* 74 ff; L Pegoraro, G Pavani and S Pennicino (eds), *Chi controlla le elezioni? Verifica parlamentare dei poteri, tribunali, commissioni indipendenti* (Bologna, Bononia University Press, 2011); S Rodriquez, 'Il controllo sulle elezioni: dalla "verifica dei poteri" ai tribunali elettorali' (2013) *Nomos*, nomos-leattualitaneldiritto.it/fascicoli/nomos-12013; L Pegoraro and G Pavani (eds), *El guardián de las elecciones. El control electoral en perspectiva comparada* (Bogotá, Universidad Libre, 2015); G Delledonne, *Costituzione e legge elettorale. Un percorso comparatistico nello Stato costituzionale europeo* (Napoli, Editoriale Scientifica, 2019) 137 ff.

[2] In this regard, see M Manetti, 'L'accesso alla Corte costituzionale nei procedimenti elettorali' in A Anzon, P Caretti and S Grassi (eds), *Prospettive di accesso alla giustizia costituzionale* (Torino, Giappichelli, 2000) 136 ff; E Catelani, F Donati and MC Grisolia (eds), *La giustizia elettorale*, Atti del Seminario svoltosi a Firenze, 16 novembre 2012 (Napoli, Editoriale Scientifica, 2013).

[3] With regard to this provision, see P Torretta, *Verifica dei poteri e Stato costituzionale. Saggio sull'articolo 66 della Costituzione* (Roma, Aracne, 2012). In a comparative perspective, see F Lanchester, 'La verifica dei poteri nel diritto comparato: modelli a confronto' (1998) *Giurisprudenza costituzionale* 2859 ff.

that scholars have identified in electoral law one the most patent 'free zones' or 'grey areas' of the Italian judicial review.[4]

Since electoral laws are at the core of modern democracies, their relevance for the political process is undisputable, and precisely because of this relevance, the judicial review, its legitimacy and its limits, are generally an issue.[5] In a system that lacks an efficient way to file appeals against electoral laws, the Constitutional Court needs to rely mainly upon itself to find the strength to overcome two kind of difficulties: on one side, the problems deriving from the structure of the system of constitutional adjudication and, on the other, the problems related to the extreme political sensitivity of the laws that regulate the composition of Parliament.

The analysis of the constitutional case-law shows that a turning point occurred a few years ago. For a long time, the Constitutional Court intervened randomly, and its intentions were inspired by self-restraint, until a new approach was adopted starting from Judgment no 1 of 2014.

II. THE CASE-LAW AFTER THE TURNING POINT

The turning point of Judgment no 1 of 13 January 2014 has its roots in the political crisis that affected Italy in the previous years. The electoral law regulating the election of Parliament was both an effect and a factor of the crisis.

Law No 270 of 21 December 2005 was adopted a few months before the date of the elections: it introduced major changes in the electoral system, that, once based mainly on single-member constituencies, became a proportional system with majority bonus. The outcome of the new electoral method was soon criticised, and criticism increased over time, even though no party was able to really initiate a reform. This situation led to a stalemate until an external factor finally

[4] On this subject, see R Balduzzi and P Costanzo (eds), *Le zone d'ombra della giustizia costituzionale. I giudizi sulle leggi* (Torino, Giappichelli, 2007); R Pinardi (ed), *Le zone d'ombra della giustizia costituzionale. I giudizi sui conflitti di attribuzione e sull'ammissibilità del* referendum *abrogativo*, Atti del seminario di Modena svoltosi il 13 ottobre 2006 (Torino, Giappichelli, 2007); A Pizzorusso, '«Zone d'ombra» e «zone franche» della giustizia costituzionale italiana' in A D'Atena (ed), *Studi in onore di Pierfrancesco Grossi* (Milano, Giuffrè, 2010) 1021 ff.

[5] A Pisaneschi, 'Giustizia costituzionale e leggi elettorali: le ragioni di un controllo difficile' (2015) *Quaderni costituzionali* 135 ff, identifies five reasons that hinder a judicial review on electoral laws: first, the electoral system is the link between society, parties and form of government; second, electoral systems must be analysed in the light of the system of parties in which they operate, so that an electoral system could never be reviewed from a theoretical perspective, but needs to be contextualised; third, complexity of modern societies implies the need for the electoral system to serve multiple needs, therefore the political choices in framing the electoral system cannot easily be reviewed form a constitutional point of view; fourth, judicial review is hampered by the need to balance opposite interests and purposes concerning the protection of minorities (through positive actions) and the right of the voters to freely express their choice; fifth, it is generally difficult, unless the system of constitutional adjudication provides for special appeals, to bring an electoral law before courts.

occurred, when a citizen contested the electoral law before the ordinary courts because of the asserted infringements of individual rights that it produced.

The case was not easy to bring before courts, since a new way of looking at the electoral law had to be experimented.[6] As a matter of fact, in order to review the constitutionality of the electoral law, the Constitutional Court had to show a two-fold activism, related, first, to innovations in interpreting the rules of the procedure before it and, second, to a stricter scrutiny of the provisions at stake. As a result, for the first time in its history, the Constitutional Court decided on the merits questions of constitutionality concerning the electoral law for the national Parliament.[7]

III. PROCEDURAL ISSUES

With regard to the rules regulating references for a preliminary ruling, Judgment no 1 of 2014 has changed considerably the way in which the relationships

[6] The reference for a preliminary ruling filed by the Court of Cassation that was at the origin of Judgment no 1 of 2014 was indeed a groundbreaking decision. A workshop on this reference was organized in Rome, on 12 June 2013 ('Le Corti e il voto. Seminario sull'ordinanza di remissione della Corte di cassazione e le prospettive della innovazione elettorale in Italia'), and several interventions were then published. See, among others, A Anzon, '"Un tentativo coraggioso ma improprio per far valere l'incostituzionalità della legge per le elezioni politiche" (e per coprire una "zona franca" del giudizio di costituzionalità)' (2013) *Rivista dell'Associazione italiana dei Costituzionalisti*; R Borrello, 'Due problemi contrapposti: ammissibilità e "zona franca"' (2013) *Nomos*; P Carnevale, 'La Cassazione all'attacco della legge elettorale. Riflessioni a prima lettura alla luce di una recente ordinanza di rimessione della Suprema Corte' (2013) *Nomos*; E Grosso, 'Riformare la legge elettorale per via giudiziaria? Un'indebita richiesta di "supplenza" alla Corte costituzionale, di fronte all'ennesima disfatta della politica' (2013) *Rivista dell'Associazione italiana dei Costituzionalisti*; C Padula, 'Spunti di riflessione sull'azione di accertamento e l'incidentalità nel giudizio di costituzionalità' (2013) *Consulta Onine*; G Repetto, 'Il divieto di *fictio litis* come connotato della natura incidentale del giudizio di costituzionalità. Spunti a partire dalla recente ordinanza della Corte di Cassazione in tema di legge elettorale' (2013) *Rivista dell'Associazione italiana dei Costituzionalisti*.

[7] … so that according to G Zagrebelsky, 'La sentenza n. 1 del 2014 e i suoi commentatori' (2014) *Giurisprudenza costituzionale* 2959, Judgment no 1 of 2014 was probably 'the most creative judgment delivered by the Constitutional Court in sixty years'. On Judgment no 1 of 2014, see, inter alia, A Anzon, 'Accesso al giudizio di costituzionalità e intervento "creativo" della Corte costituzionale' (2014) *Giurisprudenza costituzionale* 34 ff; G Azzariti, 'Ragionevolezza, scopo e valore della legge elettorale. Dopo la sentenza della Corte costituzionale n. 1 del 2014' (2014) *Costituzionalismo.it*; R Bin, '"Zone franche" e legittimazione della Corte' (2014) *Forum di Quaderni costituzionali*; B Caravita, 'La riforma elettorale alla luce della sent. 1/2014' (2014) *federalismi.it*; M D'Amico and S Catalano (eds), *Prime riflessioni sulla "storica" sentenza 1 del 2014 in materia elettorale* (Milano, Franco Angeli, 2014); L Imarisio and I Massa Pinto, 'La sentenza n. 1 del 2014 sull'incostituzionalità parziale della legge elettorale: le sue possibili narrazioni e il suo seguito legislativo' (2013) 3-4 *Democrazia e diritto* 305 ff.; FS Marini, 'La ragionevolezza come parametro incerto della costituzionalità delle leggi elettorali' (2014) *Confronti Costituzionali*; A Poggi, 'Politica "costituzionale" e legge elettorale: prime osservazioni alla sentenza n. 1 del 2014' (2014) *Confronti Costituzionali*; A Rauti, *I sistemi elettorali dopo la sentenza costituzionale n. 1 del 2014. Problemi e prospettive* (Napoli, Edizioni Scientifiche Italiane, 2014); N Zanon, 'Fare la legge elettorale "*sous l'oeil des russes*" (2014) *Rivista dell'Associazione italiana dei Costituzionalisti*.

between the ordinary proceedings and the proceedings before the Constitutional Court are conceived.

The proceedings before the Court of Cassation, the referring judge, involved an action seeking a declaratory judgment concerning the right to vote: the aim of the action was simply to establish the scope of the right, which was considered to be uncertain. The issues of the interest to sue and the availability of jurisdiction were disputed before ordinary courts, but eventually settled in favour of the claimants.

Nevertheless, the main objection against the admissibility of the question of constitutionality brought before the Constitutional Court concerned the fact that the ordinary proceedings were based on a request of a remedy that was nothing more than to ascertain the scope of the claimants' right to vote, which had been rendered uncertain by an electoral law considered to be unconstitutional. This would have been inconsistent with the doctrine of the Constitutional Court according to which the remedy sought before the ordinary courts must be separate and distinct from the question of constitutionality on which the Constitutional Court is requested to rule.[8]

In Judgment no 1 of 2014, the Constitutional Court was quite indulgent on that point and declared that the requirement was met in the case under examination, since the remedy sought in the main proceedings was

> a ruling confirming the existence of the right actioned, which [was] considered to be conditional upon the decision regarding the questions of constitutionality raised, and the ruling requested from the ordinary courts [did] not coincide entirely with the judgment of [the] Court, as it would be necessary to verify the other preconditions for the right to vote which are imposed by law.[9]

This approach was explicitly justified in the light of the object of the question of constitutionality, which related to 'a fundamental right protected under the Constitution – the right to vote – an essential corollary of which is its association with an interest of society as a whole'.[10] The inviolable nature of the right to vote made the uncertainty as to the scope of the right itself a legally significant harm.

The importance of the right at issue strengthened the power of carrying out a constitutional review also because of the need to 'cover the legal system as fully as possible': in this regard, the Court pointed out the fact that the law relating to elections to the Chamber of Deputies and the Senate would be more difficult to be reviewed by the Court in any other manner. In other words,

[8] The question of constitutionality needs to be resolved as a preliminary matter in order to reach a decision in the main proceedings (the so-called requirement of '*rilevanza*'). For the analysis of the procedural framework of references for preliminary ruling, see, in English, V Barsotti, PG Carozza, M Cartabia and A Simoncini, *Italian Constitutional Justice in Global Context* (Oxford, Oxford University Press, 2016) 54 ff.

[9] Judgment no 1 of 13 January 2014, Conclusions on points of law, para 2.

[10] ibid.

rather than focusing on the compliance with the procedural rules regulating preliminary rulings, the Court gave priority to avoiding the creation of immunities within the system of constitutional justice, 'precisely in an area which is closely related to the democratic framework as it involves the fundamental right to vote'.[11]

In subsequent case-law, Judgment no 1 of 2014 was considered a leading case. Judgment no 35 of 9 February 2017 expressly recognised its relevance as a precedent.[12] The Court had to decide on the electoral law that was passed in order to overcome the unconstitutionality declared in 2014 and to establish a new system for the next elections. When it was contested and brought before the Constitutional Court, Law No 52 of 6 May 2015 was yet in force, but had never been applied. Furthermore, the law was challenged by several courts, and one of them raised the question of constitutionality before the law became applicable. If the questions of constitutionality against Law No 270 of 2005 created some difficulties with regard of their admissibility, the questions against Law No 52 of 2015 appeared even more distant from the ordinary questions of constitutionality, because of the abstract nature of the challenge brought before the Court.[13]

[11] ibid.

[12] The continuity between the two judgments is one of the features that scholarship has pointed out: in this regard, it is noteworthy that even the *rapporteur* in Judgment no 35 of 2017 pointed out the links between the judgments in an intervention delivered during a workshop held in Seville, on 27 October 2017, among judges of the Italian, the Portuguese and the Spanish Constitutional Courts (see N Zanon, 'Il controllo di costituzionalità sulle leggi elettorali politiche in Italia. Aspetti processuali (sentenze n. 1 del 2014 e n. 35 del 2017)' www.cortecostituzionale.it/documenti/convegni_seminari/SIVIGLIA_ZANON.pdf). On Judgment no 35 of 2017, see D Casanova and L Spadacini, 'Il ballottaggio nazionale tra liste: la sentenza Corte cost. n. 35 del 2017 e il *de profundis* per i sistemi *majority assuring*' (2017) *Osservatorio dell'Associazione italiana dei Costituzionalisti*; S Ceccanti, 'I sistemi elettorali per le elezioni politiche dopo la 35/2017: una sentenza figlia del referendum, ma per il resto deludente per i proporzionalisti' (2017) *federalismi.it*; R Dickmann, 'La Corte Costituzionale trasforma l'Italicum in sistema elettorale maggioritario "eventuale" ma lascia al legislatore l'onere di definire una legislazione elettorale omogenea per le due Camere' (2017) *federalismi.it*; F Ferrari, 'Sotto la punta dell'iceberg: *fictio litis* e ammissibilità della q.l.c. nella sent. n. 35/2017' (2017) *Forum di Quaderni costituzionali*; F Ferrari, 'Perché la Corte non avrebbe dovuto giudicare nel merito l'Italicum' (18 February 2017) *laCostituzione.info*; M Luciani, '*Bis in idem*: la nuova sentenza della Corte costituzionale sulla legge elettorale politica' (2017) *Rivista dell'Associazione italiana dei Costituzionalisti* ; A Mangia, 'L'azione di accertamento come surrogato del ricorso diretto' (2017) *laCostituzione.info*; A Morrone, 'Dopo la decisione sull'Italicum: il maggioritario è salvo, e la proporzionale non un obbligo costituzionale' (2017) *Forum di Quaderni costituzionali*; A Ruggeri, 'La Corte alla sofferta ricerca di un accettabile equilibrio tra le ragioni della rappresentanza e quelle della governabilità: un'autentica quadratura del cerchio, riuscita però solo a metà, nella pronunzia sull'*Italicum*' (2017) *Forum di Quaderni costituzionali*; A Spadaro, 'Sulla intrinseca "politicità" delle decisioni "giudiziarie" dei tribunali costituzionali contemporanei' (2017) *federalismi.it*; L Trucco, '"Sentenza Italicum": la Consulta tra detto, non considerato e lasciato intendere' (2017) *Consulta Online*, 149 ff.

[13] With regard to the reference orders filed before the Constitutional Court, see R Bin, '*Italicum*: perché dalla Corte non bisogna aspettarsi nulla' (2016) *laCostituzione.info*; M Cosulich, '*Contra Italicum*, ovvero dell'ordinanza del Tribunale di Messina del 17 febbraio 2016' (2016) *Osservatorio dell'Associazione italiana dei Costituzionalisti*; S Gianello, 'L'*Italicum* "a processo": la possibilità concreta per la Corte di un ritorno alla normalità (del giudizio incidentale)' (2016) *Osservatorio dell'Associazione italiana dei Costituzionalisti*; A Poggi, 'La Corte e la legge elettorale' (2016)

The Constitutional Court confirmed the admissibility of the questions pointing out that 'the objective uncertainty on the scope of the right to vote [was] directly linked to the change in the legal system due to the same entry into force of the electoral law, in light of the contents that it introduce[d] into the legal system'.[14] Irrespective of the applicability of the new law, the fact that justified the claimants' interest in proceedings was 'in the legislative framework already in force, although not yet applicable at the time of the issue',[15] since the uncertainty regarding the scope of the right to vote, 'with the corollary of harmful potential',[16] was already actual, although designed to occur in the future, at the time when the law would have been applicable. For this reason, the removal of the uncertainty was a useful result, that could be achieved only through a judgment delivered by the Constitutional Court.

Judgment no 35 of 2017 confirmed and strengthened the idea that the (new) doctrine of the Court was basically inspired by the need to avoid, with reference to the electoral law, a 'free zone' with respect to the review of constitutionality.[17] Therefore, the Court introduced a 'variable geometry'[18] in judicial review that is justified by the need to ensure, in any case, an efficient protection to constitutional rights and principles.

IV. SUBSTANTIVE ISSUES

In Judgments no 1 of 2014 and no 35 of 2017, the Constitutional Court set out the core of the constitutional requirements related to the electoral law with reference to several features that characterised the systems introduced by the legislator.[19]

federalismi.it; GM Salerno, 'L'*Italicum* davanti alla Corte costituzionale: una sfida ad ampio raggioo' (2016) *federalismi.it*; R Bin, 'La Corte e la legge elettorale: è difficile credere ad un ritorno indietro?' (2017) *laCostituzione.info*; 'Interventi al Seminario "La Corte e l'Italicum", Roma, 11 gennaio 2017', (2017) *federalismi.it*.

[14] Judgment no 35 of 9 February 2017, Conclusions on points of law, para 3.3.

[15] ibid.

[16] ibid.

[17] On the need to avoid 'free zones' in review of electoral law, see, in particular, R Bin, '"Zone franche" e legittimazione della Corte' (2014) *Forum di Quaderni costituzionali*; G D'Amico, 'Il sindacato di costituzionalità della normativa elettorale dopo la sent. n. 1 del 2014' (2015) *Quaderni costituzionali* 1000 ff; R Bin, 'Chi è responsabile delle «zone franche»? Note sulle leggi elettorali davanti alla Corte' (2017) *Forum di Quaderni Costituzionali*; G. Sobrino, 'Il problema dell'ammissibilità delle questioni di legittimità costituzionale della legge elettorale alla luce delle sentenze n. 1/2014 e n. 35/2017 e le sue possibili ricadute: dalla (non più tollerabile) "zona franca" alla (auspicabile) "zona a statuto speciale" della giustizia costituzionale?' (2017) *federalismi.it*.

[18] See A Rauti, 'La Corte costituzionale ed il legislatore. Il caso emblematico del controllo sulle leggi elettorali' in D Butturini and M Nicolini (eds), *Giurisdizione costituzionale e potere democraticamente legittimato*, Vol I – *I soggetti, gli strumenti e i meccanismi del dialogo* (Bologna, Bononia University Press, 2017) 217 ff.

[19] The issues that are considered in the following paragraphs are examined, form a comparative point of view, by Delledonne, *Costituzione e legge elettorale* (n 1) 137 ff.

A. The Majority Bonuses

The Constitutional Court analysed the consistency with the Constitution of provisions that, in a system based on the proportional method of assignment of seats, award a majority bonus for the lists or the coalitions of lists that received the highest number of votes.

First the majority bonus allocated to the Chamber of Deputies according to Law No 270 of 2005 gave the coalition of lists or the individual list that obtained the largest number of valid votes at least 340 seats (ie, nearly 54 per cent of the total number of seats). This provision was challenged insofar as it did not render the allocation of the majority bonus conditional upon the reaching of a minimum threshold of votes, thus giving the chance to gain it even with a very narrow majority. This resulted, in the opinion of the referring court, in the impairment of democratic representation and in the infringement of the principle of equality in voting.

The Constitutional Court, in Judgment no 1 of 2014, recalled its previous judgments in which it admitted that the Constitution does not dictate the adoption of a proportional system and that the principle of equality simply requires that 'each vote potentially contributes with equal effect to the formation of elected bodies'.[20] In other words, the equality in voting 'does not extend [...] to the specific result of the electorate's expression of its wishes [...] which depends [...] exclusively on the system adopted by ordinary law'.[21]

In previous judgments concerning the admissibility of referenda aimed at changing the electoral system, the Court already pointed out the risk of an excessive over-representation of the list that gained a relative majority and therefore received a significant bonus in the allocation of seats. The legislature did not react to the Court's invitations to change this system, thus the Court had eventually to decide, in Judgment no 1 of 2014, whether the provisions complied with the minimum standards required by constitutional principles.

In areas like the electoral law, that are characterised by a broad legislative discretion, the constitutional review must be carried out involving

> a consideration of the proportionality of the means chosen by the legislator when exercising its absolute discretion *vis-à-vis* the objective requirements to be met or the goals it intends to pursue, taking account of the specific circumstances and restrictions that obtain.[22]

The Constitutional Court highlighted that the challenged provisions were intended 'to facilitate the formation of an adequate parliamentary majority, with the purpose of guaranteeing stable government for the country and

[20] See Judgment no 43 of 11 July 1961.

[21] ibid. With regard to the principle of equality in voting, see, also for a comparative analysis, D Casanova, *Eguaglianza del voto e sistemi elettorali. I limiti costituzionali alla discrezionalità legislativa* (Napoli, Editoriale Scientifica, 2020) 73 ff.

[22] See Judgment no 1130 of 22 December 1988.

streamlining the decision-making process, which is undoubtedly an objective that is consistent with the Constitution'.[23] This objective was pursued through a bonus that was very generous, irrespective of the real number of votes gained by the most voted list or coalition, since no minimum threshold in terms of votes was provided.

Precisely because of the lack of any threshold,

> the contested provisions [were] not limited to introducing a corrective mechanism [...] to the system for transforming votes into seats 'in a proportional manner', [...] with the legitimate objective of favoring the formation of stable parliamentary majorities and thus stable governments, but rather [ran] entirely contrary to the rationale underlying the electoral system chosen by the legislator in 2005 of ensuring a representative parliamentary assembly.[24]

Indeed, the system resulted 'in an excessive imbalance between the composition of the politically representative body, which lies at the heart of the system of representative democracy, and the parliamentary form of government stipulated by the Constitution on the one hand, and the wishes of the people expressed through votes, as the principal instrument for expressing popular sovereignty under Article 1(2) of the Constitution on the other hand'.[25]

Without neglecting the importance to ensure a stable parliamentary majority for Government, the Court pointed out that the principle of popular sovereignty, with its corollary of the democratic representation, demands that each vote at least potentially contribute with equal effect to the formation of elected bodies.

In order to clarify the constitutional requirements related to the electoral system, the Court made an explicit reference to the German case-law according to which,

> if the legislator adopts a proportional system, even only partially, it will create a legitimate expectation on the part of the electorate that there will not be any imbalance in the effects of each vote, that is differing assessments of the "weight" of each vote "on the outcome" when allocating seats, except insofar as necessary in order to avoid impairing the proper operation of the parliamentary body.[26]

The declaration of unconstitutionality of the provisions introducing the majority bonus was thus based on the lack of proportionality between the goal

[23] Judgment no 1 of 13 January 2014, Conclusions on points of law, para 3.1.
[24] ibid.
[25] ibid.
[26] Reference was made, in particular, to German Federal Constitutional Court, Judgment no 3/11 of 25 July 2012, but also to Judgment no 197 of 22 May 1979 and Judgment no 1 of 5 April 1952. Judgment no 1 of 2014 is one of the few examples in which the Constitutional Court has made explicit reference to a foreign judgment. For an analysis of the use of foreign law by the Constitutional Court, see V Zeno Zencovich, 'The Italian Constitutional Court' in GF Ferrari (ed), *Judicial Cosmopolitanism. The Use of Foreign Law in Contemporary Constitutional Systems* (Leiden – Boston, Brill – Nijhoff, 2019) 449 ff.

pursued (a stable government) and the sacrifices imposed on the equality in voting and on the alteration of the composition of the democratic representative bodies.

Second, in the same Judgment no 1 of 2014, the Constitutional Court reviewed the majority bonus provided by the law regulating the elections of the Senate.

According to Article 57(1) of the Constitution, '[t]he Senate of the Republic is elected on a regional basis'. The allocation of seats at the regional level imposed a consequential attribution of the majority bonus, which could not be calculated at the national level. In fact, the list of candidates or the coalition of lists receiving the largest number of valid votes in a region obtained at least 55 per cent of the seats of the region.

The way the majority bonus was allocated in the regions infringed the same principles that were infringed by the majority bonus of the Chamber of Deputies. With an additional problem related to the objective pursued:

> in providing that the majority bonus [was] to be allocated for each region, the effect [was] that the majority within the Senate [was] the chance result of the sum total of regional bonuses, which [might] end up overturning the result obtained by the lists or coalitions of lists on national level, favoring the formation of disparate parliamentary majorities in the two Chambers of Parliament, even if the overall distribution of votes [was] substantially homogeneous.[27]

As a result, the infringement of equality in voting, far from being balanced by the goal of a stable majority, was coupled by the impairment of the proper functioning of bicameralism and of the relationships between Parliament and government.

Third, the majority bonus was an issue also in Judgment no 35 of 2017.

After the declaration of unconstitutionality that stroke down the majority bonuses provided by Law No 270 of 2005 mainly because of the lack of any threshold required to gain them, Law No 52 of 2015 introduced a majority bonus for the Chamber of Deputies. The bonus was assigned, after the first round of voting, to the list that obtained at least 40 per cent of the votes. If no list obtained this percentage, the bonus was awarded to the most voted list in the second round of voting, a run-off between the two most voted lists in the first round.

The majority bonus after the first round of voting was challenged for distortion in representation, but the Constitutional Court declared the question unfounded.

Contrary to Law No 270 of 2005, Law No 52 of 2015 provided for a minimum threshold of valid votes in order to receive the bonus. Rather than

[27] Judgment no 1 of 13 January 2014, Conclusions on points of law, para 4.

allowing even a very narrow majority to obtain a comfortable majority, this bonus was intended

> to balance the constitutional principles mandating the representative nature of the Chamber of Deputies and the equality of votes, on the one hand, with the objectives (themselves of constitutional import) of the stability of the government of the Nation and the efficiency of the decision-making process, on the other.[28]

This purpose was achieved with a regulation that could not be considered as manifestly unreasonable.

Also the fact that the threshold of 40 per cent was calculated on the basis of validly cast votes, rather than on the sum total of people who have the right to vote, could not result in an unreasonable regulation, and even if the abstention from the vote could weaken, in theory, the representativeness of the list having attained the 40 per cent of votes, the choice for a different system to calculate the threshold was not imposed by the Constitution.

A possible distortion could be the result of the case in which two lists obtained more than 40 per cent of votes. The provisions concerning the majority bonus, in such an occurrence, should be interpreted as requiring the assignment of the bonus to the most voted list, although this assignment would inevitably produce a significant reduction of the number of deputies for the other list.

The Constitutional Court excluded that such a reduction could be considered as an infringement of constitutional principles, since

> it is, in any case, within the logic of an electoral system with a majority bonus that the minority lists, regardless of the percentage of votes they obtain, will receive a number of seats that is inferior to the number they would have been assigned under a proportional system with no corrective mechanisms in place.[29]

This principle could be easily extended to the case in which the percentage of the list in the second place exceeded the threshold of 40 per cent.

The distortion of representation deriving from the majority bonus was also challenged in relation to the existence of the threshold of three per cent as a condition to have access to the allocation of seats. The juxtaposition of bonus and minimum threshold did not create, in itself, an intolerable distortion of representation. In any case, 'it is not manifestly unreasonable that the legislator, in consideration of the political/party-based system that it intends to regulate with electoral rules, should resort contemporaneously, in its discretion, to both these mechanisms'.[30]

In concrete terms, the Constitutional Court recognised that Law No 52 of 2015 coupled the research of a stable majority (through the bonus) with the fight (with the threshold) against a too fragmented political landscape.

[28] Judgment no 35 of 9 February 2017, Conclusions on points of law, para 6.
[29] ibid para 7.
[30] ibid at para 6.

B. The Second Round of Voting

The regulation of the electoral process introduced by Law No 52 of 2015 was challenged also with regard to the provision for a second round of voting, insofar as it created an 'artificial' majority. The second round of voting was designed to choose between the two most voted lists or coalitions of lists, irrespective of the number of votes they gained. Thus, a concrete risk existed that the majority bonus might be attributed to a political formation that lacked a sufficient basis in the electorate.

The Constitutional Court recognised that, even if the introduction of a second round of voting was, in itself, consistent with the Constitution, its concrete regulation provided by Law No 52 of 2015 breached the principle of popular sovereignty and the equality in voting.

The Court pointed out that 'a given list [might] have access to the second round of voting despite having obtained only a slim consensus in the first round, and [might], irrespective of this fact, attain the bonus and receive double the number of seats that it would have obtained on the basis of the votes it won in the first round'.[31] This feature of the second round led to the same shortcomings that occurred with Law No 270 of 2005 and that had justified the declaration of unconstitutionality rendered with Judgment no 1 of 2014: as a matter of fact, the lack of a minimum threshold of votes to have access to the second round was similar, in terms of inconsistency with constitutional principles, to the lack of a minimum threshold to receive the majority bonus.

Precisely because of this similarity, the test of proportionality and reasonableness had to be the same. After all, the second round of voting, like the majority bonus, pursued the goal of establishing a clear political majority. Nevertheless, this legitimate purpose could not 'justify a disproportionate sacrifice of the constitutional principles of representativeness and of equality of the vote by artificially transforming a list that boast[ed] a limited consensus, or potentially even a very slim one, into an absolute majority'.[32]

Since the second round of voting followed from the lack of a list capable of obtaining a large consensus (40 per cent of votes required to obtain the majority bonus), the introduction of strict requirements in order to participate in the second round could have avoided an excessive distortion of popular representation.

The Court noted that the introduction of a potential second round of voting, intended to assign an absolute majority of seats in the representative assembly to the winning list, did not cancel out the general framework of the electoral system, that was not based on a majoritarian competition, but rather on a proportional allocation of the seats.

[31] ibid para 9.2.
[32] ibid.

Indeed, a second round with a competition of lists for the national legislative assembly needed to comply, on the one hand, to the general features of proportional systems and, on the other, with 'the holistic function pertaining to an elected assembly'.[33]

With regard to the first requirement, the Court emphasised that in proportional systems the purpose to create a political majority cannot be achieved with excessive costs in terms of equal weight of votes: the concrete regulation of the second round of voting created considerable costs, that were clearly identified through the analogy with the provisions of Law No 270 of 2005 concerning the lack of a minimum threshold to obtain the majority bonus.

As for the function of the Chamber of Deputies, the Court highlighted that this assembly grants, on equal footing with the Senate, 'confidence in the Government and exercises both the political function (Article 94 of the Constitution)[34] and the legislative function (Article 70 of the Constitution[35])'.[36] Therefore, the Chamber of Deputies has a key position within the parliamentary regime, and the regulation of a second round of voting must be in line with such a position, so that the establishment of the conditions to form a stable government (thanks to a majority of seats in the Chamber) cannot neglect the need to grant the representativeness of the assembly.

The prerequisites for a list to have access to the second round, as regulated in Law No 52 of 2015, were not consistent with this function, thus the Court stroke down the provisions concerning the second round of voting, with the consequence that the regulatory scheme that remained in force was a single round of voting, in which if the list with the highest number of votes nationwide obtained at least 40 per cent gained a majority bonus. In the event that no list exceeded this threshold, no majority bonus was awarded, and the allocation of seats would have followed the proportional method.

C. The Preferential Vote

First, with regard to preferential vote, Judgment no 1 of 2014 declared unconstitutional the provisions according to which the voters could choose the list of candidates, but not the candidates, because within the party list all candidates

[33] ibid.

[34] Article 94 of the Constitution reads as follows: 'The Government must receive the confidence of both Chambers of Parliament. | Each Chamber grants or withdraws its confidence through a reasoned motion voted on by rollcall. Within ten days of its formation the Government shall come before Parliament to obtain confidence. An opposing vote by one or both the Chambers against a Government proposal does not entail the obligation to resign. A motion of no-confidence must be signed by at least one-tenth of the members of the House and cannot be debated earlier than three days from its presentation.'

[35] Article 70: 'The legislative function is exercised collectively by both Chambers'.

[36] Judgment no 35 of 9 February 2017, Conclusions on points of law, para 9.2.

were designated and enumerated in a specific order that could not be changed, no preferential vote being allowed.

The Constitutional Court pointed out that

> in providing that a vote cast by a voter, which [was] intended to determine the overall composition of the Chamber of Deputies and the Senate, [was] a vote in favor of a list, the contested provisions [denied] the voter any right to decide on the election of his or her own representatives.[37]

The outcome of an election cannot be defined merely on the basis of the number of votes and seats that the competing lists obtained: candidates who are in the lists are also a relevant issue. Therefore, the regulation must allow voters to identify candidates when making their choice. On the contrary, 'the choice made by the voter amount[ed] to a preference vote exclusively for the list': also due to the fact that lists were presented in very large constituencies, they consisted of a very large number of candidates, which meant that it was 'difficult for candidates to be identified by voters'.[38] The lack of any preferential vote inadmissibly shifted the power to choose representatives from voters to parties.

The key feature of the system of representation is that voters must be free to choose their representatives: the challenged provisions restricted this freedom, since voters were called upon to elect all members of Parliament by voting in favour of a list of candidates, often without even knowing the candidates for whom their votes would be counted. Not to mention that, since the system allowed multiple candidacies, the elected candidates had the right to choose the constituency to represent, thus even expectations based on the order list could be frustrated.

Second, in reply to the declaration of unconstitutionality rendered by Judgment no 1 of 2014, Law No 52 of 2015 introduced a different system, providing that the lists, in the individual constituencies, were composed of a head candidate and a list of candidates among whom voters might express up to two preferences for candidates of different genders chosen from those who are not head of the list.

The Constitutional Court, in Judgment no 35 of 2017, excluded that such a regulation could infringe the constitutional principles taken into account in Judgment no 1 of 2014, since the regulation that was then annulled deprived voters of any margin of choice of their own representatives, whereas

> [t]he electoral system established by Law No 52 of 2015 [differed] from the previous one in three essential aspects: first, the lists [were] presented in one hundred multi-member constituencies of reduced dimensions, and they [were], therefore, made up of a significantly smaller number of candidates; second, the only fixed candidate [was] the head of list, whose name [appeared] on the election ballot (assuring that

[37] Judgment no 1 of 13 January 2014, Conclusions on points of law, para 5.
[38] ibid.

> he or she [was] knowable by voters in advance); and finally, voters [might] express up to two preferences for candidates of different genders among those candidates who [were] not heads of lists.[39]

D. ... And the Choice of the Seat Among Different Electoral Districts

In Judgment no 35 of 2017, the Court declared unconstitutional the provision according to which a deputy elected in more than one multi-member constituency had to declare to the President of the Chamber of Deputies, within eight days of the date of the last proclamation, which of the constituencies they had chosen. The provision was challenged insofar as it allowed

> head of list candidates elected in more than one multi-member constituency, to make a decision on the basis of a mere opportunistic assessment, and [did] not subject the choice to any objective and predetermined criterion that would respect, to the greatest extent possible, the will expressed by voters.[40]

Such an absence of objective criteria manifestly conflicted, in the opinion of the Court, with the respect of the voters' will and their right to express a choice of the person to elect. Indeed,

> [t]he arbitrary choice allow[ed] the fixed head of list elected in more than one constituency to wield not only the power to choose the constituency of his or her election ahead of time, but also, indirectly, the improper power to designate the representative of a given electoral constituency, according to a line of reasoning ultimately capable of conditioning the usefulness of the preferential votes expressed by voters.[41]

Heads of list cannot be entitled to determine the destiny of the vote of preference expressed by voters in the chosen constituency: the absolutely free choice established by Law No 52 of 2015, 'not only violat[ed] the principle of equality, but also that of the personal nature of the vote, enshrined in Articles 3 and 48(2) of the Constitution'.[42] In particular, the free choice of the district in which to be elected could be invoked by a head of list who won the election with votes of preference, but not by a fixed head of list to the detriment of candidates who did obtain preferential votes.

V. THE EFFECTS OF THE COURTS' JUDGMENTS

The declarations of unconstitutionality that stroke down several provisions of Laws No 270 of 2005 and No 52 of 2015 had a deep impact on the electoral

[39] Judgment no 35 of 9 February 2017, Conclusions on points of law, para 11.2.
[40] ibid para 12.
[41] ibid para 12.2.
[42] ibid.

system and, when it comes to Judgment no 1 of 2014, also a potential impact on the operation of Parliament.

A. The Impact on the Electoral System

With Judgment no 1 of 2014, the Constitutional Court annulled some of the key features of the electoral system then in force, such as the provision concerning the majority bonus and the lack of preferential vote.

According to constitutional case-law, the electoral law is a 'constitutionally necessary' law, thus a law that cannot lack in the institutional framework, because it is 'indispensable in order to ensure the proper functioning and continuity of constitutional bodies'.[43]

In this regard, although radically changed as a result of the declarations of unconstitutionality, the legislation remaining in force stipulated a valid mechanism for transforming votes into seats which enabled all seats to be allocated on the basis of electoral constituencies: a proportional system, essentially identical for the Chamber of Deputies and for the Senate, that lacked a mechanism for applying any majority bonus. Moreover, the system did not prevent preferential votes, since 'any apparent drawbacks [might] be resolved by applying ordinary canons of interpretation, in the light of legislation already in force',[44] so as to enable voters to cast a preference vote.[45]

The Court refused 'to assess whether that mechanism [was] advisable or effective', since its sole task was 'to verify the constitutionality of specific contested provisions and whether it [was] possible to conduct elections immediately under the residual legislation',[46] taking also into account that possible specific drawbacks might be resolved through subsequent legislation.

With Judgment no 1 of 2014, the Constitutional Court imposed a deep change in the electoral system, to the point that what resulted after the declarations of unconstitutionality was a completely new system. In any case, the Court did not replace itself to the legislator, but simply derived from the Constitution the corollaries in terms of regulation of a proportional system.

[43] In Judgment no 1 of 13 January 2014, Conclusions on points of law, para 6, the Court explicitly cited, in this regard, Judgments no 13 of 12 January 2012, no 15 and no 16 of 30 January 2008, no 13 of 28 January 1999, no 26 of 10 February 1997, no 5 of 12 January 1995, no 32 of 4 February 1993, no 47 of 2 February 1991, no 29 of 3 February 1987.

[44] Judgment no 1 of 13 January 2014, Conclusions on points of law, para 6.

[45] The Court itself suggested some interpretations aimed at this purpose. For instance, the provisions according to which of the candidates included in the list should be elected 'in the order of presentation' did not appear to be incompatible with the introduction of preference votes: in fact, the order in the list would apply only if no preference votes were cast. Moreover, nothing, in legislative provisions, prevented ballots from including a space in which a preference might be expressed.

[46] ibid.

The legislator reacted passing Law No 52 of 2015, that was, in its turn, submitted to constitutional review. The subsequent Judgment no 35 of 2017 also produced significant changes, in particular as far as the annulment of the second round was concerned. But the resulting system was still capable of being applied.

The main problem with Law No 52 of 2015 was not the result of Judgment no 35 of 2017, but rather of the fact that the electoral law for the Chamber of Deputies was strictly related with the constitutional reform that Parliament passed and that was intended, inter alia, to abolish perfect bicameralism. Since the referendum under Article 138 of the Constitution that was held on 4 December 2016 rejected the constitutional reform, perfect bicameralism was confirmed.[47] Precisely because of this event, the Constitutional Court pointed out that

> while the Constitution does not oblige the legislator to introduce identical electoral systems for the two branches of the Parliament, it does nevertheless require that the systems adopted, in order to not compromise the correct functioning of the parliamentary form of government, and despite their potential differences, must not impede, upon the outcome of elections, the formation of homogeneous parliamentary majorities.[48]

The Court thus invited, or rather pressed, the legislator to adopt a new electoral law, so as to reintroduce similar systems for selecting deputies and senators.[49]

It is what the legislator did with Law No 165 of 3 November 2017. This new law was also challenged before the Constitutional Court, because of asserted breaches in the law-making process. However, this time the law was not challenged through a reference for a preliminary ruling but through a conflict of attribution among powers of the state, a way that the Court considered inadmissible, for the lack of standing of members of Parliament and citizens that contested the law (Orders no 277 of 20 December 2017, no 280 of 21 December 2017 and no 181 of 27 July 2018).

[47] On the constitutional referendum held in 2016, see, in English, P Passaglia (ed), 'The 2016 Italian Constitutional Referendum: Origins, Stakes, Outcome' [2017] *The Italian Law Journal*, Special Issue.

[48] Judgment no 35 of 9 February 2017, Conclusions on points of law, para 15.2.

[49] With regard to the link between the constitutional reform, the electoral law and judgment rendered by the Court, see E Stradella, 'Italy after the Constitutional Referendum: Legal and Political Scenarios, from the Public Debate to the "Electoral Question"' in Passaglia (n 47) 61 ff. On the impact of the Court's judgments on the electoral law and, in particular, with regard to the need to adopt a new law consistent with the requirements emerging from the judgments, see A Chiaromonte, 'Dopo le sentenze 1/2014 e 35/2017: ancora alla ricerca di nuovo sistema elettorale' (2017) 1 *Osservatorio sulle fonti*; R Dickmann, 'La Corte costituzionale trasforma l'*Italicum* in sistema maggioritario "eventuale" ma lascia al legislatore l'onere di definire una legislazione elettorale omogenea per le due Camere' (2017) *federalismi.it*; G Ferri (ed), *Corte costituzionale e leggi elettorali. Problemi e prospettive dopo le sentenze n. 1/2014 e n. 35/2017* (Napoli, Edizioni Scientifiche Italiane, 2017).

B. Judgment no 1 of 2014 and the Operation of Parliament

Judgment no 1 of 2014 declared unconstitutional the electoral system as it had been applied for three times (in 2006, 2008 and 2013 national elections). The composition of the then current Chambers was therefore the result of elections carried out with a system that the Court had eventually found inconsistent with constitutional principles.

An issue to deal with was related to the acts that the unconstitutionally elected Chambers had passed: the idea that the lawfulness of all the previous activity could be challenged was at stake.

Nevertheless, the Constitutional Court clearly rejected this argument, stating that the annulment of the contested provisions would 'only take effect during the next general election, which [would] have to be held either according to the rules contained in the legislation remaining in force following [the] decision, or according to new electoral legislation enacted by Parliament'.[50]

Because of the delayed effects, the unconstitutionality did not 'in any way affect any actions carried out as a consequence of decisions made whilst the annulled provisions were in force, including the outcome of elections held and measures adopted by the Parliament thereby elected'.[51]

The Court thus recognised the fundamental principle of the 'continuity of the State': 'the Chambers are constitutionally necessary and essential bodies and cannot cease to exist or lose their capacity to act at any time'.[52]

VI. CONCLUSION

Activism of the Constitutional Court raised questions concerning the balance of powers between the Court itself and the legislator, with specific regard to the electoral law.

Comparing 2014 and 2017 judgments with the previous case-law, it is quite clear that something happened: electoral law, and in particular the set of provisions regulating the manner in which seats in Parliament are allotted, was a field in which the Court did not enter, so that the description of the approach adopted by the Court could be described borrowing at least one of the definitions of the American political question doctrine, '[t]he impossibility of a court's undertaking independent resolution without expressing lack of the respect due coordinate branches of government'.[53] Judgment no 1 of 2014 abandoned the traditional self-restraint and accepted to review the core of the electoral system for the Parliament.

[50] Judgment no 1 of 13 January 2014, Conclusions on points of law, para 7.

[51] ibid.

[52] ibid.

[53] See Justice Brennan's Opinion of the Court in *Baker v Carr*, 369 U.S. 186, at 217 (1962). The political question doctrine in electoral matters is also evoked by Rauti (n 18) 186 ff, even though the

The main issue is therefore to establish whether the Court could actually shift to a more activist approach.

In Judgment no 1 of 2014 and no 35 of 2017, the Court repeatedly referred to the margin of discretion that must be recognised to the legislator. These references clarify that the Court's activism could never be considered as an attempt to replace the legislator in regulating the electoral system.

It could not be otherwise, of course, but it was fair to start by pointing out that the Court's activism was displayed bearing in mind that there are limits that cannot be exceeded by a judicial body, even by a very peculiar judicial body as the Constitutional Court definitely is.

In this regard, both in Judgment no 1 of 2014 and in Judgment no 35 of 2017 the Court seemed very cautious in order to precisely deduct from constitutional principles the basis of any statement capable of impinging on legislative provisions.

The subject-matter being politically very sensitive, the Court reaffirmed its task and was very attentive to demonstrate that its activity was nothing more than interpreting the Constitution and protecting it against any infringement.

The constitutional principles that were used as standards were, however, all quite elastic principles, and they consequently implied a significant margin of discretion in their concretisation. Furthermore, the principles evoked had to be balanced, so that the task of the Court was far from being that of an automatic deduction of judicial solution from the wording of the Constitution.

In principle, the Court declared itself deferent towards legislator's choices, unless they manifestly lacked reasonableness. It is clear that it was not a strict scrutiny standard that the Court adopted in reviewing the electoral system. Referring to standards used by the US Supreme Court, probably the one that better fits with the Constitutional Court's attitude is the 'rational basis review'.[54] Indeed, the Court seems to have complied with the idea that it could 'only disregard the Act when those who [had] the right to make laws [had] not merely made a mistake, but [had] made a very clear one, – so clear that it [was] not open to rational question'.[55]

The Court recognised the power of the legislator to choose the electoral method, since the Constitution did not impose a specific system. What the Court required was, on the one hand, the compatibility of the concrete choices made with the key principles and rights involved in the electoral law and, on the other, coherence between the choice of the system and the concrete regulation,

author, taking into account some judgments concerning minor aspects of the electoral law, inclines towards the idea that the Court considered the manner in which seats were allotted as a constitutionally immaterial area (189).

[54] On the standards of review used by the US Supreme Court, see, inter alia, RA Posner, 'The Rise and Fall of Judicial Self-Restraint' (2012) 100 *California Law Review* 519.

[55] See JB Thayer, 'The Origin and Scope of the American Doctrine of Constitutional Law' (1893) 7 *Harvard Law Review* 129, 144.

otherwise the law could be illogical and, thus, irrational. For instance, the Court clearly stated that, if a proportional system is adopted, the idea of the equal weight of votes in allotting seats must be the general rule of the system, even though derogations are acceptable, provided that they do not create an excessive distortion of the general inspiration that underpins the proportional system.

Such a minimal requirement leads to conclude that the Constitutional Court did not usurp legislator's powers;[56] on the contrary, its 'activism' was justified for the simple reason that '[i]t is to some extent inevitable that the constitutional justice expand its review on all the laws that risk to break the covenant between citizens and the State'.[57]

Indeed, while reading Judgments no 1 of 2014 and no 35 of 2017 one cannot identify a real doctrine of the Court when it comes to electoral systems. The reader can constantly perceive the attention of the Court in order to assure a coherent and logical system that could be considered consistent with the constitutional requirements. That is simply what a Court should do in any case, and in particular when milestones of the constitutional framework, such as the electoral law, are at stake.

[56] This is the opinion of MC Grisolia, 'La legge elettorale tra la discrezionalità del Parlamento e i nuovi vincoli imposti dal sistem' (2017) 1 *Osservatorio sulle fonti*.

[57] See P Pasquino, 'L'estensione del dominio della Corte' (2017) 6(4) *Astrid on line. Rassegna*.

8

Electoral Legislation in the Visegrád Countries. A Limited Judicial Activism in a Constitution-Making Dominated Subject

JAN SAWICKI

I. INTRODUCTORY REMARKS

CENTRAL-EASTERN EUROPE HAS proven to be a true policy and constitutional laboratory over the past quarter of a century, with a combination of innovation and adoption of foreign patterns in various fields of interest for both government and constitutional law. This has occurred, for instance, both with respect to judicial review and electoral legislation, with fleeting intersections between the two topics. Poland and Hungary, among all the countries which rejected a socialist system in central-eastern Europe, have much in common when it comes to the path taken to leave that system in the past and start the following transition – the method of Round Tables – to the very gradual way of introducing a new constitutional order, and, finally – which is more interesting for the purposes of the present topic – to recent setbacks in the field of democratic output, or institutions and tools able to limit and counterweight dominant majorities of the day. It is on these two countries that the present chapter focuses mainly, with occasional references to other states as terms of comparison.

Poland and Hungary have also in common yet another aspect of the transition, which is relevant to the present discussion. Both countries have been pioneering in introducing in central-eastern Europe a system of centralised, constitutional review after – or even during – the collapse of socialism (Czechoslovakia, of course, had played the same role in the interwar period, and not only in this area). In Poland such an introduction, having occurred in 1986, even preceded the change in the form of state or the political system. In Hungary the Constitutional Court was established at the end of 1989, but soon emerged as a primary actor in the transformation process, with a judicial activism[1] at times even likened to that of its German counterpart (the 'invisible constitution', according to justice László Sólyom).[2] That it would lay the foundations for a state guided by rule of law was part of the plan. The Polish case is somewhat different, since the roots of the Constitutional Tribunal, being traced back at a final stage of socialism, and yet being the fruit of an autonomous initiative by the communist authorities – instead of a compromise with the opposition forces – had a more ambiguous character: as a consequence of that, at its earliest stage, the role of the Polish organ would not be that of building the rule of law in the 'western' meaning, but only that of ensuring a correct enforcement of law and legality, by the active political organs, under the principles of a socialist state. In spite of that, perhaps 'feeling' or anticipating the changes which were about to take place, the Polish Constitutional Tribunal, almost from the beginning, started to act in a rather creative way, and, although slightly less activist than its Hungarian counterpart, felt free to depart more and more from the principles which, theoretically, it was called upon to impose. This is interesting in the context of the subject of electoral legislation, a matter of paramount importance at a time of transition to political democracy. The question which arises now is the following: what is the role, if any, that constitutional justice, or the judiciary as a whole, have played in shaping the features of electoral legislation in these young and 'unripe' democracies?

II. THE CASE OF CZECHOSLOVAKIA (AND THE CASES OF CZECH REPUBLIC AND SLOVAKIA)

Free and post-communist Czechoslovakia underwent a slightly different path of transition (which finally resulted into the split between the Czech Republic and Slovakia in 1992[3]), being in itself a case-study of well rooted liberal democracy during the interwar period, far beyond some much more celebrated western countries which also have a totalitarian past. The main justification for such statement lies in the existence of a Constitutional Court since 1920, when it was introduced slightly before Austria.[4] So Czechoslovakia, and afterwards each of the two separate states, is the only country which could boast a very remote tradition in the field of judicial review of legislation.[5] In the case of the

[1] See I Stumpf, 'The Hungarian Constitutional Court's Place in the Constitutional System of Hungary' (2017) 13 (Special issue) *Polgári Szemle. Civic Review. Learned paper for economic and social sciences – Hungary*, 239–58 (eng.polgariszemle.hu).

[2] An expression later adopted by Laurence H Tribe.

[3] A Di Gregorio, 'Constitutions' in A Di Gregorio (ed), *The Constitutional Systems of Central-Eastern, Baltic and Balkan Europe* (The Hague, Eleven International Publishing, 2019) 46.

[4] Č Pištan, 'Constitutional Justice and Judicial Power. The Role of Constitutional Courts in the Process of Democratization and Europeanization' in Di Gregorio (n 3) 240, 241.

[5] It should also be remembered that in the inter-war period in Czechoslovakia an ad hoc Electoral Tribunal existed (in addition to the Court), entrusted with the task to settle disputes which could lead to forfeiture of a parliamentary seat (or recall) by MPs who had been expelled from their respective party for indignity and dishonour, but also for reasons of mere dissent. See JG Lexa,

Czech Republic, this tradition has now been renewed with a strong activism with regard to electoral legislation.

In any event, after the collapse of socialism, both Czechs and Slovaks chose, as did the majority of countries in the area, proportional representation, having in common differentiated electoral thresholds and a system of open list voting with certain consequences, with the significant difference that in the Czech case the electoral formula is inscribed in the Constitution, unlike what occurred in Slovakia. In the case of Slovakia, the unicameral 150-member National Council is elected applying the Hagenbach-Bischoff formula in a single nationwide constituency (since 1998). As for electoral thresholds, these have varied somewhat over time. Currently they stand at five per cent nationwide for single parties, seven per cent for coalitions of two or three parties and 10 per cent for coalitions of four or more parties. Voters can cast as many as four preferential votes which change priority in gaining a seat provided a candidate gets at list 10 per cent of preferential votes within their list.

Regarding the Czech Republic, a somewhat similar evolution can be observed. First of all, this country has a bicameral Parliament (Chamber of Deputies and Senate) and for each of the houses it provides an electoral formula, proportional for the lower and majority for the higher chamber. Bearing in mind the greater importance of the lower chamber, the legislation concerning the latter was the object of greater interest, and of more court challenges as well. In the late Nineties the main parties of the time, the conservative ODS and the social-democratic ČSSD, pushed for changes which would be more favourable for themselves, especially by the splitting of the national territory into more smaller districts, but this was already declared unconstitutional in 2001.[6] At the same time, the Czech state followed the same pattern of providing for differentiated electoral thresholds for individual parties and coalitions, and this lasted for some decades, until in early 2021, just months ahead of a parliamentary election, the Constitutional Court quashed a combination of measures which in its opinion departed too much from the very nature of proportional representation which is envisaged by the Constitution for this chamber.[7] The combination was referred to the use of the d'Hondt formula in 14 constituencies of unequal size together with a set of too high thresholds. Finally, the Czechs went to the

'Political Parties. The Experience of Czechoslovakia' in M Rechcigl (ed), *Czechoslovakia. Past and Present. Volume II. Essays on the Arts and Sciences* (Berlin, Boston, De Gruyter Mouton, 1968) 1945–46.

[6] Judgment no 64/2001, upon a petition by the President of the Republic (see T Lebeda, 'Voting Under Different Rules/Governing under Different Rules. The Politics of Electoral Reform in the Czech Republic' (2016) 8 *Acta Politologica* 75–101. In that ruling the Court made it clear that it was not 'choosing' an electoral formula, but only warning the law makers about the need to be coherent with the constitutional choice.

[7] Judgment Pl. Ús 44/17, 2 February 2021. See also M Antoš and F Horák, 'Proportionality Means Proportionality. Czech Constitutional Court, 2 February 2021, Pl. ÚS. 44/17' (2021) 17 *European Constitutional Law Review* 538–52.

polls in October 2021 with a set of thresholds of five per cent for single parties, eight per cent for coalitions of two parties and 11 per cent for coalitions of three or more parties. But in fact even a single, common five per cent threshold for all lists would have sufficed, since the two main coalitions have abundantly exceeded the higher thresholds and another smaller one failed even to reach five per cent.

III. ELECTORAL LEGISLATION IN HUNGARY AND POLAND. TWO SHARPLY DIVERGENT CHOICES FROM THE BEGINNING

A. The Mixed-Majoritarian System of Hungary

It is precisely in the field of electoral legislation that Hungary and Poland started differing most, right from the beginning. Poland, leaving aside the first 'semi-free' elections of June 1989, opted in favour of predominantly proportional formulas – which, by the way, was the prevailing option among the new democracies that had arisen from the collapse of real socialism – whereas Hungary chose a mixed proportional-majority electoral system, one in which, though, the majoritarian element prevailed with highly disproportionate effects.[8] In both countries the basic features of electoral legislation were in fact the fruit of a constituent decision, although put in place in the form of ordinary acts of Parliament.

In the case of Hungary, the original framework of the election law was shaped in the decisions agreed to at the NKA Round Table, composed of the communist party still in power and by the already existing opposition 'proto-parties'. The discussion was dominated, as it often happens, by calculations of self-perceived convenience more than theoretical-systemic approach. The ruling communists, in fact the Hungarian Socialist Workers' Party (MSzMP), advocated an electoral formula in which, as said above, the majoritarian system was the key component, aware of being the most rooted and best organised force. But there was consensus on the opportunity to retain single-member districts or constituencies, which were also traditional under the collapsing socialist system (although party pluralism was denied, of course). Finally, it was not difficult to achieve a compromise based on a combination of majoritarian and proportional representation, though with a blend which made the system one of the notoriously most complicated across the world. Alongside other fundamental state issues, and similarly to the Polish experience, the framework discussed and agreed to at the Round Table had to be ratified by the sitting Parliament, where the ruling party enjoyed an artificial position near to that of a monopoly, whose lack of democratic legitimacy was proved precisely by the need to adopt an electoral law

[8] A Arato, and Z Miklósi, 'Constitution Making and Transitional Politics in Hungary' in L E Miller and L Aucoin (eds), *Framing the State in Times of Transition* (Washington, United States Institute of Peace, 2010) 371.

based on alternative principles. This is to say that decision making in a context of a socialist system which was about to extinguish had to follow parallel institutional channels, but that at the same time it was often the Round Tables and the informal institutions which took on the role of constituent organs. In the field of electoral legislation this is particularly true of Hungary (the case of Poland differs for chronological reasons, as will be shown).

The Hungarian electoral law which, in 1989, passed the examination of both the Round Table negotiations and a Parliament still monopolised by the communists, quite surprisingly proved to be an enduring, rather than provisional tool, as it lasted for more than two decades, crossing through different political seasons. The complicated system was divided into as many as three criteria or tiers of allocation, partly unrelated to one another with the third related to the first: the first one, majoritarian, was based on 176 single-member constituencies under a double ballot;[9] a second ballot had to be held provided no candidate got an absolute majority in the first round, with a chance to stand for candidates who won at least 15 per cent of the vote (requirements in terms of turnout were also set out). The second tier allotted an additional maximum of 152 seats in 20 multi-member districts, whose range varied significantly: here a version of proportional representation was adopted, by the Hagenbach-Bischoff quota and with a privilege for parties winning a full quota, plus additional allotment only to remainders higher than two thirds; only parties which won at least four per cent of the national vote – raised to five per cent from the 1994 election – could take part. Finally, a variable number of seats, at least 58 but not more than 90, were awarded on a national scale, via the d'Hondt formula, to all parties passing the same threshold, under a compensation mechanism which took into account votes for candidates (and parties) who did not win seats in the single-member constituencies and the unused remainders in the multi-member districts. The change in the number of seats distributed in this way depended on the number of seats not assigned through the regional lists.[10]

[9] The excessive discrepancy among constituencies was already criticised by the Constitutional Court in a judgment of 2005 (no 22/2005), as an infringement of the equal suffrage. In it, the Court stated that although a perfect proportionality between electors and seats can never be achieved, the deviation per constituency should never exceed 15%, except derogations for the protection of concentrated minorities; that the distribution of parliamentary seats must be reviewed at least every ten years, preferably outside election periods; that the accent should be put, in each single-member constituency, not on the number of inhabitants but on the numbers of persons with the right to vote. Although the petitioner's arguments were partly rejected, the Court acted ex officio to establish an unconstitutional omission of legislative duty (at the time of the decision there was no statutory rule providing for the level of acceptable deviation from the average number of electors per constituency. Too much decisional space was left to the government by way of decrees). It also stated that the decision did not affect the constitutionality of parliamentary elections held before the required amendments of electoral statute.

[10] It must be added that the compensation mechanism under the third tier could not be really effective, as the number of seats awarded in this way was usually too low (and besides the second tier, the regional one, was already quite selective due to the low district magnitude).

As anticipated, this system proved quite resistant to the huge political change which occurred afterwards. Since the technical difficulties of the law, the aims which inspired it, the very majoritarian inclination in itself have been extremely peculiar, some aspects of the system deserve to be assessed thoroughly from the aspect of its practical consequences. Above all, the mere fact of adopting a (formally) mixed, but in fact a largely majoritarian system, emerged as a peculiarity both for a nascent democracy and for a country of the relevant area, where, at least at an early stage of transformation, forms of proportional representation appeared quite universally to be more appropriate (not least because all the 'ordinary' parliaments, and Hungary was no exception, were entrusted with the task of drafting and adopting the new democratic constitutions).

The mechanisms of rationalisation in the system of government, introduced in Hungary by way of two amendments adopted in 1990 to the socialist 1949 Constitution, paved the way for a stable government, to such an extent that this country has *never* even experienced one early election from 1990 to the present day (which is a rare event in comparative perspective, even in more consolidated democracies).[11] The exceptional stability of parliamentary terms is to be ascribed to the constitutional regulation of the system of government, beyond any doubt, but one could argue that the electoral formula, only prescribed at an ordinary legislation level, has also significantly contributed to that result.[12] Empirical evidence shows quite consistently a wide gap between vote and seat share (unless there is a very narrow margin between two main parties). As a consequence of that, it may easily happen that a simple majority in favour of the largest single party can translate into an outright majority of seats; there is no need to explain how this may facilitate the task of forming a government, and to a certain extent its stability – since a stronger cohesion and homogeneity are to be presumed (even though someone could argue that such a result would be achieved to the detriment of fair representation). But what may appear a virtue in this situation can turn into a cause of major democratic concern under differing circumstances. This is all the more likely to happen when a majoritarian system operates with an unequal vote share among parties: from a systemic perspective, it should be noted that in the first decade of this century (especially in the 2002 and 2006 elections) Hungary was approaching a two-party arena, where the two main protagonists, the socialist MSZP and the right-of-centre *Fidesz*, combined together, got more than 80 per cent of the vote and were almost evenly split between themselves: but from 2010 onwards, the balance of power was dramatically altered, with the *Fidesz* vote soaring and the rest of the political arena increasingly fragmented and marginalised.

[11] A Ágh, 'La Hongrie' in J-M De Waele and P Magnette (eds), *Les démocraties européennes* (Paris, Armand Colin, 2010) 190.

[12] For an opinion to the contrary, see G Tóka and S Popa, 'Hungary' in S Berglund, J Ekman, K Deegan-Krause and T Knutsen (eds), *The Handbook of Political Change in Eastern Europe*, 3rd edn (Cheltenham, Edward Elgar Publishing, 2013) 322.

It may be the case that a single party, by winning an absolute majority of the vote or so, obtains in fact a qualified majority, or super-majority, in terms of seats. Although generally a rare case in contemporary democracies, it is exactly what occurred in Hungary in 2010 (and twice subsequently). Now, if an ordinary sitting Parliament is called upon to draft and discuss a new constitution, as it has been the case in most central-eastern European states, such an over-representation is hardly desirable for obvious reasons. Regardless of any judgment or assessment of the Hungarian Fundamental Law, adopted in 2011, no one can deny that it is as a matter of fact a *one-party Constitution*, since only the ruling *Fidesz* party – together with its junior partner, the Christian Democratic KDNP, in fact a satellite – voted in favour of it, and has ever since embodied it, with most of the democratic opposition boycotting both the drafting process and the final vote.

Under the pretext of the new Constitution, in 2011 the ruling majority adopted a new electoral system, introduced by way of cardinal statute (Act CCIII on the Election of Members of Parliament of Hungary), which makes the system only amendable by a qualified majority of two thirds of present members of Parliament. The analysis will focus here on the electoral formula, postponing further remarks on the right to vote. The new statute missed the opportunity to adapt the system in a way which would comply with the necessity to grant an appropriate representation to minor parties. On the contrary, the new system only highlights the majoritarian features of the legislation, in a context which currently does not need that, bearing in mind the already extremely high, and stable, support a single party enjoys in the society. In any event, the first determining element of the new statute is the drastic reduction in the total number of seats, which drops from 386 to 199. In other sweeping changes, the second round of elections in single-member constituencies was abolished, giving way to a British-like first-past-the-post system;[13] the regional quota of members was repealed, and all the seats not awarded in individual constituencies were transferred to the national lists. The single-member quota of seats was brought to a total of 106, with the remaining 93 allotted via the national lists. Slightly more than half of deputies are therefore now elected under a purely majoritarian system, but the remaining part is not awarded according to strictly proportional criteria. Differentiated national thresholds have been introduced, based on five per cent of the vote for individual parties, 10 per cent for joint lists of two parties and 15 per cent for coalitions of three or more parties. Indeed, the distribution of seats in the national lists is hardly a compensatory one: all the 'unused' constituency votes are counted for the defeated candidates, but to that the votes won by winning candidates in each constituency must also be added, precisely the number of votes over and above those obtained

[13] The Venice Commission suggested several measures, also for the purpose of preventing gerrymandering. For this and other considerations, see n 16.

by the candidate who came second, plus one. In this way, the compensating mechanism helps somewhat even the party which is already the strongest in the majoritarian quota of seats. As a matter of fact, the system proved to produce majoritarian effects even more than what was in place before, as the 2014 election demonstrated (the gap between votes and seats share rose to an all-time high of 22 per cent, as opposed to a 15 per cent figure in 2010, only to fall to 17.5 and 13.7 in 2018 and 2022 respectively).[14]

Again, it should be emphasised the peculiarity of such a choice. Perhaps there is no electoral system or formula good 'for all seasons', regardless of other factors. Apart from individual preferences, both majoritarian and proportional systems, as well as mixed ones, have pros and cons. But the ruling party in Hungary, well aware of its strength and of the fact that this one is not volatile, knew in advance it did not need such an extreme formula just in order to be helped to remain in power. The mindful planning of this arrangement, under the present circumstances, seems to have been accomplished, for a party which already fluctuates around an absolute majority of the votes, with a view to facilitating a new achievement of the two-thirds qualified majority, rather than the traditional target of helping the strongest of minorities to achieve a majority. It is one thing to award a sort of prize, or bonus, in terms of outright majority to the largest single party, but a virtually permanent supermajority is quite another.

This is not a matter of secondary importance: under the current Hungarian legal order, and in particular on the basis of Article T of the Fundamental Law – but previously it was not much different either – plenty of subject matters, including electoral legislation, must be adopted by way of cardinal law by the two-thirds (of present members, in this case) supermajority[15] (included the distribution of single-member seats: gerrymandering would only be corroborated by two-thirds majority). This has been criticised both by domestic legal scholarship and by international documents, especially the Council of Europe, the Venice Commission[16] and the European Parliament. The most relevant critical

[14] And it finally ensured the two-thirds majority to the winning party, by granting it six additional seats, according to some estimates (see P Gruber, 'Les élections législatives en Hongrie: les raisons d'un échec', 7, at the webpage jean-jaures.org/sites/default/files/Note-216.pdf).

[15] G Halmai, 'Second-grade Constitutionalism? Hungary and Poland: How the EU Can and Should Cope with Illiberal Member States' in I Motoc, P Pinto de Albuquerque and K Wojtyczek (eds), *New Developments in Constitutional Law. Essays in honour of András Sajó* (The Hague, Eleven International Publishing, 2018) 159 ff.

[16] See in particular CDL-AD (2012)012-e, Joint Opinion on the Act on Elections of Members of Parliament of Hungary adopted by the Council for Democratic Elections and the Venice Commission, according to which only the general criteria for distributing electoral districts should be provided for by the cardinal law, not the actual drawing of boundaries itself, which should be made by an independent commission composed of technical experts with a balanced representation of parties (it must be recognised that the Joint Opinion praised a better distribution of seats compared

remark here, often reiterated, consists in the risk of 'cementing' the country's legal order, depriving future elections of significance. In fact, the constituent power – although exercised to some extent 'by the rules', not in any revolutionary manner or *ex nihilo* – could be used in 2011 thanks to the required qualified majority.

The strange development which occurred may thus be portrayed as follows. First, the political party which disposed of the constituent power, used it in such a way as to make sure many subjects in the new Fundamental Law would have to be regulated by 'supermajority' organic laws; eventually it adopted many such laws; but it soon realised that in order to be able to modify or change those laws in the future, or at least to be in charge of the process, the same supermajority would be needed. A continuous and reiterated majority of this kind, won de facto by a single party in some elections in a row, could grant it not only a sort of permanent constituent power, but also the possibility to change these laws at will (nor is this, in principle, undemocratic. But it may be noted that a previous wave of cardinal laws, adopted in 1989–90, although voted by similar majorities, were in fact consensual, as they were the fruit of prior agreement reached at the Round Table among several factions, whereas the last ones are not consensual at all). In general, on a comparative perspective, such cardinal or organic laws often integrate or supplement the constitution; but in the specific case of Hungary, the number of constitutional references to this source of law is so high[17] – more than 50 of them were counted – that obstacles in modifying these acts could result in what elsewhere would mean experiencing difficulty in legislating at all (even social or tax subjects must be regulated by organic laws). The question arises about what to do when, in the future, no one could be able to reach such a majority again, and it may be that some change is necessary but no agreement or compromise is achieved on how to bring it about. Otherwise, it could be the case that a consistent part of legislation is in fact hard to amend. It is quite paradoxical that in this peculiar context, what should normally be a guarantee of more (liberal) democracy, by protecting at least qualified minorities – or by spreading the idea of involving them in the decision-making process, which means more compromise and acceptance for other approaches or ideas – in fact does not mean that at all, thanks to the tricks of the electoral formula, and only cements for the unforeseeable future the will of the strongest faction.

to the one in force under the old statute law). The Opinion follows more general lines adopted in particular by the Venice Commission itself, according to which, if such a number of cardinal laws must be in force, at least they should keep to the most general and abstract level, leaving as much space as possible for detail regulation by ordinary statutory acts.

[17] KL Scheppele, 'Understanding Hungary's Constitutional Revolution' in A von Bogdandy and P Sonnevend (eds), *Constitutional Crisis in the European Constitutional Area* (Oxford, Oxford University Press, 2015) 111.

B. Poland and the (not too Coherent) Choice for Proportional Representation

Electoral legislation in Poland was quite another history. Unlike Hungary, its basic structure was not determined at the Round Table agreements, and this is for an interesting reason of historical character. The negotiations between the communist authorities and the opposition – in particular Solidarity – took place at a very early stage of 1989, between February and April, and they were indeed something both unprecedented and unpredictable. Being an experiment in partial democratisation, something new, since there were no precedents of authentic political pluralism in the area after the second world war, as the domino effect which eventually led to the collapse of the socialist system in so many states had not yet started – and it was in fact started in Poland – it was not possible at that stage to imagine a fully democratic Parliament as the fruit of agreements at the Round Table.

Therefore, the 'founding' election of Poland did not indeed provide the foundation of democracy, as the electoral law, one of the products of the Round Table, was a free but only partly competitive one. The composition of the Sejm, the lower chamber of Parliament, was largely pre-determined by the law itself. In particular, the number of seats to be won by communist PZPR and its 'satellite' partners would be allocated as much as 65 per cent of the 460 seats, and only the remaining 35 per cent would be left to the 'non-party' element, but in fact to free competition within one-member constituencies. For the new Senate, re-established after decades – but with limited powers – a majoritarian block-vote was used. In short, the outcome of the June 1989 elections saw the opposition Solidarity and its allies picking up all the free competition seats in the Sejm and all but one in the 100-member Senate. The composition of the chambers of Parliament was somewhat paradoxical, as on the one hand it rewarded far too much to the Communist party in the non-competitive tier, on the other it penalised it overwhelmingly in the competitive part of the Sejm and in the Senate because of the majority systems which had been – incautiously enough – adopted relying on its excessive self-confidence. The consequences of the unexpected outcome speeded up enormously the transformation process – and by the way also favoured changes in neighbouring countries – leading, among others, to the formation of the first non-communist led government.

But the political acceleration in Poland, and elsewhere, made the electoral compromise of 1989, along with its by-product, the 'contractual' Sejm and Parliament as a whole, seem rapidly outdated. Whereas some features of the system of government, even in future developments, remained partially influenced by the agreements of 1989, the opportunity appeared to break up a substantial part of the compromise and hold fully free parliamentary elections. That is why the true 'constituent' moment in Poland, as far as electoral legislation is concerned, is to be found at a later stage, precisely in 1991. The extreme uncertainty as to the outcome, the very unripe consistency of the parties *in statu nascendi* – more than in Hungary or Czechoslovakia – misunderstandings with President Lech Wałęsa who advocated a mixed-majority system similar to that of Hungary, let the situation slip into a pure form of proportional representation which was favoured by, and for its part determined, a state of unprecedented fragmentation and proliferation of micro-parties. The act under which the country took part in October 1991 in its first free elections since decades, provided for a Hare-Niemeyer formula implemented for 391 out of the total 460 seats in the Sejm in 37 districts, from open lists and without any threshold, and an additional 69 from national party closed lists, whose allocation was determined only by the votes cast in the districts (and only here with a five per cent threshold). The consequence of the wrong system in the wrong moment was that as many as 29 parties, micro-parties, movements, local groupings gained representation, with no one achieving critical mass to impose a clear-cut political direction.

But the mistake of 1991 was rapidly corrected by the political establishment. In 1993 a new law was adopted, which introduced several mechanisms aimed at reducing fragmentation and favouring the largest parties. Although the foundation of the law kept on pretending to be based on a 'proportional' criterion of distributing seats, in fact things changed significantly.[18] The number of Sejm districts rose to 52, new thresholds of five and eight per cent for parties and coalition respectively were introduced, and the d'Hondt formula was adopted both for district open lists and national closed lists. This, added to the fact that in the meantime the party arena began to rationalise, produced at the September 1993 election opposite results with regard the votes/seats ratio. By way of example, the two most voted parties – which eventually agreed on forming a government – gained almost 66 per cent of seats in the Sejm despite winning barely 36 per cent of the vote; and a number of lists failed to reach the differentiated thresholds, remaining deprived of any representation, even though, added together, they got more than 35 per cent of votes. This, in turn, posed at least two concerns of constitutional nature, if not of constitutionality *stricto sensu*. The first was that the Parliament so elected had to also act as a constituent assembly (indeed the Constitution was adopted in 1997); the second was that the interim 'Small Constitution', adopted in 1992 to regulate provisionally the functioning of main state institution, already imposed a proportional system for the Sejm (Article 3, then confirmed by Article 96, paragraph 2 of the 1997 Constitution). Under normal circumstances a system like that would not stand so openly in contradiction with the enshrined principle, but at that time it did (the percentage of wasted votes fell strongly eventually, only to rise

[18] See J Ciemniewski, 'Bicameralism Under the Constitutional System of Third Republic of Poland' [2014] *The Sejm Review. Fifth Special Edition*, 69 (orka.sejm.gov.pl/przeglad.nsf/0/4F65449 61C6F3EC2C1257CE0002B0A4F/%24File/ps5_2014_eng.pdf).

again to around 15 in 2015).[19] What matters here is that, apart from a problem of interpretation concerning the nature of a list – whether party or coalition – nobody then dared to challenge the constitutionality of this act, and nobody did ever since. Although the proportionality of this system is not beyond doubt, it consolidated more and more, becoming almost a tradition.

On the subject of election mechanisms to translate votes into seats, a broad tacit consensus emerged, despite weak occasional attempts to introduce more elements of a majoritarian system, especially by the centrist Civic Platform party at the turn of the new century. The effort was only successful with regard to the Senate, where – in the absence of any constitutional requirement concerning the electoral formula – a British-style first-past-the-post system, in single-member constituencies, was introduced in 2011.[20] It should be pointed out that even this formula, and the results it brought about, were never incompatible with the outcome of elections to the stronger Sejm – the political majorities have usually coincided – until the October 2019 elections, when PiS (the Law and Justice party) won an outright majority in the Sejm for the second time in a row, whereas a coalition of the left and centrist democratic parties, with joint candidates standing in each constituency, allowed them to achieve a narrow majority – 51 to 49 – in the 'upper' chamber.[21]

Over the years, some features of the system changed either for some time or in a stable way. The d'Hondt formula for the Sejm was replaced by the St-Laguë on a one-off basis for 2001, and for practical-partisan reasons, only to be re-instated eventually. The national closed list, instead, was repealed in permanently in 2000, to hand all seats over to open lists in the territorial districts, on the grounds of being an anti-democratic elitist privilege for parties aimed at guaranteeing election of people without any real support (sometimes intellectuals). In 2011, a long-lasting effort was rewarded, when the entire Polish electoral legislation, substantive and procedural, was unified under a single Electoral Code.[22] What remains characteristic of electoral law in this country, from a comparative perspective, is an extreme form of open list under which the expression of an individual preference for a candidate is nothing less than

[19] When the splitting of the left vote into two lists – each of one failing to pass the thresholds of 5% for parties and 8% for coalitions respectively – despite getting 11% of the vote combined together, allowed the right-wing PiS party to reach an overall majority in the Sejm (235 seats out of 460) with just 37.5% of the vote.

[20] On the reasons why two different electoral systems were possible and appropriated for two different chambers of Parliament in Poland – in particular because of the greater importance accorded to the *Sejm* – see M Masternak-Kubiak and J Trzciński, 'The System of Government in the Constitution of the Republic of Poland of 2 April 1997. An Analysis of the Competence of the Sejm' [1999] *The Sejm Review. First special edition* 49 (orka.sejm.gov.pl/przeglad.nsf/0/D99A48F413DBE940C12579B8003FAD99/%24File/ps1_1999_eng.pdf).

[21] For the sake of precision, it must be added that this fact did not significantly alter the course of national politics because of the inherent, structural and constitutional weakness of the Senate.

[22] A Rakowska and K Skotnicki, 'Changes in Electoral Law Introduced by the Election Code' [2014] *The Sejm Review. Fifth Special Edition* 189–213.

obligatory. The only way an elector can vote – with the exception of the Senate – is to put a cross on a box beside the name of a concrete candidate within a list. So the number of votes won by each party must always coincide with the sum of individual preferences obtained.

In more recent years the new ruling party Law and Justice (PiS) has again attempted to pass new provisions in the electoral field, for a long time with a very limited success. This is significant, since the action of the party is now known world-wide for its challenges to some basic principles in the rule of law, for example in the field of independence of the judicial power itself. But each attempt to alter the 'rules of the game' in this sector, have come under fierce social and political criticism. This is the case of the provisions of the electoral code concerning the formula for electing the Polish members to the European Parliament. However, since the state territory is divided into several districts just for that purpose – which is rather unusual in Europe – the overall number of seats is small if compared to national parliaments, the relevant provisions always provided for a preliminary allocation of seats among parties at the national level, and a subsequent distribution in the districts. A new Bill passed by Parliament in July 2018, with only the PiS votes, stated that the distribution would only take place at the narrow level of the districts, thus raising the threshold from the formal five per cent to a de facto much higher level, possibly 16.5 per cent. The measure was so unacceptable that even President Andrzej Duda – strictly linked to the party – refused to sign it into law by way of a presidential 'veto'.[23] This was important, since the level of trust placed by public opinion – but also by many legal scholars – in the Constitutional Tribunal has dropped over the last years because of other changes. So in this way one could argue that even a supposed 'shortage' of constitutional justice, as temporary as it may be, can be compensated by a head of state, when this interprets their role in an appropriate manner.

But attempts to alter electoral legislation for partisan purposes did not stop. The Electoral Code was amended in 2019 in such a way as to politicise the composition of the National Electoral Commission (*Państwowa Komisja Wyborcza*), a body entrusted with the task of managing the entire election process at all levels. Instead of all nine members appointed by three top state courts, as it was the case since 1990, this amendment left only two components to be chosen by the judiciary, and provided for parliamentary election of the remaining seven. Although these seven are to be chosen in a way that should represent as much as possible the party balance of forces present in the Sejm, without penalising the opposition, and despite the fact that they are required to be in possession of highly legal qualifications, it is still a departure from a pattern of election administration which was to bring about a sort of 'best practice' in a still young democracy.

[23] See www.euractiv.com/section/future-eu/news/polish-president-vetoes-change-to-european-parliament-election-rules/.

Pretending it was only about technical changes, in December 2022 the PiS majority adopted further amendments of a procedural nature to the Electoral Code, according to which the number of polling stations would be increased, but only in rural areas and smaller municipalities, so that the minimum number of those entitled to vote would lower from 500 to 200. In addition to this, a mandatory special system of public transport will have to be arranged – at the local governments' expense – for those who live in the most deprived and faraway places, only in order to reach the respective polling station but not to come back from it. In other changes, officials at polling stations will no longer be able to divide into groups or pile up the votes cast. Counting the ballots will have to take place by the entire staff of each polling station (*obwodowa komisja wyborcza*) in order to prevent errors (if not possibly fraud, which is believed to be exceptionally rare, however).[24] Contrary to the electoral formula for the European Parliament, President Duda signed this act into law, despite the lack of at least one year of *vacatio legis* as would be required. Another important innovation of this period, also promulgated by the President, was the one-off postponement of general municipal, district and voivodeship elections from autumn of 2023 until somewhere in the spring of 2024, by extending the term of office of mayors and local councils to 30 April 2024.[25] Both these changes deserve some short critical remarks.

With regard to the 2022 amendments to election procedure, it is widely held that the Polish administration suffers from a dramatic shortage of polling stations,[26] both in rural areas and in metropolitan areas. It is true that electoral turnout is usually comparatively higher in the latter, but these voting institutions are also the most overcrowded, even because of the high number that are entitled to vote (almost 1,500 on average). So it is not quite clear why the number of such places has only increased in areas with a determined population structure and not throughout the entire country, although this may not be totally unrelated to the fact that the PiS party fares much better in the countryside.

As far as the postponement is concerned, the justification given by government officials was related with the need to avoid overlaps between local and parliamentary elections, which are also due on some Sundays between October and November 2023. In fact, electoral procedures in Poland suffer from a high degree of technical complication, and officials involved in them must deal with plenty of tasks at once, so it is not unwise to relieve them of an excessive load of burdens. The fact is that even the spring of 2024 has European elections scheduled, so the problem of overlap could occur again soon. Even in this case suspicion has been expressed that the party in power prefers to avoid a sort of

[24] See notesfrompoland.com/2023/01/27/parliament-approves-changes-to-polands-electoral-code-as-opposition-cries-foul/.

[25] See notesfrompoland.com/2022/11/23/polish-president-approves-postponement-of-local-elections-despite-opposition-criticism/.

[26] See www.osce.org/files/f/documents/c/7/446371_1.pdf.

bandwagon effect, should the democratic oppositions prevail in local elections, as is often the case. On a legal-constitutional level, a weak justification for such a measure, of formalistic nature, lies in the fact that only the term of office of national bodies such as Parliament or the President of the Republic is set in the Constitution, whereas that of, for example, local councils, are not. On the other hand, the opposition, especially in the Senate where they prevail, maintains that departure from a constitutional principle is only possible if it is necessary to achieve another constitutional value, which is not the case in the situation at hand: neither the extension of the term of office nor the convenience of the organisers are a constitutional value.[27] Legal certainty, citizens' trust in the state and voting rights have been in turn penalised for the benefit of a doubtful political good such as ease of electoral procedure.

It should be pointed out that nobody even thought of challenging any of the aforementioned changes before the Constitutional Tribunal. This is certainly because of the entire capture of this institution by the ruling political majority since 2015,[28] which led to a an equally complete distrust in it, as much from parliamentary opposition as from other minorities or judges and other subjects who are entitled to bring an action before the Tribunal.

IV. A LIMITED JUDICIAL ACTIVISM IN A HIGHLY POLITICISED FIELD, BEFORE THE 'HOSTILE TAKEOVER' OF THE COURTS (WITH THE PARTIAL ERSATZ OF THE VENICE COMMISSION)

What has been said so far is only about the electoral formulas. Clarification is necessary, since it involves the role played by the judiciary, and in particular the once activist and powerful Hungarian Constitutional Court. In fact its activity in the subject of how votes transform into seats has been a very limited one and was generally favourable to parliamentary statute law.[29] Things slightly changed more recently, especially when the dominating political will moved on to serious reforms concerning the electorate, namely the registration of voters and the eligible to vote. But the ability to oppose objectionable political change by judicial means, in Hungary and Poland, was weakened by the victory of the illiberal forces, respectively since 2010 and 2015.

Under the new Fundamental Law (2011), the right to vote was extended to all Hungarian citizens regardless of their state of residence. Moreover, the acquisition of citizenship for ethnic Hungarians living abroad was made more simple, and the logistical conditions for casting a postal vote exceptionally friendly. This, in turn, was in sharp contrast with the much less favourable treatment reserved

[27] See again n 25.

[28] W Sadurski, *Poland's Constitutional Breakdown* (Oxford, Oxford University Press, 2019) 58–88.

[29] The four per cent national threshold was found constitutionally legitimate by the Constitutional Court in 1991 (judgment 3/1991).

to Hungarian citizens resident in the country but staying abroad at the time of voting.[30] The extension of the electoral franchise to ethnic Hungarians in the neighbouring countries has obviously to do with the trauma of the 1920 Trianon Treaty, still alive in many people's minds even after generations, whose consequence was the mutilation of Hungarian territory. At the same time, changes were introduced to provide for the registration of voters in order to be eligible to vote, as opposed to the previous automatic compilation and update of a national list of voters. Despite massive political and academic criticism, the government made it clear that this reform was high on its agenda. But the government took a risk in the choice of the legislative technique: it included the new regulation – in particular the prior registration as a precondition to the right to vote – as an additional amendment to the already adopted Transitional Provisions of the Fundamental Law. Following a petition filed by the Commissioner for Fundamental Rights to the Constitutional Court, this one found it unconstitutional, on grounds which are neither substantial nor purely procedural.

According to the Court, in a 10-5 decision,[31] a provision like the one concerning voters' registration ought not be improperly 'constitutionalised' by writing it into the Transitional provisions, at least as long as those provisions were not incorporated into the Constitution, which in principle should be made up of only one text. It is not permitted to elevate multiple provisions to the top level, which are not built into the text of the Fundamental Law,[32] as this could cause uncertainty as far as the legal order, at its top level, is concerned. Moreover, Parliament cannot introduce by way of transitional provisions norms which in fact are of permanent character and do not form an integral part of the Constitution. The question of whether the Court was enabled to set aside constitutional amendments had already been put on the table and had in fact become even more burning recently, at a time of constitution-making in a context of dramatic political change. On the above-mentioned grounds, this particular decision by the Court could be seen rather as a procedural one: Parliament, the same Parliament which had recently adopted a new Fundamental Law, did not have the 'courage' to write directly into its text a controversial political decision, which could perform a partial and subtle discrimination among citizens in exercising a key political right. But, as a matter of fact, the same Parliament passed shortly afterwards a broad fourth amendment to the Fundamental Law which incorporated the Transitional provisions directly into it, going as far as to include several other

[30] See B Majtényi, A Nagi and P Kállai, '"Only Fidesz" – Minority Electoral Law in Hungary' (March 2018) *Verfassungsblog*, who point out the 95.5% share of the vote cast in 2014 for *Fidesz* by Hungarians permanently resident abroad, as opposed to the 43.5% won in Hungary.

[31] (45/2012 on the unconstitutionality and annulment of certain provisions of the Transitional Provisions of the Fundamental Law of Hungary).

[32] I Stumpf, *Rule of Law, Division of Powers, Constitutionalism* (2014) 55(4) *Acta Iuridica Hungarica* 299, 315.

provisions which had previously been deemed unconstitutional by the Court. But it did not so in the case of electoral registration. So, in a way, the party enjoying a supermajority could feel something more substantive in the judgment of the Court, even though the latter, stating it did not want to go beyond formal-procedural criticism, in fact came quite close to a judgment based on substantial and material aspects of the Constitution.

Finally, in December 2020, in the midst of the COVID-19 pandemic, another important amendment was added to electoral legislation. Namely, Act CLXVII of 2020 changed the criteria to submit candidatures for Parliament by providing that for a national list to be registered, a party (or a national list) needs to nominate candidates in as many as 71 single-member constituencies instead of the previous 27 in 14 (out of 19) counties instead of 9.

The Venice Commission, in a Joint Opinion adopted with ODIHR (No 1040/2021),[33] criticised the vast 2020 electoral amendments on several grounds. First of all, the Commission focused on the fast-track procedure of adoption, without any public consultations which should be mandatory according to Hungarian law itself when – as in the present case – a government Bill is submitted. It also drew attention to the consequences as to public party financing, since only parties which register a national list are entitled to be awarded party funds, whereas even 'fake parties', according to the parliamentary majority, could easily obtain public money under the previous legislation. Therefore, according to the Act passed in 2020 and currently in force, the combination of limitation of the right to register national lists – in fact an informal limitation of the right to exist as a party – with the loss of any public funding as a consequence of the irrelevance of such a party, creates a situation in which these parties are either forced to join together or doomed to disappear by fighting one another, in already unfavourable conditions, in every single-member constituency. According to the Commission, although such measures are not per se unacceptable and may be compatible with basic democratic principles in rationalising the system, their concrete application in the present Hungarian context is arranged in such a way as to consolidate the Fidesz party's dominance, under different pretexts. Other measures concerning electoral procedure administration were partly criticised, as introducing too much politicisation in the composition of electoral commissions. Alongside these critical remarks, other minor amendments, of rather technical nature, were positively assessed by the Venice Commission and by ODIHR.

Of course, the official aim of such change was to favour big parties to the detriment of minor ones and so rationalise the political landscape, even though as a matter of fact only one major party existed, Fidesz itself, whereas all the others were (and are) medium or small-sized political actors. In fact, the 2020 Act actually aimed to embarrassing the opponents of the ruling Fidesz party,

[33] CL-AD (2021)039, adopted on 18 October 2021.

by hitting the weak point of their fragmentation. Since the political landscape showed a divided opposition, one can easily argue that that almost all the opposition parties, from left to the (former) far-right Jobbik, would be forced to form a broad coalition, with the risk of highlighting incompatibilities between their respective electors. Eventually a common leader was agreed upon after open primary elections by the 'United for Hungary' coalition national list, together with joint candidates for each individual constituency. And yet, despite a giant effort of unity and cohesion made by the combined forces of opposition, and in spite of favourable opinion polls, the April 2022 elections finally saw the biggest victory ever for Fidesz (and its formal coalition with the KDNP satellite party) which finished winning a 54.1 per cent share of party-list votes and 135 seats (or 67.8 per cent) in the National Assembly.

In Poland, the role played in electoral matters by the judiciary as a whole, and by the Constitutional Tribunal in particular, has been even smaller than in Hungary. What is most remarkable is the unusual deference adopted by this body in the relevant subject, much more evident than in other fields. Very rarely has the judiciary been involved in conflicts of legal-constitutional nature. One case was brought before the Tribunal, which is worth mentioning after many years. In 2006, a coalition made by three parties – the major of which was 'Law and Justice', PiS, which again won power in 2015 after eight years in opposition – changed the electoral system for all levels of local government, included the recently introduced regional level. The main innovation was the possibility for parties to reach agreements on the formation of coalitions before, not only after the vote. This was to be 'propitiated' by the fact the seats would no longer be allocated only among individual parties, but at a first stage among electoral groupings or 'blocks' of lists – *blokowanie list* – and only subsequently among each party list composing a grouping. The five per cent threshold for each list was maintained, but another one was added for coalitions (ten per cent at municipal and provincial level, 15 per cent for regional councils). The d'Hondt formula was preserved for coalitions and for individual parties which either did not or could not make alliances; but Sainte-Laguë was introduced for distributing seats among each list forming a coalition. The most striking fact, though, was that votes won by parties which did not conquer seats for failure to reach the thresholds would be used by the largest parties forming the same coalition. This was meant to favour first the parties which were capable, at the time, of forming coalitions at the expense of those which did not possess coalitional capacities – at that time it was the main party of the left, but also the centrist-liberal Civic Platform, which instead stood together with the agrarian PSL junior partner; and, second, the main parties at the expense of junior partners or minor lists inside a particular coalition (relying on the expectation that these would not pass the thresholds). In fact, the general outcome of the 2006 local government elections gave rise to criticism because of a deeply unequal treatment between parties with fewer votes but more seats as they had joined a coalition and parties (usually the left-wing SLD) which resulted in being under-represented for the opposite reason. But in general, the result proved much less favourable towards the ruling PiS than expected.

In any event, the opposition parties challenged the legislative innovation before the Constitutional Tribunal. In a judgment of 3 November 2006 (K 31/06) the Tribunal upheld the parliamentary act in full (with three dissenting opinions). First, it was based on a formalistic approach according to which the constitutional imperative of a proportional formula was only expressed for elections to the national Sejm, and was absent in the case of local elections (but it was not a matter of strict proportionality). Then it stated that creating 'blocks' of lists by individual parties is an act based on a purely voluntary basis (which as a matter of fact could prove not fully true). Then the Tribunal turned to a fully substantive approach when it stated, based on considerations of practical and political nature, that the forming of electoral 'groupings' of more parties can influence voters' behaviour – and perhaps mentality – in such a way that they will know that their vote, even if given to a party which could not gain a seat, would anyway be used by another 'grouped' party, in a sort of coalition discipline, and would not, therefore, be completely 'wasted'. Other arguments were also dismissed, like the insufficient involvement of social partners or the insufficient *vacatio legis*, since those shortcomings were not on such a scale as to justify the annulment of the statutory act. Anyway the law upheld by the judiciary was repealed by Parliament in its subsequent term and the traditional competition between individual party lists was reinstated.

But another judgment occurred in July 2011 (K 9/11)[34] concerning the above-mentioned electoral code. This time PiS members of Parliament were the initiators as opposition to the ruling Civic Platform. The Constitutional Tribunal rejected a considerable part of the applicants' arguments. It was in fact a decision of huge dimensions. First of all, the introduction of single-member constituencies for the Senate was held to be fully compatible with the Constitution, as the electoral system for the Senate could disregard a clear connection between the share of votes and number of seats for individual parties (moreover, according to the Tribunal, not even a precise uniform ratio in the number of electors for each individual constituency can be demanded as a specification of the general equal treatment principle expressed under Article 32.1 of the Constitution). Such a principle of substantive equality has not been written into the relevant Article 97 of the Constitution, nor can it be reconstructed from other provisions thereof. But in other relevant aspects the Tribunal took a different stance: namely it declared unconstitutional provisions which, inter alia, banned under the penalty of a fine the use of election posters and slogans the surface area of

[34] See webpage trybunal.gov.pl/en/news/press-releases/after-the-hearing/art/5683-kodeks-wyborczy/ for press release; trybunal.gov.pl/fileadmin/content/omowienia/K_09_11_EN.pdf for full English translation.

which exceeds two square meters as well as the broadcast of paid election radio and TV ads by state-owned and private broadcasters. The Tribunal assumed that Article 54 of the Constitution, the content of which was often summed up as 'freedom of speech', set out three freedoms which were interrelated: a) the freedom to express opinions; b) the freedom to acquire information; and c) the freedom to disseminate information. Such restrictions, according to the Tribunal, did not pass the test of proportionality as specified in Article 31.3 of the Constitution as they were too strict as far as the respect of the said liberties was concerned. The possibility of holding two-days of elections for Parliament and the President was also found unconstitutional, whereas proxy voting and the postal vote was declared fully legitimate.

V. CONCLUSION

On a more general note, what can be drawn from the cited cases is the cautious approach taken by the judiciary in general, and by constitutional courts in particular, when it comes to electoral legislation in these countries. One could synthesise as follows: in general the judiciary has recognised the role of key and decisive actors which parliaments played in this field, especially as they have also fully and symbolically embodied the role of constitution-making bodies. As such, they deserved – or were considered to be entitled to – a broad margin of discretion. The cases and levels of interventionism or activism by the courts have been displayed, only occasionally, when the courts had to ascertain the degree of coherence between the choices made at the level of higher law and their legislative translations, but never by extrapolating innovative conceptual categories or ideas by the courts themselves (even though both the Hungarian and Polish courts did so in other fields, especially in the early Nineties).

The recognition of the somewhat decisive political will has been confirmed more recently, when the Hungarian Constitutional Court had no objections with regard to the (ever more) majoritarian electoral formula for Parliament. Indeed, the Court could not broaden its scope of analysis, nor apparently so far has it been requested to do so. But it is quite implicit that the level of interference the Court could possibly ever enjoy is at present a limited one, especially in this field of the outmost importance. The current Hungarian Fundamental Law does not provide for particular norms as for the translation of votes into seats. Empirical evidence shows us that, usually, when constitutions provide something in this field, this is to make sure that some degree of proportionality is adopted in the electoral formula, not the opposite solution. When silence is kept on the subject, this is or could be proof of a positive stance in respect of majoritarian formulas. This proved particularly true in the above-mentioned case of judgment K 9/11 by the Polish Constitutional Tribunal. What is unknown today is if a line, a limit could be drawn to such a choice, and who could be able to do it.

The issue is extremely burning in the present cases of Poland and Hungary. To ascertain where limits to the political will of the majority lie, in these two countries, could be a risky and hazardous experiment, these days. Institutions such as the Venice Commission can well play a role of substitute, but only within certain limits, typically those of soft law. In the present situation, much depends indeed on the willingness of political majorities to self-restraint.

9

The Court of Justice and the European Court of Human Rights on Electoral Matters: Towards a Procedural Conception of Representative Democracy?

ROBERT BRAY AND CRISTINA FASONE

I. INTRODUCTION. THE POSITION OF SUPRANATIONAL COURTS IN CONTEXT

TYPICALLY, CONSTITUTIONAL COURTS find themselves in an awkward position when having to adjudicate on electoral rules, as their decisions are liable to alter the political dynamics and standards of democratic competition. However, the role played in this context by supranational and international courts, such as the Court of Justice of the EU (CJEU) and the European Court of Human Rights (ECtHR), which by their very nature are more distant and detached from the national constituencies where electoral rights are exercised, is even more difficult.[1] Indeed, when dealing with electoral matters and despite the differences in their jurisdictions and in the types of elections they tend to consider, both the Luxembourg and the Strasbourg courts normally take quite a deferential approach towards domestic legislatures (and courts).[2] They refer to a sort of minimal procedural concept of democracy revolving around a small number of essential standards, rather than imposing their own views on representation, for example by endorsing a consensual or, at the opposite end of the spectrum, a majoritarian imprint on the democratic systems. While a

[1] See R Bellamy, 'The Democratic Legitimacy of International Human Rights Conventions: Political Constitutionalism and the European Convention on Human Rights' (2014) 25 *European Journal of International Law* 1019.

[2] On the CJEU, see extensively, S Ninatti, *Giudicare la democrazia? Processo politico e ideale democratico nella giurisprudenza della Corte di Giustizia Europea* (Milan, Giuffrè, 2004).

hands-off approach appears to be preferable for these courts when dealing with electoral formulas and the strictly related rules, when the object of adjudication concerns individual rights, eg, the right to vote, the right to be elected and the right to an independent judge or authority for the settlement of electoral disputes, the position of the European courts varies from a light-touch review by the CJEU to the more far-reaching review performed by the ECtHR.

These two supranational courts are no exception compared with other international courts. International courts in general are in a difficult position when it comes to assessing the core of democratic procedures, such as elections, which are highly context dependent. The national history and political traditions strongly influence the choice of the design of a given electoral system and even the concept of representation through which the polity is willing to channel itself. Besides the traditional difficulty courts find in engaging with the ultimate rules of democracy in terms of legitimacy and justification, for international courts any attempt at prescribing a common or harmonised legal framework for the Contracting Parties in this very sensitive field will be liable to result in a backlash from national political institutions and communities.[3] For some international courts, such as the Inter-American Court of Human Rights and the African Court on Human and People's Rights, either the docket is fairly narrow or there are structural reasons preventing the court from playing a more far-reaching role when it comes to elections.[4]

It should also be acknowledged from the outset of the comparison how the origin and the jurisdiction of the CJEU and the ECtHR differ. Perhaps, as far as the CJEU is concerned, it is not inappropriate to start with what the late Advocate General (subsequently Judge) Federico Mancini and David Keeling wrote in 1994 in their essay *Democracy and the European Court of Justice*.[5] They begin with the undemocratic nature of the Treaty of Rome, where 'democracy' is never mentioned, 'liberty' is a value to be defended and there was nothing to prevent the accession of a non-democratic state. To a large extent the focus of the CJEU's activity was and still is to ensure the smooth functioning of the common, now internal, market and economic regional integration. It was not conceived as a human rights court nor as a court meant to supervise the unfolding of democratic procedures.

Nevertheless, just after the entry into effect of the Maastricht Treaty with its introduction of the concept of Union citizenship, which is closely connected to electoral rights, Mancini and Keeling were sanguine about the 'surprisingly

[3] See R Pildes, 'Supranational Courts and The Law of Democracy: The European Court of Human Rights' (2018) 9 *Journal of International Dispute Settlement* 154.

[4] See A Huneeus and MR Madsen, 'Between universalism and regional law and politics: A comparative history of the American, European, and African human rights systems' (2018) 16 *ICON* 143.

[5] GF Mancini and DT Keeling, 'Democracy and the European Court of Justice' (1994) 57 *Modern Law Review* 175.

important contribution of the Court of Justice to the process by which the Community has evolved into a more democratic structure than its founders apparently envisaged'. Since then, successive treaty changes, culminating in the Treaty of Lisbon with its extension of the ordinary legislative procedure, together with the *Spitzenkandidaten* device, have certainly made the EU much more democratic. At the same time, the EU has become much more committed to promoting democracy not just outside but also inside its borders, through Article 7 TEU first and, more recently, through the creative jurisprudence of the CJEU.[6]

As far as the Court of Justice itself is concerned, Mancini and Keeling's criticism that the members of the Court are completely lacking in 'links with the symbols of democratic government' is no longer entirely justified, since the panel set up under Article 255 TFEU in order to give an opinion on candidates' suitability to perform the duties of Judge and Advocate-General of the Court of Justice and the General Court before the governments of the Member States make the appointments includes a member proposed by the European Parliament.[7] Moreover, from the record of this panel, it is no longer true that the Council of Ministers holds the exclusive, uncontrolled power to appoint and reappoint the members of the Community's judiciary.[8]

The ECtHR, by contrast, had the protection of fundamental rights in its original mandate,[9] although electoral rights were not initially included in the ECHR (see next section). It has always been a human rights court and indeed since its very first case on electoral matters, *Mathieu-Mohin and Clerfayt v Belgium*, in 1987,[10] the ECtHR immediately started framing the issue in terms of human rights, though such a development could hardly have been predicted having regard to the wording of Article 3, Protocol no 1.[11] Until recently, however, the Court paid much less attention to the impact of electoral rules on the quality of democracy and decision-making. Unlike the CJEU, the procedure for appointing the judges of the ECtHR sought from the very beginning to link this Court to national democracies and politics. Indeed, the judges – one

[6] L Pech and D Kochenov, 'Respect for the Rule of Law in the Case Law of the European Court of Justice: A Casebook Overview of Key Judgments since the Portuguese Judges Case' (2021) 3 *SIEPS*.

[7] T Dumbrovsky, B Petkova, M Van der Slujs, 'Judicial appointments: The Article 255 TFEU Advisory Panel and selection procedures in the Member States' (2014) 51 *Common Market Law Review* 455.

[8] See the sixth activity report of the Art 255 Panel, available here: comite255.europa.eu/en/home. During the period covered by the report, the panel delivered opinions on 43 candidates for the offices of Judge or Advocate-General at the EU courts. 29 opinions were related to first terms of office, which entailed extensive examination and hearings by the panel. In total, eight of the opinions were unfavourable. The panel's opinions were followed by Member States' governments in all cases.

[9] See, eg, E Bates, 'The Birth of the European Convention on Human Rights – and the European Court of Human Rights' in J Christoffersen and MR Madsen (eds), *The European Court of Human Rights between Law and Politics* (Oxford, Oxford University Press, 2011) 17 ff.

[10] ECtHR, *Mathieu-Mohin and Clerfayt v Belgium*, Application no 9267/81, 2 March 1987.

[11] Amongst many, see A Ruiz Robledo, 'The Construction of the Right to Free Elections by the European Court of Human Rights' (2018) 7 *Cambridge International Law Journal* 227 ff.

per country – are elected by the Parliamentary Assembly of the Council of Europe, composed of national MPs from the Contracting Parties, from lists of three candidates proposed by each Member State which are to be compiled through transparent domestic procedures and as to ensure gender balance (Article 22 ECHR). Yet this by no means implies that the Court seeks any form of democratic legitimacy or accountability.

To complete the picture, it is noteworthy that both courts are struggling first with the challenges to the rule of law and the democratic backsliding occurring in several Member States, primarily owing to the problematic political capture of the domestic judiciaries, having regard to Article 6 ECHR and Article 19 TEU, in combination with Article 2 TEU and Article 47 of the Charter,[12] and second also with severe repercussions on the quality of national democracies.[13] In other words, when analysing the case-law of the CJEU and of the ECtHR it has to be borne in mind that the standards set have to be applied to both liberal democracies and authoritarian regimes.[14]

II. THE STANDARDS OF REVIEW

This leads us to a brief review of the standards of adjudication used by the two Courts, which also define the boundaries of their respective jurisdictions. Indeed, both Courts act under evident constraints, as is confirmed by the relatively few cases which they address on electoral matters, although they are on the rise as a proportion of the overall number of decisions.

For the CJEU, the division of competence between the EU and the Member States significantly affects the margin of manoeuvre of the Court. The only electoral controversies that have come under the radar of the CJEU so far are those connected with local elections and, most importantly, the European elections for the small part that is regulated by EU law,[15] given that a uniform electoral procedure for the European Parliament is lacking (Article 223(1) TFEU).

[12] See, eg, ECtHR, *Baka v Hungary*, Application no 20261/12, 23 June 2016, and CJEU, judgment of 19 November 2019; *A. K. and Others*, C-585/18, C-624/18 and C-625/18, ECLI:EU:C:2019:982.

[13] According to Freedom House, *Freedom in the World 2023. Marking 50 Years in the Struggle for Democracy*, March 2023, in the EU all Member States, but Hungary, which is 'partly free', have been considered as 'free', despite the clear decline in the protection of civil liberties in many countries, such as Slovenia. Within the Council of Europe, on the other hand, of the 46 Contracting Parties, 10 are 'partly free' (Albania, Armenia, Bosnia and Herzegovina, Georgia, Hungary, Montenegro, Moldova, North Macedonia, Serbia, Ukraine) and, after the departure of Russia, two, Azerbaijan and Turkey, are qualified as 'not free'.

[14] On this point, see critically P Popelier, '*L.B. v. Hungary* and the Quality of the Parliamentary Debate' (2023) 3 *Quaderni costituzionali* 674 ff.

[15] See Art 14 TEU on the European citizens' representation in the European Parliament and Art 39 of the Charter on the right to vote in and to stand for the European elections. Unlike the case of Art 40 of the Charter on municipal elections, Art 39 also requires that 'Members of the European Parliament shall be elected by direct universal suffrage in a free and secret ballot'.

Additionally, as for the narrow openings for the Court of Justice to intervene in this area, two other factors play a role: first, the difficulty for individuals to resort to the action for annulment as an instrument of individual direct complaint against the violation of rights, given the high hurdle imposed by the Treaties (Article 263(4) TFEU) and by the Court itself for non-privileged applicants.[16] Second, since prospective violations of electoral rights tend to originate in national institutions rather than in EU institutions, the Court of Justice could be involved mainly through infringement actions (Article 258 TFEU) and references for preliminary rulings from national courts (Article 267 TFEU), which, however, are unwilling to question the Court of Justice on such issues[17] or in one instance, to wait for its answer to the reference.[18]

Subject to the provisions of the Act concerning the election of the members of the European Parliament by direct universal suffrage (the '1976 Act'), the electoral procedure is to be governed in each Member State by its national provisions.[19] In *Italy and Donnici* v *Parliament*,[20] the Court of Justice dealt extensively with the distribution of responsibilities for the European elections. In that case, the European Parliament had claimed that, in verifying the credentials of MEPs, it could leave unapplied the appointment of a candidate effected by the national authorities in the event of an infringement of the free exercise of the parliamentary mandate or the principles of universal and proportional suffrage.[21] The Court held, categorically, that the Parliament had a 'complete lack of discretion in the matter' since Article 12 of the 1976 Act provided that, for the purposes of verifying the credentials of its members, the Parliament was to 'take note' of the results declared officially by the Member States and rule on any dispute which may arise out of the provisions of that Act other than

[16] *Cf* T Tridimas and S Poli, 'Locus Standi of Individuals under Article 230(4): The Return of Eurydice?' in A Arnull, P Eeckhout, and T Tridimas (eds), *Continuity and Change in EU law: Essays in Honour of Sir Francis Jacobs* (Oxford, Oxford University Press, 2008), ch 5. But see, eg, judgment of 30 April 2009, *Italy and Donnici v Parliament*, C-393/07 and C-9/08, ECLI:EU:C:2009:275.

[17] In particular Constitutional Courts, which have been repeatedly called to judge on the constitutionality of the electoral thresholds for the European elections, but have never made a reference for a preliminary ruling to the Court of Justice: German Constitutional Tribunal, judgment of 9 November 2011, Second Senate, 2 BvC 4/10; judgment of 26 February 2014, Second Senate, 2 BvE 2/13, 2 BvR 2238/13, 2 BvR 2221/13, 2 be 12/13, 2 BvE 10/13, 2 BvE 9/13, 2 BvE 8/13, 2 BvE 7/13, 2 BvE 6/13, 2 BvE 5/13, 2 BvR 2220/13; Italian Constitutional Court, judgment 10/2025; Czech Constitutional Court, Pl. ÚS 14/14 of 19 May 2015.

[18] CJEU, judgment of 19 December 2019, *Junqueras Vies*, C-502/19, ECLI:EU:C:2019:1115, where the Spanish *Tribunal Supremo* did not wait for the CJEU to give its preliminary ruling, delivering its final judgment on 13 October 2019 on the Catalan separatist leaders, including Junqueras Vies who had recently been elected as an MEP.

[19] Art 8 of the 1976 Act.

[20] *Italy and Donnici v Parliament* (n 16) paras 50–73, and S Curreri, 'Il 'caso Occhetto': rinuncia all'elezione e autonomia del Parlamento europeo' (2008) 1 *Rassegna Parlamentare* 197. See also judgment of 22 December 2022, *Junqueras i Vies v Parliament*, C-115/21 P, ECLI:EU:C:2022:1021, para 64.

[21] *Italy and Donnici v Parliament* (n 16) para 36.

those arising out of the national provisions to which the Act refers.[22] Indeed, the Court had already held that the European Parliament was under a duty to 'take note' under Article 12 of the 1976 Act of a communication from a Member State that an MEP was disqualified as a result of a criminal conviction.[23]

Although the Member States had to comply with the 1976 Act in so far as it prescribed certain electoral procedures, they had the task of organising the elections in accordance with their national law, counting the votes and making the official declaration of the results. Under Article 13(2) each Member State is to lay down appropriate procedures for filling seats which become vacant. Moreover, in the absence of EU rules, it is for the domestic legal system of each Member State to designate the competent courts and lay down procedural rules governing actions for safeguarding rights derived by individuals from EU law.[24] The only condition is that those rules must not be less favourable than those governing rights which originate in domestic law and that they do not render virtually impossible or excessively difficult the exercise of rights conferred by EU law (principles of equivalence and effectiveness). It is for the national law of each Member State to determine the rules allowing legal redress for a person who, because of a national provision that is contrary to EU law, has not been entered on the electoral register for the European elections and has therefore been excluded from participation in those elections.

Further analysis of the question of the division of competence between the EU and the Member States on electoral matters is contained in the judgment in Case C-502/19 *Junqueras Vies*, forming part of the litigation concerning the election of Catalan secessionist leaders as MEPs. Interestingly, the Court framed the case as related to immunities, where the EU and the CJEU have a broader leeway, rather than as a dispute on the verification of credentials under the 1976 Act, where, as has already been mentioned, the margin for the Court is very narrow.[25] Thus, the Court considered Article 9 of the Protocol on the privileges and immunities of the EU (the Protocol). Whereas the first paragraph of that Article provides for MEPs to enjoy immunity 'during the sessions of the European Parliament', the Court held that the second paragraph – 'Immunity shall likewise apply to members while they are travelling to and from the place of meeting of the European Parliament' – enabled a person held in provisional detention who had been elected as an MEP to enjoy immunity while travelling to the first sitting held after the official declaration of the election results, in order

[22] ibid paras 50 et seq.

[23] Judgment of 7 July 2005, *Le Pen*, C-208/03 P, ECLI:EU:C:2005:429, paras 43–58, upholding the judgment of 10 April 2003, *Le Pen v Parliament*, T-353/00, ECLI:EU:T:2003:112.

[24] *Italy and Donnici* v *Parliament* (n 16) paras 60–63.

[25] S Hardt, 'Select Fault Lines of the European Parliamentary Mandate: The Immunity of Oriol Junqueras Vies: ECJ 19 December 2019, Case C-502/19, Junqueras' (2020) 16 *European Constitutional Law Review* 170 and C Fasone and N Lupo, 'The Court of Justice on the Junqueras saga: Interpreting the European parliamentary immunities in light of the democratic principle' (2020) 57 *Common Market Law Review* 1527.

to allow the new Parliament to hold its inaugural session and, then, to verify the credentials of its Members.

If not for a question of division of competence but rather because of national constitutional concerns, the original 1950 text of the ECHR did not include the explicit protection of electoral rights. In particular, the UK Government was opposed to such a codification due to the diversity and richness of domestic legislation on voting rights and their limitations so as to prevent any harmonisation hampering national specificities,[26] such as the design of the first-past-the-post system. In the end, the Danish proposal merely to acknowledge in the Preamble the value of free and competitive elections as a political pre-condition for membership of the Council of Europe prevailed. Peace and justice in the world are seen as 'best maintained on the one hand [by] an effective political democracy and on the other by a common understanding and observance of the Human Rights upon which they depend'. Of course, what precisely is meant by 'political democracy' in the context of the Council of Europe remained, and to a large extent still remains, difficult to determine, but the ECtHR, alongside the Venice Commission, has helped to give some guidance. In any event, it was only two years later, in 1952, that three of the rights not covered by the Convention itself – property, education, and voting rights – were covered by an Additional Protocol (Protocol no 1) at the proposal of the Belgian Government. Yet, the wording of Article 3, Protocol no 1, does not provide for subjective rights, but is formulated so as to put the Contracting Parties under an obligation to 'hold free elections at reasonable intervals by secret ballot, under conditions which will ensure the free expression of the opinion of the electorate in the choice of the legislature'. It was not until 1994 that the title of the Article was amended as to read 'Right to free elections' and it was only thanks to the transformative jurisprudence of the ECtHR that three, conceptually distinct, rights could be derived from a state obligation: the right to elect the members of a legislature, including a supranational legislature like the European Parliament,[27] and subnational legislatures,[28] but excluding presidential elections;[29] the right to stand as a candidate in those elections, and the right to hold office once the election has taken place.[30]

However, it took more than three decades for the Court to reach this point. First, Article 3, Protocol no 1, was mainly used at the end of the 1960s in an inter-state application led by Denmark and supported by other countries against

[26] Council of Europe, *Collected Edition of the 'Travaux Preparatoires' of the European Convention on Human Rights* (The Hague, Brill-Nijhoff, 1985) 58–59.

[27] ECtHR, *Matthews v the United Kingdom*, Application no 24833/94, 18 February 1999.

[28] ECtHR, *Federación Nacionalista Canaria v Spain*, Application no 56618/00, 7 June 2001 and *Vito Sante Santoro v Italy*, Application no 36681/97, 1 July 2004.

[29] ECtHR, *Paksas v Lithuania*, Application no 34932/04, 6 January 2011 and *Anchugov v Russia*, Application no 11157/04, 4 July 2013.

[30] D Kurnosov, 'Pragmatic Adjudication of Election Cases in the European Court of Human Rights' (2021) 32 *European Journal of International Law* 256.

Greece where the Parliament was abolished in 1967. The country was sanctioned by the Committee of Ministers with the suspension of its rights as a Council of Europe member in 1969. This remains an interesting case insofar as Article 3 and parliamentary elections were linked to the very essence of democratic life. Second, drawing on a textual interpretation of Article 3, the European Commission of Human Rights considered the challenges invoking a violation of voting rights inadmissible (as such rights were not explicitly mentioned in the ECHR) until 1975, when the Commission shifted its interpretation and acknowledged that the right to vote and to stand in legislative elections was grounded in Article 3.[31] Third, the ECtHR did not have an opportunity to intervene in this matter until 1987, in the *Mathieu-Mohin and Clerfayt* case, where it endorsed the 1975 interpretation of the Commission, clarifying that 'the inter-State colouring of the wording of article 3 (P1–3) did not reflect any difference of substance from the other substantive clauses in the Convention and Protocols' and that the actual wording of the Article was justified by the need for states to adopt 'positive measures to "hold" democratic elections'.[32] This change in the interpretation and value of Article 3 certainly led to an upgrade of the status of electoral rights in the Council of Europe, but the arguments and reasoning of the Court have been criticised for departing from the text.[33]

Still, as will be argued, there are many constraints that the ECtHR has had to face in its case-law on electoral rights, starting from the declaratory nature of its rulings and its subsidiary jurisdiction.[34] Moreover and with the exception of pilot judgments, the codification of the margin of appreciation doctrine in the Preamble to the ECHR, following the entry into force of Protocol no 15, has made the Court's readiness to engage in this field even more cautious. It follows that it is not possible to conceptualise a specific understanding of democracy on the part of the ECtHR through the interpretation of Article 3, Protocol no 1, alone, but that Article needs to be read in conjunction with other articles of the ECHR, such as Articles 6, 10, 11 and 13.

The entry into force of Protocol no 11 to the ECHR, in 1998, with the rise of individual applications, and, before that, the big flow of accessions to the Council of Europe from the new eastern democracies caused the Court to deal with electoral challenges more often than in the past. At the same time, the work of the Venice Commission in electoral matters has been very significant over the last two decades. The emergence of a *ius commune europeum* on

[31] European Commission of Human Rights, *W, X, Y and Z v Belgium*, Application no 6745/74, 30 May 1975.

[32] ECtHR, *Mathieu-Mohin and Clerfayt* (n 10) para 50.

[33] See, eg, J García Roca, 'Del compromiso internacional de los Estados de organizar elecciones libres al derecho de sufragio de los ciudadanos (Art. 3 P1 CEDH)' in J García Roca and P Santolaya (eds), *La Europa de los Derechos: El Convenio Europeo de Derechos Humanos*, 2nd edn (Madrid, Centro de Estudios Políticos y Constitucionales, 2009) 927.

[34] A Zysset, 'Calibrating the response to populism at the European Court of Human Rights' (2022) 20 *ICON* 991.

elections detected through the Venice Commission's Code of Good Practice in Electoral Matters, adopted in 2002,[35] has been inspired by, but has also helped to shape, the case-law of the ECtHR, although it is not used by the Court as a standard of review.[36] To some extent this trend is similar to what has occurred in the EU with the CJEU's elaboration of the constitutional traditions common to the Member States, which however has been subsequently codified in Article 6 TEU and Article 52(4) of the Charter.[37]

III. THE CASE-LAW OF THE COURT OF JUSTICE

Given its jurisdiction and the composite nature of the law on the election of the European Parliament, which is predominantly national, the CJEU has been called on to resolve few cases on the right to vote and to stand as a candidate in the European elections.

Beyond that, it is possible to frame as an electoral dispute also the landmark ruling of the CJEU in the *'Les Verts'* case,[38] of 1986, on a dispute which developed between the first European direct elections in 1979 and the preparation of the European elections in 1984. The decision has been widely cited for the Court's categorisation of the European Treaties as a 'Constitutional Charter' and of the then European Community as a community based on the rule of law. More specifically, the case resulted in the annulment of the European Parliament's decision on the reimbursement of electoral expenditures because of a challenge brought by a small political formation, registered in France, which failed to elect any candidate in the national and European elections. The Court considered that the decision of the European Parliament to exclude the small Green party from the reimbursement procedure was not immune from judicial review as otherwise the electoral competition would have been impaired together with equal opportunities to access the European electoral mandate, which would have given an unfair advantage to the parties already represented in the European Parliament. The decision was annulled because it was ultra vires, in breach of Article 7(2) of the 1976 Act, which deferred regulation of electoral reimbursement, in particular for the information campaign, to the Member States. However, it is remarkable that the

[35] European Commission for Democracy through Law (Venice Commission), *Code of Good Practice in Electoral Matters*, CDL-AD (2002) 23, Strasbourg, 30 October 2022.

[36] C Fasone and G Piccirilli, 'Towards a Ius Commune on Elections in Europe? The Role of the Code of Good Practice in Electoral Matters in "Harmonizing" Electoral Rights' (2017) 16 *Election Law Journal* 247 ff.

[37] Amongst many, see J Ziller, 'Common Constitutional Traditions' in L Besselink, N Lupo, M Wendel (eds), *Research Handbook of European Constitutional Law* (Cheltenham, Edward Elgar, forthcoming).

[38] CJEU, judgment of 23 April 1986, *Parti écologiste 'Les Verts' v European Parliament*, C-294/83, ECLI:EU:C:1986:166.

CJEU linked the acknowledgment that the Community was based on the rule of law to the protection of the guarantees surrounding the European electoral process, including equal access thereto.

Yet, it cannot be overlooked that the most significant CJEU judgments in electoral matters were delivered mainly in the post-Maastricht era, where the connection between the status of citizen and that of voter emerged clearly. In *Spain v UK* the Court ruled, in an infringement action, on the UK extension of voting rights in the European elections to third country nationals resident in Gibraltar.[39] As neither the Treaty nor the Act of 1976 define precisely who is entitled to vote and to stand in the elections, this competence falls within the Member States' remit, in compliance with EU law principles, such as the principle of non-discrimination. The Court did not follow the Advocate General's argument that third-country nationals could be granted voting rights at European elections only in 'exceptional circumstances'.[40] However, the Court held that the people who are granted such electoral rights – despite not being European citizens – must have a close link with the Member State in question and that in any case the Member States must observe Community law and the classical principles of equality and proportionality.

The same reasoning on equal treatment applied to the opposite situation, which arose in the preliminary ruling case of *Eman and Selvinger*.[41] In that case what was contested was the Dutch legislation excluding certain categories of own nationals residing in one of the overseas territories associated with the Community (OCT) (Aruba) from voting in European elections. The CJEU held that Member States can define the criteria for exercising voting rights in these elections, provided that the principle of equal treatment is respected: the requirement of residence is not inappropriate per se, but the Dutch authorities had failed to justify the difference in treatment between Dutch nationals residing in one of OCT countries and Dutch citizens residing in other countries outside the EU, who, instead, were entitled to vote. This led, according to the Court, to a patent and unreasonable discrimination.

It should be noted that those two judgments were delivered in 'the current state of Community law',[42] which included, at the time, the definition of the European Parliament as composed of 'representatives of the peoples of the States brought together in the Community' and not of 'representatives of the Union's citizens' as it is under the post-Lisbon regime (Article 14(2) TFEU). This circumstance and the background to the cases lead one to reflect on the

[39] CJEU, judgment of 12 September 2006, *Spain v UK*, C-145/04, ECLI:EU:C:2006:543; see S Adam, 'Electoral Rights under the Review of the European Court of Justice: Judicial Trends and Constitutional Weakness' (2008) 3 *Croatian Yearbook of European Law and Policy* 415, 426 ff.

[40] Opinion of Advocate General Tizzano delivered on 6 April 2006, ECLI:EU:C:2006:231.

[41] CJEU, judgment of 12 September 2006, *Eman and Selvinger*, C-300/04, ECLI:EU:C:2006:545. *Cf* Adam (n 39) 432 ff., and P De Groot, N Luk, 'Twenty Years of CJEU Jurisprudence on Citizenship' (2014) 15 *German Law Journal* 825ff.

[42] *Spain v United Kingdom* (n 39) para 78.

idea of 'people' and of political community that should be given representation in the Union through the European Parliament's elections. The CJEU does not express itself precisely on the point, but a few hints can be derived from its arguments. For example, the Court is clear that the acknowledgment of electoral rights should be grounded on evident and strong bonds between the prospective voters and the territory, the historical roots and the tradition of the Member States. Moreover, the Court has also been attentive to cases of unreasonable and unjustified discrimination stemming from an exclusion from the community of EU voters. Equal treatment is a key principle in that respect and, in the view of the CJEU, limitations of voting rights should be based on objective reasons.

The boundaries of the CJEU's jurisdiction in determining the inclusion or exclusion from the community of voters in the European elections were elaborated on in the 2015 case of *Delvigne*.[43] The Grand Chamber of the Court of Justice held that French law depriving some individuals convicted by means of a final judgment of their right to vote was not incompatible with a number of principles of the EU Charter of Fundamental Rights. After noting that Article 8 of the 1976 Act provides that subject to its provisions, the electoral procedure is governed in each Member State by its national norms and that Articles 1(3) and 9 of the 1976 Act do not define, expressly and precisely, who can vote and stand as a candidate in elections to the European Parliament, this being a competence which remains with the Member States,[44] it observed that, in exercising that competence, Member States must fulfil the obligation under Article 1(3) of the Act read together with Article 14(3) TEU.[45] The Court took the view that in adopting legislation to that effect, even where it deprives an EU citizen of the right to vote in the European elections, it is fulfilling that obligation and hence implementing Union law for the purposes of the Charter.

The Court then held that the limitation on the exercise of the right to vote as enshrined in Article 39(2) of the Charter complied with Article 52(1)[46] of the Charter, asserting that the deprivation of the right to vote is 'provided for

[43] Judgment of 6 October 2015, *Delvigne v Commune de Lesparre Médoc and Préfet de la Gironde*, C-650/13, ECLI:EU:C:2015:648. See K Lenaerts, 'Linking EU Citizenship to Democracy' (2015) 11 *Croatian Yearbook of European Law and Policy* VII-XVIII, and for a more general survey of prisoners' voting rights, V Scordia, 'The cases of McHugh & others v. The United Kingdom and Thierry Delvigne v. Commune de Lesparre Médoc' in D Archibugi and AE Benli (eds), *Claiming Citizenship Rights in Europe. Emerging Challenges and Political Agents* (London, Routledge, 2017).

[44] See *Eman and Sevinger* (n 41) paras 143 and 45, and *Spain* v *United Kingdom* (n 39) paras 70 and 78.

[45] 'The members of the European Parliament shall be elected for a term of five years by direct universal suffrage in a free and secret ballot.'

[46] 'Any limitation on the exercise of the rights and freedoms recognised by this Charter must be provided for by law and respect the essence of those rights and freedoms. Subject to the principle of proportionality, limitations may be made only if they are necessary and genuinely meet objectives of general interest recognised by the Union or the need to protect the rights and freedoms of others.'

by law' and 'respects the essence' of this right because it 'does not call into question that right as such, since it has the effect of excluding certain persons, under specific conditions and on account of their conduct, from those entitled to vote in elections to the Parliament'. It held that it pursued a legitimate objective and did not conflict with the principle of proportionality since it 'takes into account the nature and gravity of the criminal offence committed and the duration of the penalty'.[47] In reaching this conclusion, the Court made no reference to the case-law of the ECtHR, but abundant reference to its own jurisprudence on the Charter, which itself contains reference to the Strasbourg case-law. For the case-law on prisoners' voting rights, the Court did have the benefit of the Advocate General's assessment, where he stated that the different national laws were so diverse that, from the point of view of EU law, regard could be had only to the common minimum shared by the Member States and, consequently, to the case-law of the ECtHR concerning Article 3 of Protocol no 1 to the ECHR.[48]

What makes this case particularly interesting is that, as he entered into office as President of the Court of Justice, Lenaerts chose to dedicate an important article to the *Delvigne* case,[49] designed to give reassurance that 'the political dimension of EU citizenship is respectful of the constitutional allocation of powers sought by the authors of the Treaties'. *Delvigne*, he wrote, helps to 'make explicit the link between EU citizenship and the democratic governance of the EU' by showing that the political dimension of EU citizenship is not limited to Articles 20–25 TFEU but also involves, notably, Articles 14(3) and 1(3) of the 1976 Act, which impose on the Member States obligations whose objective is to ensure that the basic principles inherent in a democratic electoral system are applied at EU level. By virtue of those electoral principles, the Member States are bound to ensure that MEPs are elected by direct universal suffrage in a free and secret ballot. '[T]he political dimension of EU citizenship is not only about rights, but also about ensuring that that representative democracy at EU level is effective and … legitimate'.

On this ground – notably democratic representation in the EU and the legitimacy of the vote when it comes to the European Parliament's elections post-Brexit – the 2022 CJEU ruling in *EP v Préfet du Gers* is of special significance as it reasserts the fundamental relationship between EU citizenship and voting rights.[50] The Court considered a request for a preliminary ruling

[47] CJEU, *Delvigne* (n 43) paras 47–49.

[48] Opinion of Advocate General Cruz Villalón, delivered on 4 June 2015, ECLI:EU:C:2015:363, paras 117–19, citing *Hirst v United Kingdom (No 2)* [GC] No 74026/01, 2005-IX, *Frodl v Austria*, No 20201/04 and *Scoppola* v *Italy* (No 3) [GC], No 126/05.

[49] Lenaerts (n 43).

[50] Judgment of 9 June 2022, *EP v Préfet du Gers and Institut national de la statistique et des études économiques*, C-673/20, ECLI:EU:C:2022:449. See also the order of 8 June 2021, *Price v Council*, T-231/20, ECLI:EU:T:2021:349, and the judgment on appeal, available tellingly only in French, where the applicant's claim that the Withdrawal Agreement and Decision 2020/135 should

arising out of the refusal by a local mayor, following the entry into force of the Withdrawal Agreement on 1 February 2020 and the removal of the name of the person concerned from the electoral roll in France, to register on the special electoral roll for non-French citizens of the EU a UK national who, while not being a French national, had resided in France for 38 years and was married to a French citizen. She pointed to the UK rule by which UK nationals having resided abroad for more than 15 years are no longer entitled to take part in elections in that state. The entry into force of the Withdrawal Agreement triggered for UK nationals the loss of the fundamental status of EU citizen and, with that, of the right to vote and to stand as a candidate in the European and municipal elections. It was irrelevant that UK nationals had previously exercised their right to reside in a Member State. As regards the fact that the applicant was also deprived of the vote in the UK, that was an automatic consequence of the UK's decision to withdraw from the EU and the 15-year rule was a choice of electoral law made by that state.

As already mentioned, the Court has also engaged with the other side of representative democracy, the right to stand as a candidate in the European elections, to hold the office of MEP and to exercise the mandate once elected. Besides the *Donnici* case that put the jurisdiction of the CJEU to a test on the verification of the MEPs' credentials, the already mentioned *Junqueras* case contains an important *affresco* of the CJEU's idea of democratic representation connected with the European vote. For the Court, given that the functioning of the Union is founded on the principle of representative democracy (Article 10 TEU), the status of MEP arises from being elected by direct universal suffrage in a free and secret ballot, while the term of office of the Members of that institution constitutes the main attribute of that status. Consequently, the acquisition of the status of MEP, for the purposes of Article 9 of the Protocol on privileges and immunities, occurs because of and at the time of the official declaration of the election results carried out by the Member States. The 1976 Act makes it clear that the term of office of MEPs begins and ends at the same time as that five-year legislative period.

The Court confirmed its case-law to the effect that the objectives of the Protocol are to ensure that the institutions of the EU have full and effective protection against hindrances or risks to their proper functioning and independence.[51] On that basis the immunities granted to MEPs are intended to ensure the independence of the European Parliament in the performance of its tasks, as the European Court of Human Rights noted as regards

be partially annulled was dismissed out of hand as inadmissible judgment of 15 June 2023, *Price v Council*, C-502/21 P, ECLI:EU:C:2023:482, upholding the order of the General Court.

[51] Judgment of 10 July 1986, *Wybot*, 149/85, EU:C:1986:310, paras 12 and 22; order of 13 July 1990, *Zwartveld and Others*, C-2/88 IMM, EU:C:1990:315, para 19, and judgment of 22 March 2007, *Commission v Belgium*, C-437/04, EU:C:2007:178, para 56).

different forms of parliamentary immunity established in democratic political systems.[52]

The MEPs' immunity also serves to ensure the effectiveness of the right to stand as a candidate in elections guaranteed by Article 39(2) of the Charter of Fundamental Rights, which constitutes the expression in the Charter of the principle of direct universal suffrage in a free and secret ballot enshrined in Article 14(3) TEU and Article 1(3) of the 1976 Act, by allowing persons who have been elected Members of the European Parliament to complete the steps necessary to take their seats.

Accordingly, a person who was officially declared elected to the European Parliament while the subject of a measure of provisional detention in the context of proceedings in respect of serious criminal offences, but who was not authorised to comply with certain requirements under national law following such a declaration – namely to swear allegiance to the Spanish Constitution – and to travel to the European Parliament, in order to take part in its first sitting, must be regarded as enjoying immunity under the second paragraph of Article 9 of the Protocol. The Court further held that the immunity laid down in the second paragraph of Article 9 of the Protocol precludes, inter alia, that a measure of provisional detention may impede the freedom of MEPs to travel to the place where the first sitting of the new parliamentary term is to take place, in order to complete the formalities required by the 1976 Act.

In the latest decision in the saga of the Catalan MEPs,[53] the General Court provided a narrower reading of the parliamentary immunities and of the formal acquisition of the parliamentary status compared to the *Junqueras* case, where the CJEU appeared to envisage an automatism between the declaration of the official results of the elections and the start of the MEP's mandate and to consider any further national requirement to this end void. On 6 July 2022 the General Court ruled in a case concerning candidates whose names appeared on the original list of candidates elected to the European Parliament, but had had both their request for withdrawal of the arrest warrants concerning them and their request to sign the declaration of allegiance to the Spanish Constitution remotely refused.[54] They challenged – failing on both counts – an instruction of the President of European Parliament refusing them access to the welcome and assistance service offered to incoming MEPs and the grant of temporary accreditation and the refusal of the President to recognise their status as MEPs contained in a letter. The Court held that the President of Parliament did not have the power to state that the Kingdom of Spain could not lay down the

[52] ECtHR, *Karácsony and Others v Hungary*, Application no 42461/13, 17 May 2016, para 138, and ECtHR, *Uspaskich v Lithuania*, Application no 14737/08, 20 December 2016, para 98.

[53] See Fasone and Lupo (n 25) 1527 ff.

[54] Judgment of 6 July 2022, *Puigdemont i Casamajó and Comín i Oliveres v European Parliament*, T-388/19, ECLI:EU:T:2022:421 (under appeal as Case C-600/22 P). See A Di Chiara, 'I deputati catalani al parlamento europeo: sulla verifica dei poteri a Strasburgo', *Lacostituzione.info*, 28 June 2019.

requirement to swear an oath to respect the Constitution and the General Court had no jurisdiction to assess the legality of that requirement under national or EU law. Those questions fell within the jurisdiction of the national courts or the Court of Justice hearing an application for failure to fulfil obligations under Article 258 TFEU or when asked for a preliminary ruling on interpretation under Article 267 TFEU. The Court further noted that Article 223(2) TFEU gave Parliament exclusive competence to establish the Statute for MEPs and hence the general conditions for the performance of MEPs' duties, but not the formalities prior to taking office.

IV. THE CASE-LAW OF THE EUROPEAN COURT OF HUMAN RIGHTS

Although the ECtHR case-law on elections, in particular on Article 3, Protocol no 1, is just a tiny portion of its jurisprudence, over the last three decades electoral cases have increased significantly and, at times, the rulings of the Court have sparked controversies. Without any pretention to offer a comprehensive analysis, this section will map the most significant of the cases based on Article 3, Protocol no 1, by looking at the object of the review, ie, whether it is the design of the electoral system as such or, by contrast, access to the right to vote and to stand as a candidate for elections and the right to hold and exercise the electoral mandate. The idea then is to assess the ECtHR's conception of democracy emerging from this case-law and compare it with that of the CJEU.

First of all, the Court has been clear that Article 3, Protocol no 1, does not envisage any preferred electoral systems nor does it pose any eligibility criteria to stand for elections, both of these questions being left entirely to Member States.[55] As stated in *Mathieu-Mohin and Clerfayt v Belgium*,

> any electoral system must be assessed in the light of the political evolution of the country concerned; features that would be unacceptable in the context of one system may accordingly be justified in the context of another, at least so long as the chosen system provides for conditions which will ensure the 'free expression of the opinion of the people in the choice of the legislature'.[56]

As far as the design of electoral systems is concerned, arguably one of the best known cases is *Yumak and Sadak v Turkey*,[57] where the Grand Chamber held that the electoral threshold of 10 per cent imposed nationally for Turkish parliamentary elections (of a unicameral legislature) did not interfere with the free choice of the people to elect their representative and hence no violation of Article 3, Protocol no 1, had occurred, even though in practice the threshold made

[55] ECtHR, *Berlusconi v Italy*, Application no 58428/13, 27 November 2018.
[56] ECtHR, *Mathieu-Mohin and Clerfayt v Belgium* (n 10) para 54.
[57] ECtHR, *Yumak and Sadak v Turkey*, Application no 10226/03, 8 July 2008.

it particularly difficult for opposition parties to enter the Parliament. As long as five fundamental principles, also enshrined in the Venice Commission's Code of Good Practice in Electoral Matters – universal, equal, free, secret, and direct suffrage – are respected in the elections the Court leaves a very broad discretion to the Contracting Parties as to their electoral arrangements. It confirmed that any electoral system can pursue legitimate aims. Electoral systems should be assessed on a case-by-case basis.

However, the ECtHR has been much more critical of the lack of predictability and certainty of electoral rules on the ground that they are essential preconditions for the well-functioning of the democratic order so as to enable voters to make an informed choice and prospective candidates to participate in the electoral competition on an equal footing. In *Ekoglasnost v Bulgaria*,[58] the Court condemned Bulgaria for the lack of stability of electoral rights in the period immediately prior to the polls. In that case the ECtHR invoked the Code of Good Practice in Electoral Matters as a minimum limit that cannot be transgressed by the legislation of the Member States. The Code identifies three types of fundamental rules for the electoral process – on the methods for electoral scrutiny, the composition of electoral commissions, and the division of polling stations into constituencies – and 'prohibits' amendments during the year preceding the elections. On the basis of these preconditions, which are merely minimum requirements, the Court confirmed the link between conventional legality and the stability of the Bulgarian cardinal rules on the voting system during the pre-electoral year, as changes therein could lead to the perception of a link with contingent interests, which, in extreme cases, could 'benefit the political parties in power' and therefore constitute a 'practice incompatible with democratic order'. Hence, although the new conditions introduced by the 'late' amendments for taking part in the elections were recognised as pursuing a legitimate aim, the Court considered the changes to the Bulgarian electoral law to be in violation of Article 3, Protocol no 1, as they had been introduced only two months before the elections.

For the Court, electoral rights can be subject to limitations, but under conditions that 'do not curtail the rights in question to such an extent as to impair their very essence and deprive them of their effectiveness'. The Court should satisfy itself that they are 'imposed in pursuit of a legitimate aim; and that the means employed are not disproportionate'.[59] In particular, most of the alleged limitations that come under the scrutiny of the Court essentially refer to equality of treatment of voters and candidates.[60] For example, in *Sitaropoulos and Giakoumopoulos v Greece*, where Greek citizens residing abroad alleged that

[58] ECtHR, *Ekoglasnost v Bulgaria*, Application no 30386/05, 6 November 2012.

[59] ECtHR, *Mathieu-Mohin and Clerfayt v Belgium* (n 10) para 52.

[60] See also, *Matthews v UK* (n 27), where UK citizens residing in Gibraltar were denied the possibility to vote in the European elections and, for discrimination between candidates willing to stand for election, see *Aziz v Cyprus*, Application no 69949/01, 22 June 2004.

their inability to vote for the Parliament from their place of residence amounted to disproportionate interference with the exercise of their right to vote, the Court considered that no infringement of Article 3, Protocol no 1, had been committed. It did so on the basis of a comprehensive comparative law analysis of Member States' legislation showing that most countries subject the exercise of the right to vote to residence requirements and hence that the country could be allowed a wide margin of appreciation. By contrast, a legislative ban on candidates with more than one nationality standing in parliamentary elections has been held to conflict with Article 3, Protocol no 1, as an unjustified and disproportionate measure.[61]

On very limited occasions, however, where the protection of electoral rights was found to be impaired in its essence vis-à-vis the democratic process, the Court has issued pilot judgments and found against the Member State. In *Sejdić and Finci v Bosnia and Herzegovina*, the ECtHR had to review the exclusion of the right of the two complainants, national citizens, to stand for election to the second chamber of the Federal Parliament and the federal collective Presidency owing to their Roma and Jewish origins.[62] Indeed, the state Constitution acknowledged (and still recognises) the right to stand in those elections as being vested only in the 'constituent peoples' of Bosnia and Herzegovina, notably Bosniacs, Croats and Serbs, owing to the past genocide and ethnic cleansing, with a view to the restoration of peace in a post-conflict context. For the Court, such a total ban could by no means withstand the proportionality assessment as it lacked an objective and reasonable justification. Consequently, the Court found a violation of Article 14 ECHR – which, on the basis of the consolidated case-law of the ECtHR, is never used as a stand-alone clause of review – in conjunction with Article 3, Protocol no 1, as well as of Article 1, Protocol no 12, for the exclusion from the presidential elections, which otherwise would have fallen outside the scope of the ECHR due to the focus of Article 3 on legislative elections only. The landmark ruling, which has yet to be implemented after 15 years, does not contain any specific conceptualisation of democracy which the Court sought to protect despite the electoral matters, the very peculiar situation of Bosnia and Herzegovina and the allegation contained in the dissenting opinions of lack of contextualisation of the (majority) judgment with regard to domestic ethnic divisions and political representation.[63]

No elaboration of what is expected by the Court in terms of 'democratic society', either as a public good to protect or as a limit on the enjoyment of

[61] ECtHR, *Tănase v Moldova*, Application no 7/08, 27 April 2010.

[62] ECtHR, *Sejdić and Finci v Bosnia and Herzegovina*, Applications nos 27996/06 and 34836/06, 22 December 2009.

[63] In ECtHR, *Kovačević v Bosnia and Herzegovina*, Application no 43651/22, 29 August 2023, the Court acknowledged the violation of the applicant's right under Art 1, Protocol no 12 with regard to the composition of the lower chamber of the federal Parliament considering that the emphasis on ethnic representation impaired the effective political participation of all citizens.

political rights, is provided for in what is probably the best known line of the ECtHR jurisprudence on elections, namely the ban on prisoners voting.[64] In this field, the Court has assured the Member States of a wide margin of appreciation,[65] clarifying in *Hirst no 2*,[66] the pilot judgment, that no violation of Article 3, Protocol no 1, is to be detected unless, as in that case, disenfranchisement is to be considered 'general, automatic and indiscriminate', and, hence, disproportionate.[67] In the subsequent case-law, with the exception of *Frodl v Austria*,[68] the Court adopted a very cautious approach with regard to prisoners' disenfranchisement in long-standing democracies and, to a lesser extent, in democracies on a clear path of consolidation. For instance in *Scoppola v Italy (no 3)*, the Grand Chamber referred to the 'historical development, cultural diversity and political thought within Europe' to justify its deference to national legislation.[69] Similar reasoning can also be found in the case of *Zdanoka v Latvia*[70] involving a limitation of the right to stand as a candidate in the elections in Latvia where the person concerned had formerly been a member of the Communist Parties of the former Soviet Union and Latvia, which were held responsible for the attempted *coup d'état* of 1991. Dealing with what had recently become a EU Member State, the ECtHR affirmed with regard to this limitation, excluding the applicant from standing as a candidate, that national authorities are better placed to assess the difficulties faced in 'establishing and safeguarding the democratic order'. In such circumstances, Member States

> should therefore be left sufficient latitude to assess the needs of their society in building confidence in the new democratic institutions, including the national parliament, and to answer the question whether the impugned measure is still needed for these purposes, provided that the Court has found nothing arbitrary or disproportionate in such an assessment (para 102).[71]

[64] Zysset (n 34) 999.

[65] ibid.

[66] ECtHR, *Hirst No 2 v the United Kingdom*, Application no 74025/01, 6 October 2005, not yet fully implemented, on which see, critically, Bellamy (n 1) 1019 ff. and Kurnosov (n 30) 276 ff.

[67] The same reasoning also applies to cases of a 'permanent and irreversible ban': see ECtHR, *Paksas v Lithuania*, Application no 34932/04, 6 January 2011. A similar approach applies as well to the compatibility of national measures disenfranchising people with mental disability. See ECtHR, *Alajos Kiss v Hungary*. Application no 38832/06, 20 May 2010 compared to *Caamaño Valle v Spain*, Application no 43564/17, 11 May 2021.

[68] ECtHR, *Frodl v Austria*, Application no 20201/04, 8 April 2010, where Austria was condemned for violating Art 3, Protocol no 1, because the disenfranchisement of the prisoner, Mr Frodl, had not been declared by a judge and there was no connection between the criminal offence and the sanction on elections.

[69] ECtHR, *Scoppola v Italy (no 3)*, Application no 126/05, 22 May 2012.

[70] ECtHR, *Zdanoka v Latvia*, Application no 58278/00, 16 March 2006.

[71] However, two years later, in *Adamson v Latvia*, Application no 3669/03, 1 December 2008, the ECtHR considered as clearly arbitrary the legal exclusion of a former member of a military unit affiliated to the KGB before the collapse of the Soviet Union from the right to stand as a candidate in parliamentary elections.

The ECtHR has adopted a very different attitude, however, in recent years when dealing with limitations of electoral rights in illiberal democracies and authoritarian regimes. For example, a strict approach was followed in *Söyler v Turkey*[72] where Turkey imposed a general voting ban on all those who committed intentional crimes, and in relation to Russia and its Constitutional Court: the Russian constitutional provisions on prisoners' disenfranchisement have been at the centre of a fierce 'battle' with the Strasbourg Court. This – disputably – led the Russian Constitutional Court, in 2016, to consider the ECtHR judgment in *Anchugov and Gadkov v Russia*, where the country was found to have violated the ECHR, as unenforceable.[73] That the ECtHR uses different scrutiny methods depending on whether the measures under review emanate or not from a consolidated democracy has been clearly shown by empirical studies[74] and has been criticised for the risk the strategy may entail for the Court's overall authority.[75]

Another important strand of case-law of the ECtHR on elections and Article 3, Protocol no 1, deals with verification of the MPs' credentials once elected and electoral disputes. Both aspects ultimately refer to the right to fulfil the electoral mandate derived from the right to stand as a candidate in the elections and here often Article 3, Protocol no 1, is invoked by the parties and considered by the Court together with other provisions, in particular Article 13 ECHR, on effective remedies. As regards the verification of credentials, in *Grosaru v Romania* the applicant claimed that Article 13 ECHR had been violated in conjunction with Article 3, Protocol no 1, as he had no effective and impartial remedies against the refusal to allocate a seat in Parliament to him as a representative of the Italian minority in Romania.[76] According to the majority of the Court, the Romanian electoral legislation violated the standards invoked as no court could intervene in the proceedings, so there was no effective system of appeal. By the same token, in *Mugemangango v Belgium*,[77] where the complaint called for the recount of ballot papers where the candidate was 14 votes short of taking a seat, the Court found a violation of Article 3, Protocol no 1, both alone and in conjunction with Article 13 as the parliamentary body examining the request lacked impartiality insofar as it included members of Parliament whose

[72] ECtHR, *Söyler v Turkey*, Application no 29411/07, 17 September 2013.

[73] See ECtHR, *Anchugov and Gladkov*, Application no 11157/04, 4 July 2013 and the judgment of the Constitutional Court of the Russia Federation, Judgment No 12-П, 19 April 2016. For a more critical assessment of Russia-Council of Europe dynamics, even before 2016, see A Matta and A Mazmanyan, 'Russia: In Quest for a European Identity' in P Popelier, S Lambrecht and K Lemmens (eds), *Criticism of the European Court of Human Rights. Shifting the Convention System: Counter-dynamics at the National and EU Level* (Cambridge, Intersentia, 2017) 481.

[74] Ø Stiansen and E Voeten, 'Backlash and Judicial Restraint: Evidence from the European Court of Human Rights' (2020) 64 *International Studies Quarterly* 770.

[75] Popelier (n 14).

[76] ECtHR, *Grosaru v Romania*, Application no 78039/01, 2 June 2010.

[77] ECtHR, *Mugemangango v Belgium*, Application no 310/15, 10 July 2020.

election could have been called into question. The procedure was deficient in terms of safeguards for the parties and the body involved enjoyed too broad a discretion, without a mandate sufficiently clarified by the law.

In cases dealing with electoral disputes the Court has emphasised the need to ensure procedural safeguards, in particular the impartiality and neutrality of the procedure when the results of the elections are contested and of the body in charge of deciding on the enrolment of candidates on the electoral register and of resolving the dispute.[78] For example, in *Russian Conservative Party of Entrepreneurs and Others*, concerning the allegation that the Central Electoral Commission had acted beyond its jurisdiction and failed to punish any electoral frauds, the first section of the ECtHR held that Russia had violated Article 3, Protocol no 1, read alone and also in conjunction with Article 13 ECHR.[79] The same violations were found in *Petkov and Others* where the electoral authorities in Bulgaria failed to comply with the Supreme Administrative Court's final ruling ordering reinstatement of the three applicants declared ineligible on the list of candidates for the parliamentary elections.[80] Likewise the lack of a pre-defined and detailed procedure to invalidate the results of parliamentary elections was considered in breach of Article 3, Protocol no 1, in *The Georgian Labour Party* case, where the Central Electoral Commission had cancelled the outcome of the elections in two districts without providing sufficient reasons and without offering legal remedies.[81]

The last – very recent – line of case-law on Article 3, Protocol no 1, which deserves attention here relates to parliamentary immunity, in particular to inviolability. The Court has repeatedly asserted that the rights guaranteed by Article 3, Protocol no 1, 'would be merely illusory if elected representatives or their voters could be arbitrarily deprived of them at any moment'.[82] The provision covers both the individual right to stand for election and, once elected, to sit as a member of Parliament: with this proviso, parliamentary inviolability, which is present in most Contracting Parties although with a different degree of protection of the MPs' position, is crucial to this guarantee. Until a few years ago, cases where an MP was deprived of their liberty were predominantly adjudicated on the ground of Article 6 ECHR, the right to fair trial.[83] Regarding Article 3, Protocol no 1, the central issue to be ascertained by the ECtHR is

[78] See, amongst many, ECtHR, *Ofensiva Tinerilor v Romania*, Application no 16732/05, 15 March 2016.

[79] ECtHR, *Russian Conservative Party of Entrepreneurs and Others group v Russia*, Applications nos 55066/00 and 55638/00, 11 January 2007.

[80] ECtHR, *Petkov and others v Bulgaria*, Applications nos 77568/01, 178/02 and 505/02, 11 June 2009.

[81] ECtHR, *The Georgian Labour Party v Georgia*, Application no 9103/04, 8 October 2008.

[82] ECtHR, *Lykourezos v Greece*, Application no 33554/03, 15 June 2006, para 56.

[83] See, eg, ECtHR, *Tsalkitzis v Greece*, Application no 11801/04, 16 November 2006; *Kart v Turkey*, Application no 8917/05, 8 July 2008, *Syngelidis v Greece*, Application no 24895/07, 11 February 2011,.

whether the effects of the pre-trial detention of a candidate in parliamentary elections or of an elected member of Parliament essentially impair the possibility for the member to perform their parliamentary duties. The article does not prevent the imposition of measures depriving elected representatives of their liberty as such, but especially domestic courts have to weigh up the public interest pursued through the restrictive measures against the right of the person subject to custody and explore whether less restrictive means could have been used. Moreover, the ECtHR attaches considerable importance in this balancing exercise to whether the criminal charges against the MPs have a political basis.[84] In *Selahattin Demirtaş*, the Grand Chamber found multiple violations of the Convention, namely of Article 5, paragraphs 1 and 3, Article 10, on the freedom of expression, and, notably of Article 18 in combination with Article 5 ECHR.[85] Interestingly it also considered Article 3, Protocol no 1, violated where, by virtue of a constitutional amendment, passed in 2016 in Turkey with retroactive effects, Selahattin Demirtaş was stripped of his parliamentary immunity. A member of the Turkish National Assembly from 2007 to 2018, he was a prominent political figure in the country, the leader of a left-wing pro-Kurdish political party, the main opposition party in Parliament at that time, and a former candidate in the presidential elections. Charged with being a member of an armed terrorist organisation and of public incitement to commit an offence, he had been placed in pre-trial detention since 2016. The Court held that the prolonged pre-trial detention was unreasonable, disproportionate and a consequence of political charges. Although the claimant was formally able to keep the status of MP, 'it was effectively impossible for him to take part in the activities of the National Assembly on account of his pre-trial detention', which thereby 'constitutes an unjustified interference with the free expression of the opinion of the people and with his own right to be elected and to sit in Parliament'.[86]

V. CONCLUSION. A PROCEDURAL UNDERSTANDING OF DEMOCRACY AND THE CHALLENGE OF BACKSLIDING FROM THE RULE OF LAW

The analysis of the case-law of the CJEU and the ECtHR on electoral rights has revealed few important differences, but also remarkable similarities, especially as regards the conception of democracy that seems indirectly to flow from the respective case-law. As a result of the nature of the European integration process, its original mission, and the division of competences between the EU and the Member States on electoral matters, the European Court of Justice has ruled

[84] ECtHR, *Uspaskich v Lithuania* (n 62) para 94.
[85] ECtHR, *Selahattin Demirtaş v Turkey* (No 2), Application no 14305/17, 22 December 2020.
[86] ibid para 397.

on a very limited number of electoral cases, mainly dealing with the verification of credentials of MEPs, voting rights as citizens' rights, and immunities for incumbent MEPs, where it has typically exhibited quite a deferential approach to national authorities.

For the ECtHR, as a human rights court, electoral cases have been routinely addressed under Article 3, Protocol no 1, but they constitute only a marginal part of its rich case-law. The attitude of the Court to elections has been described as 'erratic',[87] being at times extremely cautious vis-à-vis domestic law, yet on other occasions quite intrusive into national constitutional systems. It can be argued that the level of scrutiny has also been informed by the quality of the democratic regime, with a few exceptions such as *Hirst*,[88] being softer towards consolidated democracies but much stricter on illiberal or authoritarian regimes.

Neither of these supranational courts provide for an explicit conceptualisation of democracy from the case-law which uses the Treaties' clauses on electoral rights as the standard for review. They both acknowledge that elections are 'the foundations of an effective and meaningful democracy governed by the rule of law'[89] and that they contribute to the quality of the political debate.[90] After the CJEU's decision in *Delvigne*,[91] the President of the Court stressed the importance of the political dimension of citizenship with its bundle of electoral rights for representative democracy in the EU,[92] but without offering further details of the vision of democracy he endorsed.

The two Courts have also come to address similar electoral cases – rarely citing each other – for example, on the requirement for residence and citizenship in order to be able to vote and stand as a candidate in elections, prisoners' disenfranchisement, verification of credentials, and inviolability. Moreover, they have also insisted on similar conditions to justify the limitation of electoral rights, notably the protection of the ultimate essence and effectiveness of the right, the pursuit of a legitimate aim, the lack of less restrictive means and the presence of effective remedies.

In their case-law on electoral rights both Courts have stressed the importance of providing voters and candidates with equal opportunities to participate in the electoral competition, precluding discriminatory measures lacking sound justifications, on the predictability and stability of the electoral rules and on the substantive ability to perform the electoral mandate so as to represent the voters' will (compared with the purely nominal attribution of the MPs' status). In the case of the ECtHR, which has now ruled extensively

[87] Pildes (n 3) 157 and 179.

[88] ECtHR, *Hirst v United Kingdom* (No 2) (n 66).

[89] See, recently, ECtHR, *Mugemangango v Belgium* (n 77) para 67, and *Selahattin Demirtaş v Turkey* (No 2) (n 85) para 382.

[90] ECtHR, *Mathieu-Mohin and Clerfayt v Belgium* (n 10) para 47.

[91] CJEU, *Delvigne* (n 43).

[92] Lenaerts (n 43).

on the legal guarantees provided in electoral disputes, starting from effective legal remedies, considerable attention has been paid also to the fairness of the electoral procedures, the inclusion of minorities, the impartiality of the body which reviews the compilation of the lists of voters and candidates as well as the electoral results and the lack of conflicts of interests.[93]

All this seems to point to the protection of a procedural vision of democracy, as described by Saffon and Urbinati drawing on Kelsen and Bobbio:[94] such a vision, 'based on every individual's equal participation in fair and competitive elections for selecting political representatives and thereby contributing to the production of decisions via majority rule – is the best way of respecting equal liberty in a context of pluralism and dissent'.[95] This understanding of democracy, inferred indirectly from the jurisprudence of the CJEU and the ECtHR, departs from a minimalist conception of democracy that focuses mainly on the dimension of competition to select political leaders[96] as well as from an epistemic view on democracy as a truth-seeking process[97] or, further, from a substantive vision of democracy considering democratic procedures, including elections, as targeting specific political ends (as it is with mobilisation for populists).[98] The reading of democracy that seems endorsed by the two Courts values particular procedural safeguards before, during and after the electoral process as tools for ensuring that the representatives' deliberations are informed by wide participation and pluralism of opinions.

In the final analysis, whilst no clear inferences can be drawn on this point from the CJEU rulings on election-related matters, this interpretation is in line with the ECtHR jurisprudence on Articles 10 and 11 ECHR, on freedom of expression and freedom of assembly. Unlike Article 3, Protocol no 1, the fact that the wording of the two articles contains a clear reference to limitations of those rights justified in a 'democratic society' has prompted the ECtHR to elaborate on the meaning of this expression. On these provisions, the Court has devised an interpretative threshold to ascertain when the preservation of a 'democratic society' is ensured, pointing to the 'tolerance, pluralism and broadmindedness' of the deliberation.[99] As has been shown,[100] these standards have been regularly

[93] But see also on this point CJEU, *Parti écologiste 'Les Verts' v European Parliament* (n 38).

[94] See, respectively, H Kelsen [1920], *The Essence and Value of Democracy* in N Urbinati and C Invernizzi Accetti (eds), trans B Graf (London, Rowman & Littlefield, 2013) and N Bobbio, *Liberalism and Democracy*, trans M Ryle and K Soper (London, Verso, 2005).

[95] MP Saffon and N Urbinati, 'Procedural Democracy, the Bulwark of Equal Liberty' (2013) 41 *Political Theory* 441, 442.

[96] JA Schumpeter, *Capitalism, Socialism, and Democracy* (New York, Harper & Brothersplus, 1942).

[97] See, eg, D Estlund, *Democratic Authority: A Philosophical Framework* (Princeton NJ, Princeton University Press, 2008).

[98] E Laclau, *On Populist Reason* (London, Verso, 2005) Part II.

[99] Since ECtHR, *Handyside v United Kingdom*, Application no 5493/72, 7 December 1976, para 50. See Zysset (n 34) 994.

[100] Pildes (n 3) 154, 162 ff.

used by the Strasbourg Court when applying Article 10 ECHR in the context of political procedures and the status of MPs, for example on campaign finance[101] and on non-accountability of elected representatives.[102] Despite the textual constraints – which the Court has pragmatically bypassed since 1987 – in future the standards of a 'democratic society' could be more explicitly referred to in the case-law on Article 3, Protocol no 1, also by taking into account, on the one hand, the increasing recourse to this article, also as a stand-alone clause, for reviewing national measures interfering with political processes[103] and, on the other, the steady decline in the quality of democratic procedures in several Contracting Parties. There are hints of such a potential development, which could ultimately benefit the predictability of the ECtHR (erratic) case-law, especially if it were to be used consistently across the Contracting Parties. For instance, in *Selahattin Demirtaş v Turkey* (No 2), the Court drew on the 'interdependence' between Article 10 ECHR and Article 3, Protocol no 1, to state that, in view of the importance attached to the freedom of expression of MPs, particularly from the opposition, 'the requirements of pluralism, tolerance and broadmindedness' can render the pre-trial detention of a member of Parliament incompatible with Article 3, Protocol no 1, besides violating Article 10.[104]

Although it lacks a comparable reference to the requirements of a 'democratic society' with regard to electoral rights both in the Treaties and in the CJEU jurisprudence, the EU may also be increasingly confronted in the future with the alteration of the electoral competition by countries backsliding from the rule of law; it therefore may need an elaborated and explicit standard to use as a yardstick when considering the principle of democracy in the light of Articles 2 and 10 TEU. Indeed, this may be triggered by the initiation of infringement proceedings against Poland, also on the ground of a violation of the democratic principle, on account of the approval, on 14 April 2023, of the so-called *Lex Tusk* as it appears to target the leader of the main opposition party in the country and to be likely to affect the election campaign and the outcome of the 2023 parliamentary elections.[105]

[101] ECtHR, *Bowman v UK*, Application no 24839/94, 19 February 1998.

[102] ECtHR, *Karácsony and Others v Hungary*, Application nos 42461/13 and 44357/13, 17 May 2016.

[103] See, eg, *Political Party 'Patria' and Others v Moldova*, 5113/15, 14963/15, 15910/15 et al., 4 August 2020, dealing with the arbitrary disqualification of a political party three days before the parliamentary elections due to alleged financial irregularities and undisclosed use of foreign funds. This was reviewed by the ECtHR under Art 3, Protocol no 1, which it held to have been violated.

[104] ECtHR, *Selahattin Demirtaş v Turkey* (No 2) (n 85) para 392.

[105] N Vissers, 'Enforcing Democracy. How the European Commission is Testing out the Legal Waters' *Verfassungsblog*, 13 June 2023 and G Piccirilli, 'Una nuova procedura di infrazione nei confronti della Polonia: la problematica vicenda della c.d. 'Lex Tusk'' (2023) 3 *Quaderni costituzionali*, forthcoming.

Part III

Beyond Europe

10

Judicial Review and Presidential Elections in Africa

BERIHUN ADUGNA GEBEYE

I. INTRODUCTION

DURING THE 1876 American presidential election, the Democrat Samuel Tilden and the Republican Rutherford B Hayes both claimed victory to the highest executive office in the land. The Democratic-controlled House of Representatives and the Republican-controlled Senate established an Electoral Commission composed of some members of each house and Supreme Court Justices to resolve the presidential election dispute. The 15-member Electoral Commission finally decided in favour of Hayes by an eight-to-seven vote and made him President. In the 2000 presidential election dispute between George W Bush and Al Gore, however, the Supreme Court alone decided who should be the President of the US in a five-to-four vote. One key difference between these two presidential election disputes is the increasing role of the Supreme Court in American democracy and the attendant expansion of its judicial power.[1] But the expansion of judicial power is a global phenomenon and part of what Ran Hirschl characterises as 'new constitutionalism' based on juristocracy.[2] Courts around the world today decide on fundamental moral, political, and policy matters that could define and divide polities, including on elections such as *Bush v Gore*.[3] With the reintroduction of democratic constitutions in the 1990s, courts in Africa, some more than others, have been playing an important role as legal and constitutional arbiters, ranging from judging the

[1] See WH Rehnquist, *Centennial Crisis: The Disputed Election of 1876* (New York, Vintage, 2005).

[2] R Hirschl, *Towards Juristocracy: The Origins and Consequences of the New Constitutionalism* (Cambridge, MA, Harvard University Press, 2007).

[3] See R Hirschl, 'The Judicialization of Mega-Politics and the Rise of Political Courts' (2008) 11 *Annual Review of Political Science* 93, 100; AJ Jacobson and M Rosenfeld (eds), *The Longest Night: Polemics and Perspectives on Election 2000* (Berkeley, University of California Press, 2002).

constitutionality of constitutional amendments[4] to adjudicating presidential election disputes.

In 2017, the Supreme Court of Kenya nullified the presidential election result in which the incumbent President Uhuru Kenyatta was declared the winner of the presidential race. In 2020, the Supreme Court of Malawi also affirmed the nullification of a disputed presidential election decided by the High Court. While these are cases where the courts nullified a presidential election outcome, there are also several examples in which they affirmed a contested result, such as, for example, in Ghana, Namibia, Zambia, and Zimbabwe, to mention but a few.[5] There are also several presidential election petitions that courts have struck down before considering the merits on procedural grounds. Presidential elections are usually challenged in Africa, and today, more than ever, there is a greater likelihood that courts will decide on these contested elections. This means that presidential elections may require the contesting parties to undertake not only election campaigns and promises to obtain the votes of their citizens, but also to prepare a legal argument to convince courts that they won the election in a free, fair, and democratic process or that they lost the election because of some election-related illegalities or irregularities. In election periods, courts then may have to be ready to solve any possible election disputes, not least because these require a timely resolution. For better or worse, there is an increasing trend toward the judicialisation of presidential elections on the continent.

While the jurisprudence on presidential election disputes in Africa is still developing, courts have used two major doctrines for adjudicating such disputes thus far. The first, which is applied in many jurisdictions, is the 'substantive impact doctrine', adopted by courts such as the Supreme Courts of Ghana, Zimbabwe, and Namibia, where a disputed presidential election result would be annulled only if the violations of electoral laws and regulations would substantively affect the electoral process and the electoral result. The second, which is new to the continent, is what I called the 'process-outcome doctrine', adopted by the Supreme Courts of Kenya and Malawi, where a disputed presidential election result would be annulled either because the violations of electoral laws and regulations have negatively impacted the integrity of the electoral process, or they have affected the result of the election. This chapter explores how courts resolve presidential election disputes using the substantive impact and the process-outcome doctrines and suggests why a more dynamic judicial doctrine may be necessary for the institutional security and legitimacy of the judiciary, as well as the maintenance of the general political and institutional stability necessary for sustainable democracy. But first, the chapter discusses the reasons,

[4] See *David Ndii and Others v Attorney General and Others*, Petition No E282 of 2020 (High Court of Kenya).

[5] See OB Kaaba and CM Fombad, 'Adjudication of Disputed Presidential Elections in Africa' in CM Fombad and N Steytler (eds), *Democracy, Elections, and Constitutionalism in Africa* (Oxford, Oxford University Press, 2021) 361–99.

drivers, and dynamics behind the judicialisation of presidential election disputes in Africa.

II. THE JUDICIALISATION OF PRESIDENTIAL ELECTIONS

The end of political pluralism and the institutionalisation of one-party systems in the two- or three-decades following independence made military coups the major mechanisms of transfer of power in Africa. While the opening of the political space for multi-party competition with the third wave of democratisation in the 1990s enabled the peaceful transfer of power in many African countries, elections in several other countries did not bring about a transfer of power.[6] Although many constitutions have term limit provisions, several African leaders have managed to change or evade them through 'constitutional coups', ie, via amendments approved by Parliament or the judiciary or in national referenda, to remain in power.[7] The military has even returned to politics in a number of countries.[8] Thus, the judicialisation of presidential elections is one of the emerging trends in electoral politics in *some* African countries. It will be useful to explain the reasons for the judicialisation of presidential elections in these countries before discussing how courts resolve such election disputes and how this may, in turn, impact democratic consolidation in these countries in the long term.

There is no one single explanation for the judicialisation of presidential elections in Africa. But we can at least identify three major factors that have led to this phenomenon: those related to the empowerment of courts to adjudicate election disputes, the motivations of petitioners, and the broader socio-political context. As judicial review and the rights revolution have provided the institutional framework for courts to proactively protect these rights by checking legislative and executive (in)action,[9] the constitutional empowerment of courts as final arbiters of election disputes has enabled them to check whether presidents are elected in a free, fair, and democratic process. The adjudication of electoral disputes, be it parliamentary or presidential, is one of the main tasks of constitutional review institutions in many African countries.[10] Additionally, many African constitutions have introduced formal mechanisms to ensure the

[6] T Lodge, 'Alternation and Leadership Succession in African Democracies' (2013) 24 *Irish Studies in International Affairs* 21–40.

[7] See F Reyntjens, 'Respecting and Circumventing Presidential Term Limits in Sub-Saharan Africa: A Comparative Survey' (2020) 119 *African Affairs* 275.

[8] For instance, in Niger (2010), the Central African Republic (2013), Egypt (2013), Mali (2012 and 2020), Guinea Bissau (2012), Burkina Faso (2015), Zimbabwe (2017), Sudan (2019 and 2021), and Guinea (2021).

[9] R Hirschl, 'The Judicialization of Politics' in RE Goodin (ed), *The Oxford Handbook of Political Science* (Oxford, Oxford University Press, 2011) 264.

[10] B Kante and HK Prempeh, 'Other Competencies of Constitutional Review Institutions', in M Böckenförde et al., *Judicial Review Systems in West Africa: A Comparative Analysis* (International IDEA, 2016) 101–05.

personal and institutional independence of the judiciary, at least in terms of constitutional design.[11] Nonetheless, the practical independence of the judiciary is neither an essential element (although very useful) for the judicialisation of presidential elections, nor is such judicialisation a marker of democratic consolidation. But the existence of formal judicial review power over elections and the conduct of periodic elections are necessary conditions for the judicialisation of presidential elections in Africa.[12] In other words, formal constitutional institutions and rules impact and structure electoral politics. For example, it is very unlikely to see presidential election petitions in Tanzania, because their Constitution prohibits the court from hearing such petitions, or in Eritrea, because there have been no presidential elections there to begin with since the country was founded in 1993.[13] However, despite the executive dominance over the judiciary,[14] every presidential election in Nigeria since 1999, except for the one in 2015, has been contested in court and the petitions dismissed each time. Similarly, every presidential election in Kenya since the adoption of the 2010 Constitution has been contested in court and the results either affirmed or nullified by it, and the emergence of an independent judiciary is an important factor in this judicialisation.[15]

The existence of judicial review power over presidential elections requires one or more motivated petitioner(s) to activate the judicialisation process. While courts in many African countries are not simply a rubber stamp for the executive or total bystanders in national political affairs, we also know that judicial independence and public confidence in African judiciaries are not strong, at least not yet. This means that petitioners may have different motivations in choosing the judicial route to resolve presidential election disputes and we could identify three main motivations here. First, like any other litigation,[16] presidential election contenders and/or their political parties may think that they have a reasonably winnable case before a court of law. They may believe that the conduct of the presidential election violated constitutional and electoral laws and regulations and that they have evidence to prove the allegedly committed illegalities and irregularities.[17] If they could present a strong legal case and supporting evidence, they may think that the court has no option but to nullify

[11] HK Prempeh, 'Marbury in Africa: Judicial Review and the Challenge of Constitutionalism in Contemporary Africa' (2006) 80 *Tulane Law Review* 57–58.

[12] On the purpose of periodic elections, see N Cheeseman, G Lynch and J Willis, *The Moral Economy of Elections in Africa: Democracy, Voting and Virtue* (Cambridge, Cambridge University Press, 2021).

[13] Art 41(7) of the Constitution of the United Republic of Tanzania.

[14] BA Gebeye, *A Theory of African Constitutionalism* (Oxford, Oxford University Press, 2021) 158–63.

[15] See K Kanyinga and C Odote, 'Judicialisation of Politics and Kenya's 2017 Elections' (2019) 13 *Journal of Eastern African Studies* 235.

[16] See E Spier, 'Litigation' in AM Polinsky and S Shavell (eds), *Handbook of Law and Economics*, Vol 1 (Amsterdam, Elsevier, 2007).

[17] See also LA Nkansah, 'Dispute Resolution and Electoral Justice in Africa: The Way Forward' (2016) 41 *Africa Development / Afrique et Développement* 97, 121–22.

the election result. But they will never know this without filing a petition to the court. In two such instances, the court decided in favour of the petitioners: in Kenya in 2017 and in Malawi in 2020.

Second, although petitioners may not have a reasonable expectation of winning the case, either because of reasons related to the independence of the judiciary or issues related to the strength of their legal argument and their supporting evidence, they may still go to court with the objective of exposing the illegalities and irregularities in the conduct of the presidential elections.[18] By doing so they could maintain the momentum of their political base, expose the unfairness of the election to the public, and alert and mobilise civil society, the media, and international development partners about the state of presidential elections in their respective countries, which could create better conditions for the next election.[19] Even when the courts declined to invalidate the disputed presidential election results, as happened, for example, in Ghana (2012), Kenya (2013), and Namibia (2020), they found a number of illegalities and irregularities in the conduct of the elections that could cast some doubt on the fairness and legality of the elections, which, in turn, could impact the legitimacy and credibility of the electoral winner. Additionally, these decisions have led either to electoral reform, as in Ghana, the undertaking of some prospective corrective measures, as in Namibia, or a change of judicial doctrine, as in Kenya.[20] Moreover, some of the petitioners eventually became presidents in the following elections, such as Nana Akufo-Addo of Ghana and Muhammadu Buhari of Nigeria. Hence, regardless of the judicial outcome, presidential election petitions play an important role in the electoral politics of different states.

Third, and finally, petitioners, especially in countries which have undertaken new constitutional or judicial reforms, such as Kenya,[21] may want to test if the judiciary can perform its constitutionally allocated duties and if it could play some role in important national political and policy matters.[22] As courts are strategic actors, which want to maintain and enhance their constitutional role and their national political significance and international reputation, they may consider presidential election petitions as important sites of dialogue, which could further encourage similar petitions in the future.[23]

[18] See also ibid.

[19] See JT Gathii, 'Implementing a New Constitution in a Competitive Authoritarian Context: The Case of Kenya' in T Ginsburg and AZ Huq (eds), *From Parchment to Practice: Implementing New Constitutions* (Cambridge, Cambridge University Press, 2020) 230; Y Dotan and M Hofnung, 'Legal Defeats – Political Wins: Why Do Elected Representatives Go to Court?' (2005) 38 *Comparative Political Studies* 75.

[20] See RE Van Gyampo, 'The State of Electoral Reforms in Ghana' (2017) 52 *Africa Spectrum* 95.

[21] Kanyinga and Odote (n 15) 238–39; Gathii (n 19) 226–27.

[22] See Gathii (n 19) 226–27; T Ginsburg, 'Courts and New Democracies: Recent Works' (2012) 37 *Law & Social Inquiry* 720.

[23] Hirschl (n 9) 266–67; T Ginsburg, *Judicial Review in New Democracies: Constitutional Courts in Asian Cases* (Cambridge, Cambridge University Press, 2003) 73.

The existence of formal judicial review power over elections and the different motivations of the petitioners alone may not set the judicialisation of presidential elections in motion. The judicialisation of politics, as Hirschl observed, requires some enabling socio-political context that is conducive to and supportive of courts as major decision-making bodies.[24] The prevailing socio-political dynamics in each country at a given time could either encourage or discourage presidential contenders to file a petition. The 2017 Kenyan presidential election is an interesting case in this regard. Two days after the voting had ended, international election observation missions had declared that the election was largely free, fair, and credible and that the incumbent President Uhuru Kenyatta had won the election.[25] They urged the main presidential contender Raila Odinga to concede defeat. But when Odinga rejected such calls, these election observation missions, along with other nations, especially the US and the EU, pressured him to seek redress from the Supreme Court rather than resorting to mass protest.[26] There were also similar calls within the country, especially from church, business, and civil society leaders, that Odinga should follow the legal processes to resolve the dispute.[27] After the 2007 post-election violence, which was a raison d'être for the adoption of the 2010 Constitution, Odinga could not easily disregard the legal processes for resolving election disputes and resort to mass protest, which could invite similar or even greater post-election violence. Moreover, the memories of the 2007 post-election brutality remained alive,[28] and could have formed a reminder for the presidential contenders to resort to the Supreme Court, which is the last line of defence against post-election clashes and political instability. On the other hand, Goodluck Jonathan of Nigeria could have challenged the 2015 presidential result (as Buhari did each time he lost a presidential race), but instead he conceded defeat in an unprecedented way in Nigerian political history, partly because the country was in a state of dangerous political and security dynamics and, consequently, may not have sustained further electoral warfare in courts.[29] Thus, the prevailing peace

[24] Hirschl (n 9) 268–70.

[25] D Kahura, 'See No Evil: How International Election Observers Lost Credibility During the August Elections', *The Elephant*, 21 September 2017, www.theelephant.info/features/2017/09/21/see-no-evil-how-international-election-observers-lost-credibility-during-the-august-elections/ (accessed 2 March 2022).

[26] S Owino and H Misiko, 'NASA Gives into Pressure over Election Petition Case', *Daily Nation*, 18 August 2017, nation.africa/kenya/news/nasa-gives-in-to-pressure-over-election-petition-case-439424?view=htmlamp (accessed 2 March 2022).

[27] T Gathii (n 19) 228–29.

[28] D Branch, 'The Fire Next Time: Why Memories of the 2007-8 Post-Election Violence Still Remain Alive', *The Elephant*, 29 July 2017, www.theelephant.info/features/2017/07/29/the-fire-next-time-why-memories-of-the-2007-8-post-election-violence-still-remain-alive/ (accessed 2 March 2022).

[29] K Busari, 'Why I Conceded Defeat to Buhari in 2015 – Jonathan', *Premium Times*, 27 October 2017, www.premiumtimesng.com/news/top-news/247451-i-conceded-defeat-buhari-2015-jonathan.html (accessed 2 March 2022); T Cocks and B Felix, 'Nigerian President Warns Against Bloodshed Ahead of Saturday's Vote', *Thomson Reuters*, 27 March 2015, www.reuters.com/article/us-nigeria-election-idUSKBN0MN19620150327 (accessed 2 March 2022).

and security situation, public opinion, and international pressure could affect a presidential contenders' decision on whether or not to take the judicial route to resolve a disputed election result.

In sum, formal judicial empowerment, motivated petitioners, and the broader socio-political dynamics trigger, facilitate, and structure the judicialisation of presidential elections. Now we turn to exploring how courts apply the substantive impact and process-outcome doctrines to resolve a disputed presidential election, which, in turn, reveals their views on democracy.

III. JUDICIAL DOCTRINES FOR ADJUDICATING PRESIDENTIAL ELECTION DISPUTES

A. The Substantive Impact Doctrine

In outlining the principles for annulling election results, the Supreme Court of Ghana noted that '[f]or starters I would state that the Judiciary in Ghana, like its counterparts in other jurisdictions, does not readily invalidate a public election but often strives in the public interest, to sustain it'.[30] Similarly, the Constitutional Court of Zimbabwe observed that '[i]t is not for a court to decide elections; it is the people who do so. It is the duty of the courts to strive in the public interest to sustain that which the people have expressed as their will'.[31] Similar attitudes of the judiciary toward the nullifications of presidential election results are widely shared across the region. In many countries, the court's 'idea of democracy' largely builds on and defends the applicable law of democracy in each jurisdiction with the citation of some comparable foreign case law. In Anglophone Africa in particular, where presidential election disputes are most prevalent, the law regulating election nullification is based on either the received common law or statutory law informed by the principles of the common law. The so-called 'substantive impact doctrine' is the primary legal and jurisprudential tool for many courts to resolve presidential election disputes.

While the substantive impact doctrine may have some peculiar features in different jurisdictions, as we shall see below, its essential element is included in *Halsbury's Laws of England*, as follows:

> No election is to be declared invalid by reason of any act or omission by the returning officer or any other person in breach of his official duty in connection with the election or otherwise of the appropriate elections rules if it appears to the tribunal having cognizance of the question that the election was conducted substantially in

[30] *Nana Addo Dankwa Akufo-Addo & Others v John Dramani Mahama & Others* (Writ J 1/6/2013) [Supreme Court of Ghana] 40.

[31] *Nelson Chamisa v Emmerson Dambudzo Mnangagwa and Others* (CCZ 21/19) 136.

> accordance with the law as to the elections, and that the act or omission did not affect the result.[32]

According to the substantive impact doctrine, an election will be nullified only when the illegalities and/or irregularities in the conduct of the election have a substantive or adverse impact on the election and election result. Their existence alone may not lead to the invalidation of the said elections. Hence, a petitioner challenging a presidential election result must prove, first, the existence of illegalities and/or irregularities in the conduct of elections and, second, that these have affected the election result. At the core of the substantive impact doctrine is the burden of proof expected from the petitioner(s) and the discretionary powers of judges in identifying permissible and impermissible violations of constitutions, electoral laws, rules, and regulations. A brief analysis of some recent presidential petition cases from Ghana, Zimbabwe, and Namibia suffices to show how the substantive impact doctrine is applied in presidential election disputes in Africa.

Since 1992, Ghana has held presidential elections every four years, and has changed the incumbent party three times, which is a pioneering example of the peaceful democratic transfer of power on the continent. The 2012 presidential election result, however, was ultimately affirmed by the Supreme Court applying the substantive impact doctrine. A few days after the conclusion of the presidential election, the Electoral Commission declared John Dramani Mahama, the incumbent President, who had 5,574,761 votes (50.70 per cent), as President of the Republic. But Nana Addo Dankwa Akufo-Addo, the main opposition presidential contender, who received 5,248,898 votes (47.74 per cent), challenged the election result before the Supreme Court, along with his running mate and the chairperson of his party. The main grounds for their petition were over-voting, voting without biometric verification, the absence of the signature of a presiding officer, the duplication of serial numbers on the pink sheets and of polling station codes, and the presence of unknown polling stations.[33] The petitioners asked the court to declare that John Dramani Mahama was not validly elected but instead to declare Nana Addo Dankwa Akufo-Addo as the validly elected President and to make the necessary consequential orders to this effect. In a nutshell, the petitioners argued that: (i) there were violations of electoral laws and regulations in the conduct of the 2012 presidential elections which substantively affected the result of the elections, as well as that; (ii) the voting in 11,916 polling stations was vitiated by gross irregularities and malpractices, and that elections were conducted in some unknown locations that were not part of the 26,002 polling stations prepared for the presidential elections, which fundamentally affected the validity of the results of the elections in those polling stations.

[32] HS Giffard Halsbury and JPH Mackay of Clashfern, *Halsbury's Laws of England*, 4th edn (London, LexisNexis Butterworths, 2007) para 670.

[33] *Nana Addo Dankwa Akufo-Addo & Others v John Dramani Mahama & Others* 3.

They contended that there were 4,670,504 unlawful and irregular votes and if these were annulled, it would be Mr Akufo-Addo, not Mr Mahama, who would satisfy the requirements of the law to be declared as the President of Ghana. The respondents denied all the allegations and claimed that the election was conducted in conformity with the applicable laws and regulations.

As in *Bush v Gore*, *Nana Addo Dankwa Akufo-Addo and Others v John Dramani Mahama and Others* sharply divided the Supreme Court. In a five-to-four vote, the court decided that Mr Mahama was the validly elected President. In reaching this decision, the court focused on the three grounds of the petitioners, namely the allegations of over-voting, voting without biometric verification, and the absence of the signature of a presiding officer, while excluding the other grounds because either it found no merit in considering them or it did not consider them to have any substantial effect on the declared results.[34] After consulting its own case law related to constitutional and statutory interpretation and some foreign election cases, the court adopted the substantive impact doctrine.[35] The majority found that while there were instances of over-voting and voting without biometric verification, these instances did not adversely impact the outcome of the election result. Similarly, the Court held that although the signature of a presiding officer in polling stations is a constitutional requirement and the absence of such a signature amounts to a constitutional violation, this in and of itself cannot invalidate the otherwise sacred votes of citizens. The Court further stated that:

> [T]he underlying purpose of the signatures of the presiding officer and the polling agents on the pink sheets is to provide evidence that the results to which they relate were those generated at the relevant polling station in compliance with the constitutional and other statutory requirements, otherwise each 'signature in itself has no magic about it'.[36]

The absence of such a signature is an administrative error that has been corrected in some collation centres and can still be corrected by the order of this Court.[37] As the petitioners did not question the authenticity of the results which did not bear the presiding officer's signature, the Court observed, invalidating those votes on this technical ground might amount to crushing 'substantive justice'.[38] The majority concluded that the election was conducted in substantial compliance with the electoral laws and regulations and that the results of the election did reflect the will of the Ghanaian people.

The minority, however, found that the illegalities and irregularities in the conduct of the 2012 presidential election were substantial and that these affected

[34] ibid 4.
[35] ibid 40–45.
[36] ibid 18.
[37] ibid 37.
[38] ibid 18.

the results of the election. Many in the minority held the view that the evaluation of the impact of the nullified votes was such that neither Mr Mahama nor Mr Akufo-Addo had obtained the necessary 50 per cent plus one valid vote threshold to be President of the Republic according to Article 63(3) of the Constitution. Justice Anin Yeboah, for his part, stated that:

> [I] would have readily proceeded to grant the reliefs sought in its entirety but the ONLY problem is that from the available evidence, the widespread violations, omissions and malpractices appeared to be of such proportions that it would not be proper for me to declare the first petitioner as winner of the elections in controversy in terms of the reliefs sought. I find the malpractices, omissions and violations enormous which rock the very foundation of free and fair elections as enshrined in our constitution which was itself breached through over-voting, lack of presiding officer's signature and lack of biometric verification which takes its validity from Article 51 of the very constitution.[39]

For different reasons, the minority was convinced that the election was not conducted in substantive compliance with the law and that the election did not produce a winner that could be declared as President-elect according to the Constitution.

In the absence of a clear statutory law on election nullification, as Justice Adinyira also noted,[40] the Court followed the substantive impact doctrine to strike some balance between democracy and the rule of law. Given the burden of proof expected from the petitioners and the discretionary power of the judges, as noted above, the substantive impact doctrine often largely defers to electoral management bodies on issues related to the conduct of elections. But even if one accepts the views of the minority, a rerun of the election may have been the more suitable order under the circumstances. This could have required, as the Court observed from the outset, the consideration of some other legitimate public interests, which are no less fundamental than the rerun of elections, such as public finance and the impact that such a decision may have on the political dynamics of the country.[41] Despite the sharply divided views on the judgment, however, the Court noted that the petition exposed the need for electoral reform and recommended some areas for reform.[42]

Nelson Chamisa v Emmerson Dambudzo Mnangagwa and Others is another case of a presidential petition where the Constitutional Court of Zimbabwe applied the substantive impact doctrine. On 30 July 2018, Zimbabwe held presidential, parliamentary, and local elections. On 3 August 2018, the Electoral Commission declared Emmerson Dambudzo Mnangagwa, the incumbent President, who received more than half of the votes cast, as the duly

[39] ibid 505.

[40] ibid 144.

[41] See also M Azu, 'Lessons from Ghana and Kenya on Why Presidential Election Petitions Usually Fail' (2015) 15 *African Human Rights Law Journal* 150, 165.

[42] *Nana Addo Dankwa Akufo-Addo & Others v John Dramani Mahama & Others* 48.

elected President of the Republic. Nelson Chamisa, the opposition candidate, challenged the validity of the election results before the Constitutional Court on more than 18 grounds, which ultimately revolved around two main arguments: (i) that the election was not free, fair, and credible; and (ii) that there were illegalities, irregularities, or malpractices in the conduct of the elections.[43] The petitioner asked the court to declare that the 2018 presidential election was neither conducted in accordance with the law nor was it free and fair, and to declare him as the duly elected President instead of Emmerson Dambudzo Mnangagwa. Unlike the case in Ghana, the Court unanimously dismissed the petition on evidentiary grounds.

The Court asked the petitioner to prove: (i) the alleged illegalities and irregularities in the conduct of the election; and (ii) whether these had affected the result of the election. These two tests, which constitute the substantive impact doctrine, unlike Ghana, are found in section 177 of the Electoral Act, which reads:[44]

> An election shall be set aside by the Court by reason of any mistake or non-compliance with the provisions of this Act if, and only if, it appears to the Court that, (a) the election was not conducted in accordance with the principles laid down in this Act; and (b) such mistake or non-compliance did affect the result of the election.

After considering the evidence before it, the Court decided that the petitioner even failed to prove the first test, that is, the alleged illegalities and irregularities, with 'clear, sufficient, direct and credible evidence' and it found it unnecessary to consider the second test, that is, whether these had affected the result.[45] This passage from the judgment is instructive of how the Court rendered such a decision:

> Without the primary evidence, the applicant did not have proof of the reality of what actually transpired on the day of the vote. He did not have the evidence that is required by the law as cogent evidence for challenging the validity of a Presidential election result …[46] The applicant did not so much rely on the allegation that the Presidential election was not free, fair and credible on the basis of the generalised and unproved allegations he made against the Commission. The essence of the case was that the applicant was the winner of the Presidential election. That is the allegation he failed to prove.[47]

Like the Supreme Court of Ghana, the Constitutional Court of Zimbabwe made references to some foreign election petitions, but ultimately resolved the case relying on the Electoral Act that enshrines the substantive impact doctrine.

[43] *Nelson Chamisa v Emmerson Dambudzo Mnangagwa and Others* 47–48.

[44] See Electoral Act consolidated as at 28 May 2018, available at www.veritaszim.net/node/2424 (accessed 2 March 2022).

[45] *Nelson Chamisa v Emmerson Dambudzo Mnangagwa and Others* 135.

[46] ibid 99.

[47] ibid 135.

Panduleni Filemon Bango Itula and Others v Minister of Urban and Rural Development and Others is the latest case from Namibia where the substantive impact doctrine was applied. Like the previous cases, this case offers an interesting context in the application of the substantive impact doctrine. All the petitioners in this case were candidates in the 2019 presidential election, and they asked the Supreme Court to set aside this election and order a new one without undue delay. The main basis for their petition was constitutional and related to section 97 of the Electoral Act of 2014, which deals with the use of voting machines in elections. The Minister of Urban and Rural Development excluded section 97(3) and (4) from application when this Act was promulgated as law in 2014. Section 97(3) requires the use of a verifiable paper trail along with the voting machines and section 97(4) provides that in a case where the results of the paper trails and the results of the voting machines do not match, the results of the paper trails will be accepted as the election outcome. The petitioners argued that both the selective implementation of section 97 of the Electoral Act by the Minister of Urban and Rural Development and the use of voting machines in the 2019 presidential election without a paper trail by the Electoral Commission were unconstitutional.[48] They also alleged that there were several irregularities related to the voting machines during the election. The respondents argued that the petitioners were unreasonably delayed in challenging the selective implementation of section 97.[49] The 2014 presidential election was conducted under similar circumstances and some of the applicants who participated in that election did not challenge its legality. Additionally, the respondents submitted that the lawfulness of voting machines without a paper trail was already confirmed by the decision of the High Court in *Maletzky & Others v Electoral Commission of Namibia & Others* 2015 (2) NR 571 (HC) and that this remained the law on this matter as there had been no challenge to this decision.[50] They also denied the allegation of irregularities related to the voting machines.

Although the Supreme Court concluded that the selective implementation of section 97 by the Minister of Urban and Rural Development was unconstitutional, it found the Electoral Commission's decision to conduct the election without the paper trails acceptable, and, consequently, declined to invalidate the presidential election. In selectively implementing section 97, the Court noted that the Minister not only exercised a power that belongs to the legislature, but also undermined the whole purpose of voting machines as additional, not sole, safeguards for conducting free and fair elections. If the Minister's decision was unconstitutional, the Court asked whether this determination could lead to the invalidation of the presidential election. Here the Court applied the

[48] *Panduleni Filemon Bango Itula and Others v Minister of Urban and Rural Development and Others* (A 1/2019) [Supreme Court of Namibia] 4.
[49] ibid 5.
[50] ibid.

'materiality test', ie, the substantive impact doctrine, as included in section 115 of the Electoral Act, which provides:

> No election may be set aside by any competent Court by reason of any mistake or non-compliance with this Part, if it appears to the Court that the election in question was conducted in accordance with the principles laid down therein and that the mistake or noncompliance did not affect the result of the election.

The issue became whether the conduct of the election without paper trails, which is unconstitutional, had adversely impacted the election and its outcome. The Court found that it had no adverse impact as '[t]he applicants have not shown that the absence of a verifiable paper trail has adversely affected their fundamental right to vote particularly with reference to irregular use of voting machines or their unreliability'.[51] The Court held that the Electoral Commission not only conducted the election in accordance with the applicable law at the time, but also executed its duty without any wrongdoing.

However, unlike the courts in Ghana and Zimbabwe, the Supreme Court of Namibia has gone beyond the substantive impact doctrine in exercising its discretionary power: it put the actions and conducts of the petitioners before the election on trial to test their commitment to and responsibility for participating in democratic elections. If the absence of a paper trail is an important and fundamental issue for the applicants, the Court observed, they should have challenged it before and after the 2015 and 2016 elections, or even much ahead of the 2019 elections. The applicants filed their petition on the eve of the election, only a month before the elections. By doing so, the Court alluded to the fact that the applicants failed to perform their duty to act in a timely manner, which would have created an opportunity to remedy any potential violations of law in the conduct of the elections.[52] The Court noted in particular that '[t]he first applicant, whilst pursuing the remedies provided for in the Act, could also have done so far more expeditiously after becoming aware of the lack of a paper trail and not have waited more than three weeks before launching his application to the Tribunal, given the far reaching relief sought by him – of interdicting the elections'.[53] Essentially, the court as a referee expected all presidential contenders to play a 'fair game', but the applicants did not play this game fairly. The Supreme Court added these 'fair play' criteria in its application of the substantive impact doctrine when it affirmed the election result and ordered a prospective relief about the use of paper trails along with voting machines in future elections.

Although there could be some reasonable disagreements about how each of these three cases are decided, the courts relied on their respective electoral laws or the received common law to affirm their respective disputed presidential

[51] ibid 40.
[52] ibid at 44–45.
[53] ibid 45–46.

election results. We could make three general conclusions from these cases. First, the fact that all parties accepted these court decisions means that there is some sort of commitment to the rule of law in each of these countries, which we should not take for granted. On a continent where political actors use violence or the threat of such to solve a political problem or to achieve a political objective, the rejection of these brutal means and the acceptance of court decisions by the opposition presidential candidates are reasons for celebration. Moreover, this also shows that courts play an important role in resolving election disputes. Second, while there is a long-established bias in Africa that courts decide in favour of incumbents, these cases reveal that we must also pay serious attention to the claims of the opposition as well. For example, while the opposition candidates in Ghana and Zimbabwe claimed that the elections were marred by serious illegalities and irregularities, they still wanted their respective courts to declare them the winners of such elections. In a similar vein, while the opposition candidates in Namibia had ample time, even years, to challenge the selective implementation of section 97, they approached the Court at the last minute. Like the incumbents, the opposition may also want to win by all available means. Hence, decisions on the affirmation of election results may not be necessarily biased, and we must give them the recognition and attention they deserve. Third, and finally, as noted in the last section, beyond a mechanical application of the substantive impact doctrine, courts may have to adopt a more dynamic doctrine that maintains their institutional security and legitimacy and positions them to play a key role in the democratic experimentation of their respective countries. This is because the mechanical application of the substantive impact doctrine not only normalises electoral illegalities and irregularities, which could hinder the potential of progressive and incremental democratic consolidation, but it also undermines the legitimacy and the credibility of the judiciary for it to be considered as another arm of the incumbent.[54]

B. The Process-Outcome Doctrine

While the substantive impact doctrine is the dominant one, there is a new and emerging doctrine for resolving presidential election disputes in Africa. As this doctrine takes electoral processes and electoral outcomes on their own seriously, it could be called a 'process-outcome doctrine'. According to the process-outcome doctrine, a presidential election could be invalidated if the illegalities or irregularities in the said elections undermined the integrity of the electoral process or affected the electoral result. The judicial philosophy that animates the process-outcome doctrine is that democracy is not only about results but is also about the processes through which such results are gained.

[54] See also Kaaba and Fombad (n 5) 375–80.

In this doctrine, electoral processes are as fundamental as electoral outcomes and a presidential election could be nullified on violations related to electoral processes alone. Hence, a court that applies a process-outcome doctrine acts as 'a guarantor of democracy', thereby being willing to intervene to defend its version of democracy, more than a court that applies the substantive impact doctrine. Accordingly, although the burden of proof remains with the petitioner and a presidential election could not be invalidated for minor infractions, as in the substantive impact doctrine, the petitioner here does not have to prove that the illegalities or irregularities have affected both the process and the result of the election: proving either of these would suffice to invalidate the election. Thus, a court that applies the process-outcome doctrine is more likely to nullify a presidential election than a court that applies the substantive impact doctrine. As this doctrine was invented by the Supreme Court of Kenya and followed by the courts in Malawi, we will examine how these courts develop and apply this doctrine in their respective presidential petition cases.

So far, every presidential election in Kenya after the adoption of the new Constitution in 2010 has been litigated at the Supreme Court. Although the parties and the facts in the 2013 and 2017 presidential petitions are strikingly similar, the Supreme Court adopted a different judicial outlook and doctrine.[55] In 2013, the Supreme Court viewed its role primarily as an 'oversight body'[56] where judicial restraint is a virtue in Kenya's new democratic experimentation and, consequently, deployed some interpretative tools that could sustain rather than disturb the outcome of the election. But in 2017, the Court considered its role as 'a guarantor of democracy' where judicial intervention is necessary to realize the constitutional vision of democracy. For this, the Court developed the process-outcome doctrine to test whether the 2017 presidential election was conducted in accordance with the Constitution and all other electoral laws and regulations.

On 8 August 2017, Kenya held its second presidential election under its new 2010 Constitution. On 11 August 2017, the Independent Electoral and Boundaries Commission (IEBC) declared Uhuru Kenyatta the winner of the election. However, Raila Odinga and his running mate rejected the IEBC's declaration and filed a petition before the Supreme Court. They challenged the declared result on several grounds, which revolved around two main allegations: the election was not held in accordance with the principles laid down in the Constitution and electoral laws, and there were several illegalities and irregularities in the conduct of the election. The petitioners, among others, alleged that the IEBC failed to conduct the election in a 'simple, accurate,

[55] On why it changed its views, see R Stacey and V Miyandazi, 'Constituting and Regulating Democracy: Kenya's Electoral Commission and the Courts in the 2010s' [2021] *Asian Journal of Comparative Law* 1.

[56] *Raila Odinga and Others v Independent Electoral and Boundaries Commission of Kenya and Others* [2013] eKLR, Petition 5 of 2013, para 310.

transparent, verifiable, secure and accountable' manner, as provided in the Constitution and the Elections Act, and that the IEBC failed to promptly verify and simultaneously electronically transmit the results from polling stations to the Constituency Tallying Centers and National Tallying Center as required by the Elections Act.[57] Because the IEBC disregarded the Constitution and the Elections Act by making itself 'a law and institution unto itself' in the conduct of the election, the petitioners argued, the result did not reflect the will of the people and should be nullified.[58] The respondents, however, claimed that the election result did reflect the will of the majority and even if there were some irregularities, these did not affect the result of the election enough to warrant nullification. In an unprecedented judgment on the continent, the Court in a four-to-two vote nullified the declared result of the 2017 presidential election and ordered a rerun election.

To arrive at this judgment, the Supreme Court, unlike its counterparts in Ghana, Zimbabwe, and Namibia, started its analysis by noting that elections are not only about numbers, but also about processes. In its own words, '[e]ven in numbers, we used to be told in school that to arrive at a mathematical solution, there is always a computational path one has to take, as proof that the process indeed gives rise to the stated solution. Elections are not events but processes'.[59] As a result, the Court held that the electoral processes for casting, counting, verifying, and transmitting a vote are as important as the result of the election itself.[60] This is precisely why, the Court noted, the Elections Act established an integrated electronic electoral system that should be 'simple, accurate, verifiable, secure, accountable and transparent', which are 'the selfsame constitutional principles' included in Articles 10, 38, 81 and 86 of the Constitution.[61] After considering the evidence before it, the Court held that the failure of the IEBC to verify the results before its chairperson declared them violated Article 138(3) (c) of the Constitution, and its failure to electronically and simultaneously transmit the results from all the polling stations to the National Tallying Centre violated section 39 (1C) of the Elections Act.[62] The Court further held that '[t]hese violations of the Constitution and the law call into serious doubt as to whether the said election can be said to have been a free expression of the will of the people as contemplated by Article 38 of the Constitution'.[63] For these reasons, the Court found that the 2017 presidential election was not conducted in accordance with the principles laid down in the

[57] *Raila Odinga & Another v Independent Electoral and Boundaries Commission & Others* [2017] eKLR, Presidential Petition 1 of 2017, para 218.

[58] ibid para 214.

[59] ibid para 224.

[60] ibid para 227.

[61] ibid para 237.

[62] ibid para 292.

[63] ibid para 292.

Constitution and electoral laws. On this basis alone, the Court held, 'we have no choice but to nullify it'.[64]

A court that applies the substantive impact doctrine will not stop with the finding of illegalities and irregularities. As discussed in the previous section, it will examine whether these illegalities and irregularities have affected the election result. However, the Supreme Court of Kenya did not find it necessary to investigate the impact of these violations on the election result. Even when the Court examined the impact of the other illegalities and irregularities on the election result, it stated that:

> [T]he correct approach … is for a court of law, to not only determine whether, the election was characterized by irregularities, but whether, those irregularities were of such a nature, or such a magnitude, as to have either affected the result of the election, or to have so negatively impacted the integrity of the election, that no reasonable tribunal would uphold it.[65]

It held that the quality of the electoral process is as important as the quantity of the electoral outcome.[66] The Court asked 'what if the numbers are themselves a product, not of the expression of the free and sovereign will of the people, but of the many unanswered questions with which we are faced'.[67] It found that the illegalities and irregularities committed by the IEBC 'were of such a substantial nature that no Court properly applying its mind to the evidence and the law as well as the administrative arrangements put in place by IEBC can, in good conscience, declare that they do not matter, and that the will of the people was expressed nonetheless'.[68] Regardless of their impact on the election result, the Court found that the 2017 presidential election did not meet the requirements of the law in that it was neither simple nor accurate and verifiable. The Court therefore declined to validate it and ordered a rerun election.

If the 2017 presidential election did not pass the *Wednesbury* unreasonable test in the sense that 'no Court properly applying its mind to the evidence and the law as well as the administrative arrangements put in place by IEBC can, in good conscience, declare that they do not matter, and that the will of the people was expressed nonetheless', the Supreme Court in the 2022 presidential petition noted that the petitioners did not prove to the required standard whether the alleged illegalities and irregularities affected the presidential election result or the integrity of the electoral process. As in 2017, the Court applied the process-outcome doctrine in adjudicating the 2022 presidential petition but reaffirmed the electoral result.[69] The decisive factor in the resolution of the 2022 presidential petition was the standard of proof. The Court

[64] ibid para 303.
[65] ibid para 373.
[66] ibid para 378.
[67] ibid para 378.
[68] ibid para 379.
[69] *Odinga & 16 others v Ruto & 10 others* [2022] KESC 56 (KLR) PRESIDENTIAL ELECTION PETITION E005, E001, E002, E003, E004, E007 & E008 OF 2022, para 301.

has adopted an 'intermediate standard' of proof, which is 'higher than the civil standard of balance of probabilities, but lower than the criminal standard of proof beyond reasonable doubt' to adjudicate presidential election petitions since 2013.[70] While the process-outcome doctrine favours the petitioner more than the respondent in its quest for ensuring greater compliance with the rule of law in the conduct of presidential elections, the adoption of an 'intermediate standard' of proof rather than the civil standard of balance of probabilities (adopted by many courts on the continent) puts more burdens to the petitioner in Kenya. Although the Court in the 2022 presidential petition concluded that 'the irregularities and illegalities cited by the petitioners were not proved to the required standard, or at all',[71] the adoption of an 'intermediate standard' of proof meant that it would sustain a presidential election even if there were some illegalities and irregularities that affect either the presidential election result or the integrity of the electoral process based on the civil standard of balance of probabilities. Such higher standard of proof, in turn, meant that the Supreme Court of Kenya (unlike as it first appears) could be tolerant of electoral illegalities and irregularities more than any court on the continent in some respects.

Saulos Klaus Chilima and Other v Arthur Peter Mutharika and Other[72] is another case where the High Court of Malawi, sitting as a Constitutional Court, applied the process-outcome doctrine to resolve a presidential petition. On 21 May 2019, Malawi held presidential, parliamentary, and local elections. On 27 May 2019, the Electoral Commission declared Arthur Peter Mutharika, the incumbent President, who gained 1,940,709 votes, as the duly elected President of Malawi. Dissatisfied with the outcome of the election, Saulos Klaus Chilima (who received 1,018,369 votes) and Lazarus McCarthy Chakwera (1,781,740 votes) separately petitioned the High Court seeking nullification of the presidential election. The petitioners challenged the declared result on account of several irregularities during the conduct of the presidential election, especially related to the count, audit, and transmission of results from polling stations to tallying centres, all of which, according to them, affected the integrity of the electoral process and outcome. They argued that the tampering of votes and the absence of the signatures of presiding officers, among other irregularities, meant that the 2019 presidential election was not duly conducted in accordance with the applicable laws on election and, therefore, should be nullified. The Court consolidated the two petitions and decided in their favour by invalidating the presidential election result and ordering a rerun election, which the Supreme Court upheld on appeal.[73]

[70] ibid para 287.

[71] ibid para 297.

[72] *Saulos Klaus Chilima and Other v Arthur Peter Mutharika and Other* (2019) [Constitutional Reference No 1 of 2019] (High Court of Malawi).

[73] *Saulos Klaus Chilima and Other v Arthur Peter Mutharika and Other* (2020) [MSCA Constitutional Appeal No 1 of 2020].

The High Court, like the Supreme Court of Kenya, applied the process-outcome doctrine to resolve the presidential petition. While the judgment of the Supreme Court of Kenya could be a source of inspiration to the courts in Malawi, the Elections Act in Malawi also created possibilities for them to choose the process-outcome doctrine. Unlike the Election Acts of Zimbabwe and Namibia, which prescribe the substantive impact doctrine to adjudicate a presidential petition, the Elections Act in Malawi is silent about the judicial doctrine that should be applied to resolve such petitions. Section 100 of the Elections Act, which deals with presidential petitions, regulates only the procedural matters regarding such petitions. Even if the courts could still follow the road taken by the Supreme Court of Ghana, they found the substantive impact doctrine inappropriate as they consider electoral processes as important as electoral outcomes.[74] In this regard, the Supreme Court noted that '[a]n election can only be free, fair and credible if it fully complies with the dictates of the constitution and applicable electoral laws as well as principles of transparency and accountability'.[75] By applying the process-outcome doctrine, and after examining the evidence before it, the Court found that the systematic and widespread irregularities and anomalies in the conduct of the presidential election had affected both the electoral process and electoral outcome.[76] Moreover, the Court noted that the declared result could even be nullified on the irregularities that affect the electoral process or the electoral outcome.

While the courts in Malawi followed the Supreme Court of Kenya in applying the process-outcome doctrine, they have followed a different path related to the standard of proof in presidential election petitions. Unlike the Supreme Court of Kenya,[77] which considers election petitions as sui generis in nature and, consequently, applies an 'intermediate standard of proof', the courts in Malawi adopt the balance of probabilities. The justification for this according to the Supreme Court is that '[s]etting the standard too high for a petitioner to substantiate his grievance in such a matter might well impinge on the average Malawian's right to access justice when his constitutionally based rights have been violated'.[78] This makes the courts in Malawi more willing to intervene and, concomitantly, nullify a presidential election more than any other court on the continent. In other words, they demand a higher degree of compliance with the rule of law than any other court in the conduct of a presidential election.

Despite differences in their standard of proof, courts in Kenya and Malawi pay more attention to the procedural and substantive aspects of democracy more than courts in Ghana, Zimbabwe, and Namibia. Their nullification

[74] ibid 84–85.

[75] ibid 85.

[76] *Saulos Klaus Chilima and Other v Arthur Peter Mutharika and Other* (2019) paras 1478–479.

[77] *Raila Odinga & Another v Independent Electoral and Boundaries Commission & Others* (2017) paras 148–53.

[78] *Saulos Klaus Chilima and Other v Arthur Peter Mutharika and Other* (2020) 39.

judgments show the potential and limits of judicial review in Africa. On the one hand, by virtue of these judgments alone, the courts in Kenya and Malawi could not only inspire public confidence in them, which, in turn, could enhance their credibility and legitimacy, but they could also send a signal to the executive and administrative institutions and politicians to respect the Constitution and the rule of law in the performance of their duties and in the exercise of their powers related to and beyond elections. Indeed, these judgments have enhanced the national prestige and international reputation of the courts in the two countries.[79] As these courts have strongly asserted their position as the third branch of government, the other branches and institutions could pay serious attention to their actions and modes of operation. This is simply because a court that invalidates a presidential election could be more willing to intervene in other matters, especially in protecting or enforcing constitutional rights and correcting the abuse of power. On the other hand, the judiciary as the least dangerous branch has inherent limitations to enforcing its decisions as it lacks a 'purse or a sword'. The enforcement of its decisions depends on other institutions and broader socio-economic and political factors at a given time. Even worse, the judiciary may face a backlash that could challenge its institutional security and independence. All these are important considerations in the exercise of judicial power.

In this regard, while the judgment of the Supreme Court of Kenya is jurisprudentially groundbreaking, it did not have an impact on the 2017 presidential election, as Odinga boycotted the rerun election, alleging that the IEBC was unfit to conduct a free and fair election. Yet, the nullified election cost Kenya '$1 billon in aggregate', making it one of the most expensive elections in Africa.[80] In addition, the Supreme Court has been attacked by the incumbent President and his associates and has been increasingly politicised ever since its nullification judgment.[81] Furthermore, in a dramatic turn of events, the March 2018 handshake between Kenyatta and Odinga ushered in the so-called 'Building Bridges Initiative' (BBI) that aims to transform the political landscape of Kenya and its new constitutional order.[82] Once fierce political opponents, Kenyatta and Odinga have joined together in rewriting the 2010 Constitution through the Constitution of Kenya Amendment Bill, 2020, which the Supreme Court struck down as unconstitutional. While Kenyan judges brilliantly and skilfully

[79] See, eg, D Pilling, 'Malawi court decision is a victory for African democracy', *Financial Times*, 4 February 2020, available at www.ft.com/content/89670eee-4739-11ea-aeb3-955839e06441 (accessed 2 March 2022); K de Freytas-Tamura, 'Kenya Supreme Court Nullifies Presidential Election', *The New York Times*, 1 September 2017, available at www.nytimes.com/2017/09/01/world/africa/kenya-election-kenyatta-odinga.html (accessed 2 March 2022).

[80] AL Dahir, 'Kenya is set to hold one of the most expensive elections in Africa', *Quartz Africa*, 18 July 2017, qz.com/africa/1030958/kenyas-elections-will-cost-1-billion-in-government-and-campaign-spend/ (accessed 2 March 2022).

[81] See K Kanyinga and C Odote, 'Judicialisation of Politics and Kenya's 2017 Elections' (2019) 13 *Journal of Eastern African Studies* 235.

[82] See the details of the BBI www.bbi.go.ke (accessed 2 March 2022).

defended their Constitution from what they called unconstitutional constitutional amendment or dismemberment, they and their constitutional order have been under a lot of pressure following the political and constitutional developments since the 2017 nullification judgment.[83]

In contrast, the judgment of nullification in Malawi has been jurisprudentially and practically successful. It is practically successful because, unlike Kenya, the chairperson of the Electoral Commission, which ran the disputed presidential election, resigned due to criticisms by the opposition and the new chairperson was determined to conduct a credible rerun election. Additionally, and even most importantly, unlike Kenya, the military in Malawi stood with the people rather than with those in power. These conditions have facilitated the rerun election in Malawi, which the opposition presidential candidate won.[84]

Why the nullification judgments have different impacts in Kenya and Malawi in the rerun election is a cautionary tale that courts should not mechanically apply the process-outcome doctrine. But they should adopt a more dynamic doctrine grounded in their national contexts at a given time.

IV. CONCLUSION: TOWARDS A DYNAMIC JUDICIAL DOCTRINE FOR ADJUDICATING PRESIDENTIAL ELECTION DISPUTES

A presidential election petition is no ordinary petition. As Ran Hirschl observed in his comment on *Bush v Gore*, 'short of the Supreme Court declaring war, it would be difficult to imagine the court making a more momentous decision on behalf of the American populace'.[85] In its long history, the American Supreme Court made this kind of decision only once. But courts in Africa make such momentous decisions more often. While the substantive impact and process-outcome doctrines are both legally defensible, the former is favourable to the respondent, whereas the latter is favourable to the petitioner. As a presidential election petition has a personal and public dimension, the decision to apply one or the other doctrine has serious consequences from the outset regarding who should or should not be the President of the Republic. On the one hand, courts that apply the substantive impact doctrine are usually perceived as incumbent-friendly and are accused of normalising electoral illegalities and irregularities, and, on the other, courts that apply the process-outcome doctrine are blamed for subverting the people's will. Moreover, even when one considers

[83] See, eg, S Maombo, 'Uhuru has 'list of hate', Mutunga says over six judges', *The Star*, 8 June 2021, www.the-star.co.ke/news/2021-06-08-uhuru-has-list-of-hate-mutunga-says-over-six-judges/ (accessed 2 March 2022).

[84] See also N Cheeseman, 'Can the Courts Protect Democracy in Africa?', *The Africa Report*, 21 May 2021, www.theafricareport.com/90612/can-the-courts-protect-democracy-in-africa/ (accessed 2 March 2022).

[85] R Hirschl, 'Resituating the Judicialization of Politics: Bush v. Gore as a Global Trend' (2002) 15 *Canadian Journal of Law & Jurisprudence* 191, 217.

the process-outcome doctrine as a more fitting doctrine for its high expectation of compliance with the law in the conduct of a presidential election, judgments based on this doctrine could risk non-compliance or may not have a practical impact on the election, as the Kenyan case clearly shows. Hence, courts should adopt a dynamic judicial doctrine that maintains and enhances their institutional security and legitimacy and sustains the democratic trajectory of their respective states.

A turn to a dynamic judicial doctrine is not only necessitated by the sui generis nature of presidential election petitions, but also the role of courts in non-established democracies. As Tom Daly argues, courts in non-established democracies (as in Africa) are expected to both *judge* and *facilitate* the democratisation process, that is, to 'both assess what is required to support the democratization process at any given point and to judge when the democratization context requires a different approach'.[86] This *double role of judging and facilitating the democratisation process* essentially requires a dynamic judicial role[87] that both responds to the needs of the time and simultaneously advances the constitutional vision of democracy in the long term. In presidential election petitions especially, a dynamic judicial doctrine and judicial role are extremely necessary given presidential contestants' capacity and willingness to both advance and hinder the democratisation process, including the role of the judiciary in it.

A dynamic judicial doctrine for the adjudication of presidential election disputes, then, may have to involve a two-tiered adjudicatory process.[88] The first process involves the court's role of judging. In a constitutional democracy, the role of the court is to resolve disputes in a manner that maintains the coherence of the legal system as a whole and in a way that protects the Constitution and democracy.[89] In this role, courts should strive to reach a constitutionally and legally principled outcome in the disposition of the case before them. Here, for example, courts may consider either the substantive impact or the process-outcome doctrines, or another doctrine that best fits with their own constitutional, legal, or other jurisprudential considerations. But this is not and should not be the end of the adjudicatory process. After reaching a principled outcome in its *judging role*, the second process for the court is to consider its *facilitating role* in the democratic building process. In this role, among others, the court may consider the impact of the principled outcome on its institutional security and legitimacy and the democratic trajectory of the state in the short and long terms. In its *facilitating role*, the court is more a partner than an arbiter that collaborates with the other branches and institutions in

[86] T Daly, *The Alchemists: Questioning Our Faith in Courts as Democracy-Builders* (Cambridge, Cambridge University Press, 2018) 1.

[87] See Landau, 'A Dynamic Theory of Judicial Role' (2014) 55 *Boston College Law Review* 1501.

[88] See also R Mann, 'Non-Ideal Theory of Constitutional Adjudication' (2018) 7 *Global Constitutionalism* 14–15.

[89] A Barak, *The Judge in a Democracy* (Princeton, Princeton University Press, 2006) chs 1–2.

the practice of constitutional democracy. This requires the court to account for some practical factors and, concomitantly, make some empirical calculations as part and parcel of the adjudicatory process. In this regard, the Namibian Supreme Court's use of a 'fair play' criterion along with the substantive impact doctrine is an example of how courts could include other important factors in the adjudicatory process. Beyond being a Hercules or a Sisyphus, as Yvonne Tew observed in the context of Asia,[90] courts in Africa need to strike a proper balance between constitutional principle and empirical reality in a way that maintains and enhances their institutional security and legitimacy and sustains the democratic building process.[91]

[90] See Y Tew, *Constitutional Statecraft in Asian Courts* (Oxford, Oxford University Press, 2020).

[91] See R Dixon, 'Strong Courts: Judicial Statecraft in Aid of Constitutional Change' (2021) 59 *Columbia Journal of Transnational Law* 298–363; Mann (n 88).

11

Electoral Constitutional Justice as the Tool to Protect Mexican Democracy

IRENE SPIGNO*

I. PRELIMINARY REMARKS

IN MEXICO, ELECTORAL constitutional justice, that is, the provision of judicial procedure instruments which enable the judiciary to review the constitutionality of electoral laws, is one of the central points of the consolidation of the democratic order. Introduced in 1996, the provision of electoral constitutional justice has modified a tradition which had existed for more than a century, according to which all electoral regulations were exempt from judicial review. The constitutional and legal reform of that year which generated this revolutionary change was characterised by three fundamental issues: first, it established a comprehensive system of electoral justice, at the top of which is the Supreme Court of Justice of the Nation (henceforth the Supreme Court or SCJN), with one of the central pieces being the Electoral Court of the Judicial Power of the Federation (henceforth the Electoral Tribunal or TEPJF, from its name in Spanish *Tribunal Electoral del Poder Judicial de la Federación*); second, it consolidated a contentious judicial system for the resolution of electoral disputes, with the consequent strengthening of the Electoral Court itself; and, third, it created procedural instruments allowing for the judicial review of the constitutionality of electoral laws and acts, that is, through the incorporation of authentic electoral constitutional guarantees, as well as the expansion and purification of the system through which electoral matters can be challenged.

Therefore, when we talk about the judicial review of electoral laws in Mexico, we are talking about a complex panorama whose protagonists are two courts: on the one hand, the Electoral Tribunal, a specialised body of the Judicial Power of the Federation, in charge of resolving electoral controversies and protecting the political-electoral rights of citizens and, on the other hand, the Supreme

* The author acknowledges Chris Callan for the linguistic review.

Court, the highest constitutional court and highest judicial authority of the Judicial Power of the Federation.

Although the judicial review of electoral law legislation had been established since 1996, it was only in 2007 that the relationship between the SCJN and the TEPJF were clearly defined. The constitutional reform of December 1994 introduced the instrument of the *Acción de Inconstitucionalidad* in the Mexican legal system to allow for an abstract control of constitutional regularity of general norms.[1] Expressly, electoral rules were excluded from this review. In neither the legislative initiative sent by the federal executive power, nor in the documents of the legislative process was it possible to find a reason for the aforementioned exclusion. The most plausible explanation is found in two contextual circumstances. The first of those is that the ultimate definition of the validity of elections was a political qualification (entrusted to the electoral colleges). This meant that since the latter part of the nineteenth century, the idea had been generated that the judiciary should not intervene in political matters. The second is that the SCJN was resistant to getting involved in these conflicts.

This idea generated a conflict between the SCJN and the TEPJF regarding the constitutional review of the electoral laws that was resolved only with the 2007 constitutional reform.[2] These amendments included in Article 99 of the Constitution the provision according to which the Electoral Tribunal (the Superior Chamber or the Regional Chambers[3]) could decide on the non-application of electoral laws when they were contrary to the Constitution, as long as the resolutions issued in the exercise of this power were limited to the specific case. Therefore, the 2007 constitutional reform gave the TEPJF the power to decide on the non-application of electoral laws contrary to the Constitution, as long as the SCJN, when resolving an action of unconstitutionality, has not ruled on the unconstitutionality of that rule.

The resolutions issued by the Electoral Tribunal Regional Chambers determining the non-application of the electoral regulation due to a finding that it is contrary to the Constitution do not expel it from the legal order but determine that this rule does not apply to the specific case. These sentences can be appealed before the higher court. The rulings issued by the Superior Chamber when resolving these appeals are, however, definitive. That said, they do not determine

[1] The procedure for the Action of Unconstitutionality is provided for in Art 105 of the Constitution. It is exclusively heard by the Supreme Court and deals with an abstract constitutional control over general rules. A rule issued at the federal or local level may be examined by the Supreme Court through the review the of laws within the 'block of normative regularity' or 'block of constitutionality'. See M Díaz Beltrán, 'El parámetro de regularidad constitucional credo en fuente jurisprudencial' (2018) 11 *Revista Misión Jurídica* 205.

[2] See *Decreto que reforma los artículos 6, 41, 85, 99, 108, 116 y 122; adiciona el artículo 134 y deroga un párrafo al artículo 97 de la Constitución ôlítica de los Estados Unidos Mexicanos*, published in the Official Gazette of the Federation on 13 November 2007. The corresponding legal reform was published in the Official Gazette of the Federation on 14 January 2008.

[3] On the structure of the Electoral Tribunal see below.

the exclusion of the electoral regulation, but only order their non-application to the specific case. Article 99 indicates that the Superior Chamber will inform the SCJN of said resolutions, although it does not suggest for what purposes. Thus, while the TEPJF can carry out a specific constitutional review which only determines the non-application of the norm considered unconstitutional to the particular case and *inter partes*, this is without prejudice to the provisions of Article 105, which recognises the possibility that the SCJN can carry out an abstract and effective *erga omnes* constitutional review of the electoral norms.[4]

However, to understand the meaning that the electoral constitutional jurisprudence has for the Mexican democratic system, in the following pages, we will be making some general considerations about the Mexican constitutional, political and electoral system to understand the current meaning of the electoral constitutional justice system (II). Subsequently, we will analyse the role played in the Mexican system by the TEPJF, highlighting, in particular, the cases in which it has declared the unconstitutionality of the electoral norms (III). Finally, the actions of the unconstitutionality of the SCJN (IV), and the text will close with some final reflections on the concept of democracy that this jurisprudence has allowed to build (V).

II. THE MEXICAN ELECTORAL JUSTICE SYSTEM: AN OVERVIEW

The current Mexican electoral justice system can be primarily explained and understood by considering the history of the nineteenth and twentieth centuries. During this period, it is possible to identify four crucial political moments which help with understanding the contemporary Mexican democratic context.

The first one is the post-independence period, a period of significant 'political instability' which lasted for more than 40 years (1821–64) and prevented the construction of democratic rules. The conflicts with Spain, the US, and France and the internal conflict between liberals and conservatives revealed the absence of the necessary conditions for democratic stability.[5] This first stage was also characterised by the electoral fraud of Antonio López de Santa Anna, who was 11 times President of the Republic.[6]

[4] In addition, constitutional reform in 2021 amended para 7 of Art 99 to establish that 'When a Chamber of the Electoral Tribunal upheld a criterion on the unconstitutionality of any act or resolution or the interpretation of a precept of this Constitution and said criterion might be contradictory with one held by the chambers or the Plenary of the Supreme Court of Justice, any of the Ministers, the chambers or the parties, may denounce the contradiction in the terms indicated by law, so that the Plenary of the Supreme Court of Justice of the Nation decides definitively which criterion should prevail. The resolutions issued in this case will not affect the issues already resolved.'

[5] G Palomo Gonzalez, 'La inestabilidad político-militar durante la primera república central, 1835–1839. La lógica del pronunciamiento en la figura del general José Urrea' (2008) 36 *Estudios de Historia Moderna y Contemporánea de México* 85.

[6] See also ESR Garmendia, 'Elecciones y lecciones de democracia en México' (2013) 26 *Veredas: Revista del Pensamiento Sociológico* 101.

The second moment coincided with the first stage of political stability, which saw an authoritarian regime. The so-called *Porfiriato* period (1876–1911), due to the name of the President and dictator Porfirio Díaz, distinguished itself by perpetuating the power of a single person through fraudulent elections.[7] It was a period of peace and internal political control based on social, cultural, and economic progress.[8] But there was no democracy and no political alternation.

The third critical moment refers to the revolutionary movement promoted by Francisco I Madero, in 1910, which burst onto the scene during the dictatorship of Porfirio Díaz at a time when the country was going through a moment of crisis and repression by the government.[9] It should be said that it was here, together with the other liberation movements in this period, that the foundations of the political rights that we have inherited today were gestated.[10] In the same way, Maderism was a push and a call to all Mexicans to take care to concern themselves with public affairs.

The fourth moment started in 1929 and lasted almost 70 years, in a period known as the 'perfect dictatorship'.[11] Mexico never knew an authoritarian breakdown like the majority of Latin America States, but rather it experienced an uninterrupted period of nearly 70 years through which it was governed by one political party: the Institutional Revolutionary Party (PRI from its name in Spanish *Partido Revolucionario Institucional*). During the PRI regime (1929–2000), there was no party alternation. Various political practices were established to ensure control and power over the country was maintained (such as the President of the Republic electing his successor).[12]

This system started to collapse at the end of the 1980s and especially with the 1988 presidential election, where the PRI won once again. Still, it was an election tainted by fraud (with the election of Carlos Salinas de Gortari). Starting in 1988, Mexico began a transition to democracy based on alternation of political parties, which would be consolidated in 2000, with the electoral victory of Vicente Fox Quesada of the National Action Party (PAN from its name in Spanish, *Partido de Acción Nacional*) in the presidential elections. Thus, through the alternation of political parties which started at the beginning of the twenty-first century and which lasted from 2000 to 2012 with the government of the National Action Party, political life and especially political rights evolved, and the space for public debate opened up. In 2006 a left-wing

[7] S Kuntz Ficker and E Speckman Guerra, 'El porfiriato' (2017) *Nueva historia general de México* 487–536.

[8] FA Ávila Espinosa, 'Porfirio Díaz y la modernización porfirista' in A Beretta Curi (ed), *Agricultura y modernización, 1840-1930* (Montevideo, Universidad de la República, 2010) 165.

[9] See F Katz, *De Díaz a Madero* (México, Ediciones Era, 2004).

[10] CC Cumberland, *Madero y la revolución mexicana* (México, Siglo XXI, 1984).

[11] See RR Lagier, 'México ¿la dictadura perfecta?' (2019) 38 *Amérique Latine Histoire et Mémoire. Les Cahiers ALHIM*, online.

[12] RG de Barros Gomes, 'La Dictadura Perfecta: un análisis de las estrategias de permanencia del régimen priista en México' (2018) 4 *Faces de Clio* 148.

alliance (the Coalition for the Good of All[13]) started to appear as a resistance front against the hegemonic parties.[14] The presidential elections of 2006 were highly competitive. Practically tied, both Felipe Calderón of the National Action Party and Andrés Manuel López Obrador of the Coalition for the Good of All reached the final stretch.[15]

In addition to this, for the 2018 elections, the introduction of independent candidates opened up a new era in the country's political life. It marked the victory of the current president Andrés Manuel Lopez Obrador, from the political party Morena, which constitutes a historical fact for Mexico.[16] The results not only made possible, for the first time, the arrival to power of a force located on the left but also destroyed the power of the old Institutional Revolutionary Party.

These four stages were accompanied and promoted by eleven electoral reforms between 1977 and 2014. Eight of them were far-reaching and involved constitutional and legal changes (which took place in 1977, 1986, 1990, 1993, 1994, 1996, 2007, and 2014), while three only changed specific aspects and made legal modifications: that of 2002, to establish gender quotas in legislative candidacies; that of 2003, to raise the requirements to form political parties; and that of 2005, to regulate the vote of Mexicans abroad.[17]

This high number of electoral reforms, especially if compared with European standards, is quite a common phenomenon in Latin America. Between 1978 and 2015, more than 250 electoral reforms were registered in the region.[18] In Mexico, the intense electoral reformism is a reflection of that process of political change described above, and which sought pluralism and inclusion as its primary goal,

[13] The Coalition for the Good of All was a left-wing electoral alliance formed by the Mexican political parties of the Democratic Revolution (*Partido de la Revolución Demócratica* – PRD), Labor (*Partido del Trabajo* – PT) and Convergence, built around the candidacy of the PRD and former head of government of the Federal District Andrés Manuel López Obrador, to compete in the 2006 elections.

[14] MR Mercado, 'La distribución del voto en las entidades federativas. Análisis sobre las elecciones presidenciales en México, 1988-2006' (2007) 21 *El Cotidiano* 17.

[15] RM Valles Ruiz, 'Elecciones presidenciales 2006 en México. La perspectiva de la prensa escrita' (2016) 20 *Revista mexicana de opinión pública* 31. See also AF Andrade, '¡Habemus presidente! El conflicto post-electoral en México' (2006) 30 *La Chronique des Amériques*, online. Available at www.orison.uqam.ca/IMG/pdf/chro_Flores_30_06.pdf.

[16] NE Hernández Trejo, 'La histórica elección presidencial de 2018' (2020) 65 *Revista mexicana de ciencias políticas y sociales* 397.

[17] See I Méndez de Hoyos, *Transición a la democracia en México* (México, Fontamara, 2006); G Moctezuma Barragán (ed), *Derecho y legislación electoral, 30 años después de 1968* (México, Miguel Ángel Porrúa, 1999); R Becerra, P Salazar and J Woldenberg, *La mecánica del cambio político en México* (México, Ediciones Cal y Arena, 2000).

[18] Three groups can be identified: hyperactive political systems, in which there have been more than 20 changes during the relevant period (as in Ecuador and Peru); moderate systems (the majority), which have made between six and 19 modifications (as in Argentina, Brazil, Colombia and Chile); and passive systems, with five or less reforms (as in Uruguay and Paraguay): see F Freidenberg and T Došek, 'Las reformas electorales en América Latina (1978-2015)' in K Casas-Zamora et al (eds), *Reformas políticas en América Latina: tendencias y casos* (Washington, DC, OEA, 2016).

as a consequence of the political hegemony of one official party during much of the twentieth century, which had effectively led to the exclusion of political groups, social activists and segments of the population.

Although the beginning of the Mexican transition was marked in 1988, the origins of the political change were in 1968,[19] the year which saw a social movement in which university students, professors, intellectuals, homemakers, workers, peasants, merchants and professionals made specific demands such as freedom for political prisoners and the reduction or elimination of authoritarianism.[20] In simple terms, the movement sought democratic change in the country after decades of the same ruling party, more significant political and civil liberties, less inequality, and the departure of the government of the Institutional Revolutionary Party, which it considered authoritarian.[21]

The transition that began there was developed through various attempts. The parties concerned adjusted the game's rules according to the political context and to their convenience, and to the results, which translated into multiple constitutional and legal reforms on electoral matters.[22]

In addition to pluralism, Mexican electoral reformism has sought other objectives that have changed over time: inclusion (notoriously in the reforms of 1977, 1986, and 1990),[23] certainty and transparency (1990, 1993, 1994),[24] equity (1993, 1996, 2007), the impartiality of the authorities (1994 and 1996)[25] and legality (1986, 1996).[26]

[19] S Loaeza, 'México 1968: los orígenes de la transición' (1989) 30 *Foro internacional* 66.

[20] I Semo, *La transición interrumpida: México 1968-1988* (México, Universidad Iberoamericana, 1993).

[21] M Basáñez, *La lucha por la hegemonía en México, 1968-1990* (México, Siglo XXI, 1990).

[22] LC Ugalde, 'Introducción: el reformismo electoral mexicano, 1977-2019' in LC Ugalde and S Hernández Quintana (eds), *Elecciones, justicia y democracia en México. Fortalezas y debilidades del sistema electoral, 1990-2020* (México, TEPJF, 2020).

[23] The 1977 reform encouraged the creation of political parties and the inclusion of proscribed groups (such as the Mexican Communist Party which regained its legal registration after years of living in the shadows) and created 100 proportional representation deputies to give voice to the minorities in Congress. The same logic was strengthened by successive changes: see Ugalde (n 22) 39.

[24] The second objective of Mexican electoral reformism was to create certainty and transparency in the organisation of electoral processes and thus eliminate any practice of electoral fraud, through the professionalisation of the electoral machinery. This objective was reached with the creation of an electoral institute; on the evolution of the electoral institute see C Astudillo, 'Cinco premisas en torno a la metamorfosis del IFE en autoridad electoral nacional' (2014) 6 *Revista Mexicana de Derecho Electoral* 3.

[25] The third objective of electoral reform was to establish equal conditions of competition. It was a long process, mainly related to the fact that all the parties that have governed federally or from various state governments were quite reluctant to abandon overnight the privileges that gave them access to government resources. It was only with the reforms of 1986, 1990 and 1993 that factors were gradually introduced to estimate the amounts of public and private financing: see RM Mirón Lince and K Valverde Viesca, 'Partidos políticos, financiamiento y reforma' in RM Mirón Lince and L Valdés (eds), *Partidos y Elecciones* (México, Universidad Autónoma Metropolitana, 1996).

[26] The fourth objective of electoral reformism was the impartiality of the electoral authorities. In the evolution of the electoral institute, the key turning point was the 1996 reform which attributed autonomy: the presidency was no longer held by the Secretary of the Interior and his place was taken

The electoral justice system was created on its own to guarantee the objective of legality. Its first foundations can be found in 1986 with the reform of Article 60 of the Constitution, which provided for the creation of the Electoral Contentious Court (it was an autonomous body with administrative nature),[27] then the Federal Electoral Tribunal in 1990 (an independent judicial body on electoral matters),[28] and finally the TEPJF in 1996, a specialised organ of the judiciary and the highest judicial authority. In subsequent reforms, Electoral Tribunal powers were expanded.[29] Electoral justice and its jurisprudence have played a relevant role in the definition and scope of the rights of political participation and the conditions for the validity of elections and represent the central core of consolidation of the Mexican democratic order.[30]

III. THE CONCRETE CONSTITUTIONAL REVIEW OF ELECTORAL LEGISLATION

Since its inception, the Mexican Electoral Tribunal has done an extraordinary job, becoming a proper constitutional and conventional court which maximises the political-electoral rights of citizens in an egalitarian way and guarantees the democratic principles of any electoral process.

by a president councilor also elected by a qualified majority of the Chamber of Deputies, like the other eight electoral councilors: see Astudillo (n 24).

[27] M Barquín Álvarez, 'La renovación política de 1986-1987 y la creación del Tribunal De lo Contencioso Electoral' in E Elías Musi (ed), *Evolución histórica de las instituciones de la Justicia Electoral en México* (México, TEPJF, 2002). See also M Acosta Romero, 'Reflexiones sobre el Tribunal de lo Contencioso Electoral Federal de México' (1989) 29 *Cuadernos de CAPEL* 11 and JL De la Peza Muñoz Cano, 'Justicia y jurisprudencia electoral' (1989) *Revista del Tribunal de lo Contencioso Electoral Federal.*

[28] During this time, Mexican electoral jurisdiction has been progressively reinforced by several constitutional reforms that led to the Electoral Tribunal becoming the highest judicial authority in electoral matters: in 1993, presidential self-qualification disappeared, and the Tribunal was entrusted with the competence to declare the presidential qualification. On this evolution see JF Franco González Salas, 'Creación y evolución de la jurisdicción especializada en materia electoral en México' (2013) 1 *Revista Justicia Electoral* 339.

[29] On this evolution see SO Nava Gomar, 'La evolución de la justicia electoral en México, 1996–2019' in LC Ugalde and S Hernández Quintana (eds), *Elecciones, justicia y democracia en México. Fortalezas y debilidades del sistema electoral, 1990-2020* (México, TEPJF, 2020). See also E Andrade Sánchez, 'La Reforma Política de 1996 en México' (1997) 25 *Cuadernos Constitucionales México-Centroamérica* 11; R Becerra et al., *La reforma electoral de 1996. Una descripción general* (México, Fondo de Cultura Económica, 1997); HA Concha Cantú, 'Una aproximación a la administración de justicia en México' in D Valadés and R Gutiérrez Rivas (eds), *Justicia. Memoria del IV Congreso Nacional de Derecho Constitucional I* (México, UNAM, 2001); JP Huber Olea y Contró, *Derecho contencioso electoral* (México, Porrúa, 2005); J Patiño Camarena, *Nuevo derecho electoral mexicano 2006*, 8th edn (México, UNAM, 2006); and R Terrazas Salgado, *Introducción al estudio de la justicia constitucional electoral en México* (Mexico, Ángel Editor, 2006).

[30] Scholarship on the electoral case law is immense: see *ex plurimis* MP Acosta Vázquez et al, *TEPJF. Un tribunal para la democracia* (México, TEPJF, 2021).

The Electoral Tribunal constitutes the highest judicial authority on the matter and is a specialised organ of the Federal Judicial Power. According to Article 99 of the Mexican Constitution, it works permanently with a Superior Chamber, five Regional Chambers, and a Specialized Regional Chamber on freedom of expression. Regarding its integration, the Constitution establishes that the judges of the Court will be elected by the vote of two-thirds of the present members of the Senate at the proposal of the Supreme Court of Justice of the Nation. Their period of appointment lasts nine years, they are non-extendable, and their renewal is staggered. The decisions of the Tribunal are final, so they constitute the last instance through which declarations can be made on the validity of a specific election.

Regarding judges' autonomy, independence, and impartiality, which are the preconditions for the existence of effective and impartial resolutions of the electoral challenge, the Electoral Tribunal has the inherent guarantees that correspond to the judicial bodies of other matters. These guarantees consist of the separation of other powers of the state, the respective attributions of an administrative and budgetary nature. Likewise, to guarantee the electoral judges' absolute independence, impartiality, and professionalism, they are assured of their duration in office (nine years non-extendable), the salaries granted to them, and stability in their positions.[31]

What is very important to highlight is the institutional role that the Electoral Tribunal has played so far. It is the guarantor of electoral peace and ultimately decides all electoral controversies. It also guarantees the governability of the peaceful electoral transition because, as we have seen, Mexico has previously renewed its democracy through fraud, or by not even appointing a successor, as in the dynasties. Therefore, it is the guarantor of electoral consistency and peace and has become the instrument of electoral fairness and the freedom of elections. It is also the guarantor of political rights in the country; it is essential to highlight its case law on issues of gender equality, which has promoted the formation of crucial principles and on political violence against women, the LGBTQIA + community, freedom of expression, and political rights of indigenous peoples.[32]

As far as its competence on the constitutional review of electoral laws is concerned, it was introduced by the constitutional reform of 2007, which amended Article 99 of the Constitution, to grant the TEPJF the power to disapply the rules on electoral matters where they are considered in violation of the Constitution, except the provisions of Article 105, section II.[33]

[31] On the functioning of the Electoral Tribunal see JJ Orozco Henríquez, *Justicia electoral comparada de América Latina* (México, Instituto de Investigaciones Jurídicas, Universidad Nacional Autónoma de México, 2019) 140 ff.

[32] See, *ex plurimis*, MP Acosta Vázquez et al, *Sentencias fundacionales. La creación del derecho electoral* (México, TEPJF, 2021).

[33] See L Córdova Vianello and P Salazar Ugarte (eds), *Estudios sobre la reforma electoral 2007. Hacia un nuevo modelo* (México, TEPJF, 2008).

This reform intervened by resolving the conflict between the TEPJF and the SCJN regarding the constitutional review of electoral laws derived from the standard that the Electoral Tribunal adopted in 1998, awarding itself the powers to carry out this review. More specifically, in 1998 the Superior Chamber of the TEPJF resolved three constitutional electoral review trials. It determined the inapplicability of the provisions contained in the electoral laws, considering them contrary to the Constitution.[34]

Months later, the *Contradicción de tesis 2/2000-PL* was presented before the SCJN.[35] The SCJN declared the *Contradicción* inadmissible, considering that it was impossible to confront a criterion upheld by a judicial body competent to hear the unconstitutionality of a law with a standard upheld by a body that lacks that attribution (that is, the TEPJF). When resolving the *Contradicción*, it was pointed out that the SCJN was the only body empowered to analyse the constitutionality of the laws, suspending the thesis of the Electoral Court.[36] The resolution that the Court gave to the *Contradicción de tesis 2/2000-PL* was highly debated and criticised. The most important criticism was that this had led to the creation of a significant loophole in Mexican electoral law, since there was no effective means to challenge the unconstitutionality of electoral laws.[37]

It is possible to identify three stages in which the constitutional review of electoral norms was applied in different ways within the Mexican legal system. During the first stage, only the abstract and concentrated constitutional review of the laws on electoral matters was applied through the *acción de inconstitucionalidad* procedure by the SCJN. But, despite the criteria issued by the SCJN, the TEPJF, before the 2007–08 electoral reform and the constitutional human rights reform,[38] carried out a constitutional and conventional review of electoral legislation through an interpretative process, applying fundamental human rights principles (the consistent interpretation, in a systematic and functional way to maximise the human rights contained in international treaties, using principles such as pro persona).

[34] See the *Tesis de jurisprudencia S3ELJ 5/99*.

[35] The *Contradicción de Tesis* procedure arises from the need to establish an integrated jurisprudential system. It is an abstract procedure intended to preserve the interpretative unity of the Mexican legal order, through which the SCJN – functioning in Plenary session or in Chambers – resolves opposing jurisprudential criteria issued either by the SCJN itself or by other federal judges, narrowing the different interpretations that legal provisions may have. The decision issued throughout the *Contradicción de Tesis* procedure constitutes new case law, with a mandatory nature which is based on a hierarchical criterion.

[36] According to the SCJN 'the Electoral Court, on the one hand, violated article 105 of the Political Constitution of Mexico and, on the other hand, violated article 235 of the Organic Law of the Judicial Power of the Federation by contravening a pronouncement of the [SCJN] that has the characteristics of firmness and constitutional obligation' (*Contradicción de tesis 2/2000-PL*).

[37] See KM Gilas, *Control de constitucionalidad en materia electoral* (México, Tribunal Electoral del Poder Judicial de la Federación, 2011) 19.

[38] Published in the Official Gazette of the Federation on 10 June 2011.

In a second moment, following the arrival of the constitutional electoral reform of 2007 and the legal reform of 2008, all the Chambers of the TEPJF were attributed the obligation to carry out a constitutional review of the specific case,[39] in which, in the first instance, an interpretation was made in accordance and second, if there was no possible application of a norm that would more broadly protect the violated right, it could not apply the unconstitutional electoral norm that had been used in the matter that was resolved. In this way, constitutional review in electoral matters was reinforced.

The third stage began with the constitutional reform on human rights.[40] The beginning of this third stage begins with *Expediente Varios 912/2010* with which the SCJN established the triphasic methodology to carry out the exercise of constitutional and conventional review of legislation.[41] In the first instance, the judges of the country, like all the other authorities of the Mexican State, must proceed to applying a consistent interpretation in a broad sense. This means that they must interpret the legal order in light of and in accordance with the human rights established in the Constitution and in the international treaties signed and ratified by Mexico, favouring people at all times with the broadest protection. In the case that there are several legally valid interpretations, the judges must proceed to make an interpretation that conforms in the strict sense. This means that based on the presumption of constitutionality of the laws, the one that makes the law in accordance with the human rights established in the Constitution and in the international treaties that are binding for Mexico should be preferred, in order to avoid influencing or violating the essential content of these rights. The non-application of the law is the *extrema ratio*, when the previous alternatives are no longer possible.

Applying these criteria to electoral matters, all electoral authorities, state and federal, both administrative and judicial, will have the obligation to carry out the constitutional and conventional review of electoral legislation through 'consistent interpretation' and observing the constitutional block. However, only the electoral courts have the power to disapply regulations that are found to be unconstitutional. In addition, in the exercise of reviewing electoral

[39] The following paragraph was added to Art 99 of the Constitution: 'Without prejudice to the provisions of article 105 of this Constitution, the chambers of the Electoral Tribunal may resolve the non-application of laws on electoral matters contrary to this Constitution. The resolutions that are issued in the exercise of this power will be limited to the specific case on which the trial will deal with.'

[40] The human rights constitutional reform was ordered by the *Decreto por el que se modifica la denominación del Capítulo I del Título Primero y reforma diversos artículos de la Constitución Política de los Estados Unidos Mexicanos*, published in the Official Gazette of the Federation on 10 June 2011 and which modified Arts 1, 3, 11, 15, 18, 29, 33, 89, 97, 102 and 105. On this reform see, *ex plurimis*, P Salazar Ugarte (ed), *La reforma constitucional sobre derechos humanos. Una guía conceptual* (México, Instituto Belisario Domínguez, 2014).

[41] See J Dondé, 'Comentarios al expediente varios 912/2010' in P Salazar Ugarte, R Niembro Ortega and CE Alonso Beltrán (eds), *Diez sentencias emblemáticas de la Suprema Corte* (México, UNAM, 2019).

constitutionality, the Electoral Court must respect those guiding principles that are intended to make effective the application and protection of human rights.[42]

The TEPJF, with reference to the constitutional review of electoral rules, has outlined these standards elaborated by the SCJN[43] to apply them to the electoral norms when they implement human rights, introducing a relevant variant to the scheme designed by the SCJN with the *Expediente Varios 912/2010*. For the Superior Chamber, after the impossibility of carrying out a consistent interpretation (in a broad or strict sense), and before determining the non-application of the legal precept in question, a proportionality test must be carried out that justifies the negative analysis (if applicable) of constitutionality and conventionality of the regulation analysed.[44]

In the first place, and when the meaning of the law is in accordance with the constitutionality block, it should be considered valid. Second, when the law is not openly contrary to the Constitution, but implements, regulates or delimits to some extent the exercise of a human right, to determine its constitutional regularity it must be subject to a proportionality test, in which it is verified whether the rule meets a legitimate legal purpose, as well as the need, suitability and proportionality required to achieve it. In the third and last place, when there is no possibility that the alternatives are directly consistent with the system, the non-application of the general rule must be stated.[45]

The application of these standards has allowed the Superior Chamber to rule on the non-application of a norm in a small number of cases if compared to the high number of decisions and it does so only when it cannot resolve via interpretation. This data can also be justified in consideration of the fact that, by exercising a constitutional review in electoral justice, interpretive results are produced more frequently in specific cases and especially in matters in which the extreme of non-application is not revealed. This means that no criticism of unconstitutionality or unconventionality is attributed to the textual content of the rule at stake. Thus, the Superior Chamber internalises relevant international norms that allow the protection of political-electoral rights in interpretive way in specific cases.

Finally, if on the one hand the attitude of the Court has been to limit the inapplicability of the laws that it considers unconstitutional and to prefer to proceed with the consistent interpretation, on the other hand it has been developing an extensive jurisprudence of the spatial limits of the declaration of unconstitutionality originally limited to the specific case, extending said effects to third parties

[42] See A Herrera García, 'Sentencias fundacionales del control de convencionalidad en la jurisprudencia del Tribunal Electoral del Poder Judicial de la Federación' in Acosta Vázquez et al (n 32).

[43] *Tesis XXI/2016*, 'Control constitucional y convencional de normas electorales. Método para determinar la regularidad de una norma que instrumenta un derecho humano' (2016) 18 *Gaceta Jurisprudencia y Tesis en materia electoral* 74.

[44] See Herrera García (n 42) 254 ff, 264.

[45] These standards have been outlined in the decision *SUP-REC-538/2015*, 23 October 2015.

who did not intervene in the process. According to the case law of the Superior Chamber, the effects of a declaration of unconstitutionality are not necessarily exclusive to the parties; they can generate general effects (*erga omnes*). For this to be possible, the following conditions must be met: first, they must be people who are in the same legal situation. Second, there must be an identity of the fundamental rights violated or that may be affected due to the application of a rule declared contrary to the Federal Constitution or international treaties. Third, there is the need of a similar factual circumstance with respect to the event that generated the violation. And finally, the identity in the claim of the person who obtained, by means of a judicial ruling, the non-application of the unconstitutional or unconventional electoral norm is needed.[46]

IV. THE ABSTRACT CONSTITUTIONAL REVIEW OF LEGISLATION

The *Acción de Inconstitucionalidad* procedure arose with the constitutional reform of December 1994 to provide an abstract control of the constitutional consistency of general rules.[47] However, when it was pointed out that said control mechanism would create a potential conflict between a general rule and the Political Constitution of the United Mexican States, at first, electoral rules were expressly excluded – albeit without explicit justification – as it was decided that said matter would remain outside the control of acts and general rules by way of constitutional controversy. The reasons have already been explained above.

To build a comprehensive system of justice in relation to electoral matters, which would allow electoral laws to be invariably subject to the provisions of the Constitution, to protect the electoral political rights of Mexican citizens, to establish the constitutional review of acts and resolutions and decisions of the local electoral authorities, as well as to allow the final resolution of a judicial issue in the presidential election, the constitutional and political-electoral reform of 1996[48] opened up the possibility that electoral norms would be subject to abstract control by way of an action of unconstitutionality.

Since 2007,[49] when the relationship between the TEPJF and the SCJN was defined,[50] the SCJN has received around 500 actions of unconstitutionality in electoral matters. The years which see reforms of political-electoral issues or that precede electoral processes see a significant increase in the number of

[46] See Herrera García (n 42) 273 ff.

[47] Published in the Official Gazette of the Federation on 31 December1994. See above.

[48] Published in the Official Gazette of the Federation on 22 August1996.

[49] In the present chapter, we take this date into account so that the analysis goes hand in hand with the study of the jurisprudence of the TEPJF, since 2007 is the year in which the relationship between the SCJN and the Electoral Tribunal is defined in terms of constitutional control.

[50] See JR Cossío Díaz, *Constitución, democracia y jurisdicción electoral* (México, Editorial Porrúa, 2010) 157 ff.

unconstitutional actions. The vast majority of activities falling into this category were carried out by political parties (more than 80 per cent). Among the most critical actions of unconstitutionality analysed by the SCJN after the 2014 reforms are those related to the distribution of powers between the federal and local regimes, provided for in both the General Law of Political Parties[51] and the General Law of Electoral Institutions and Procedures[52] and, to a lesser extent, also the General Law of Electoral Crimes.[53]

The most relevant challenges have dealt with the scope of freedom of expression. By declaring the unconstitutionality of the conduct of 'denigrating' institutions or political parties through political or electoral propaganda provided for in Article 41, second paragraph, base III, section C, first paragraph of the Constitution, and leaving only the prohibition of the 'slander [against] people',[54] the Supreme Court determined that this provision only protected people against slander, not institutions and political parties. Additionally, it pointed out the importance of protecting the freedom of expression of political parties, emphasising that this contributes to promoting the democratic participation of people, as, through the information they provide, they contribute to the exercise of the vote being free and for citizens to have the necessary information to evaluate their representatives.[55] More recently, in terms of prohibitions on political and electoral propaganda, the Court declared invalid the precepts that provided as a sanction, an assumption that political or electoral propaganda is capable of slandering political parties or institutions, considering that the constitutional protection against slander only protects people, so it was not possible for protection to cover subjects other than these. Thus, it considered that it was a restriction on the freedom of expression of political parties without justification (*Acciones de Inconstitucionalidad 133/2020, 134/2020, 165/2020 y 273/2020*).

Another relevant issue has been the new electoral organisation arising from the consolidation of the Electoral National Institute and the rules subsequently imposed on the local political electoral bodies,[56] in terms of access to the

[51] Published in the Official Gazette of the Federation on 23 May 2014.

[52] Published in the Official Gazette of the Federation on 23 May 2014.

[53] Published in the Official Gazette of the Federation on 27 June 2014.

[54] According to Art 41, s C of the Mexican Constitution: 'In the political or electoral propaganda that the parties and candidates disseminate, they must refrain from expressions that slander people.' The reform was published in the Official Gazette of the Federation on 10 February 2014.

[55] This principle was established in the following decisions: *Acción de Inconstitucionalidad 35/2014 y sus acumuladas 74/2014, 76/2014 y 83/2014*; *Acción de Inconstitucionalidad 38/2014 y sus acumuladas 91/2014, 92/2014 y 93/2014*; *Acción de Inconstitucionalidad 90/2014*; *Acción de Inconstitucionalidad 50/2015 y sus acumuladas 55/2015, 56/2015 y 58/2015*; *Acción de Inconstitucionalidad 64/2015 y sus acumuladas 65/2015, 66/2015, 68/2015 y 70/2015*; *Acción de Inconstitucionalidad 67/2015 y sus acumuladas 72/2015 y 82/2015*; *Acción de Inconstitucionalidad 129/2015 y sus acumuladas 130/2015, 131/2015, 132/2015, 133/2015 y 137/2015*.

[56] With the reform of February 2014 to Art 41, fraction V, s D, of the Constitution, the power to regulate everything related to the national professional electoral service was reserved to the Electoral National Institute, providing that it would be composed of the public servants of the executive and

media,[57] financing and the new model for auditing the income and expenses of the political parties and their candidates,[58] as well as the mixed electoral systems of relative majority and proportional representation to integrate the federal legislative bodies[59] and those of the federative entities (the latter of which was particularly important in the reforms to the electoral regime of Mexico City and in several states that modified their schemes and reduced the number of deputies and members of the City Councils to be elected in 2018).[60]

technical bodies of the Institute, and of the electoral bodies of the states. This principle was established in the following decisions: *Acción de Inconstitucionalidad 35/2014 y sus acumuladas 74/2014, 76/2014 y 83/2014*; *Acción de Inconstitucionalidad 51/2014 y sus acumuladas 77/2014 y 79/2014*; *Acción de Inconstitucionalidad 50/2015 y sus acumuladas 55/2015, 56/2015 y 58/2015*; *Acción de Inconstitucionalidad 126/2015 y su acumulada 127/2015*; and *Acción de Inconstitucionalidad 50/2016 y sus acumuladas 51/2016, 52/2016, 53/2016 y 54/2016*.

[57] Regarding the access to media, the Supreme Court considered valid that, during the pre-campaigns and federal electoral campaigns, 30% of the total time on radio and television available to the political parties had been distributed equally, and the remaining 70% had been distributed in proportion to the percentage of votes obtained in the immediately preceding election for federal deputies. It was also considered valid that, in the pre-campaigns and campaigns for local elections, the basis for the distribution of 70% of the time assigned to the political parties was the percentage of votes obtained by each one in the immediately preceding election for local deputies. These principles were established in the *Acción de Inconstitucionalidad 22/2014 y sus acumuladas 26/2014, 28/2014 y 30/2014*.

[58] Regarding the financing of political parties, the SCJN held that in s II of Art 41 of the Constitution the public financing of national political parties should be divided into three large items: 1) for the maintenance of permanent ordinary activities; 2) for activities aimed at obtaining the vote during electoral processes; 3) for activities of a specific nature, consisting of education, training, socioeconomic and political research, as well as editorial tasks of the parties. In addition, the SCJN determined as unconstitutional the provisions of the General Law of Political Parties by which two new concepts of economic administrations were instituted, namely, those of 'party structure' and 'electoral structures'. The decision not to consider this criterion in accordance with the Constitution is based on the fact that it would mean increasing ordinary spending with disbursements that are not continuous or permanent, and subtracting an equivalent amount from intermittent funds for obtaining the vote, which would not be audited for effects of the control of the resources applied during the campaigns. This principle was established in the *Acción de Inconstitucionalidad 22/2014 y sus acumuladas 26/2014, 28/2014 y 30/2014*. More recently and with reference to the 2020–21 electoral process, the SCJN has issued the following principle on financing: a) reduction to ordinary public financing of local political parties (*Acción de Inconstitucionalidad 165/2020*); b) prohibition of receiving private financing in case of not having the right to public financing (*Acción de Inconstitucionalidad 132/2020*, a criterion in contrast to that established by the Superior Chamber of the TEPJF when resolving the file *SUP-JRC-4/2017*); c) annual limits on the financing that parties can receive from their members and supporters (*Acción de Inconstitucionalidad 156/2020*).

[59] This principle was established in the *Acción de Inconstitucionalidad 22/2014 y sus acumuladas 26/2014, 28/2014 y 30/2014*.

[60] This principle was established in the following *Acciones de Inconstitucionalidad*: *13/2014 y sus acumuladas 14/2014, 15/2014 y 16/2014*; *65/2014 y su acumulada 81/2014*; *86/2014 y su acumulada 88/2014*; *36/2015 y sus acumuladas 37/2015, 40/2015 y 41/2015*; *42/2015 y sus acumuladas 43/2015 y 44/2015*; *67/2015 y sus acumuladas 72/2015 y 82/2015*; *129/2015 y sus acumuladas 130/2015, 131/2015, 132/2015, 133/2015 y 137/2015; 55/2016*. On the other hand, Art 116 of the Constitution, s II, third paragraph, provides for the obligation to integrate state legislatures with deputies elected by both principles (relative majority and proportional representation). The constitutional and legal reform that gave rise to Mexico City as a 'federative entity that enjoys autonomy in everything related to its internal regime and its political and administrative organization' (Art 122 of the Political Constitution of the United States Mexicans), introduced the determination that the Congress of

In the *Acción de Inconstitucionalidad 22/2014 y sus acumuladas 26/2014, 28/2014 y 30/2014*, the SCJN stated that, given the lack of exhaustive regulation in the Constitution regarding independent candidates, the federal and local legislatures would have a wide margin of freedom to configure this figure, albeit without departing from the constitutional principles in electoral matters. The Court endorsed the power granted to the secondary legislator to regulate independent candidates, based on the fact that Articles 35, section II, 41 and 116, section IV, of the Constitution, as well as the second transitory of the decree that reformed it,[61] provided for only elementary guidelines to which these candidates had to adhere. Thus, those laws establishing for independent candidates to require one per cent of the citizen support from the nominal list of voters to participate in the presidential election were considered constitutionally valid; as were those when it came to requiring two per cent support from the same list corresponding to the state (for seats with a relative majority of senators) or the electoral district (for seats with a relative majority of deputies). The foregoing adheres to the legally demanded requirements of independent candidates who want to obtain their official registration, to which must be added those established in Article 385 of the General Law of Electoral Institutions and Procedures.[62]

The 2020–21 electoral process was the largest in the history of Mexico due to the number of positions to be elected (21,368) and the number of potential voters (close to 94 million people). Twenty-seven Mexican states made reforms to their respective electoral legislation. In some cases, new laws were even issued on the matter.[63] Among the issues addressed in these reforms were the modification of the start date of local electoral processes, provisions related to political violence against women based on gender, prohibitions regarding political and electoral propaganda, regulation of coalitions, electoral training, financing, affirmative actions for indigenous people, modification to the cap on campaign expenses and a reduction in the remuneration of electoral consultants, among others.

More than 60 actions of unconstitutionality were brought challenging the normative changes of the rules that would have governed the 2020–21 electoral

Mexico City would be integrated by an equal number of deputies elected by the principle of relative majority and the principle of proportional representation, which was endorsed by the Supreme Court when resolving the *Acciones de Inconstitucionalidad 15/2017 y sus acumuladas*.

[61] Published in the Official Gazette of the Federation on 10 February 2014.

[62] Some *acciones de inconstitucionalidad* established important standards regarding the uniform regime of coalitions and the common candidacy in local elections. This principle was established in the following decisions: *Acción de Inconstitucionalidad 17/2014*; *Acción de Inconstitucionalidad 36/2014 y sus acumuladas 87/2014 y 89/2014*; *Acción de Inconstitucionalidad 39/2014 y sus acumuladas 44/2014, 54/2014 y 84/2014*; *Acción de Inconstitucionalidad 59/2014*; *Acción de Inconstitucionalidad 17/2015 y su acumulada 18/2015*; *Acción de Inconstitucionalidad 64/2015 y sus acumuladas 65/2015, 66/2015, 68/20153 y 70/2015*; *Acción de Inconstitucionalidad 69/2015 y sus acumuladas 71/2015 y 73/2015*; *Acción de Inconstitucionalidad 103/2015*.

[63] As in Chiapas and San Luis Potosí.

contest. In the first instance, the regulations that modified the beginning of the local electoral process were challenged. The SCJN declared valid the normative provision that postponed the beginning of the electoral process in Sinaloa from September to December of the year prior to the election, recognising the freedom of the state Congress to make such a change (*Acción de Inconstitucionalidad 135/2020*). However, when resolving the *Acción de Inconstitucionalidad 165/2020 y su acumulada*, the SCJN declared invalid the rule that extended the start date of the electoral process in Jalisco. This by concluding that although the local Congresses have ample freedom to establish the start dates of the electoral processes and the duration of the pre-campaigns and campaigns, it is up to the local electoral institutes to determine the factual issues that are presented prior to the beginning of the electoral processes and during these, to defer to them in the determination of any adjustments concerning the beginning, development and conclusion of said processes, which arise from problems observable in the real context faced by the federal entities and which may lead to the need to postpone the initiation of such processes in case of social problems, public safety or general health.

The SCJN has also ruled on the eligibility of people convicted of committing gender-based political violence against women. When resolving the *Acción de Inconstitucionalidad 140/2020 y su acumulada 145/2020*, the Court considered that a provision that limited the eligibility of people for having been convicted of gender-based political violence against women should be interpreted in accordance with the Constitution, in the sense that they should only lose eligibility in cases of the commission of the crime of gender-based political violence against women and after a final sentence. The relevance of this criterion lies in its possible discrepancy with what is established by the Electoral Court, which has constructed a criterion according to which any sanction – whether administrative, electoral or criminal – incurred from criminal conduct concerning gender-based political violence against women translates into the impossibility of participating as a candidate or candidate.[64]

With the *Acción de Inconstitucionalidad 132/2020, 133/2020, 134/2020, 140/2020 y su acumulada 145/2020*, regarding the regulation of coalitions by local Congresses, the Supreme Court declared invalid different rules that established requirements not foreseen in the general laws for the formation of coalitions, modified the terms established for their registration and, in a general way, sought to regulate them, based on the argument that the regulation of coalitions is within the exclusive competence of the Congress of the Union. However, when resolving the *Acción de Inconstitucionalidad 236/2020 y su acumulada*, the SCJN declared the validity of a provision of the Constitution of Baja California which, regarding the assignment of deputies through the principle of proportional representation, establishes that in the case of coalitions,

[64] See TEPJF, *SUP-REC-91/2020*, 29 July 2020.

the first allocation to each political party must also be determined based on the registered coalition agreement. The foregoing, considering that said legislative rule does not substantially regulate the figure of coalitions, but is an instrumental norm to give meaning to the system of assigning deputies by the principle of proportional representation.

Among the most recent cases also noteworthy are the *Acción de Inconstitucionalidad 140/2020 y su acumulada 145/2020* with which the SCJN declared invalid various rules that regulated electoral training in favour of the Local Electoral Institutes, by virtue of the fact that this matter is reserved to the National Electoral Institute, and the *Acciones de Inconstitucionalidad 136/2020, 148/2020, 158/2020 y su acumulada 241/2020* on the omission to carry out a prior consultation with the indigenous peoples and communities, which led the Court to declare invalid, legislative modifications which, being likely to affect the interests of the indigenous and Afro-Mexican peoples and communities disproportionately, meant the local Congresses had failed to comply with their obligation to consult with them prior to the establishment of affirmative actions.

Finally, the Court also ruled on the regulation of the campaign spending ceiling,[65] the remuneration of the members of the Electoral Institute,[66] the competence to establish types and penalties in matters of electoral crimes,[67] the cancellation of the registration of incomplete City Council payrolls[68] and the reduction of the number of members of City Councils.[69]

[65] In deciding the *Acción de Inconstitucionalidad 132/2020*, the Court pointed out that the states have freedom of configuration to determine the limits of campaign expenses, as long as they are subject to the parameters of reasonableness and proportionality.

[66] In the *Acción de Inconstitucionalidad 128/2020 y acumuladas*, the Court declared invalid the rule that established a decrease in the remuneration of the electoral counselors of Baja California, considering that with such a decrease their autonomy and impartiality were affected.

[67] See *Acción de Inconstitucionalidad 80/2019*, where the Court declared invalid the provisions of the Penal Code of Chihuahua that punished physical, psychological, emotional, or economic damage, which would result in the prevention of the exercise of women's political rights, with a prison sentence. This by concluding that the local Congresses lack the competence to determine criminal issues.

[68] See *Acción de Inconstitucionalidad 132/2020*, with which the Court declared valid the Electoral Law of the State of Querétaro according to which if the integration of a City Hall list is incomplete, its registration will be cancelled. The foregoing, considering that said provision does not restrict the right to vote or to be voted for as a candidate on the list, since it only establishes a consequence in the event that this situation is not corrected prior to the election. This is added to the fact that, in accordance with the principle of certainty, it is important that citizens know all the candidates that make up the City Council's list in order to exercise an informed vote. This is a criterion that contradicts the *Jurisprudencia 17/2018* of the TEPJF on '*Candidaturas a cargos de elección popular. los partidos políticos tienen la obligación de presentar fórmulas completas, a fin de garantizar la correcta integración de los ayuntamientos*', which establishes that in the event of the identification of incomplete forms or where there are duplicate applications in a form, if the requirement to correct them is omitted, it is possible that incomplete forms may be registered, considering that, in this way, the right to be elected of those who were duly nominated in completed forms is safeguarded, with the electoral administrative authorities being the ones who must implement measures that ensure the proper integration of the municipalities for their operation.

[69] In deciding the *Acción de Inconstitucionalidad 278/23020 y sus acumuladas*, the SCJN determined that the reduction in the number of trustees and aldermen of the municipalities of the State

V. CONCLUSION

Despite the important challenges that are currently being faced (especially with regard to maintaining its autonomy and independence from political control and maintaining the high standard of its decisions), in recent decades Mexico has consolidated itself – both nationally and internationally – as a solid democratic system.

This has been possible thanks to the consolidation of the electoral constitutional justice system. In particular, both the TEPJF through its Superior Chamber and the six Regional Chambers, as well as the SCJN, (especially in the years following the 2011 constitutional reform on human rights), have adopted important standards and issued decisions that have changed the course of federal and local elections.

These are decisions in which the protection and exercise of political-electoral rights have been maximised and enhanced, addressing issues such as gender equality, the political-electoral rights of indigenous peoples, gender equality, freedom of expression in electoral contests, the suspension of political-electoral rights and the origin of the means of challenge, among others.

The constitutional review of electoral legislation carried out by the TEPJF has specific characteristics that explain how the main effect of this control is of an interpretive type and rarely applicable. For this reason, the action of unconstitutionality has become, de facto, part of the legislative process in electoral matters, by constituting itself as the way through which a party can seek to nullify those provisions whose content contravenes the constitutional text, in order to prevent them forming part of the rules conducting the electoral process.

In addition, thanks to a more careful analysis of the electoral constitutional jurisprudence, we can see how they are able to correct omissions, antinomies and, sometimes, contradictions that the hyper-detailed electoral normative framework presents.[70] Very important aspects that have shown deficiencies are, among others, the system of prerogatives and control of political parties and candidates; the uniform system of coalitions – especially at the local level – and the figure of the common candidacy that does not exist at the federal level, but which has been recognised as being able to exist at the local level; the formulas to integrate the legislative bodies through the proportional representation system; as well as, in a special way, the normative regime of independent candidates.

of Mexico does not violate the principle of proportional representation, since the Constitution grants freedom to the local legislator to define the number and percentages of aldermen who occupy the position, as long as they are reasonable.

[70] On the 'schizophrenia' of the Mexican electoral legislator see I Spigno, 'El *test restrictivo* de la propaganda política (gubernamental y calumniosa). Una lectura crítica' in LE Ríos Vega (ed), *La justicia constitucional de los derechos políticos. Una agenda contemporánea* (México, Tirant lo Blanch, 2017) 261.

Also in the context of the new organic structure, both nationally and locally, the Supreme Court has had to resolve some extremely complex situations, which are made even more difficult precisely because of the lack of a clear or complete legal framework.

The proliferation of *acciones de inconstitucionalidad*, therefore, is a multi-factorial product. Among those factors that influence the high level of litigation in electoral matters are: the proliferation of electoral reforms, the issuance, not infrequently, of unclear, incomplete or contradictory regulations in the Mexican and state Constitutions; and the lack of comprehensive political consensus. In fact, where one or more political forces representing 33 per cent of the members of the legislative bodies are left out of the most important decisions or remain dissatisfied with the final result, they can seek the judicial route to reverse those with which they are dissatisfied. Finally, the *accion de inconstitucionalidad* has been used as an instrument to impose political pressure to resolve other pending issues on the legislative or executive agenda, often without a real legal basis for the challenges of unconstitutionality and even where those issues have been voted upon favourably by previous political agreements. But it must also be recognised that the parties, in general, are giving more and more importance to legal aspects, which is why they are increasingly concerned with having more and better advisors and litigants in electoral matters.

Similarly, it should not be forgotten that this litigious situation is also presented with great intensity in an additional avenue of constitutional control of equal relevance, given that the TEPJF, in exercise of its constitutional powers, can disapply those laws or electoral norms that they consider to be contrary to the Constitution, in the cases in which: a) they were not the subject of an action of unconstitutionality; b) that, having been so, the specific challenge was dismissed for not reaching the qualified majority of eight votes in plenary session of the Court or; c) that it did not reach a vote of six or more votes in plenary, in favour of declaring its validity.

It must be recognised that both the decisions of the Supreme Court and the Electoral Tribunal are not always peaceful; in many cases, they are subject to significant critical scrutiny, not just by political actors, but in academic and professional forums. This synergy can be very healthy, since it allows a comparison between the different criteria that are used in judicial headquarters on the various controversial issues. At the same time, when the academic studies are not serious and purposeful – while remaining critical and calling into question – there is a risk that the credibility of the institutions and electoral processes is undermined, essential factors for a true constitutional regime to exist. Legislative deficiencies mean that judicial or administrative decisions are not easy or even accepted by all. This can undoubtedly affect the democratic-electoral consistency and represent a very serious challenge for the Mexican democratic system.

12

Electoral Justice and the Supreme Federal Court in Brazilian Democracy

LUCAS HENRIQUE MUNIZ DA CONCEIÇÃO

I. INTRODUCTION

BRAZILIAN CONSTITUTIONAL HISTORY is permeated by liberal advances and drastic authoritarian interventions, which led to the development of particular approaches to liberal democracy and a specific framework of separation of powers. After the 1988 constitutional settlement, the Brazilian judicial power has maintained a firm grip on the country's political system, translated both in the Supreme Federal Court's extensive jurisdiction over an analytic constitution that regulates multiple areas of law and the overall management of the electoral system itself by a specialised justice spearheaded by the Superior Electoral Court (SEC).

As such, the positioning of the judicial branch is extensive and has been an object of study and criticism by political scientists and legal academics alike. On the one hand, political scientists have focused on institutional analysis, perceiving the design and framework of electoral justice in Brazil vis-à-vis its effectiveness in promoting legitimacy and trust in the electoral procedures of the country.[1] On the other hand, legal academics have focused on the judicialisation of the political competition promoted by the SEC and the Supreme Federal Court, engaging with the numerous alterations of electoral laws by resolutions and judicial decisions.[2]

This chapter summarises the historical foundations of the Brazilian framework for electoral management bodies. Furthermore, it analyses the intersection

[1] MTA Sadek, *A Justiça Eleitoral e a Consolidação Da Democracia No Brasil* (São Paulo, Fundação Konrad-Adenauer-Stiftung, 1995); M Taylor, 'A Justiça Eleitoral' in L Avritzer and F Anastasia (eds), *Reforma política no Brasil* (Belo Horizonte, Editora UFMG, 2006).

[2] DV Fleischer and L Barreto, 'El impacto de la justicia electoral sobre el sistema político brasileño' [2009] *América Latina Hoy: Revista de Ciencias Sociales* 117; LR Barroso, 'Judicialização, Ativismo Judicial e Legitimidade Democrática' (2012) 5 *(SYN)THESIS* 23; V Marchetti, 'Governança Eleitoral: O Modelo Brasileiro de Justiça Eleitoral' (2008) 51 *Dados* 865.

between the SEC and the Supreme Federal Court, perceiving how the accumulation of administrative and judicial power in both institutions affects Brazilian constitutional democracy. The relationship between the two courts has been ambivalent, with moments of confrontation, deference, and interdependence, despite the relevant autonomy of both institutions.

As such, the chapter is divided as follows. Section II presents a historical and analytical introduction to the Brazilian electoral justice framework and its positioning through different Brazilian constitutions. It expands on the regulatory power of the SEC, contextualising the monopolisation of electoral governance in the country. Section III addresses the democratic regime established in Brazil with the Constitution of 1988, focusing on the transformative aspiration embedded in the country's legal culture, specifically concerning the Supreme Federal Court prerogative to materialise this constitutional promise. Section IV analyses the repercussions of this constitutional design vis-à-vis the electoral justice framework in a period marked by unstable politics – the general elections of 2022. Section V concludes.

II. THE BRAZILIAN SUPERIOR ELECTORAL TRIBUNAL: INSTITUTIONAL DESIGN AND JUDICIAL ACTIVISM

Brazil has held elections since its colonisation period when citizens could vote on local representatives and, in the year prior to its independence, representatives for the Constituent Courts of Lisbon in 1821. Still, only after the country formalised its Republican form of government in 1891, dismantling the constitutional monarchy established after independence, the electoral justice system became a project heavily debated among the country's political class.[3]

During the first Republic, Brazil harboured an oligarchical state in which constitutionalism became 'the product of a conciliation-compromise between a modernising and social authoritarianism, and a conservative bourgeois liberalism'.[4] While the Constitution of 1891 adopted a centralised federalist and presidential system inspired by the US Constitution, the constitutional predicaments diverged from the reality of Brazilian society. Economic and political elites consisting of landowners, politicians, and army officers maintained an authoritarian behaviour towards civil society and exacerbated the conservative features of the Constitution.[5] As such, the federal executive power's intervention in state

[3] TC de Souza Cardoso Vale, 'Pré-história e história da Justiça Eleitoral' (2011) *ANPUH* bibliotecadigital.tse.jus.br/xmlui/handle/bdtse/4853.

[4] AC Wolkmer, *Constitucionalismo e direitos sociais no Brasil* (São Paulo, Acadêmica, 1989) 35. R Gargarella, 'Latin America: Constitutions in Trouble' in MA Graber, S Levinson and MV Turshnet (eds), *Constitutional Democracy in Crisis?* (Oxford, Oxford University Press, 2018).

[5] R Gargarella, *Latin American Constitutionalism, 1810–2010: The Engine Room of the Constitution* (Oxford, Oxford University Press, 2013) 36–38.

politics was used as a political tool to enforce the rule of factions favoured by authorities in the then country's capital of Rio de Janeiro, while state governments performed unconstitutional acts with the avowal of the national executive in exchange for political support.[6]

Therefore, the political class was dominated by representatives of the state of São Paulo and Minas Gerais, who alternated presidential positions as both were relevant economic regions of the country during the period extending from 1891 to 1929.[7] This state of affairs was maintained by intensive electoral frauds stemming from local political disputes to the federal level. By then, voting was not mandatory, and the political franchise excluded women, establishing voting rights only for literate men over 21. In a country populated by recently liberated black people (slavery was abolished in 1888) and poor immigrants from Europe, the Middle East and Asia, the franchise also excluded large sections of society and maintained voting rights over the political and economic elite.[8] Beyond this, an open ballot system facilitated the intense manipulation of those who could vote, with local landowners and political leaders heavily influencing the electorate's decision-making.[9] As such, with the electoral process being managed by the local administration and the legislative power, the manipulation of the electoral results was maintained with practices such as the falsification of the electoral minutes by the local voting precinct, misrepresenting the counting of votes in remote and small cities, and the so-called 'beheading of candidates' (*degola* in Portuguese) in which the Legislative verification committees refused to recognise the election of a candidate despite a majority in votes.[10]

In 1930, the political environment in the country was drastically changed by the so-called 'Revolution of 30', which had as its motto the establishment of mechanisms to protect and extend an 'electoral truth'.[11] The 'revolt' was portrayed as the product of a complete mistrust of the electoral procedures that led to the 1930 general election. The then-losing candidate (Getúlio Vargas) seized the national executive power, dissolved Congress, and established the electoral justice as the authority to ensure electoral authenticity. All these measures were taken within a provisional government.[12]

Brazil's first electoral code was established in 1932, setting the framework for the electoral process in municipalities, states and the federal union. The

[6] PA Martin, 'Federalism in Brazil' (1938) 18 *The Hispanic American Historical Review* 143; GMA Rodrigues, MA Garcia Lopes Lorencini and A Zimmermann, 'The Supreme Federal Court of Brazil: Protecting Democracy and Centralized Power' in NT Aroney and J Kincaid (eds), *Courts in Federal Countries* (Toronto, University of Toronto Press, 2018).

[7] L Basbaum, *Historia Sincera da Republica: 1889–1930*, 4th edn, (São Paulo, Alfa-Omega, 1975).

[8] J Marconi Nicolau, *História do voto no Brasil* (Rio de Janeiro, Zahar, 2002).

[9] Basbaum (n 7).

[10] P Ricci and J Porto Zulini, 'Partidos, competição política e fraude eleitoral: a tônica das eleições na Primeira República' (2014) 57 *Dados* 443.

[11] Vale (n 3).

[12] ED Salgado, 'The Judicial Branch as a (Pretty) Bad Political Regulator: Notes from Brazil' [2022] *Revista de Derecho Político* 339, revistas.uned.es/index.php/derechopolitico/article/view/33579.

code transferred the competence for the administration of the electoral process from the Legislative to the Judiciary by establishing the Electoral Justice as a specialised branch of the judicial system. The institution's attributions included the preparation and realisation of elections, registering the electorate and the candidates, counting the votes, and formally recognising elected candidates.[13] In addition, the electoral justice was also responsible for solving legal disputes concerning all steps in the electoral procedures, with the institution thus combining both administrative and judicial functions.[14]

This framework was consolidated in 1934 with the writing of a new constitution and the formal election of Getúlio Vargas, who transitioned from interim chief to the first President of the new Brazilian Republic. The 1934 Constitution solidified the role and function of electoral justice to both administer and adjudicate all the electoral processes in the country.[15] The main argument supporting the role of judges in managing elections and ensuring a competitive and fair democratic process was that unlike the executive and legislative, the judicial branch would be politically neutral and disinterested in drafting rules or issuing decisions in favour of one particular representation of the political spectrum. As such, a specialised branch of the judicial system was perceived by jurists as the most efficient way to administer elections in all entities of the federation (in Brazil, municipalities, states, and the Federal Union).[16]

However, the Constitution of 1934 was short-lived, and the electoral justice was dissolved along with the National Congress in 1937 when Getúlio Vargas implemented the 'Estado Novo' dictatorship. Until 1945, no elections were held in the country, and the regime was characterised by increasing centralisation of powers. Although a period in which Brazilian social rights were extended, with the establishment of labour rights and welfare policies, Vargas's rule was marked by an affinity with the European fascist movement, the broadcast of nationalist views regarding immigration and trade, anti-Semitic sentiment, disdain for democratic values and political liberties, and a national security discourse that condoned arbitrary rule.[17]

Prior to the end of his regime, Vargas issued an executive decree reinstating the electoral justice and imposing specific rules for presidential and congressional elections, such as the requirement that all political parties must have a national expression (being represented in National Congress and not only in state legislatures and executive mandates) as well as the restriction on the right for individuals to present candidacies for office, which became a monopolised

[13] Article 5 of Presidencia Brasil, 'Decreto No. 21.076/1932'.

[14] ibid.

[15] JF de Assis Brasil, *Democracia Representativa: Do Voto e Da Maneira de Votar* (Lisboa, Imprensa Nacional, 1931); JF de Assis Brasil, *A Democracia Representativa Na República (Antologia)* (Brasília, Editora do Senado Federal, 1998).

[16] Fr Cavalcanti Pontes de Miranda, *Comentários à Constituição Da República Dos Estados Unidos Do Brasil*, vol II (Rio de Janeiro, Guanabara, 1937); Vale (n 3).

[17] FVidal Luna and HS Klein, *Brazil Since 1980* (Cambridge, Cambridge University Press, 2006).

prerogative exercised by political parties.[18] Although instituted at the last breath of an authoritarian regime, these institutions were replicated in further developments in electoral law and are still perceived nowadays.

Thus, the rules and general framework of electoral justice were inserted in the democratic Constitution of 1946 and were later replicated during the long dictatorial period between 1964 and 1985. During the military dictatorship in the 1960s, a new Electoral Code was established, maintaining the federalised organisation of the electoral justice as a branch of the judicial system, even though combining state and federal judges in the administration of elections and adjudication of legal issues concerning electoral disputes in all levels of the federation. With Brazil's re-democratisation and promulgation of its current 1988 Constitution, the system has remained unchanged despite its authoritarian origins and the relative centralisation of powers to the federal government in managing all election cycles in the country.[19]

A. Administration and Adjudication: An Organisational Analyses

As a special branch of the Brazilian judicial system, the electoral justice framework comprises the Superior Electoral Court (SEC), Regional Electoral Courts (REC), electoral judges, and electoral juntas.[20] The SEC is the apex court of the system, based in Brasília and composed of seven justices. In turn, RECs are distributed in each of the 26 Member States of the union plus the federal district of Brasilia, all also composed of seven judges. Finally, electoral judges act within the municipalities of each state following the territorial distribution of districts of the state judicial system, while electoral juntas are organised periodically for each electoral period.

Competencies are shared among these courts, which act as administrators and adjudicators of elections for municipal, state and federal offices. Among others, the SEC has the jurisdiction to: (i) administer and adjudicate issues concerning the registration of political parties, their national directorates and the candidacies for the offices of president and vice-president of the Republic; (ii) issue judgements on appeals against decisions of RECs; (iii) approve the demarcation of electoral zones within the states defined by the RECs; (iv) request the assistance from the federal union to enforce its own decisions or state electoral court decisions that request it; and (v) take any measure it deems necessary and convenient for the execution of electoral legislation.[21] In addition to these

[18] Salgado (n 12).

[19] ibid.

[20] Constituição da República Federativa do Brasil [Federal Constitution of the Brazilian Republic] 1988 Art 118.

[21] Congresso Nacional Brasil, 'Código Eleitoral Brasileiro' [Brazilian Electoral Code] Arts 22 and 23.

comprehensive mandates aligned with its jurisdictional character, the SEC also conflates the attribution to prepare and distribute voting material, publishing norms related to preparatory acts and rules for each election cycle, the counting and disclosure of electoral results, and the formal induction of elected candidates for the office of president and vice president.

The RECs perform similar adjudicatory duties on elections held at the state level (for offices such as state governor and members of state legislatures). As such, it has the jurisdiction to: (i) manage and adjudicate the registration of political party's state and municipal directories and the candidacies for state governor and vice-governor, representatives at state legislative assemblies, and representatives of the state for the National Congress; (ii) issue judgements on appeals against decisions from electoral judges; (iii) constitute the electoral juntas; and (iv) formally request the SEC for the use of force for implementing its decisions.[22] Electoral judges are the electoral authorities for the electoral districts within states, organised according to the allocation of state judges. They are in charge of the registration of voters, the transference of residence between electoral districts, and adjudicating on electoral crimes and other transgressions provided by the Electoral Code.[23]

Although these institutions are prescribed in the Brazilian Constitution and federal law, the electoral justice in Brazil does not have a consolidated composition.[24] Its executive members (justices and judges) have a mandate of two years and originate from different bodies of the judicial system, in addition to lawyers who are admitted to the Brazilian Bar Association (Figure 1 below).

The SEC comprises seven executive members: three are chosen from the Supreme Federal Court after a majority election within the institution. Two are chosen from the Superior Court of Justice also through a majority election within that judicial institution, and two lawyers are appointed by the President of the Republic and chosen among a list of six candidates maintained by the Supreme Federal Court.[25]

At the state level, RECs follow a similar rationale, with its seven members having a mandate of two years. Of those, two judges are drawn from the State Court of Appeals, selected through a majority election among the justices of the appellate courts of each state. Two are state judges. A federal judge and two lawyers fill the final vacancies. At this level, the lawyers are also appointed by the president of the Republic but chosen among a list of six organised by the Court of Appeals for each state. Lastly, electoral judges are also not explicitly

[22] ibid Arts 29 and 30.

[23] ibid Art 32.

[24] Constituição da República Federativa do Brasil [Federal Constitution of the Brazilian Republic] Art 118; Brasil, 'Código Eleitoral Brasileiro' [Brazilian Electoral Code] (n 22); Lei das Eleições [Elections Act]. Lei No 9.504/97 1997; Lei dos Partidos Politicos [Political Parties Act]. Lei No 9.096/95 1995.

[25] Constituição da República Federativa do Brasil [Federal Constitution of the Brazilian Republic] Art 119, s II.

appointed for the electoral justice system, being drawn from state judges that accumulate functions in their district.

Figure 1 Partial organogram of the Brazilian Judicial System, indicating the origin of executive members of the Electoral Justice branch

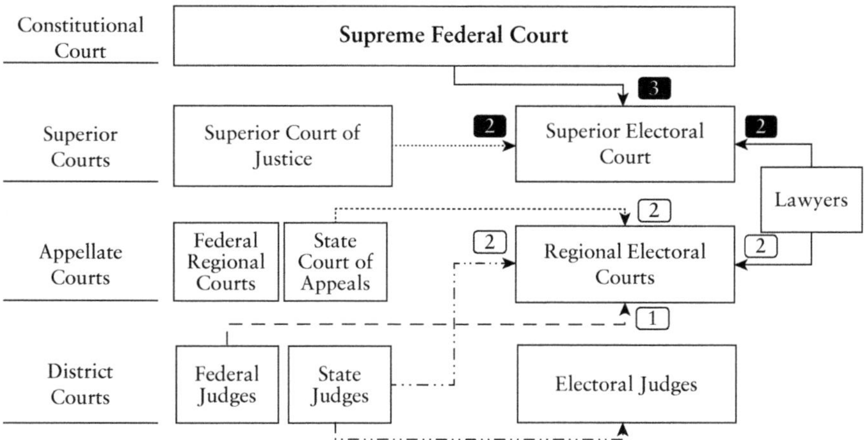

The fixed mandate of two years, the heterogeneous institutional background of its members, and the form of selection are mechanisms established to avoid political affiliations and preferences in the administration and adjudication of electoral procedures.[26] Nevertheless, the system is still heavily centralised in the union, which can be perceived by the prerogative of the executive to appoint the lawyers composing the SEC and REC from a pre-organised list maintained by the Supreme Federal Court and the Court of Appeals for each state, respectively.

The confluence between the Supreme Federal Court and the SEC raises concerns for the overall functioning of Brazilian democracy.[27] The former is composed of a total of 11 justices appointed by the President of the Republic and confirmed by the Senate, with life-long mandates. The latter comprises seven members and includes three justices of the Supreme Federal Court plus three alternates. As such, arguably, six constitutional court justices are exposed to electoral governance, which brings at least two issues concerning the stability of Brazilian democracy. First, this framework tests the limits for the legitimacy of judicial review proceedings against decisions of the electoral justice, as

[26] AP de Almeida Lopes, 'Governança Eleitoral e Ativismo Judicial: Uma Análise Comparada sobre o Impacto de Decisões Judiciais nas Regras do Processo Eleitoral Brasileiro' (2019) 62 *Dados*, www.scielo.br/j/dados/a/MdtLDf4JHnydNzQPVvXvLJG/?lang=pt.

[27] V Marchetti, *Justiça e Competição Eleitoral*, 1st edn (Santo André, Editora UFABC, 2015); ED Salgado, *Administración de las elecciones y jurisdicción electoral: un análisis del modelo mexicano y una crítica a la opción brasilera* (Ciudad de México, Universidad Nacional Autónoma de México Instituto de Investigaciones Jurídicas, 2016) 205–16, ru.juridicas.unam.mx:80/xmlui/handle/123456789/13088.

members of the constitutional court performing the review are directly involved in the contested legal act and do not excuse themselves.[28] Second, it exposes the country's constitutional court to political debates in a manner that amplifies the risk of it being implicated in party politics.[29] In order to showcase how these dynamics affect Brazilian democracy, the following sections will develop on the electoral process and the role of the Supreme Federal Court in either contesting or asserting the activities of the electoral justice system.

B. The Management of the Electoral Process

The comparative study of electoral governance is grounded on the analytical distinction between the variables concerning three levels of electoral governance, namely, rule-making, rule implementation, and rule adjudication.[30] Democracies employ different institutions that may amalgamate some levels, combining one or more state powers in the governance of electoral disputes.[31] In Brazil, the three variables are concentrated on the electoral justice system and its institutions, following the country's specific federative arrangement.[32]

In terms of rulemaking, the Brazilian Constitution defines most of the norms concerning the electoral system and the political rights of citizens. These constitutional provisions are complemented by federal law (the Electoral Code, the Elections Act, and the Political Parties Act) and secondary legislation established within the electoral justice system.[33]

The SEC maintains broad regulatory powers provisioned in Article 23, IX of the Electoral code, which provides that the court shall 'issue the regulations it deems necessary for the enforcement of this Code'. This prerogative is exercised in relation to electoral processes in all of the federation through 'judicial resolutions' that, in some circumstances, have an ultra vires effect.[34] In addition, Article 23, XII of the Electoral Code also provides the SEC with a consultancy role in which political parties may refer to the interpretation or application of electoral rules, with the court's manifestation having normative value and being also published as judicial resolutions.

[28] Salgado (n 12).

[29] R Hirschl, 'The Judicialization of Mega-Politics and the Rise of Political Courts' (2008) 11 *Annual Review of Political Science* 93, doi.org/10.1146/annurev.polisci.11.053006.183906.

[30] S Mozaffar and A Schedler, 'The Comparative Study of Electoral Governance – Introduction' (2002) 23 *International Political Science Review* 5, 7, doi.org/10.1177/0192512102023001001.

[31] R López-Pintor, *Electoral Management Bodies as Institutions of Governance* / (Bureau for Development Policy, UNDP, 2000) digitallibrary.un.org/record/440927.

[32] Salgado (n 12).

[33] Brasil (n 21); Lei dos Partidos Politicos [Political Parties Act]. Lei No 9.096/95; Lei das Eleições [Elections Act]. Lei No 9.504/97.

[34] Desiree Salgado argues that the electoral justice framework should not have the power to legislate electoral rules, arguing that secondary norms developed in electoral courts must have a constitutional foundation. ED Salgado, *Princípios Constitucionais Eleitorais*, 2nd edn (Belo Horizonte, Fórum, 2015); Salgado (n 12).

An example relates to the regulation of party loyalty and the conditions for an elected official losing their mandate. Brazil's electoral system is designed as a hybrid system of representation.[35] Representatives elected for the Chamber of Deputies (the lower house of the National Congress), state legislative assemblies, and municipal legislative assemblies are elected in an open-list proportional representative system. In contrast, representatives elected for the Senate and the offices of city mayor, state governors, president and vice-president are elected by a majority vote.[36]

As such, when electing the representatives for the 513 seats in the Chamber of Deputies, although citizens can vote for one specific candidate, their vote is counted towards the political party hosting the candidacy, with the candidate preference being registered only for the party's distribution of seats gained in the electoral cycle. In this scenario, party loyalty becomes essential for elected representatives since seat allocation is linked with the votes the political party has secured from all of the candidates it presented for office.

Nevertheless, the 1988 Constitution regulates the specific conditions necessary for removing representatives in the National Congress. Article 55 of the Federal Constitution does not differentiate between the representatives elected through the proportional system (those in the Chamber of Deputies) and those elected through a majority system (those in the Senate), and as such, does not provide the possibility of a loss of congressional mandate in case of eventual changes in party affiliation.[37] From 1989 to 2007, the Supreme Federal Court maintained the interpretation that party affiliation and loyalty could not be invoked as a reason for removing an elected representative from the Chamber of Deputies from office.[38] This interpretation followed a broad understanding of the freedom of association, a fundamental right constitutionally prescribed, and the historical conditions that led to the drafting of the 1988 Constitution.[39]

During military dictatorship, party loyalty was introduced into the constitutional system as 'political party discipline', assigning the SEC as the institution

[35] Jì Kunicová and S Rose-Ackerman, 'Electoral Rules and Constitutional Structures as Constraints on Corruption' (2005) 35 *British Journal of Political Science* 573, 584–85.

[36] L Avritzer, 'The Double Crisis of Representation and Participation in Brazil' (2019) 55 *Representation* 251, doi.org/10.1080/00344893.2019.1572646.

[37] The constitutional provision establishes that a representative may lose their mandate only when they: (i) violate any of the prohibitions constitutionally provisioned; (ii) have become involved in a procedure declared incompatible with parliamentary decorum; (iii) fail to attend, in each legislative session, a third of the ordinary sessions of the house to which he belongs, except for a licence or authorised institutional mission; (iv) lose their political rights or have them suspended; (v) have been criminally convicted and have exhausted all possible appeals. Additionally, (vi) the Electoral Justice may decree the impeachment of the mandate per the Constitution. Constituição da República Federativa do Brasil [Federal Constitution of the Brazilian Republic] Art 55.

[38] *Mandado de Segurança* [1989] Supremo Tribunal Federal 20.927/DF, Min Moreira Alves.

[39] In verbis: 'Article 5: Everyone is equal before the law, without distinction of any kind, guaranteeing Brazilians and foreigners residing in the country the inviolability of the right to life, liberty, equality, security and property, in the following terms: [...] XVII: Freedom of association for lawful purposes is complete, paramilitary associations being prohibited;' Constituição da República Federativa do Brasil [Federal Constitution of the Brazilian Republic].

responsible for overseeing and approving the policy whitepapers of the political parties in the bipartisan regime.[40] Upon the nation's return to democratic rule, party loyalty was revoked in favour of a normative framework focusing on political party autonomy. The imposed bipartisan regime was overcome by the established freedom to create, fuse, incorporate and extinguish political parties, and those gained more autonomy by being able to regulate for themselves the norms and interpretation of party loyalty. Without a political party's regulation and a specific constitutional provision for loss of mandate in case of changes in party affiliation, the Supreme Federal Court maintained the political right of representatives to move to different political parties in the course of their mandate.

Therefore, after 1988, even though those representatives received their seat allocation through a proportional system, which distributes congressional seats through the strength of political parties and not for the candidate themselves, a representative in the lower chamber that decided to change their political affiliation during mandate was able to retain their seat in Congress. As such, the proportional representation of political parties was affected.

In 2007, the SEC challenged the Supreme Federal Court jurisprudence when a political party consulted it regarding its possibility of retaining a seat in the Chamber of Deputies after a congressman moved his affiliation from the party. The consultation decision was published as the Judicial Resolution no 22.526. It asserted that in cases of proportional representation, mandates and their respective seats are won by the political party and not by a specific candidate. As such, despite the standing jurisprudence of the Supreme Federal Court, the lack of constitutional provisions and federal legislation, the SEC decided that the bond of a candidate to the party for which an election is registered is the only element of that mandate's political identity. In sum, the SEC resolution considered that the seats in the lower house are won by the political party and thus neglected the possibility that the electorate might want a candidate in Congress despite their changing affiliation.

The resolution was brought under the purview of the Supreme Federal Court in the same year (2007) through three *writs of mandamus* petitioned by political parties seeking to regain seats from representatives that had changed affiliation during their mandates. Deciding the matter, the Constitutional Court changed its previous position and corroborated the SEC resolution defining that congressional mandates are won and maintained by the political party, not the representatives. As such, the Court declared the possibility of a representative losing a seat in Congress in case of changes to party affiliation without a valid justification, conditioning that in the absence of federal legislation on

[40] Art 153 of Constitutional Amendment no 01/1969. A Campos Silva and P Pereira dos Santos, 'O princípio da fidelidade partidária e a possibilidade de perda de mandato por sua violação' (2013) 11 *RIHJ – Revista do Instituto de Hermenêutica Jurídica* 13, ojs.editoraforum.com.br/rihj/index.php/rihj/article/view/523.

the matter, the SEC should issue a new resolution providing the legal framework and procedure for political parties to remove representatives, giving elected representatives the right to repel and present possible valid justifications that would allow changes of affiliations.[41]

Upon the Supreme Federal Court's new interpretation, the SEC enacted two new resolutions on the matter (nos 22.610/2007 and 22.733/2008), establishing extensive procedural and jurisdictional norms and designating the valid justifications that would allow for a representative to finish his mandate despite changing political party affiliation. These justifications included: (i) the incorporation or fusion of the political party with another; (ii) the creation of a new political party; (iii) substantial change of political ideology or program from the political party; and (iv) grave discrimination from the party towards the elected representative. In addition, resolution no 22.610 also extended its applicability towards representatives elected through a majority system (In Brazil, those in the Senate and Executive offices).[42]

Although another constitutional claim was brought against these new resolutions, the Supreme Federal Court maintained its new position regarding their constitutionality. It issued a pragmatic decision recognising, by a majority, that the SEC resolution is constitutional because it only legislates the matter temporarily, in compliance with former decisions by the court, and while the legislature had not issued a regulation.[43] This position was maintained until May of 2015 when the Supreme Federal Court issued another decision on a constitutional challenge to the resolutions of the SEC addressing specifically the institute of party loyalty regarding candidates elected through a majority representational system. Only then did the Supreme Federal Court refurbished its position, stating that the extension of the principle of party loyalty, and its ability to remove a representative from office, relates only to mandates in the proportional system of representation, with its application in the majority system being unconstitutional and inapplicable in Brazilian democracy as it may hinder popular sovereignty.[44]

On the other hand, later in the same year, Congress published Law no 13.165, regulating party loyalty for the first time after the SEC resolutions. The legislation suppressed two of the previous valid justifications stated within

[41] *Mandado de Segurança* [2007] Supremo Tribunal Federal 26.602, Min Eros Grau; *Mandado de Segurança* [2007] Supremo Tribunal Federal 26.603, Min Celso de Mello; *Mandado de Segurança* [2007] Supremo Tribunal Federal 26.604, Min Carmen Lúcia.

[42] Art 13 of the resolution established that it would apply for representatives elected through the proportionality system since March of 2007, while for representatives elected through the majority representation system (those in the Senate), it would be applicable only after mid-October of the same year. Tribunal Superior Eleitoral Brasil, 'Resolução 22.610/TSE'.

[43] *Ação Direta de Inconstitucionalidade* [2008] Supremo Tribunal Federal 3.999, Min Joaquim Barbosa; *Ação Direta de Inconstitucionalidade* [2008] Supremo Tribunal Federal 4.086, Min Joaquim Barbosa.

[44] *Ação Direta de Inconstitucionalidade* [2015] Supremo Tribunal Federal 5.081, Min Luís Roberto Barroso.

the secondary norms, that is, the possibility to change party affiliation in case of: (i) incorporation and fusion of political parties; and (ii) the creation of a new political party.[45] It implemented a new justification in which representatives may change party affiliation within 30 days before the deadline to affiliate with a political party to run for a new election. As such, representatives at the end of their current mandate became able to change their affiliations to run for office representing another political party in the forthcoming election.

The changes in party loyalty discipline showcase electoral justice's predominant role in Brazilian electoral law. The SEC was responsible for re-introducing the legal institute of party loyalty, regulating the right of political parties to remove elected representatives from office, and defining the procedural avenue for disputes concerning this right to be adjudicated. Afterwards, it was responsible for applying this novel legal framework, eventually handling the adjudication of these matters as political parties petitioned the SEC and RECs to curtail the mandate of elected representatives in case of an unjustified change in party affiliation.

III. THE SUPREME FEDERAL COURT AND SUPERIOR ELECTORAL COURT IN CONSTITUTIONAL POLITICS

As demonstrated, the management of the electoral process is entirely maintained in the judicial system. As such, there are political dynamics between the SEC and the Supreme Federal Court when handling the adjudication of cases pertaining to electoral law. The regulatory powers of the former are an explicit example of judicial activism, which has been deemed justifiable and coherent in the historical context of Brazilian federalism and separation of powers. This activism is institutionally coupled with the overall judicialisation of politics in Brazil, which has perceived a more prominent role of the latter in promoting social change after the promulgation of the 1988 Constitution.

A. The Supreme Federal Court in the 1988 Constitutional Framework

With the reestablishment of democracy, the Supreme Federal Court has become increasingly influential in shaping Brazilian politics, a trend also perceived comparatively in other countries.[46] The 1988 Constitution established an

[45] The change followed a political debate concerning the tendency of further political disintegration by the multiplication of parties after the SEC's 2007 resolution. AA Rotta, 'A Conexão entre Migração Partidária e os Novos Partidos Depois da Edição da Resolução n. 22.526/2007 do TSE' (2022) 4 *Campos Neutrais – Revista Latino-Americana de Relações Internacionais* 15, periodicos.furg.br/cn/article/view/14040.

[46] Tracking the phenomena in a comparative study, Hirschl signals the emergence of juristocracy in a scenario of transition from authoritarianism to democracy in countries such as Greece, Portu-

extensive system of safeguards that, like other Latin American constitutions towards the end of the twentieth century, maintained a transformative premised within the constitutional landscape. Thus, a vast number of norms and principles were accredited with a constitutional standing, making it possible for the Supreme Federal Court to enforce them, notwithstanding legislative and executive inaction. In other words, if rights were not protected by the Executive or Legislative powers, the Judiciary was responsible for ensuring the effectiveness of the constitution and its provisions.[47] As such, the constitution displays an aspirational nature with specific objectives to be pursued by the state, such as the construction of a free and just society based on solidarity, national development, the eradication of poverty and substandard living conditions, the reduction of social and regional inequality, and the promotion of public welfare by combating discrimination arising from, among others, race, gender, skin colour, and age.

While other countries in Latin America maintained the transformative objective in their new constitutional arrangements through a system that prioritises Executive and Legislative action, in Brazil, the task of building a fairer and just society was secured by the accumulation of functions in the Supreme Federal Court, which maintains a broad jurisdiction as a constitutional court and a specialised trial court.[48]

As a constitutional court, the Supreme Federal Court interprets the Constitution both through abstract and diffuse judicial review proceedings, thus issuing decisions in abstract interpretations of legislative and executive acts from the federal government and as an appellate court in cases involving a legal dispute that requires the interpretation of a constitutional clause (in many times, involving political rights and electoral law).

Additionally, with the mandate to secure the aspirational promises of the constitution, the Supreme Federal Court employs ample jurisdiction that considers the necessary effect of its decisions and the human rights prescribed in the constitutional text. An example of this can be perceived through the 'constitutional remedies' provisioned in Article 5, which allow the Court to immediately give effect to the application of fundamental rights despite legislative or executive omissions.[49] Given the transformative nature of the constitutional mandate

gal, and Spain, in Europe, many Latin American states, and South Africa. See: R Hirschl, *Towards Juristocracy: The Origins and Consequences of the New Constitutionalism* (Cambridge, MA, Harvard University Press, 2007).

[47] C Merlin Clève, *Para Uma Dogmática Constitucional Emancipatória* (Belo Horizonte, Fórum, 2012); O Vilhena, 'Descriptive Overview of the Brazilian Constitution and Supreme Court' in O Vilhena, B Upendra and F Viljoen (eds), *Transformative Constitutionalism: Comparing the apex courts of Brazil, India and South Africa* (Pretoria, Pretoria University Law Press, 2013).

[48] Gargarella (n 5); Di Werneck Arguelhes, 'Transformative Constitutionalism: A View from Brazil' in P Dann, M Riegner and M Bönnemann (eds), *The Global South and Comparative Constitutional Law* (Oxford, Oxford University Press, 2020).

[49] These are *Habeas Corpus, Habeas Data*, which guarantees access to information about oneself; *Writ of Mandamus*, which protect all constitutional rights not secured by other judicial remedies;

towards the Supreme Federal Court, Barroso defends that the institution has, beyond a counter-majoritarian duty to promote human rights, an enlightened role that must expand the interpretation and 'move history forward' to recognise new rights beyond those explicit in the constitutional text.[50] One example of this performance is the recognition of same-sex civil unions, which was achieved by radically changing the interpretation of the federal civil code by considering the principle of equality in the Brazilian Constitution.[51]

In its capacity as a constitutional court, the expansion of the court's influence in the political agenda can also be traced to the amplification of the list of actors with direct standing before the court, with representatives and political parties using the Supreme Federal Court to rediscuss political deliberations that have been surpassed in the representative sphere. Vilhena tracks these dynamics by assessing that political parties tend to recourse to the Supreme Federal Court when they see themselves as opposed to the government, observing this trend specifically between the Worker's Party and the Democratic and Social Democratic parties during Fernando H Cardoso's presidency between 1995–2002 and Lula's presidency, between 2003–10, respectively.[52]

On the other hand, as a specialised court, the Supreme Federal Tribunal has the power to adjudicate cases involving prominent state officials, handling their criminal cases and investigation. This competence has inserted the Supreme Federal Court in the political arena, especially during trials concerning corruption scandals between 2006 and 2018. The institution corroborated other judicial institutions' mutation of procedural laws and principles as a mechanism to overcome the polycentric disputes threatening the country's constitutional stability.[53]

This intense concentration of powers works in tandem with the centralisation of the federative system. An ambiguous compromise between autonomy and centralisation has marked Brazilian federalism.[54] While the 1988 Constitution reaffirms state autonomy, pluralism, and the decentralisation of executive and legislative functions, decision-making procedures within the Executive and the

and Writ of Injunction, which ensures the efficacy of fundamental rights against a legislative omission that obstructs the immediate application of rights.

[50] LR Barroso, 'Reason Without Vote: The Representative and Majoritarian Function of Constitutional Courts' in T Bustamante and B Gonçalves Fernandes (eds), *Democratizing Constitutional Law: Perspectives on Legal Theory and the Legitimacy of Constitutionalism* (Switzerland, Springer International Publishing, 2016).

[51] D Werneck Arguelhes and L Molhano Ribeiro, 'Courts as the First and Only Legislative Chambers? The Brazilian Supreme Court and the Legalization of Same-Sex Marriage' (2017) 50 *Verfassung und Recht in Übersee / Law and Politics in Africa, Asia and Latin America* 281.

[52] Vilhena (n 47) 90; Confirming in the case of Brazil the dynamics of party politics and its judicialisation. C Tate and T Vallinder, *The Global Expansion of Judicial Power* (New York, London, New York University Press, 1995); Y Dotan and M Hofnung, 'Legal Defeats – Political Wins: Why Do Elected Representatives Go to Court?' (2005) 38 *Comparative Political Studies* 75, doi.org/10.1177/0010414004270969.

[53] M Tushnet, *The New Fourth Branch: Institutions for Protecting Constitutional Democracy*, 1st edn (Cambridge, Cambridge University Press, 2021) 97–110.

[54] Rodrigues, Lorencini and Zimmermann (n 6).

Supreme Federal Court have contributed to the increasing concentration of powers in the federation.[55] This phenomenon can be perceived by the increasing prominence of the Brazilian Supreme Federal Court as a political actor through its more explicit insertion in electoral debates and a restrictive interpretation of state autonomy when deciding on federal disputes.[56]

An example relates to the proportionality of municipal legislative assemblies vis-à-vis their population. Municipalities are the smallest entities of the Brazilian federation and have their autonomy, jurisdiction, and legislative authorities established in the federal Constitution.[57] There were broad constitutional limits for the size of municipal legislative assemblies, with each municipality having the prerogative to organise its legislative within these parameters.[58] The SEC recognised the legitimacy of municipal legislative assemblies setting the size of their forums within the broad limits set by the Constitution. This important decision allowed for unusually large assemblies in municipalities with small populations, raising administrative costs and creating a divergence in the proportional representation in municipalities with similar populations. It also diverged from the principle of proportional representation present at both federal and state legislative bodies.[59]

In the state of São Paulo, the state prosecutor's office filed a lawsuit on behalf of the civil society (Public Civil Action, or Ação Civil Pública), arguing that the number of representatives in municipal legislative assemblies should be proportional to the size of the population, in addition to the parameters set by the Constitution. In that state, the electoral justice had already formalised the candidature of new municipal representatives in a small municipality that had enlarged its legislative body within the broad limits set by the Constitution without a significant change in population size. The Supreme Federal Court decided that proportionality and federative symmetry should be applied even within the

[55] JA Castillo de Macedo and EMQ Barboza, 'Federação Brasileira: Design Constitucional e Centralização' in M Immordino, N Gullo and G Armao (eds), *Le Autonomie Speciali Nella Prospettiva del Regionalismo Differenziato* (Napoli, Editoriale Scientifica, 2021).

[56] FR de Limas Tomio, IN Robl Filho and RL Kanayama, 'Controle De Constitucionalidade Abstrato E Concentrado No Brasil, Espanha, Itália, México E Portugal' (2017) 36 *Cuestiones Constitucionales* 301.

[57] Constituição da República Federativa do Brasil [Federal Constitution of the Brazilian Republic] Arts 29–31.

[58] Then, Art 29 established that Municipalities with up to a million citizens could have legislative assemblies with a minimum of 9 and a maximum of 21 representatives; Municipalities with a population between 1 and 5 million citizens could maintain legislative assemblies with a minimum of 33 and a maximum of 41 representatives; and in municipalities with more than 5 million citizens, assemblies could be composed of a minimum of 42 and a maximum of 55 representatives.

[59] Following the broad parameters, a municipality with 500,000 citizens could, for example, have a legislative assembly composed of 21 representatives, while a municipality with 900,000 citizens may organise their legislative assembly to have only nine representatives. Such disparities became common, especially with small municipalities enlarging their legislative bodies, creating more expenditures.

discretionary limits set by Article 29 of the Constitution, thus establishing more defined size limits for municipal legislative assemblies.[60]

A dissenting opinion in the court argued that the Supreme Federal Court was undermining the autonomy of municipalities, leading to an excessive centralisation of power.[61] Nevertheless, in the aftermath of the decision, the SEC changed its interpretation and issued a new resolution following the premises of the decision.[62] In contrast, the National Congress approved a constitutional amendment (Amendment no 58/2009), modifying Article 29, IV, of the Constitution to create 24 proportionality bands limiting the number of representatives in municipal legislative assemblies with more strict limits.

IV. COURTS AS GUARANTORS OF CONSTITUTIONAL DEMOCRACY

Until now, this chapter has digressed on two examples in which the SEC and the Supreme Federal Court have had overlaying jurisdiction over electoral legislation application, political parties' organisation, and constitutional law interpretation. These two examples do not reflect the full entanglement between the two courts regarding constitutional and electoral law in the administration of electoral processes.[63] However, it demonstrates how the political choice of extending the prerogative of the electoral justice courts when developing new regulations is impacted by external factors that often sway the Supreme Federal Court to a more deferential or interventionist agenda.

While in the case concerning party loyalty, the Supreme Federal Court maintained a deferential stance towards electoral justice, applying the standards set by the SEC and building upon their initial premise to change the constitutional and legislative framework concerning the loss of mandate, in the case concerning the federal arrangement and autonomy of municipalities, its decision overruled the interpretation of the courts in the electoral justice system and demanded the SEC to issue a new resolution implementing its disposition. It overruled the electoral justice, extending its centralising approach towards the country's federalist arrangement.[64]

In Brazil's current political crises, the role of the Supreme Federal Tribunal has become contested.[65] The Court expands its prerogative to interpret and apply the Constitution in a more expansive approach that does not limit itself to safeguarding the fundamental rights provisioned in the Constitution. As such,

[60] *Recurso Extraordinário* [2002] Supremo Tribunal Federal 197.917-8/SP, Min Maurício Corrêa.

[61] Dissenting opinion by Min Sepúlveda Pertence, ibid.

[62] Tribunal Superior Eleitoral Brasil, 'Resolução 21.702/TSE'.

[63] Marchetti (n 27).

[64] Rodrigues, Lorencini and Zimmermann (n 6); Castillo de Macedo and Barboza (n 55).

[65] L Avritzer, 'Inovando Na Direção Errada: Supremo Tribunal Federal e Ministério Público No Brasil' in M Corrêa Marona and A Del Río (eds), *Justiça no Brasil: Às Margens da Democracia* (Belo Horizonte, Arraes Editores, 2018).

it inserts itself more prominently in the political arena to protect constitutional democracy, broadly understood.[66] This expansion of powers, however, takes over a prerogative that is constitutionally conferred to the Federal and State Prosecutor's Office, and in issues concerning political authorities, the General Prosecutor of the Republic (PGR), the head of the institution.[67]

The Prosecutor's Office is established in the Brazilian Constitution as an almost fourth branch of power. It conflates its function as the judicial representative of the Executive power in state and federal criminal proceedings with a broader mandate to secure the rule of law and Brazilian democracy. Exercising a representative role for the public interest in general, the institution maintains a direct constitutional mandate to protect collective rights and interests, such as the protection of indigenous people and the environment. Additionally, in Brazil's checks and balances framework, the prosecutor's office maintains functional and administrative autonomy, not being subjected to either of the other three branches of power.[68]

Concerning the SEC, the Supreme Federal Court's expansion of powers has justified a more deferential approach towards electoral justice, which can be perceived by both institutions' activism in tackling the spread of disinformation. The pervasiveness of disinformation campaigns has been an issue in Brazilian politics since, at least, the country's 2014 general election cycle.[69] In 2018, disinformation intensified as it became the foremost campaign strategy of then-candidate Jair Bolsonaro, with the organisation of a complex structure of dissemination tactics with a populist and extreme right-wing discourse.[70]

With the beginning of Bolsonaro's mandate in 2019 and the radicalisation of politics in a more confrontational framework, the Supreme Federal Court established a judicial criminal inquiry into the distribution of fake news against the institution's credibility and its justices, broadly interpreting the territorial component of its internal rules of procedure to assert jurisdiction in online environments. As a mechanism to promote the autonomy of judicial courts in the overall system of checks and balances, the Brazilian Constitution establishes the prerogative for tribunals to regulate their proceedings and jurisdiction

[66] Tushnet (n 53).

[67] Arts 127–130 Constituição da República Federativa do Brasil [Federal Constitution of the Brazilian Republic]; Avritzer (n 65).

[68] Vilhena (n 47) 78.

[69] D Arnaudo, 'Brazil: Political Bot Intervention During Pivotal Events' in PN Howard and SC Woolley (eds), *Computational Propaganda: Political Parties, Politicians, and Political Manipulation on Social Media* (Oxford, Oxford University Press, 2018).

[70] C Machado et al, 'A Study of Misinformation in WhatsApp Groups with a Focus on the Brazilian Presidential Elections' *Companion Proceedings of The 2019 World Wide Web Conference* (Association for Computing Machinery, 2019) doi.org/10.1145/3308560.3316738; LH Muniz Conceição, 'Social Media, Politics, and Law: The Role of Data in the Brazilian Constitutional Democracy' [2022] *Journal of Iberian and Latin American Research*, www.tandfonline.com/doi/abs/10.1080/13260219.2022.2097296.

through internal rules, given the constraints of federal procedural law and the Constitution itself. In the case of the Supreme Federal Court, its by-laws allow it to define procedures related to, for example, the manipulation of the docket agenda and the investigation of criminal violations within the premises of the court.[71] With the inaction of the PGR regarding the disinformation campaigns undermining the authority and integrity of the court, the Supreme Federal Court, through an initiative of Justice Alexandre de Moraes, used its by-laws to extend its jurisdiction and assume more extensively the role of democracy's guarantor.[72]

On the other hand, Congress began deliberations on a Bill (PL 2630/2020) to counter disinformation by re-addressing elements of the framework for internet service providers in Brazil. The 'Fake News Bill' was drafted and approved in the Senate but is still pending deliberations in the Chamber of Deputies. The Bill has been re-drafted, and new proposals have encompassed a more extensive debate in Brazilian society concerning internet regulation after the country's Internet Bill of Rights, published in 2014.[73] In order to respond more practically to disinformation during the 2022 General Elections cycle, the SEC issued a new resolution that included streamlined content removal procedures, expanded powers for the chief of the Electoral justice, the ability to suspend platforms for non-compliance, and increased scrutiny of social media platforms overall. This resolution surpassed previous deliberations and aims to combat disinformation in a more effective manner.[74]

The ultra vires effect of the resolution is contested. The PGR petitioned the Supreme Federal Court to declare the electoral justice regulation unconstitutional. It argued that the resolution establishes sanctions not previously defined in primary legislation, such as the Internet Bill of Rights and the Constitution, hindering freedom of expression by enlarging the oversight of the SEC over communications on social media platforms.[75] Additionally, it argued that the resolution disrespected due process since it allowed for the President of the SEC, Supreme Court Justice Alexandre de Moraes, to issue individual decisions instead of collegial ones that consider the input of the other six electoral justices. The Supreme Federal Court rejected the PGR's claims, establishing that

[71] D Werneck Arguelhes and IA Hartmann, 'Timing Control without Docket Control: How Individual Justices Shape the Brazilian Supreme Court's Agenda' (2017) 5 *Journal of Law and Courts* 105, www.journals.uchicago.edu/doi/full/10.1086/690195; Art 43. Supremo Tribunal Federal Brasil, 'Regimento Interno Do Supremo Tribunal Federal'.

[72] T Khaitan, 'Guarantor Institutions' (2021) 16 *Asian Journal of Comparative Law* S40; LH Muniz Conceição, 'You Want It Darker? The Brazilian Supreme Court Kills the Flame: The Temporary Suspension of Telegram Services in Brazil' (*I-CONnect: Blog of the International Journal of Constitutional Law*, 12 April 2022) www.iconnectblog.com/2022/04/you-want-it-darker-the-brazilian-supreme-court-kills-the-flame-the-temporary-suspension-of-telegram-services-in-brazil/.

[73] MA Loschiavo Leme de Barros and others, 'Fake News in Brazil's 2018 Presidential Elections: A Systems Theory Approach to Judicial and Legal Responses' (2023) 32 *Social & Legal Studies* 116, journals.sagepub.com/doi/abs/10.1177/09646639221094152.

[74] Tribunal Superior Eleitoral Brasil, 'Resolução 23.714/TSE'.

[75] Marco Civil Law da Internet [Brazilian Internet Bill of Rights]. Lei No 12.965/2014 2014.

the resolution's purpose of constraining the flow of disinformation was compatible with the Brazilian Constitution and federal electoral legislation.

As a result, Moraes, a constitutional court justice and President of the SEC between 2022 and 2024 became Brazilian democracy's chief guardian. Before the vote in the general elections of 2022, he oversaw the judicial investigation of disinformation, issuing decisions in the established judicial criminal inquiry. As President of the SEC, he cut a deal with the military to run additional tests on electronic voting machines and avoid legitimacy questions concerning the vote. On election day, he ordered the federal highway police to explain why officers were stopping buses full of voters in certain districts, which was being raised as a possible attempt at voter suppression by Bolsonaro supporters within the police force. After the vote, Moraes arranged for government leaders to announce the winner jointly, showcasing the unity of constituted powers against any attempt from the losing candidate and political establishment to contest the electoral result.[76]

All of these measures have had a duplicitous effect. The general elections of 2022 were secured by the pragmatic responses orchestrated by the SEC in conjunction with the Supreme Federal Court. However, this directly implicated both institutions in party politics, especially Justice Alexandre de Moraes, which became the number one enemy for the 49.1 per cent of the electorate that voted for Bolsonaro.[77]

After the country's first dictatorship in the 1930s, history repeated itself as tragedy in 1964, with the military coup, and again as farce, with the botched attempt by former President Jair Bolsonaro in 2023 to destitute the newly elected government.[78] In all, the court's performance did not preclude the attempt from the former President to delegitimate the results and overturn the newly established government. On 8 January 2023, as Bolsonaro supporters invaded the buildings of Congress, the Supreme Federal Court, and the Planalto Palace demanding the destitution of the new incumbent, a strong Executive, in partnership with the Legislative power, was able to counter further political instability and re-establish order.

V. ADJUDICATED DEMOCRACY

Brazil's electoral justice system is a complex and crucial part of the country's democratic governance. Its evolution from a system designed to combat electoral fraud to the institution responsible for the administration and adjudication

[76] J Nicas, 'He Is Brazil's Defender of Democracy. Is He Actually Good for Democracy?' *The New York Times* (22 January 2023) www.nytimes.com/2023/01/22/world/americas/brazil-alexandre-de-moraes.html.

[77] Tribunal Superior Eleitoral, '2022 General Elections Result – TSE' (31 October 2022) resultados.tse.jus.br/oficial/app/index.html#/eleicao/resultados.

[78] Recasting the common referral of Marx concerning history, politics, and the hegelian dialectic. K Marx, *The Eighteenth Brumaire of Louis Bonaparte* (New York, International Publishers Co, 1994).

of all aspects of the electoral process at the municipal, state, and federal levels has been a significant achievement. It corroborated the maintenance of constitutional democracy, and through time it has demonstrated its resilience and adaptability throughout periods of democracy and authoritarianism, making significant progress in ensuring that Brazil's electoral process is as free, fair and transparent as it can be.

Contrastingly, Brazilian democracy has been heavily expanded by the transformative role performed by judicial courts. With a broad constitutional mandate, the Supreme Federal Court partly realised the promises established in the 1988 constitutional text and, as such, judicialised a significant part of the country's political life. Barroso, a justice of the Supreme Federal Court, argues that the judicialisation of politics in Brazil is a fact that stems directly from the country's institutional design and should not be confused with a deliberate exercise of political will, distinguishing judicial activism and the judicialisation of politics.[79] This distinction, however, appears to have reached its limits as the court extends its authority to better position itself as a guarantor of democracy despite the configuration of the country's separation of powers attributing this task to the Prosecutor's Office.

Descriptively assessing the performance of the Supreme Federal Court in protecting and expanding human rights in Brazil, Vilhena has distinguished four distinct phases since the promulgation of the 1988 Constitution. In the immediate years after the new Constitution was established (1988–90), the Court focused on harmonising the previous legal framework with the new constitutional paradigm.[80] The second phase starts in the 1990s, with the Court dedicating its deliberations towards regulating economic affairs during the extensive economic upheaval.[81] The third period relates to the country's economic changes, with the Court overseeing the constitutional reform that led to the creation of regulatory agencies, extensive privatisation of public companies, and social security reform. The fourth and final period observed by Vilhena starts from the beginning of the new millennium and relates to the Supreme Federal Court's engagement with a fundamental rights agenda.[82]

In conclusion, concerning the organisation of the electoral justice system in the country, this chapter distinguishes the current period of the constitutional

[79] LLB Barroso, 'Constituição, Democracia e Supremacia Judicial: Direito e Política no Brasil Contemporâneo' in AL Fernandes Fellet, D Giotti de Paula and M Novelino (eds), *As Novas Faces do Ativismo Judicial* (Salvador, Juspodivm, 2011) 234; LR Barroso, *O Novo Direito Constitucional Brasileiro: Contribuições Para a Construção Teórica e Prática Da Jurisdição Constitucional No Brasil* (Belo Horizonte, Fórum, 2012).

[80] This phase included rulings regarding the legal regime of public servants and the distribution of competencies between members of the federation and the three branches of power. Vilhena (n 47) 98–100.

[81] During the Fernando Collor de Melo presidency, multiple monetary plans were created to curb high inflation rates, which led to the change of the country's currency in 1994 with the 'Plano Real' ibid.

[82] Vilhena (n 47).

court as a new phase. Beyond protecting fundamental rights, both institutions inserted themselves more radically in the mega-politics regarding issues such as transference of power and electoral competition.[83] Although an advantageous position during the sensitive period of the general elections in 2022, the consolidation of the Supreme Federal Court and the SEC in this political dynamic raises concerns for its legitimacy and capability of de facto guarding Brazilian democracy against authoritarian assaults.

[83] Hirschl (n 29).

13

Election Law, Judicial Review, and Canadian Democracy

SARAH BURTON AND MICHAEL PAL

I. INTRODUCTION

CONTEMPORARY REPRESENTATIVE DEMOCRACY is, inevitably, structured by the law. Constitutions, electoral statutes, regulations issued by Electoral Management Bodies, and other legal mechanisms determine how elections operate, how votes are translated into representation in the legislature, the working of politics between elections, and so on. Canadian democracy is no exception. The Canadian courts have been called upon repeatedly to interpret the laws structuring Canadian democracy. In doing so they have attracted significant criticism, given the high political stakes, but also have had a hand in shaping the operation of democracy itself.

This chapter provides an overview of what constitutional adjudication of electoral laws has accomplished to date in Canada, and considers what questions remain unanswered. After this introduction, it proceeds in three parts. First, it provides a structural and historical overview of the law of democracy in Canada, with a focus on its foundational documents. Prior to 1982, the law of democracy was primarily framed by the Constitution Act 1867,[1] through which courts possessed limited tools to challenge democratically passed law other than on federalism grounds. Following Canada's patriation of the Constitution via the Constitution Act 1982[2] with its entrenched bill of rights, the Canadian Charter of Rights and Freedoms,[3] the judiciary took on a much more robust role in defining and protecting democratic rights.

Despite their significant involvement in developing the law of democracy, several issues have persisted. Part two explores four enduring puzzles that remain unanswered in Canadian election law. Each of these issues – the role and

[1] The Constitution Act 1867, 30 & 31 Vict, c 3.
[2] The Constitution Act 1982, Sch B to the Canada Act 1982 (UK), 1982, c 11.
[3] Canadian Charter of Rights and Freedoms, Part 1 of the Constitution Act 1982, being Sch B to the Canada Act 1982 (UK), 1982, c 11 (Charter).

regulation of political parties; the functioning of the notwithstanding clause; the regulation of online political speech; and the representation of Indigenous voices, strain either existing electoral jurisprudence or the institutional power of courts. While inroads have been made, there are practical and structural hurdles that impede their resolution.

The last part of the chapter concludes by placing the Canadian Constitution in a comparative lens. Other national constitutions have tended to provide more detail on their democratic requirements and on how elections function. In hindsight, our Constitution would have benefited from this detail. Given the difficulty in Canada of amending the Constitution, these textual limitations are here to stay. Courts will as a consequence continue take a central role in developing matters of electoral law and fairness.

II. A HISTORY OF CANADIAN ELECTION LAW

A. Democracy in the Pre-Charter Era

The structure of democracy as set out in the Canadian Constitution is the starting point for any analysis of Canadian election law. Canadian election law is primarily set out in statute. The text of the Constitution sets the framework within which election law operates.

As a result of its British constitutional lineage, the Canadian Constitution is comprised of written and unwritten sources.[4] The Constitution Act 1867, formerly entitled the British North America Act, establishes Canada as a federation and a parliamentary democracy with a Constitution 'similar in principle' to that of the UK.[5] It sets out a bicameral Parliament with an appointed Senate representing the regions of the country and a democratically elected House of Commons.[6] Flowing from its federal system of government, each province has its own elections and legislatures.

Relatively little is actually specified by the text, however, on the conduct of elections, the electoral system, and the transfer of power. For the most part,

[4] *Reference re Secession of Quebec* [1998] 2 SCR 217 [32]; *Ref re Remuneration of Judges of the Prov. Court of P.E.I.; Ref re Independence and Impartiality of Judges of the Prov Court of PEI* [1997] 3 SCR 3 [92]; *New Brunswick Broadcasting Co v Nova Scotia (Speaker of the House of Assembly)* [1993] 1 SCR 319; VA MacDonnell, 'Rethinking the Invisible Constitution: How Unwritten Constitutional Principles Shape Political Decision-Making' (2019) 65 *McGill Law Journal* 175; R Albert and M Pal, 'The Democratic Resilience of the Canadian Constitution' in M Graber, S Levinson and M Tushnet (eds), *Constitutional Democracy in Crisis?* (New York, Oxford University Press, 2018) 123–24.

[5] The Constitution Act 1867 (n 1), Preamble; Secession Reference (n 4) [44]; P Lagassé, 'The Crown and Prime Ministerial Power' (2016) 39 *Canadian Parliamentary Review* 17, 18; PC Oliver, '"A Constitution Similar in Principle to that of the United Kingdom": The Preamble, Constitutional Principles, and a Sustainable Jurisprudence' (2019) 65 *McGill Law Journal* 207.

[6] Constitution Act 1867 (n 1) s 17.

'The representative and democratic nature of our political institutions was simply assumed',[7] and the answers to these questions are located within the Constitution's many unwritten conventions, practices, customs, and norms.[8] For example, Canada's first-past-the-post electoral system derived from the Westminster model is not specified by the Constitution.

Prior to 1982, the Westminster tradition of parliamentary sovereignty was paramount in Canadian law. Without a constitutionally entrenched bill of rights, judges had more limited tools with which they could protect individual rights. During this period, the principle of federalism emerged as a mechanism by which individual rights, including those relevant to elections, were safeguarded. For example, provincial and/or municipal laws that restricted the distribution of pamphlets,[9] freedom of the press,[10] display of election signs,[11] propagating political materials,[12] political donations,[13] and disenfranchisement[14] were challenged in court on the basis that they exceeded provincial jurisdiction.[15]

The pre-1982 era is also noteworthy for its discriminatory approach to Indigenous governance and enfranchisement.[16] Since 1876, Canada's relationship with First Nations has been framed by the Indian Act, which imposed several colonial electoral policies aimed at excluding or assimilating Indigenous persons.[17] For example, prior to 1960 the Act declared that 'registered Indians'[18] could not vote in federal elections unless they forfeited their treaty rights and 'Indian status'.[19]

[7] *Secession Reference* (n 4) [62].

[8] For a discussion of the distinction between conventions, practices, customs and norms, see: P Lagassé, 'The Crown and Government Formation: Conventions, Practices, Customs, and Norms' (2019) 28 *Constitutional Forum* 1.

[9] *Saumur v Quebec (City of)* [1953] 2 SCR 299.

[10] *Reference re Alberta Legislation* [1938] SCR 100.

[11] *McKay v R* [1965] SCR 798.

[12] *Switzman v Elbling* [1957] SCR 285.

[13] *OCAW Local 16-601 v Imperial Oil Ltd* [1963] SCR 584.

[14] *Cunningham v Homma* [1903] AC 151, PC.

[15] See also: *CFRB Ltd v Canada (Attorney General) (No. 2)* [1973] 3 OR 819 (CA) which unsuccessfully argued that federal broadcasting restrictions which applied to elections unconstitutionally infringed on provincial jurisdiction when applied to provincial elections. For an example of federalism arguments being invoked to protect rights outside the context of election law, see: *Walter v Alberta (Attorney General)* [1969] SCR 383.

[16] In Canada, Indigenous persons refers to individuals who identify as First Nations, Métis, and Inuit.

[17] Indian Act RSC 1985 c I-5. The term 'Indian' is used here because it was, and remains, the title of legislation in Canada. The term itself is offensive to many Indigenous persons.

[18] The Indian Act creates a registry of all persons entitled to be registered as such under the Act. The rules for registration flow from parentage (ibid ss 5, 6). The Indian Act does not apply to Inuit or Métis persons, or First Nations persons who do not have status under that Act.

[19] This was known as 'voluntary enfranchisement'. See KL Ladner and M McCrossan, 'The Electoral Participation of Aboriginal People' (Working Paper Series on Electoral Participation and Outreach Practices) (Ottawa, Chief Electoral Officer of Canada, 2007) 11. Similar exclusionary rules existed at the provincial level: *A History of the Vote In Canada* (Gatineau, Chief Electoral Officer of Canada, 2021) 74–75. First Nations persons who joined the military were also enfranchised, but until 1924, they were disenfranchised when they returned to their reserves (*History of the Vote*, 110).

Federal legislation also imposed a governance structure onto the internal functioning of First Nations via band council elections.[20]

B. The Charter-Era

Canada's constitutional paradigm shifted dramatically in 1982 with the passage of the Constitution Act 1982,[21] and its entrenched bill of rights, the Canadian Charter of Rights and Freedoms.[22] The Charter changed the relationship between courts and Parliament. Infringements of guaranteed rights and freedoms that are not demonstrably justified in a free and democratic society can be struck down by the courts for non-compliance with the Charter.[23] The Constitution Act 1982[24] also codified an amendment process that has proven exceedingly difficult to satisfy for most reforms of any significance.[25]

The Supreme Court of Canada has held that certain unwritten principles inform interpretation of the Constitution, including its text and unwritten portions.[26] The list of unwritten principles includes the principle of democracy, which is of particular importance to election law.[27] The legitimacy and uses of the unwritten principles are the subject of considerable uncertainty

Inuit persons were enfranchised in 1950, and Indigenous Métis and other Indigenous persons excluded from the Act were enfranchised on their own timelines. These groups also faced unique discrimination related to their enfranchisement, as did women subject to the Indian Act. For details on enfranchisement policies for these groups, and on provincial enfranchisement policies for Indigenous persons, see Ladner and McCrossan, 11–12. See also: *History of the Vote*, 109–10. The relationship of women who fell under the Indian Act is more complicated. Until 1985, a status 'Indian' women's right to vote, and their status more generally, were tied to their husband's status and decision to enfranchise: *History of the Vote*, 109–10.

[20] Indian Act (n 17) ss 74–80; Indian Band Election Regulations CRC c 952; Report of the Standing Senate Committee on Aboriginal Peoples, *First Nations Elections: The Choice is Inherently Theirs* (May 2010) (Chair, The Honourable Gerry St. Germain, PC) 15–19.

[21] Constitution Act 1982 (n 2).

[22] Charter (n 3).

[23] ibid s 1.

[24] Constitution Act 1982 (n 2).

[25] Constitution Act 1982 (n 2) s 38. Most amendments require a resolution be passed by the House of Commons, the Senate, and at least two-thirds of the provincial legislative assemblies representing at least 50% of the population. Pre-1982, constitutional amendment was an evolving set of conventions: DM Kilgour and J Terrence, 'The Canadian Constitutional Amending Formula: Bargaining in the Past and the Future' (1984) 44 *Public Choice* 457, 463. On the difficulty of amendment, see: R Albert, 'The Conventions of Constitutional Amendment in Canada' (2016) 53 *Osgoode Hall Law Journal* 399; R Albert, 'The Difficulty of Constitutional Amendment in Canada' (2015) 53 *Alberta Law Review* 85.

[26] See *Secession Reference* (n 4) [55]–[82] (federalism, constitutionalism and the rule of law, protection of minorities, and democracy); *Babcock v Canada (AG)* 2002 SCC 57, [2002] 3 SCR 3 (parliamentary sovereignty); *Reference re Remuneration of Judges of the Provincial Court of PEI* [1997] 3 SCR 3 (judicial independence); *New Brunswick Broadcasting Co* (n 4) (parliamentary privilege); *Mikisew Cree First Nation v Canada (Governor General in Council)*, 2018 SCC 40, [2018] 2 SCR 765 [42] (duty to consult).

[27] M Pal, 'The Unwritten Principle of Democracy' (2019) 65 *McGill Law Journal* 269; *Secession Reference* (n 4) [61]–[69].

and debate.[28] While in years past they had been 'generally understood to be justiciable',[29] the Supreme Court has thrown cold water on any suggestion that the unwritten principles can be used to invalidate legislation.[30] Instead, a majority of the Supreme Court recently relegated the unwritten principles to the background, where they may be used to interpret constitutional provisions and to develop constitutional doctrines, but not as a free-standing basis to strike down laws.[31] The unwritten principle of democracy therefore remains important in interpreting constitutional provisions related to elections, but the text has primacy.

Within the text of the Constitution, the Charter has three main provisions that expressly protect access to Canada's democratic institutions and the accountability of government and elected representatives. Section 3 of the Charter states that, 'Every citizen of Canada has the right to vote in an election of members of the House of Commons or of a legislative assembly and to be qualified for membership therein.'[32] Sections 4 and 5 together provide that federal and provincial elections must be held at least every five years,[33] and that Parliaments and/or legislatures must sit at least once during a 12-month period.[34] Sections 3–5 therefore ensure periodic and regular elections with a broad electorate and require that the government convene the legislative body.

Other Charter rights and freedoms, while not specific to elections, nonetheless have important bearing on electoral rights. Section 2(b) of the Charter guarantees a general right to free expression, which has implications for political speech and the flow of money in politics.[35] Other rights, such as section 15's equality guarantee[36] and section 2(d)'s freedom of association[37] are less frequently invoked, but nonetheless form part of the fabric of the law of democracy. Freedom of association, for example, protects the right of individuals to join political parties or interest groups.

[28] See, eg, J LeClair, 'Canada's Unfathomable Unwritten Constitutional Principles' (2002) 27 *Queen's Law Journal* 389 (on the legitimacy of unwritten principles); V Kazmierski, 'Draconian but Not Despotic: The 'Unwritten' Limits of Parliamentary Sovereignty in Canada' (2009) 41 *Ottawa Law Review* 245 (application of unwritten principles).

[29] Macdonnell (n 4) 180; Pal (n 27).

[30] *Toronto (City) v Ontario (Attorney General)*, 2021 SCC 34, 462 DLR (4th) 1 [50], [57]–[59], [63], [78], [84].

[31] ibid [55], [56]. See, however, dissenting comments which suggest the issue may not be settled [170].

[32] Charter (n 3) s 3.

[33] ibid s 4(1).

[34] ibid s 5.

[35] ibid s 2(b): 'Everyone has the following fundamental freedoms: … (b) freedom of thought, belief, opinion and expression, including freedom of the press and other media of communication.'

[36] Charter (n 3) s 15(1). See, eg, *Kahkewistahaw First Nation v Taypotat*, 2015 SCC 30, [2015] 2 SCR 548.

[37] Charter (n 3) s 2(d): 'Everyone has the following fundamental freedoms: … (d) freedom of association'; Y Dawood, 'Democracy and the Right to Vote: Rethinking Democratic Rights under the *Charter*' (2013) 51 *Osgoode Hall Law Journal* 251, 254, citing C Feasby, 'Constitutional Questions About Canada's New Political Finance Regime' (2007) 45 *Osgoode Hall Law Journal* 514, 539.

The rights and freedoms in the Charter are worded broadly, which provides courts wide latitude in deciphering their content. All Charter rights are beholden to a proportionality analysis in which rights are subject 'to such reasonable limits prescribed by law as can be demonstrably justified in a free and democratic society'.[38]

Early election law jurisprudence focused on setting the parameters of where section 3's protection for the right to vote and stand as a candidate operated. The courts have read the text referring to elections for 'members of the House of Commons or of a legislative assembly' as limiting the scope of section 3. It applies only to federal and provincial elections under this doctrine. Other important electoral events, such as referendums,[39] school board,[40] band council,[41] and municipal[42] elections lay outside of its protection.

The text of section 3 guaranteeing that 'Every citizen of Canada' be able to vote set the foundation for wide access to the franchise. In early Charter litigation, judges struck down blanket disenfranchisement laws that had excluded mentally incompetent persons,[43] federal judges,[44] and (eventually) prisoners. The debate over prisoner enfranchisement was particularly hotly contested and remained in litigation for over a decade.[45] The Court's vigorous protection of the right to vote remains controversial.[46] The Supreme Court most recently struck down a prohibition on voting by non-resident citizens.[47] In the Charter-era, all blanket bans on voting by groups of Canadian citizens have been struck down,[48] with the exception of persons under 18.

The jurisprudence has also deepened section 3's protections. All Charter rights are interpreted in a broad and purposive manner having regard to their context.[49] Early on, the Supreme Court declared that 'More is intended [in the right to vote] than the bare right to place a ballot in a box.'[50] The first meaningful

[38] Charter (n 3) s 1.

[39] *Haig v Canada (Chief Electoral Officer)* [1993] 2 SCR 995.

[40] *Baier v Alberta* 2007 SCC 31, [2007] 2 SCR 673 [39].

[41] *Kahkewistahaw First Nation* (n 36) in which s 15(1) is invoked, not s 3.

[42] *Toronto City* (n 30).

[43] *Canadian Disability Rights Council v Canada* [1988] 3 FC 622.

[44] *Muldoon v R* [1988] 3 FC 628 (TD); *Hoogbruin v British Columbia (Attorney General)* (1985) 24 DLR (4th) 718, 70 BCLR 1 (BCCA).

[45] *Belczowski v Canada* [1992] 2 FC 440; *Sauvé v Canada (Attorney General)* [1993] 2 SCR 438; *Sauvé v Canada (Chief Electoral Officer)* 2002 SCC 68, [2002] 3 SCR 519.

[46] See, eg, CP Manfredi, 'The Day the Dialogue Died: A Comment on *Sauvé v Canada*' (2007) 45 *Osgoode Hall Law Journal* 105.

[47] *Frank v Canada (Attorney General)* 2019 SCC 1, [2019] 1 SCR 3.

[48] *Fitzgerald v Alberta* 2002 ABQB 1086, 10 Alta LR (4th) 155; *Fitzgerald v Alberta* 2004 ABCA 184, 27 Alta LR (4th) 205. Voter suppression tactics, on the other hand, have received softer treatment from the judiciary, although the Supreme Court has yet to rule on the matter. See, eg, *MacEwing v Canada (AG)* 2013 FC 525, 433 FTR 59 (FC); *Henry v Canada (AG)* 2014 BCCA 30, 370 DLR (4th) 742 (voter identification).

[49] *Hunter et al v Southam Inc* [1984] 2 SCR 145.

[50] *Dixon v British Columbia (Attorney General)* [1989] 4 WWR 393, 403.

clue as to section 3's content came to light in the *Carter* decision,[51] where the Supreme Court of Canada faced an allegation that variances in electoral district size violated this section.[52] The Court upheld the regime, holding that section 3 does not guarantee voter parity, but rather guarantees a right to 'effective representation'.[53] This concept of effective representation has remained at the core of section 3.[54]

The second major clue as to section 3's content came to light in the context of party participation thresholds.[55] *Figueroa* was a challenge to legislation that imposed a threshold on obtaining registered party status. The Supreme Court held that the threshold violated section 3 because it undermined the ability of individual citizens to play a 'meaningful role' in the electoral process.[56]

These dual concepts – effective representation and meaningful participation – remain the foundational touchstones of section 3's protection. Because these concepts are themselves broad, their content has proven malleable and difficult to predict[57] and section 3 jurisprudence has attracted scholarly criticism on this basis.[58]

The guarantee of freedom of political expression in section 2(b) of the Charter has also proven critical to electoral law in Canada. The Charter's free speech provision is broad and protects all non-violent attempts to convey meaning from government interference. The Supreme Court has frequently been asked to apply this protection to laws which restrict political expression. Courts have repeatedly affirmed that political expression sits 'at the core' of this guarantee.[59] As such, political speech jurisprudence has espoused a broad protection for individual and media communications about elections.

Under the auspices of section 2(b), the courts have also permitted restrictions by governments on the flow of money in politics. In this regard, the spending limits imposed on third parties (individuals, groups, or associations other than

[51] *Reference Re Prov Electoral Boundaries (Sask)* [1991] 2 SCR 158 (*Carter*).

[52] The notion that the redistricting amounted to partisan gerrymandering was not discussed in detail by the Supreme Court, although there is evidence it favoured the ruling party. For discussion of this feature and the Court's (non)reaction to it, see M Pal, 'Breakdowns in the Democratic Process and the Law of Canadian Democracy' (2011) 57 *McGill Law Journal* 299.

[53] *Carter* (n 51) 183.

[54] See, eg, *Harvey v New Brunswick (Attorney General)* [1996] 2 SCR 876; *Figueroa v Canada (Attorney General)* 2003 SCC 37, [2003] 1 SCR 912; *Haig v R* [1993] 2 SCR 995.

[55] *Figueroa* (n 54).

[56] ibid [58].

[57] See, eg, the characterisations of effective representation in *Frank* (n 47) [154], [169]. See also: competing conceptions of effective representation in *Harvey* (n 54) [27] and *Thomson Newspapers Co v Canada (Attorney General)* [1998] 1 SCR 877 [19], [82]. As for meaningful participation, see: *Harper v Canada (Attorney General)*, 2004 SCC 33, [2004] 1 SCR 827 [70]–[74]. See, also the 'informational component' to meaningful participation in *Working Families Coalition (Canada) Inc v Ontario (Attorney General)* 2023 ONCA 139 (Working Families #2 CA).

[58] M Rush and C Manfredi, *Judging Democracy* (Toronto, University of Toronto Press, 2008) 116; Pal (n 52) 304; C Feasby, 'Freedom of Expression and the Law of the Democratic Process' (2005) 29 *The Supreme Court Law Review* 237, 258.

[59] *Harper* (n 57) [66].

political parties) have attracted more than their share of litigation.[60] In a series of cases on third party spending, the Supreme Court carved out a space in which electoral laws may significantly restrict free speech in service of an 'egalitarian' model of politics, in which spending limits are viewed as an essential means to 'promote electoral fairness by creating equality in the political discourse'.[61] The egalitarian model of elections is now firmly embedded in the Canadian electoral canon.[62] The egalitarian model has included limits on donations to political parties and their candidates, as well as spending limits for political parties, candidates, and third parties during the statutorily defined election campaign period.

The challenge of balancing freedom of political expression within the egalitarian model of campaign finance law is an ongoing issue. Canada's federal election legislation recently extended political and third-party spending limits for the first time to a defined period in the months *before* an election campaign officially begins. This type of 'pre-writ' spending limit has already been successfully challenged under two provincial statutory regimes.[63] The Supreme Court is likely to address the constitutionality of pre-writ spending limits in the coming years.

Free speech jurisprudence has also taken an increasingly hard line against claims which assert that the government has an obligation to facilitate political expression.[64] In *Toronto City*, for example, Canada's largest city launched an action against the provincial government claiming that legislation which radically redrew municipal electoral districts mid-election contravened section 2(b).[65] The Supreme Court rejected the claim, because they alleged the claimants were seeking access to a particular platform of expression.[66] Unlike 'negative' claims from government interference, 'positive' speech claims are only given constitutional protection where 'the claim [is] grounded in the fundamental *Charter* freedom of expression, such that, by denying access to a

[60] *Libman v Canada (Attorney General)* [1997] 3 SCR 569, *Harper* (n 57), *Somerville v Canada (Attorney General)* [1996] 184 AR 241 (CA); *National Citizens Coalition v Canada (Attorney General)* [1984] 32 Alta LR (2d) 249, 11 DLR (4th) 481 (KB).

[61] *Libman* ibid [47]–[50]; *Harper* (n 57) [63]; C Feasby, '*Libman v. Quebec (A.G.)* and the Administration of the Process of Democracy under the *Charter*: The Emerging Egalitarian Model' (1999) 44 *McGill Law Journal* 5, 32; Feasby (n 58) 250.

[62] See, eg, *BC Freedom of Information and Privacy Assn v British Columbia (Attorney General)* 2017 SCC 6, [2017] 1 SCR 83.

[63] *Working Families Ontario v Ontario* 2021 ONSC 4076 (Working Families #1) but see: The Canadian Press 'Ford government pushes through controversial election spending bill with notwithstanding clause' (*CBC News* 14 June 2021) www.cbc.ca/news/canada/toronto/notwithstanding-clause-vote-ontario-1.6064952; *Working Families Coalition (Canada) Inc v Ontario* 2021 ONSC 7697 (Working Families #2); Working Families #2 CA (n 57); *Reference re Election Act (BC)* 2012 BCCA 394; *British Columbia Teachers' Federation v British Columbia* 2011 BCCA 408, 343 DLR (4th) 237. For more on the *Working Families* series of cases, see III.B, below.

[64] *Toronto City* (n 30).

[65] Note that because the legislation dealt with municipal elections, s 3 of the Charter was not available to ground the claim: *Toronto City* (n 30) [88].

[66] *Toronto City* (n 30) [32].

statutory platform … the government has substantially interfered with freedom of expression'.[67] The distinction between positive and negative rights has long been the subject of critique and debate.[68] Nonetheless, this distinction in the case law between positive and negative rights is now entrenched in the case law. Because the Supreme Court has imposed a very high standard to prove a positive rights claim under section 2(b), protection for that kind of free expression claim is likely to be curtailed in the coming years both within and outside the electoral arena.

This brief overview demonstrates that courts have been a driving force in developing the content of electoral law in Canada, along with legislatures. The Constitution's scant detail on the contours of how our democracy functions means there is ample space for disagreement requiring judicial resolution. Despite the significant work that has been done, the state of Canadian election law is piecemeal. While many aspects of Canada's election laws are well-developed, others lag behind. The next section considers four enduring puzzles and how they impact Canada's law of democracy.

III. ENDURING PUZZLES

A. Courts and Political Parties

Courts have struggled to locate their footing in relation to the inner workings of political parties. Political parties are not mentioned in the Constitution and election law largely steers clear of regulating intra-party activities, with some notable exceptions.[69] By keeping internal party processes out of statutory control, the theory is that political parties remain independent from the state and function as private entities accountable to their members.[70] There is, however, an undeniable public interest in ensuring the viability of political parties that reflect the full scope of public opinion and which possess internal party processes that are fair and transparent. Parties exist in a constant tension as private entities accountable to their members with control over their own internal affairs, but which are highly regulated by election law and play a role of undeniable public importance in a democracy.

[67] ibid [25].

[68] S Holmes and CR Sunstein, *The Cost of Rights: Why Liberty Depends on Taxes* (New York, WW Norton & Co, 1999).

[69] Statutory regulation of political parties are focused on matters such as party registration, reporting requirements, and financial administration (Canada Elections Act SC 2000 c 9, ss 385–446), see also *Mackay v Ahenakew* [2004] 71 OR (3d) 130, (CA) [31].

[70] *Longley v Canada (Attorney General)* 2007 ONCA 852, 288 DLR (4th) 599 [71], quoting D Beatty, 'Political Parties and Constitutional Reform' in T Fleiner (ed), *Five Decades of Constitutional Law: Reality and Perspectives* (1945–1995) (Tokyo, International Association of Constitutional Law Fourth World Congress, 1999) 292–94.

In the courtroom, the issue manifests as a struggle to classify political parties as merely voluntary private organisations – with all the benefits and trappings thereof – or something more. Earlier caselaw leaned on the unique nature of political parties. In *Ahenakew v MacKay*, for example, aggrieved members of Canada's Progressive Conservative party approached the court to nullify that party's merger with Canadian Reform Conservative Alliance.[71] They drew on a line of cases holding that voluntary associations are simply a web of contracts between each and every member and, on that basis, a valid merger required unanimous agreement from members. The framework was rejected as being inapplicable to political parties. Political parties may be voluntary associations, but they are given significant statutory powers and duties which accords them their own legal status and requires that they have the authority to 'control and regulate their internal affairs'.[72]

The issue became significantly more complicated, however, when party members began approaching court seeking judicial review of internal party disputes. Courts have been wrestling with the nature of political parties to determine whether they can judicially review internal party disputes on public law grounds or if they are limited to private law actions and remedies, such as breach of contract or tort. 'Judicial review' involves courts assessing the decisions of public entities to ensure that they follow basic legal principles and respect the limits of their jurisdiction.[73] Public law remedies include the power to force the public body, in this case the party, to take or, refrain from, certain actions.[74]

Two strains of reasoning emerged in response to this issue. The dominant strand treats political parties the same as any other voluntary, private association, which lack recourse to judicial review. For example, in *Knox v Conservative Party of Canada*[75] the court declined to judicially review a candidate nomination process despite a number of abnormalities. Aggrieved parties may only approach a court seeking private law remedies, such as those for breach of the party constitutions, bylaws, and rules, in this line of thinking.[76]

Another line of cases undertakes a more nuanced evaluation as to whether a political party is a public decision maker. These cases apply a list of contextual factors to determine whether a decision of an association is of 'a sufficiently public nature' to ground jurisdiction for judicial review.[77] *Graff v New Democratic*

[71] *Ahenakew* (n 69).

[72] ibid [32].

[73] Constitution Act 1867 (n 1) s 96; *Knox v Conservative Party of Canada* 2007 ABCA 295, 422 AR 29 [14].

[74] For more information on remedies in judicial review, see D Mullan, *Administrative Law* (Toronto, Irwin Law, 2001) ch 16.

[75] *Knox* (n 73).

[76] ibid [27].

[77] Citing to *Setia v Appleby College* 2013 ONCA 753, 370 DLR (4th) 356; *Air Canada v Toronto Port Authority* 2011 FCA 347, [2013] 3 FCR 605.

Party is an example of this approach.[78] There, the applicant sought judicial review of an internal party decision to reject his application to be a leadership candidate. The court found it had jurisdiction to judicially review the decision on the basis that the decision at issue was of 'a sufficiently public nature'.[79]

The Supreme Court of Canada has thrown support behind the *Knox* approach, albeit in a different context. *Highwood Congregation of Jehovah's Witnesses (Judicial Committee) v Wall*[80] was an application for judicial review launched by a claimant disfellowshipped from his religious association. The Supreme Court rejected the claim and expressly limited judicial review to state rather than private action.[81] In so doing, it lumped the caselaw on political parties alongside other voluntary organisations, holding them all to be inappropriate for judicial review.

Wall therefore leaves the impression that judicial review is no longer an option when political parties act unfairly in their internal workings.[82] This means that judicial oversight of internal party governance is confined to cases where a private cause of action exists.[83] There are obvious limits to this approach. Political parties can, for example, isolate themselves from a claim for breach of contract by expressly permitting derogations from their requirements in their constitutions, by-laws, and rules.

In addition, we are faced with uncertainty if not downright inconsistency in how political parties ought to be characterised in relation to other associations. The Court in *Ahenakew* declined to intervene on the basis that political parties are not the same as other private voluntary associations. In *Wall*, the Court essentially stated the opposite. The result is an ever-narrowing playing field by which unfair party practices may be challenged.

On a deeper level, *Wall* is especially unsatisfying because it paints all private voluntary entities with the same brush. A political party and a sports organisation may both be voluntary and private, but their function in our democracy is manifestly different. Political parties essentially serve as gatekeepers to elected office in Canada.[84] Few independent candidates are ever elected. They also operate as an essential 'vehicle for the participation of individual citizens in the

[78] *Graff v New Democratic Party* 2017 ONSC 3578, 28 Admin LR (6th) 294. See also: *Barron v Warkentin*, 2004 ABQB 603, 372 AR 40.

[79] *Graff*, ibid [10]. See also: *Trost v Conservative Party of Canada* 2018 ONSC 2733, 424 DLR (4th) 562, which adopts the same contextual approach but reaches the opposite conclusion.

[80] *Highwood Congregation of Jehovah's Witnesses (Judicial Committee) v Wall* 2018 SCC 26, [2018] 1 SCR 750. See also: *Ethiopian Orthodox Tewahedo Church of Canada St Mary Cathedral v Aga*, 2021 SCC 22, 459 DLR (4th) 425 which reiterates that membership decisions of a religious association are not subject to the review of a court, absent an underlying legal right.

[81] *Wall* ibid [13]–[17].

[82] M Chowdhury, 'A Wall Between the 'Public' and the 'Private': A Comment on *Highwood Congregation of Jehovah's Witnesses (Judicial Committee) v Wall*' (2019) 9 *Western Journal of Legal Studies* 1, 9.

[83] *Glover v The Progressive Conservative Party of Manitoba* 2021 MBQB 246 [14]–[16].

[84] TD Hancock, '"Blood Sport": The Struggle for Political Party Transparency in Ontario' (2020) 14 *Journal of Parliamentary and Political Law* 367, 379.

political life of the country'.[85] In light of this, there is an argument that public interest weighs in favour of ensuring their processes, especially those related to nomination of candidates, are transparent and fair.

The inadequacy of *Wall*'s analysis for political parties is already becoming evident via a strain of judicial resistance emerging from lower courts. *Karahalios v Conservative Party of Canada* dealt with an ousted leadership candidate who approached the Court alleging a breach of the party's leadership contest rules.[86] The Court held that, where a significant private law right (in this case contract) is involved, it may review the decision to ensure the private association acted in accordance with obligations of procedural fairness, the principles of natural justice, and reached its decision on a bona fide basis.[87] These concepts have deep roots in public law, and may result in an analysis that effectively 'grafts' these concepts into the private law setting.[88] *Melek v Conservative Party of Canada* expands on this, in holding that mere membership in a political party that has a constitution and bylaws constitutes a contract,[89] a significant breach of which merits judicial intervention.[90] Given the interests at stake, clearly this matter is not settled and will continue to appear before Canadian courts.[91]

B. Section 33

Another enduring puzzle relates to the application of section 33 of the Charter, colloquially known as the 'notwithstanding clause'. When invoked, section 33 permits a law to operate despite the fact that it infringes certain Charter rights and freedoms.[92] While extraordinary in its potential, historically the notwithstanding clause has been rarely invoked, which has resulted in an ambiguous

[85] *Figueroa* (n 55) [40].

[86] *Karahalios v Conservative Party of Canada* 2020 ONSC 3145, [2020] OJ No 2270 (QL).

[87] In so doing, the Court latched on to a reference in *Wall* (n 80) [26] to *Shergill v Khaira* [2014] UKSC 33 [48]. See also: *Lee v Yeung* 2012 ABQB 40, 531 AR 171 [51]–[55]. See also: *Bajwa v BC Liberal Party* 2022 BCSC 194 [39]–[42].

[88] *Hancock* (n 84) 378.

[89] Note, however, that the Supreme Court of Canada subsequently rejected this blanket understanding in *Aga* (n 80) [43].

[90] *Melek v Conservative Party of Canada* 2021 ONSC 1959 [14]. The Court in *Melek* was also presenting arguments on breach of procedural fairness, but did not need to address them [31].

[91] See, eg, *Glover* (n 83).

[92] Charter (n 3) s 33(1): 'Parliament or the legislature of a province may expressly declare in an Act of Parliament or of the legislature, as the case may be, that the Act or a provision thereof shall operate notwithstanding a provision included in section 2 or sections 7 to 15 of this *Charter*. (2) An Act or a provision of an Act in respect of which a declaration made under this section is in effect shall have such operation as it would have but for the provision of this *Charter* referred to in the declaration. (3) A declaration made under section (1) shall cease to have effect five years after it comes into force or on such earlier date as may be specified in the declaration. (4) Parliament or the legislature of a province may re-enact a declaration made under section (1). (5) Section (3) applies in respect of a re-enactment made under section (4).'

understanding of its contours. Its recent resurgence in the electoral arena requires answers to previously overlooked questions.

The notwithstanding clause is a uniquely Canadian compromise struck as part of the constitutional bargain when the Charter was signed. The section itself was a late-stage concession granted to reluctant political leaders to ensure the Charter's passage.[93] While the Charter cemented the role of the courts in invalidating legislation that breached rights and freedoms enumerated in the document, section 33 partially preserved Parliament's traditional power in a Westminster parliamentary system to have 'the last word'.[94] Parliament and the provincial legislatures can pass laws notwithstanding their infringement of section 2 and 7–15 of the Charter. This power is tempered with a five-year sunset clause, at which point the legislative override must be renewed.[95] Notably, the notwithstanding clause may only be applied to certain guaranteed rights. Democratic rights, including section 3's voting guarantee, are exempt from its application.

On its passage, section 33 garnered significant fame (or infamy) in media, political and academic circles.[96] Lauded as a legislative counterweight to fallible courts[97] or derided as a 'a dagger pointed at the heart of our fundamental freedoms'[98] section 33 was, and remains, deeply controversial.

Given the Charter's popularity, legislative bodies perceived significant political risks in invoking it. Outside of Quebec, the notwithstanding clause has largely sat on the shelf unused in the 40 years since its passage. Between 1982 and 2000 it was invoked on 16 specific occasions.[99] Thirteen of these instances

[93] JL Hiebert, 'Compromise and the Notwithstanding Clause: Why the Dominant Narrative Distorts our Understanding' in CP Manfredi and JP Kelly (eds), *Contested Constitutionalism: Reflections on the Canadian Charter of Rights and Freedoms* (Vancouver, UBC Press, 2009) 107, 109; JL Hiebert 'The Notwithstanding Clause: Why Non-use Does Not Necessarily Equate with Abiding by Judicial Norms' in P Oliver, P Macklem, and N Des Rosiers (eds), *The Oxford Handbook of the Canadian Constitution* (Oxford, Oxford University Press, 2018) 697.

[94] Hiebert (n 93) 121; R Leckey and E Mendelsohn, 'The Notwithstanding Clause: Legislatures, Courts, and the Electorate' (2022) 72 *University of Toronto Law Journal* 189; PH Russell, 'Standing Up for Notwithstanding' (1991) 29 *Alta Law Review* 293; R Albert 'Advisory Review: The Reincarnation of the Notwithstanding Clause' (2008) 45 *Alberta Law Review* 1037, 1038.

[95] Charter (n 3) s 33(3), (4).

[96] B Slattery, 'Canadian *Charter of Rights and Freedoms* – Override Clause Under S. 33 – Whether Subject to Judicial Review Under Section 1' (1983) 61 *Canadian Bar Review* 391; D Greschner and K Norman, 'The Courts and Section 33' (1987) 12 *Queen's Law Journal* 155; JD Whyte, 'On Not Standing For Notwithstanding' (1990) 28 *Alta Law Review* 347; Russell (n 94). The existence of s 33 is central to Canadian constitutional and democratic theory. See, eg, PW Hogg and AA Bushell, 'The *Charter* Dialogue Between Courts and Legislatures (Or Perhaps the *Charter* of Rights Isn't Such A Bad Thing After All)' (1997) 35 *Osgoode Hall Law Journal* 75. For a contrary view, CP Manfredi, 'The Day the Dialogue Died: A Comment on *Sauvé v Canada*' (2007) 45 *Osgoode Hall Law Journal* 105.

[97] Russell (n 94) 301.

[98] D Johansen and P Rosen 'The Notwithstanding Clause of the *Charter*' *Parliamentary Information and Research Service* (16 October 2008) 17.

[99] T Kahana, 'The Notwithstanding Mechanism and Public Discussion: Lessons from the Ignored Practice of Section 33 of the *Charter*' (2001) 44 *Canadian Public Administration* 255, 257.

occurred in Quebec,[100] where it was used on an omnibus basis as a form of political protest,[101] pre-emptively to forestall a potential finding of unconstitutionality,[102] and as a response to an unpopular judicial decision.[103] Outside of Quebec, the notwithstanding clause has been invoked in relation to back-to-work legislation,[104] land planning,[105] and marriage equality.[106]

For reasons of public perception and political risk, section 33 acquired a taboo status, characterised by a 'deeply entrenched reticence' to use it, and a widespread view that it was 'beyond rehabilitation or revival'.[107]

The contours of Canada's most controversial constitutional provision are arguably under-theorised and undetermined. For example, there is significant disagreement on when it may be invoked and how it interacts with the judiciary. Some academics have taken the view that section 33 may be validly invoked on a pre-emptive basis, meaning it might be included in legislation prior to any review of that legislation by the courts.[108] Such pre-emptive use anticipates invalidation and invokes section 33 as a response. Others have argued that, while there is a history of pre-emptive usage, section 33 may only be validly invoked *after* a court has ruled a law unconstitutional.[109] Still others have argued that invoking section 33 – pre-emptively or otherwise – cannot shield a law from judicial scrutiny, but that it merely restricts judges from imposing remedies other than a declaration of inconsistency.[110]

These debates have now spilled outside academia and into the electoral arena. Starting in 2018, various Canadian jurisdictions have started openly considering and, on some occasions, applying the notwithstanding clause in relation to (among other things) elections.

[100] ibid 258–59.
[101] Kahana (n 99) FN 1; Hiebert (n 93) 698.
[102] Hiebert (n 93) 698; Kahana (n 99) 258.
[103] *Ford v Quebec (Attorney General)* [1988] 2 SCR 712.
[104] SGEU Dispute Settlement Act, SS 1986, c 111, s 9(1) (back to work legislation).
[105] Land Planning and Development Act, SY 1982, c 22 s. 39(1) (This Act was never brought into force); Kahana (n 99) 258, 265.
[106] Marriage Act RSA 2000, c M-5 s 1.1, as amended by Marriage Amendment Act, 2000; T Kahana, The Notwithstanding Mechanism, above n 99 at 258, 267.
[107] Hiebert (n 92) 93, 695, 704, 706; H Leeson, 'Section 33, The Notwithstanding Clause: A Paper Tiger?' in P Howe and PH Russell (eds), *Judicial Power and Canadian Democracy* (Montreal & Kingston, McGill-Queen's University Press, 2001) 297, 318–19; Albert (n 94) 1038.
[108] Hiebert (n 92) 93, 697.
[109] Kahana (n 99) 276.
[110] G Webber, E Mendelsohn and R Leckey, 'The Faulty Received Wisdom around the Notwithstanding Clause' (*Policy Options* 10 May 2019) policyoptions.irpp.org/magazines/may-2019/faulty-wisdom-notwithstanding-clause/; R Leckey and E Mendelsohn, 'The Notwithstanding Clause: Legislatures, Courts, and the Electorate' (2022) 72 *University of Toronto Law Journal* 189; G Webber, 'Notwithstanding Rights, Review, or Remedy? On the Notwithstanding Clause and the Operation of Legislation' (2021) 71 *University of Toronto Law Journal* 510. But see: M St-Hilaire and X Foccroulle Menard 'Nothing to Declare: A Response to Grégoire Webber, Eric Mendelsohn, Robert Leckey, and Léonid Sirota on the Effects of the Notwithstanding Clause' (2020) 29 *Constitutional Forum* 38; Working Families #2 CA (n 57) [48]–[59].

While section 33 cannot be invoked in relation to voting rights, it can be used in relation to the free expression guarantee. In 2018, the leader of Canada's largest province threatened to invoke section 33 after a court used free speech guarantees to strike down a law that redrew electoral districts during a municipal election.[111] In early 2021, section 33 reappeared in the electoral arena when a lower court held that legislation which imposed spending limits on third parties for a specified period prior to the election unjustifiability violated the free expression guarantee.[112] Rather than proceeding through channels of appeal, the legislature invoked the notwithstanding clause to override the decision. Litigation was relaunched, this time alleging the spending limit violated a novel 'informational component' of voting rights under section 3.[113] This rationale was accepted on appeal, thus sidelining the operation of the notwithstanding clause.[114] The court added that there are no substantive limits that restrain invoking the notwithstanding clause in the electoral arena.[115]

While it is unclear if this decision will make it to the Supreme Court, it is obvious that there are additional chapters to be written on section 33's resurgence in the electoral arena. This is a trend that requires further investigation and will likely play a role in the evolution of voting rights jurisprudence. On a broader level, section 33's recent use has drawn into focus the limits of the Charter's protections in relation to political participation.

C. Online Political Expression

Legislatures, governments, and courts have struggled to adequately respond to the issues posed by online political speech. The Charter's free speech provisions are broad, and protect all non-violent attempts to convey meaning from government interference.[116] Political speech garners especially robust protection, online as well as offline.[117] While freedom of political expression both offline and online is foundational to a democracy, ensuring both free speech and a functioning public sphere is increasingly a challenge.

For example, female politicians face a barrage of extreme, misogynistic, violent, and/or otherwise discriminatory comments online. Such treatment

[111] *City of Toronto et al v Ontario (Attorney General)*, 2018 ONSC 5151 [3].
[112] *Working Families* #1 (n 63).
[113] *Working Families Coalition (Canada) Inc v Ontario* 2021 ONSC 7697.
[114] *Working Families* #2 CA (n 57).
[115] ibid [48]–[59].
[116] *Irwin Toy Ltd v Quebec (Attorney General)* [1989] 1 SCR 927, 97; *Libman* (n 60) [31]. See also *Toronto City* (n 30) for discussion of a narrowed range of protections when individuals claim there is a positive obligation on the government to facilitate expression.
[117] *Thomson Newspapers* (n 57) [92]; *Harper* (n 57) [66].

likely discourages participation in electoral politics by women. While Canada possesses criminal restrictions on hate speech, criminal prosecutions are rare[118] and the courts have set a high bar for prosecutions under human rights law.[119]

Other online harms are being propagated against politicians which are, at present, shielded by free speech protections. For example, politicians are being impersonated online, either as part of monetary scams or to inflict reputational damage.[120] Legislation prohibits such misleading communications, but because of fear of breaching section 2(b) of the Charter, these rules only apply during election periods.[121] Separately, a law prohibiting the publication of false statements about candidates during federal elections was struck down as unconstitutional because it lacked a knowledge requirement as part of the offence.[122]

Of course, political actors may be propagators as well as victims of online harm. In this regard, Canadian laws have also not kept pace with the move to partisan activities online. Given a lack of comprehensive guidance, Canada's Electoral Management Body (Elections Canada) has adopted a cautious stance to regulating online content.[123] In the face of this hesitancy, political actors are able to avoid spending limits regulatory requirements by producing content on certain online platforms such as YouTube and Facebook.[124] The result is content that, had it appeared on television, would be subject to regulations regarding election advertising, but is not treated as such because it was shared organically online. In addition, given nuances of online advertising such as microtargeting, there are holes in Elections' Canada's ability to monitor what advertisements political parties are placing online.[125]

[118] Criminal Code RSC 1985 c C-46, s 319(2): 'Every one who, by communicating statements, other than in private conversation, wilfully promotes hatred against any identifiable group is guilty of (a) an indictable offence and is liable to imprisonment for a term not exceeding two years; or (b) an offence punishable on summary conviction.'; *R v Keegstra* [1990] 3 SCR 697; *R v AB* 2012 NSPC 31 [15]: '… [I]t is not illegal simply to say things that are grossly rude, wildly offensive, blatantly false, callously hurtful, or even disgustingly hateful'.

[119] *Saskatchewan (Human Rights Commission) v Whatcott* 2013 SCC 11, [2013] 1 SCR 467 [80]–[82]: 'the expression captured under legislation restricting hate speech must rise to a level beyond merely impugning individuals: it must seek to marginalize the group by affecting its social status and acceptance in the eyes of the majority'.

[120] R Gilmore, 'Fraudsters are impersonating politicians online to scam Canadians' (*CTV News* 12 July 2019) ctvnews.ca/politics/fraudsters-are-impersonating-politicians-online-to-scam-canadians-1.4506130.

[121] Canada Elections Act SC 2000 c 9, s 481(1).

[122] *Canadian Constitution Foundation v Canada (Attorney General)* 2021 ONSC 1224.

[123] Elections Canada, *Interpretation Note 2020-05 Partisan and Election Advertising on the Internet* (November 2020). For more on this, see: M Pal, 'Social Media and Democracy: Challenges for Election Law and Administration in Canada' (2020) 19 *Election Law Journal* 200.

[124] Pal ibid.

[125] For more, see: E Judge and M Pal, 'Voter Privacy and Big-Data Elections' (2021) 58 *Osgoode Hall Law Journal* 1.

D. Indigenous Political Representation

The issue of Indigenous political representation also looms over Canadian election law. Like many settler states, the Government of Canada is in an ongoing struggle to renew and reconcile its relationship with Indigenous Peoples.[126] But while other countries are embarking on national efforts to formalise and even constitutionalise Indigenous perspectives in political decision making,[127] efforts in Canada have stalled.

Canada's historical track record of Indigenous political participation and representation in government is abysmal.[128] While the percentage of Indigenous political representatives has been increasing in recent years, numbers still lag behind the proportion of the national population.[129] Voter turnout is also lower among Indigenous persons than other Canadian demographic groups.[130]

Many interwoven causes have been advanced to explain these failings. The historical backdrop of Indigenous enfranchisement as a tool of racist assimilation has cast a long shadow over Indigenous electoral participation.[131] Canada's Westminster-styled democracy does not reflect Indigenous traditions or values.[132] Participation in Canada's electoral system can be viewed as undermining Indigenous rights to self-determination and self-government.[133] Partaking in federal and provincial elections may conflict with notions of identity and citizenship.[134] Logistical and communication barriers leaves out many northern Indigenous communities.[135] Ongoing inequalities and lack of Indigenous presence in politics helps creates a negative feedback loop that discourages participation.[136]

[126] *Principles Respecting the Government of Canada's Relationship with Indigenous Peoples* (2018) 3.

[127] Austl, Joint Select Committee on Constitutional Recognition relating to Aboriginal and Torres Strait Islander Peoples, *Final Report* (2018) Austl, National Indigenous Australians Agency, *Indigenous Voice Co-Design Final* (2021); Austl, Constitution Alteration (Aboriginal and Torres Strait Islander Voice) 2023.

[128] Until the 2015 federal elections, there had been only 34 Indigenous members of Parliament in the entire history of Canada since Confederation, and only 15 Indigenous senators: M Morden, 'Indigenizing Parliament: Time to Re-Start a Conversation' (2016) 39(2) *Canadian Parliamentary Review* 24, 25. At present, 12 of its 338 elected Members of Parliament identify as Indigenous: B Hobson, 'Canada election: 3 new Indigenous MPs likely elected for NDP, Tories' (*Global News* 22 September 2021) globalnews.ca/news/8213533/canada-election-indigenous-mps/.

[129] The most recent census data suggests that Indigenous persons are 5% of Canada's population. 3.5% of Canada's Members of Parliament identify as indigenous. See also: MS Williams, 'Indigenous Representation, Self-Determination, and Electoral Reform' in A Potter, D Weinstock and PJ Loewen (eds), *Should we Change how we Vote?: Evaluating Canada's Electoral System* (Montreal, McGill-Queen's University Press, 2017) 126, 127.

[130] Ladner and McCrossan (n 19) 32; A Hunter, 'Exploring the Issues of Aboriginal Representation in Federal Elections' (2003) 5 *Electoral Insight: Aboriginal Participation in Elections* 27.

[131] Hunter, ibid; Ladner and McCrossan (n 19) 30.

[132] *Report of the Royal Commission on Aboriginal Peoples* Vol 2 (1996), 357 (RCAP).

[133] Ladner and McCrossan (n 19) 21.

[134] ibid; Hunter (n 130) 30; Williams (n 129) 126.

[135] Hunter (n 130); Ladner and McCrossan (n 19) 22.

[136] Ladner and McCrossan (n 19) 24.

In short, Canada's electoral system alienates and lacks legitimacy for many Indigenous peoples and also contains structural barriers that hinder their participation both as voters and representatives. Clearly, change is needed. While a number of solutions have been advanced, meaningful reform has remained elusive.

Some of this stagnation flows from Canada's constitutional structure. Many problems of Indigenous political representation flow to the very roots of Canada's relationship with Indigenous nations, and repairing these faults requires constitutional amendment. The fact that constitutional amendment with non-trivial effects is a political near-impossibility has stymied several proposed solutions to enhance Indigenous representation. In 1992 the Charlottetown Accord would have guaranteed Indigenous representation in the Senate as part of a package of constitutional amendments.[137] In 1996, The Royal Commission on Aboriginal People recommended the creation of a third chamber of Parliament elected and populated by Indigenous persons.[138] Neither were implemented.

At the sub-constitutional level meaningful reforms have also largely failed to materialise. Canada's first-past-the-post (single member plurality) system has been criticised for its impact on Indigenous voters. The Law Commission of Canada recommended switching to a proportional or mixed system of representation to remedy this failing.[139] Separate efforts to switch from this system collapsed in 2017.[140] Another proposed answer involves altering voting districts to amplify Indigenous voices. The Royal Commission on Electoral Reform and Party Financing recommended the creation of Indigenous districts on top of general electoral ridings to remedy the structural inequalities that impede participation (as candidates and as voters) in the traditional electoral system.[141]

A related plan would adjust or create new geographic districts to increase the concentration of Indigenous community voices. In Canada, both federal and provincial electoral boundaries are set by statutory boundary commissions that operate at arms' length from government. These commissions may alter

[137] K McRoberts and P Monahan, *The Charlottetown Accord, the Referendum, and the Future of Canada* (Toronto, University of Toronto Press, 1993).

[138] RCAP (n 132) 359; Williams (n 129) 133.

[139] J Dalton, 'Alienation and Nationalism: Is It Possible to Increase First Nation Voter Turnout in Ontario?' (2007) 27 *Canadian Journal of Native Studies* 247; L Marchand, 'Proportional Representation' (1990) 13 *Canadian Parliamentary Review* 1.

[140] For discussion, see: The Canadian Press, 'Trudeau abandons electoral reform promise – no change to voting system in time for 2019 election' (*National Post* 1 Feb 2017) nationalpost.com/news/politics/trudeau-abandons-electoral-reform-promise-to-change-voting-system-in-time-for-2019-election; S Kilpatrick, 'Conservatives vow to block electoral reform without referendum' (*The Globe and Mail* 30 December 2015) www.theglobeandmail.com/news/politics/conservatives-vow-to-block-electoral-reform-without-referendum/article27968324/.

[141] Williams (n 129) 132.

electoral district size in order to accommodate 'geography, community history, community interests and minority representation' and the government cannot fetter their discretion to make such recommendations.[142] The record of such commissions in facilitating Indigenous representation is very mixed. Recently, one such commission expressly denied any obligation to reach out to, much less a duty to consult with, Indigenous communities.[143] Given the complexities that surround Indigenous political engagement and representation, it is unlikely statutory boundary commissions can be relied on alone to solve the problem of representation.

Thus, while there is widespread acknowledgment that something needs to be done, the way forward in Canada has stalled. The mechanisms for change largely lie beyond the institutional authority of courts, which leaves matters in the hands of the executive and legislative powers. While countries such as Australia are moving forward with a referendum that, if approved, will constitutionalise an Indigenous voice in government, Canada is at a stalemate, hamstrung by a mix of constitutional restraints and political inaction.[144] In this regard, it is startling that Canada's most recent road-map to reconciliation – the Calls to Action of the Truth and Reconciliation Commission – does not expressly refer to either electoral reform or Indigenous political representation.[145]

Whatever the path ahead, any plan clearly must engage Indigenous peoples and communities, and proceed with their support.[146] Looking forward, it is possible that renewed traction will come from the federal government's recent passage of the United Nations Declaration of Indigenous Peoples' Act. That Act requires the government to take measures to ensure its laws are in accordance with UNDRIP,[147] which, among other things, guarantees Indigenous peoples the right to 'participate fully, if they so choose, in the political … life of the State'.[148]

[142] *Carter* (n 51) 184; *Reference re the Final Report of the Electoral Boundaries Commission*, 2017 NSCA 10; Ministry of the Attorney General, *Final Report of the Far North Electoral Boundaries Commission for the Province of Ontario* (2017).

[143] Report of the Federal Electoral Boundaries Commission for the Province of Nova Scotia, Published Pursuant to the Electoral Boundaries Readjustment Act (2023), [40]–[50].

[144] (n 127).

[145] The Calls to Action do call on upon federal, provincial, territorial, and municipal governments to 'fully adopt and implement the *United Nations Declaration on the Rights of Indigenous Peoples* as the framework for reconciliation': Truth and Reconciliation Commission of Canada: Calls to Action (2015), 43; UN General Assembly, United Nations Declaration on the Rights of Indigenous Peoples (2 October 2007) A/RES/61/295, Art 5: 'Indigenous peoples have the right to maintain and strengthen their distinct political, legal, economic, social and cultural institutions, while retaining their right to participate fully, if they so choose, in the political, economic, social and cultural life of the State' (UNDRIP).

[146] Williams (n 129) 137.

[147] United Nations Declaration on the Rights of Indigenous Peoples Act RSC 2021, c 14.

[148] UNDRIP (n 147) Art 5.

IV. CANADIAN CONSTITUTIONAL DESIGN IN COMPARATIVE PERSPECTIVE

This chapter provides an overview of how Canada's Constitution and courts shape its democracy. Given the brevity with which the Canadian Constitution addresses democracy and elections, much of this content has been shaped by the judiciary. Because Canada's current constitutional text is here to stay, we can expect a continuation of this trend. While some enduring puzzles lie within the court's grasp, such as the development of free speech doctrine, many issues that continue to hound election law are those which strain the limits of courts in the face of constitutional silence.

For example, newer constitutional projects have chosen to include terms on the existence, funding, and functioning of political parties within their constitutional text. South Africa[149] and Mexico[150] provide examples of this approach. By including the regulation of political parties in the constitutional text, courts have a clear gateway to monitor the processes by which electoral candidates are selected, an issue which continues to confound Canadian law.

Other essential features of modern democracy, from the existence of independent Electoral Management Bodies,[151] to the guarantee that elections be free and fair,[152] to the mechanics of how to vote,[153] are often included in the national constitutions of leading democracies. In this regard, the Constitution Act 1982 is showing its age in comparison to more contemporary constitutions and, even by the standards of 1982, missed some of the innovations occurring in constitution-making to protect democracy around the globe.

Other states are able to address constitutional gaps by way of amendment. While Australia, for example, is also reckoning with political representation of Indigenous communities, they have developed a path to constitutionalise Indigenous voices.[154] The reality that Canada has little reasonable prospect of successful constitutional amendment severely stunts our ability to make similar progress.

In short, given Canada's constitutional amending impasse, courts will continue to have to rule on matters of electoral law and fairness. They will be under significant pressure to move the practice of democracy forward in response to the ongoing challenges that it faces.

[149] Constitution of the Republic of South Africa 1997, Arts 19(1), 236.

[150] Political Constitution of the United Mexican States 1917, ch II, Art 41(I-IV).

[151] Constitution of Mexico (n 150) Art 41 (V); Constitution of South Africa (n 149) ss 180, 190, 191; The Constitution of India, 1950, s 324. For more discussion and examples, see M Pal, 'Electoral Management Bodies as a Fourth Branch of Government' (2016) 21 *Review of Constitutional Studies* 85.

[152] Constitution of South Africa (n 149) s 19(2); Constitution of Mexico (n 150) Art 41.

[153] Constitution of South Africa (n 149) s 19(3); Constitution of Mexico (n 150) Art 41(I); Constitution of India (n 151) ss 327, 328.

[154] (n 127).

14

Challenging Political Equality in Electoral Legislation: The Case of the US Supreme Court

GRAZIELLA ROMEO AND DAVIDE ZECCA

I. INTRODUCTION

FEW TOPICS REPRESENT more controversial terrain for bitter disputes in American constitutional law than the relationship between lawmakers and the judiciary in matters related to political processes and electoral legislation. This is unsurprising given the extremely sensitive nature of the issues at stake for the equilibrium among separated institutions sharing powers and ultimately for the endurance of democracy.[1]

Previous studies have covered a broad spectrum of topics on this subject matter, including issues as varied as the extent and limits of legislative enforcement of the XV Amendment through the 1965 Voting Rights Act (VRA); the evolution of federal legislation and case law concerning campaign financing; the standard of scrutiny for state measures that impose specific burdens on the exercise of the suffrage (eg, ID laws); the interpretation of the Congressional Elections Clause (Article I, section 4 Const) and its impact on the allocation of powers between federal and state legislatures; and the relationship between democracy and election law in general.[2]

[1] The interaction between different governmental institutions, which had been described as indicated by RE Neustadt, *Presidential Power* (New York, Wiley, 1964) 42, has progressively come to be qualified more accurately as a relationship between separated institutions competing for shared powers, see CO Jones, *The Presidency in a Separated System* (Washington DC, Brookings Institution, 1994) 16.

[2] ED Katz, 'Enforcing the Fifteenth Amendment' in M Tushnet, M Graber and S Levinson (eds), *Oxford Handbook of the U.S. Constitution* (New York, Oxford University Press, 2015); RL Hasen, '"Citizens United" and the illusion of coherence' (2011) 109 *Michigan Law Review* 581; EB Foley, 'Due Process, Fair Play, and Excessive Partisanship: A New Principle for Judicial Review of Election Laws' (2017) 84 *University of Chicago Law Review* 655, 675 ff; RG Natelson, 'The Original Scope of the Congressional Power to Regulate Elections' (2010) 13 *University of Pennsylvania Journal of Constitutional Law* 1; MT Morley, 'The New Elections Clause' (2016) 91 *Notre Dame Law Review Online* 79; D Schultz, *Election Law and Democratic Theory* (London, Routledge, 2014).

Against this backdrop, the chapter analyses the adjudication of electoral issues by focusing on political equality as understood by the United States (US) Supreme Court in the past few decades. Possibly due to its nature as a competitive democracy, the US has struggled to overcome a formalistic interpretation of the principle of political equality which is frequently frustrated in practice.[3] The deference towards elected institutions' policy determinations in this matter often translates into a tolerance of incumbents' entrenchment, with a substantial effect on political equality. Such deference is based on the assumption that remedies to incumbents' entrenchment can only be found in the political process as traditional patterns of separation of powers cannot be altered by counter-majoritarian institutions.

To identify the perimeter of the research and to narrow down the wide pool of judicial decisions that require scrutiny, a few preliminary considerations are necessary. In particular, the present chapter addresses gerrymandering because this phenomenon elucidates the conflict between judicial deference to the dynamics of political processes and judicial attempts to construe the constitutional text as providing an inherent commitment to political equality. The investigation singles out the election of Representatives to the House as opposed to the election of Senators and the presidential ticket. The mandatory adoption of election by districts of Representatives to the House emphasises the relevance of apportionment choices made by state legislators in this regard, whereas no manipulation of the boundaries of a constituency is possible for state-wide elections.[4]

Setting the scene at the House of Representatives highlights the risks underlying the identification of the political community entitled to vote for the election by incumbents themselves, who most often have an obvious interest in the final result.[5] Therefore, decisions affecting reapportionment and redistricting plans are of the most importance for this analysis as they allow the perimeter of the *demos* that deserves representation in legislative assemblies to be discerned. Resorting to an often-abused terminology of generational barriers to voting rights, the assessment of the existence of political equality may not be fully satisfied by verifying whether the relevant state and federal provisions, both at constitutional and legislative level, are neutral regarding access to ballots (ie, first generation barriers to voting rights). Instead, it requires an investigation of the effective possibility of all citizens to influence the outcome of the electoral process; more specifically, whether partisan

[3] For the illustration of different kinds of competitive democracy, see R Dixon and D Landau, 'Competitive democracy and the constitutional minimum core' in T Ginsburg and A Huq (eds), *Assessing Constitutional Performance* (Cambridge, Cambridge University Press, 2016).

[4] Apportionment Act of 1842 (ch 47, 5 Stat 491). Single-member districts are mandatory for the election of the US House of Representatives since the adoption of the Uniform Congressional District Act of 1967 (Pub L 90–196; 81 Stat 581).

[5] A Kouroutakis, 'Legitimate and Illegitimate Political Self-entrenchment and Its Impact on Political Equality' (2021) 15 *Vienna Journal on International Constitutional Law* 1.

considerations should play any role in redistricting policies and to what extent it is permissible to dilute the opportunities of specific communities of interest to see their collective interests represented in legislative assemblies (ie, second generation barriers to voting rights).[6]

Indeed, due consideration is given to the different approaches to redistricting techniques according to the specific group or community of interest allegedly discriminated against. In doing so, the construction of the relevant statutory and constitutional provisions by the Supreme Court is also considered. The issue is further discussed by reference to the struggle for a consensus on how to measure the effects of gerrymandering techniques with respect to fair redistricting and the difficulties of adopting a workable standard for courts called to adjudicate on these controversies. The latter concern is increasingly relevant for the pursuance of political equality within a given community as it affects the organisation of elections and requires the judiciary to account for the timing of judgments likely to alter the shape of electoral constituencies.[7]

The chapter is then organised as follows: it first clarifies the source of federal authority to regulate elections by identifying the constitutional interests that such a regulation protects (II). The distribution of normative powers between different institutional bodies in the field of electoral legislation is relevant to clarify the limits to federal and state regulation in this domain. The analysis questioning the existence of an election federalism also better frames the discussion on the relationship between legislative and judicial power. Indeed, state bodies are important actors in the system of checks and balances, a system that prevents any power prevailing over the others.[8] The chapter subsequently proceeds to address the issue of gerrymandering by distinguishing among different forms of this practice as well as highlighting how they impact disparately on political equality (III). It further builds on this to discuss the Supreme Court case law concerning gerrymandering (IV). The federal judiciary has shown a certain reluctance to 'enter th[e] political thicket'.[9] However, a momentous shift of the federal case law began in the 1960s, and this was coupled with the VRA.[10] Without neglecting such a complex history, the chapter investigates a set of relevant Supreme Court decisions to assess the contemporary judicial attitude towards the adjudication of electoral disputes. The goal is to explore the nature and extent of constitutional scrutiny of a large component of US electoral legislation. Finally, the chapter offers some

[6] S Issacharoff, 'Polarized Voting and the Political Process: The Transformation of Voting Rights Jurisprudence' (1992) 90 *Michigan Law Review* 1833.

[7] See the so-called 'Purcell doctrine', *Purcell v Gonzalez*, 549 U.S. 1 (2006), as argued also in *Merrill v Milligan*, 142 S. Ct. 879 (2022), Kavanaugh J, Concurring Opinion; RL Hasen, 'Reining in the Purcell Principle' (2016) 43 *Florida State University Law Review* 427.

[8] WJ Brennan Jr, 'State Constitutions and the Protection of Individual Rights' (1977) 90 *Harvard Law Review* 489.

[9] *Colegrove v Green*, 328 U.S. 549, 556 (1946).

[10] *Baker v Carr*, 369 U.S. 186 (1962).

conclusions on the idea of democracy as encapsulated in the analysed decisions (V). Judicial findings in cases where the ability of citizens to participate, albeit indirectly, in public-decision making through the channels of representative democracy is at stake affect the proximity or distance of a constitutional legal system from an ideal political equality of the members of the community.[11] Reflecting on institutions' commitment to attain not only de jure but also de facto political equality among its citizens provides hints as to the conception of democracy within the US constitutional and legal framework.[12] This also explains the nature of the relationship between deliberative and adjudicatory bodies, as construed in the most recent electoral case law of the Supreme Court.

II. RIGHT TO VOTE AND POLITICAL PARTICIPATION BETWEEN STATE AND FEDERAL LEVEL

Although explicitly mentioned by the Constitution, US citizens' right to vote originates from states.[13] Such origin has a double meaning. First, the right to vote is conceptually grounded in citizens' membership of a state political community (with the notable exception of the District of Columbia). Second, the Elections Clause empowers states to determine the 'Times, Places, and Manner' of congressional elections.[14] Under the Elections Clause, however, state power coexists with Congressional authority to make or alter state regulations.

Scholars have pointed out that in the Antebellum era, state power to regulate elections was interpreted as a device to strengthen states' commitment to establishing a sound political system in which congressmen were legitimised by clear rules.[15] Following the political changes on the brink of civil war, Congress interpreted its authority in broader terms to set aside state legislation enacted to protect slavery.[16] The adoption of the XIV and XV Amendments further interfered with state power by authorising Congress to legislate to remove discrimination and secure voting rights. Against this backdrop, the Supreme

[11] The features of an ideal democracy ensuring political equality among its citizens are discussed by RA Dahl, *On Political Equality* (New Haven, Yale University Press, 2006) 8 ff.

[12] The most apparent example of cleavages of the kind may be traced back to the disregard of the principles enshrined within the XIV and XV Amendment in the former confederate states between the Reconstruction era, which brought about the infamous Jim Crow's legislation adversely affecting the access of African Americans to the ballots, and the advent of the Civil rights movements, see A Derfner, 'Racial Discrimination and the Right to Vote' (1973) 26 *Vanderbilt Law Review* 523; A Keyssar, *The Right to Vote: The Contested History of Democracy in the United States* (New York, Basic Books, 2009) 83 ff.

[13] XV Amendment, XIX Amendment, XXIV Amendment and XXVI Amendment.

[14] Art I, s 4.

[15] F Tolson, 'The Spectrum of Congressional Authority over Elections' (2019) 99 *Boston University Law Review* 317, 342.

[16] ibid 354.

Court upheld congressional intervention in electoral matters when state laws were directed at hindering Black Americans' exercise of the right to vote.[17] Congress reinforced such a trend with the Enforcement Acts of 1870 and 1871, both enacted under the Reconstruction Amendments and the Elections Clause.[18] Whereas the first Act addressed a wide spectrum of voting fraud, the second provided for federal oversight of congressional elections to also prevent the violation of the XV Amendment.[19]

Despite congressional effort to strengthen its legislative authority over electoral legislation, the Supreme Court was initially deferential to state prerogatives when the challenge brought about did not concern racial discrimination.[20] In the Reconstruction era, concerns over keeping the original dualistic federalism played a major role in shaping the Court's attitude. Over the years, however, the Court changed its approach. In *Ex parte Siebold*, an 1879 case concerning a state judge interfering and resisting the supervisors of election in the performance of their duty during federal elections of congressmen, the Court stated that federal officers' role is secured by regulations adopted pursuant to the Elections Clause.[21] At the same time, the Court clarified that, in the case of conflict between state and federal law, the latter superseded the former to the extent to which this is necessary to avoid the clash of laws. In fact, the two laws can coexist to create an 'harmonious system perfectly capable of being administered and carried out as such'.[22]

Judicial activism in the era of the Civil Rights Movement further challenged the width of state prerogatives, even though the Supreme Court's main concern was dismantling state regulations infringing upon voting rights rather than securing federal power over elections in general. In *South Carolina v Katzenbach*, for example, the Court upheld the VRA against a challenge brought by South Carolina seeking a declaration of unconstitutionality of selected provisions of the Act.[23] The challenges included section 4(a)(c)(d) VRA, which suspended literacy and other voting tests in some states, identified according to a formula provided for by the VRA. South Carolina claimed that singling out some covered jurisdictions was a violation of state equal sovereignty and an impermissible intrusion into state legislation. The Court found that the VRA reflected Congress' intention to end racial discrimination in

[17] *United States v Reese*, 92 U.S. 214, 218 (1876) ('It is only when the wrongful refusal at such an election is because of race, color, or previous condition of servitude, that Congress can interfere …').

[18] Enforcement Act of 1870 (ch 114, 16 Stat 140); Enforcement Act of 1871 (ch 22, 17 Stat 13).

[19] X Wang, 'The Making of Federal Enforcement Laws, 1870–1872' (1995) 70 *Chicago-Kent Law Review* 1013; E Swinney, 'Enforcing the Fifteenth Amendment, 1870–1877' (1962) 28 *The Journal of Southern History* 202.

[20] *United States v Cruikshank*, 92 U.S. 542 (1876). See also ED Katz, 'Reinforcing Representation: Congressional Power to Enforce the Fourteenth and Fifteenth Amendments in the Rehnquist and Waite Courts' (2003) 101 *Michigan Law Review* 2341, 2389–391.

[21] *Ex parte Siebold*, 100 U.S. 371 (1879).

[22] ibid 386.

[23] *South Carolina v Katzenbach*, 383 U.S. 301 (1966).

voting as prescribed by the Fifteenth Amendment. The Court further clarified that, to effect the constitutional prohibition of racial discrimination, Congress 'may use any rational means', even against states' powers.[24] *Katzenbach* was part of a larger set of decisions curtailing state prerogatives in the regulation of elections, mostly adopted to protect political equality and the principle of 'one man, one vote'.[25]

The decision in *Katzenbach* was reached by reference to the Fifteenth Amendment as legal ground for Congress' exercise of power over electoral legislation, with no mention of the Elections Clause as additional ground. Indeed, case law dealing with discrimination has been constantly characterised by judicial reliance on the Reconstruction Amendments, with no reference to the Elections Clause as appropriate ground for congressional power, thus leaving the Clause less explored.[26] In *Arizona v Inter Tribal Council of Arizona, Inc.*, the Supreme Court considered a case where the Elections Clause was invoked.[27] The case concerned a challenge to Arizona law requiring voters to present proof of citizenship to register to vote. A group of residents sought a declaration that the legislation was pre-empted by federal law, namely by the National Voter Registration Act of 1993 (NVRA). The Court affirmed the Ninth Circuit's conclusion in favour of pre-emption. Even the presumption against pre-emption, Justice Scalia held in the majority opinion, is easily rebutted in the case of electoral legislation as Congress is acting upon an explicit constitutional mandate. Justice Scalia, however, also stressed in a *dictum* that Arizona defence was correct in interpreting the Elections Clause as granting Congress authority only concerning time, place and manner of voting. Scalia clarified that such a clause implies that 'Arizona is correct that the Elections Clause empowers Congress to regulate how federal elections are held, but not who may vote in them. The latter is the province of the States.'[28] Consequently, constitutional doubts would arise if a federal statute precluded a state from obtaining the information necessary to identify who is entitled to vote. The conflict can be avoided by interpreting the NVRA as avoiding such a clash of laws. In particular, it can be construed as permitting the federal Election Assistance Commission to include on the Federal Form required for voters' registration information 'necessary to enable the appropriate state election

[24] ibid 324.

[25] *Reynolds v Sims*, 377 U.S. 533 (1964); *Kirkpatrick v Preisler*, 394 U.S. 526 (1969); *Wells v Rockefeller*, 395 U.S. 542 (1969). Those decisions have also attracted criticism even by scholars who, despite sharing the Court's concerns regarding discrimination, pointed out at the frequent judicial intervention into political decisions such as redistricting in cases of variation of population: RG Dixon Jr , 'The Warren Court Crusade for the Holy Grail of "One Man-One Vote"' (1969) *Supreme Court Review* 220, arguing that 'it is now becoming obvious that the Court needs help from the political system in managing the equality concept in apportionment-districting'.

[26] F Tolson, 'Election Law Federalism and the Limits of the Antidiscrimination Framework' (2018) 59 *William & Mary Law Review* 2211.

[27] *Arizona v Inter Tribal Council of Arizona, Inc.*, 570 U.S. 1 (2013).

[28] ibid 13–17 Slip Op.

official to assess the eligibility of the applicant'. Scalia's *dictum* concerning the Elections Clause, however, suggested an inclination on the part of conservative justices to open the door to a narrow interpretation of the scope of federal authority.

The severe curtailment of congressional power over electoral regulation, however, occurred a few days after *Arizona v Inter Tribal Council* and without bringing up the Elections Clause. In *Shelby County v Holder*, the Supreme Court held that section 4(b) VRA violated the 'fundamental principle' of equal sovereignty by prescribing that certain states apply for federal preclearance before implementing electoral laws. The same formula, used to identify the covered jurisdiction, had survived *Katzenbach* only to be struck down in *Shelby*, thus freeing states from federal control concerning non-discriminatory voter qualification standards and procedural regulations that govern elections. Chief Justice Roberts, writing for the majority, maintained that the origin of the preclearance mechanism of section 4(b) VRA was a historical context characterised by hideous discrimination targeting the Black population; however, such conditions of systematic segregation are no longer in place. To maintain such control over state legislation would imply a path dependency that undermines state powers without achieving any constitutional interest that still needs to be realised.

The existence of multiple sources of constitutional authority granting Congress the power to intervene in electoral legislation does appear to impact the Supreme Court's approach to the relationship between state and federal powers. States, therefore, play a major role in electoral regulation. In *Shelby*, the Elections Clause did not grant constitutional authority to the preclearance mechanism of the VRA. Instead, the majority insisted on the need to restore to states their equal sovereignty frustrated by selective control over their legislation.

The optimist vision of the progress of political equality offered by Chief Justice Roberts coexists with the persistence of important litigation concerning state manipulation of legislative districts, fuelled by the abolition of federal preclearance over state regulation. This spike in federal litigation concerning redistricting and apportionment plans is closely connected to the neutralisation of the preventive oversight mechanism of section 5 VRA by *Shelby*. This, in turn, leaves only an ex-post judicial remedy available to voters, according to the general prohibition on voting discriminatory practices in section 2 VRA.[29] To properly assess the US Supreme Court's approach towards redistricting litigation, it is therefore necessary to identify the features of manipulatory apportionment techniques and discuss to what extent the Court has applied the constitutional provisions discussed above or has resorted to statutory interpretation of the provisions of the VRA.

[29] DE Ho, 'Voting Rights Litigation after Shelby County: Mechanics and Standards in Section 2 Vote Denial Claims' (2014) 17 *New York University Journal of Legislation & Public Policy* 675.

III. DEFINING THE PROBLEM WITH GERRYMANDERING

Gerrymandering is usually defined as the practice of manipulating legislative district boundaries with a view to political gain.[30] It is by no means an exclusive US phenomenon as examples of manipulation of district boundaries can be found in a number of democracies. The impact of gerrymandering, however, is higher within majoritarian, either single-member or multi-member, electoral systems also characterised by a certain level of diversity in the population.[31] The impact can be amplified in countries where the uneven distribution of the population density potentially overrepresents rural areas inhabited by a homogeneous population.[32] These characteristics explain why gerrymandering has been enacted in at least three different ways in the history of the US.

The first form of gerrymandering has been perpetrated through malapportionment, where districts' boundaries are designed to incorporate the population unequally, either by intentionally drawing districts with an uneven population, by not updating districts to reflect demographic changes, or by using apportionment criteria to the benefit of one political party.[33]

The second type of manipulation of districts has targeted an ethnic or racial minority to marginalise their political power. This is the so-called 'racial gerrymandering', which occurs typically by either 'cracking' or 'packing' voters. In the first scenario (cracking), minority voters are distributed across multiple districts to dilute their political impact on electoral results. In the second scenario (packing), minority voters are included in a district where the ethnic or racial minority accounts for the majority of the district's population (supermajority districts). In this manner, their political significance is engulfed by the majority. Racial gerrymandering can also occur also when majority–minority districts, where the white non-Hispanic population is below 50 per cent of residents, are reapportioned to rebalance the demographic disproportion to the detriment of minorities.[34] Therefore, resort to a racial criterion is not an unequivocal sign of unconstitutionality. In fact, the constitutional framework does not allow for the predominance of race as a criterion for deciding electoral boundaries.[35]

[30] See A Keena, M Latner, AJ McGann and CA Smith, *Gerrymandering the States* (Cambridge, Cambridge University Press, 2021) 15. For a detailed discussion of the concept of gerrymandering see E Voyakis, ch 3 in this volume. See also S Bickerstaff, *Election Systems and Gerrymandering Worldwide* (Cham, Springer, 2020).

[31] On the impact of gerrymandering on multi-member districts, see 'Effective Representation and Multimember Districts' (1970) 68 *Michigan Law Review* 1577.

[32] G Epps, 'One person, one vote' (2015–2016) *Supreme Court Preview* 66.

[33] Examples include the so called 'rural gerrymandering' which occurs when redistricting maps do not take into consideration the drop of rural population and the parallel growth of urban districts, see Keena, Latner, McGann and Smith (n 30) 17.

[34] R McKeever, 'Race and Representation in the United States: The Constitutional Validity of Majority–Minority Congressional Districts' (1999) 33 *Journal of American Studies* 491.

[35] See, eg, *Miller v Johnson*, 515 U.S. 900, 920–28 (1995), and *Evenwel v Abbott*, 136 S. Ct. 1120 (2016); see also O Wilson and F Andrew, 'Population Predominance in Racial Gerrymandering' (2015) 3 *Civil Rights Litigation* 2.

This form of racial gerrymandering was outlawed with the VRA. The Supreme Court has contributed to the development of a racial gerrymandering jurisprudence that has identified discriminatory intent as the criterion to rule unconstitutional district maps that manipulate boundaries. However, the practice continues, as demonstrated by the number of cases that reach the Court on an almost yearly basis.[36]

The third example of gerrymandering is characterised by the manipulation of district boundaries based on historically attested political preferences.[37] This practice is labelled 'partisan gerrymandering' because it allows legislators to draw districts by considering the political orientation of the population in a given area.[38] Thereby, voters of a certain political party can be cracked or packed to dilute their impact and power, even if for each district an even distribution of the population is preserved. Such a practice has not been outlawed, and the Supreme Court has so far refused to rule it straightforwardly unconstitutional. In fact, whereas racial gerrymandering is understood as manipulation motivated by an invidious logic, partisan gerrymandering is frequently depicted as a dynamic inherent in political competition which lacks a manageable judicial standard.[39]

An examination of practice clarifies that the framing of gerrymandering as a constitutional issue is not an easy task. Manipulation of district boundaries can indeed pursue the legitimate end of rebalancing electoral power in an inhomogeneous population.[40] Even the reapportionment of districts that does not adjust boundaries to the change in population can legitimately aim to preserve the structure of a majority–minority district. In fact, the first conceptual problem is to understand if, and when, gerrymandering violates

[36] See the cases reported by the National Conference of State legislatures which are now available at www.ncsl.org/research/redistricting/redistricting-and-the-supreme-court-the-most-significant-cases.aspx.

[37] Partisan gerrymandering has been raising major concerns since data regarding electoral preferences have become sufficiently precise and easily accessible to political parties, also thanks to technological developments, see M Altman, K MacDonald and M McDonald, 'From Crayons to Computers: The Evolution of Computer Use in Redistricting' (2005) 23 *Social Science Computer Review* 334.

[38] A manipulation of districts boundaries occurs even where districts are drawn to guarantee safe seats for the elected officials of both parties through cracking or packing votes along partisan lines. In such a case, gerrymandering can be described as a form of 'incumbent protection', which is less problematic from a constitutional standpoint as it impacts equally on either party, see Keena, Latner, McGann and Smith (n 30) 20; see also N Persily, 'In Defense of Foxes Guarding Henhouses: The Case for Judicial Acquiescence to Incumbent Protecting Gerrymanders' (2002) 116 *Harvard Law Review* 649.

[39] For racial gerrymandering, see *Shaw v Reno*, 509 U.S. 630 (1993); for partisan gerrymandering, see *Vieth v Jubelirer*, 541 U.S. 267 (2004), where the majority stated that 'We do not disagree with [the] judgment' that 'partisan gerrymanders [are incompatible] with democratic principles.' Kennedy J noted in his concurring opinion that the majority's conclusion that partisan gerrymandering that disfavours one party is permissible is inconsistent with the premise concerning the unlawfulness of an excessive injection of politics in districting, see Kennedy J, Concurring opinion.

[40] R Hanson, 'Rorschach Tests, Art Criticism, and the Jurisprudence of Gerrymandering' (2012) 2 *Wake Forest Journal of Law & Policy* 357.

constitutional principles. Supreme Court case law has identified the principle of equal representation as the constitutional limit to gerrymandering practices since the 1963 pivotal case *Gray v Sanders*.[41] Equal representation implies that each person counts for one vote so that his or her participation in elections equally contributes to the creation of a majority. The principle logically derives from the majority rule, which in turn rests upon the premise of political equality. Moreover, gerrymandering not only affects the possibility of the fair representation of minorities, either racial or political, but it also undermines their political power in general. In other words, not only do voters lose their opportunity to be represented, but they also become politically irrelevant. In fact, by losing from the outset their ability to decide who governs, gerrymandered voters lose the opportunity to obtain policy concessions they are interested in and that would be ideally indispensable for the running parties to win them over. In a gerrymandered district, the running parties know those voters will not influence their political result.

According to arguments often advanced in litigation, the practice does not undermine the valid expression of single votes.[42] Indeed, gerrymandering can be detected only if the aggregate composition of votes is grouped along the lines of racial or partisan membership. The Supreme Court has followed this logic by stating that legislators cannot draw lines of congressional districts in such a manner as to give greater voice to some voters to the detriment of others.[43] In litigation, however, the definition of what exactly determines the allocation of a greater voice is contentious, especially because the effects of gerrymandering must be proven with regard to specific districts.

In particular, to advance a gerrymandering claim, plaintiffs must prove that their districts have been cracked or packed and, therefore, that the practice has harmed them as voters. Standing to sue is then recognised only to those who have suffered a representational injury in a challenged district.[44] A generalised gerrymandering practice, even if recognised as a matter of fact, cannot ground per se a claim for violation of political equality. Stated differently, gerrymandering is framed as a constitutional issue that, although affecting individuals, can be proven only by examining the aggregate effects of the practice concerning the contested districts. Consequently, a generalised gerrymandering plan which, for example, precludes the representation of a minority but cannot be adequately proved with reference to single districts will escape constitutional adjudication.[45]

[41] *Gray v Sanders*, 372 U.S. 368 (1963).

[42] RH Pildes, 'Why Rights Are Not Trumps: Social Meanings, Expressive Harms, and Constitutionalism' (1998) 27 *The Journal of Legal Studies* 725, 755 ff.

[43] *Wesberry v Sanders*, 376 U.S. 1 (1964).

[44] *United States v Hays*, 515 U.S. 737, 739 (1995), and *Gill v Whitford*, 138 S. Ct. 1916, 1930–31 (2018).

[45] See GA Spann, 'Gerrymandering Justiciability' (2020) 108 *Georgetown Law Journal* 981.

Moreover, in the case of partisan gerrymandering, the problem of the identification of the harm is particularly exacerbated as the group who would need to prove the harm is qualified by partisan membership. In the pivotal case *Vieth v Jubelirer*, Justice Scalia persuaded a plurality of the Supreme Court that partisan gerrymandering could be challenged only if a right to proportional representation of partisan groups existed.[46] As such a right is not established in the Constitution, and therefore the participation of a group simply identified by partisan affiliation is not secured, Scalia concluded that the Court cannot address the claim, and subsequently treated partisan membership as a demographic characteristic not different from race or gender. The conclusion is controversial as partisan membership is the determinant of electoral results, so the manipulation of the composition of voters based on such a criterion is intrinsically dangerous for the fairness of the election. If voters of a certain party are unable to determine or influence the result of an election by expressing their views, their political equality is violated and democracy is thus endangered. Although the Supreme Court has conceded that partisan gerrymandering has the potential to inject excessive levels of politics into the allocation of districts and votes, it has so far disagreed internally on the framing of the constitutional violation that such practice entails.

In substantive terms, gerrymandering has been so far conceptualised as a violation of the Equal Protection Clause of the XIV Amendment, whereas attempts to frame it as a violation of the I Amendment are far less common. In his concurring opinion in *Vieth*, Justice Kennedy argued that the latter may be more relevant in partisan gerrymandering cases.[47] The I Amendment protects individuals from burdens derived from their participation in the electoral process, their voting history, their association with a political party, or their expression of political views. This argument emphasises how democracy can be nourished only by effective political participation and how partisan gerrymandering prevents citizens from banding together to promote their interests towards the candidates that share their views. Both the XIV and the I Amendment arguments construe gerrymandering as a potential violation of the principle of equality. What the two options leave unsolved is whether gerrymandering violates an individual or a collective right.

Some scholars have argued that gerrymandering harms democracy as much as the groups targeted by such practice.[48] Some studies, for example, draw a correlation between gerrymandered districts and controversial policy outcomes.[49] Such a correlation is not linked to the particular quality of a party; rather, it is connected to the lack of meaningful electoral competition.

[46] *Vieth v Jubelirer* (n 39).

[47] ibid.

[48] AJ McGann, CA Smith, M Latner and A Keena, *Gerrymandering in America: The House of Representatives, the Supreme Court and the Future of Popular Sovereignty* (New York, Cambridge University Press, 2016).

[49] See Keena, Latner, McGann and Smith (n 30) 141.

In constitutional terms, however, the problem of gerrymandering is not one of the drawbacks of its implementation; it is rather the sustainability of the institutional system, which is built on fair competition for power.

Viewed in such a context, the problem with framing gerrymandering lies in the following paradox: it is mainly conceptualised as a violation of the individual right to political equality yet occurs only insofar as the effect of such a violation propagates to a group. Such a paradox magnifies the problem with the justiciability of gerrymandering claims, which largely rests on the possibility of identifying the interest group that can be shown to have suffered a representational injury.

IV. POLITICAL EQUALITY AND GERRYMANDERING LITIGATION BEFORE THE SUPREME COURT

Addressing the constitutional adjudication of gerrymandering requires an assessment of its justiciability in federal courts. Establishing whether a justiciable right to political equality and a collective interest in political participation exist is therefore preliminary to examining the approach of the US Supreme Court to gerrymandering litigation.

The Court was initially sceptical of the above-mentioned rights, arguing that redistricting disputes were peculiarly political issues. Notably, it clarified that no court could draw a map for congressional seats *ex novo*, but the judiciary could only invalidate a map enacted by a state legislature, with the undesirable consequence of triggering a state-wide election of the Representatives.[50] The main rationale for refraining to step into the 'political thicket' lay in the allocation of remedial powers for the malapportionment of congressional districts to Congress and the legislatures of the states (Article I, section 4 Const.). The inability of Congress to ensure the compliance of states or its historical negligence in providing for reasonable apportionment criteria applicable nationwide were deemed irrelevant. Despite the absence of an express constitutional mandate that congressional districts be of roughly equal population, a minority of the justices maintained that state apportionment must strive to ensure an approximate equal representation of citizens in Congress to avoid the survival of 'rotten boroughs'.[51] The applicability of the political question doctrine to reapportionment disputes was later discarded in *Baker v Carr*, which held that malapportionment cases did not concern the allocation of powers between different branches of government but rather whether inherently political actions exceeded the constitutional authority granted to a given branch of government.[52]

[50] Above n 9.

[51] ibid, Black J, Dissenting Opinion; see also A Lewis, 'Legislative Apportionment and the Federal Courts' (1957) 71 *Harvard Law Review* 1057.

[52] Above n 10.

Regarding racial gerrymandering, the justices recognised that state apportionment powers, although indeed wide and discretionary, are by no means absolute as they must comply with constitutional obligations granting explicit rights to citizens (eg, the XV Amendment). Therefore, the political question doctrine does not shield state apportionment from federal judicial scrutiny when racially motivated disenfranchisement is alleged.[53]

Political equality was originally conceptualised by the Warren Court in the context of malapportionment.[54] First, in *Gray v Sanders* the Court invalidated a county-unit system of voting for state-wide offices by deriving from the Equal Protection Clause the principle that all those residing within a geographical subdivision must have an equal vote.[55] Therefore, no preferred class of citizens may exist as, once voters' qualifications are established, the conception of political equality implies each vote has equal weight ('one person, one vote'). Notably, the command that the House of Representatives be elected 'by the People' of each state (Article I, section 2) has been interpreted by the Court as exemplifying that the fundamental goal of the House is to pursue equal representation for equal numbers.[56] Equal representation was held to also apply to the apportionment of state legislative districts, trumping even contrary state constitutional provisions, as the Equal Protection Clause provides for the equal participation of all qualified voters in the election of state legislators.[57] Despite negating the opportunity of any de minimis variance threshold for congressional districts' apportionment, the Court later recognised that minor deviations from mathematical equality for state legislative districts are admissible.[58] Therefore, a twofold standard of scrutiny has emerged: for congressional districts, the parameter is strict compliance to Article I, section 2 (*Wesberry v Sanders*); conversely, a more lenient standard applies to state districts under the Equal Protection Clause (*Reynolds v Sims*).[59] In this regard, the Roberts Court has recently upheld redistricting plans referring to the total population of a state as opposed to the number of qualified voters.[60]

Regarding racial gerrymandering, the adoption of the VRA was a landmark accomplishment. The preclearance mechanism (section 5 VRA) applicable

[53] *Gomillion v Lightfoot*, 364 U.S. 339 (1960).

[54] RL Engstrom, 'The Supreme Court and Equipopulous Gerrymandering: A Remaining Obstacle in the Quest for Fair and Effective Representation' (1976) 2 *Arizona State Law Journal* 277.

[55] Above n 41.

[56] *Wesberry v Sanders*, (n 43).

[57] *Reynolds v Sims*, (n 25).

[58] Respectively, *Kirkpatrick v Preisler* (n 25); *Karcher v Daggett*, 462 U.S. 725 (1983); and *Mahan v Howell*, 410 U.S. 315 (1973); *White v Regester*, 412 U.S. 755 (1973); *Gaffney v Cummings*, 412 U.S. 735 (1973). In the recent case *Harris v Arizona Independent Redistricting Commission*, 136 S. Ct. 1301 (2016), the Supreme Court has validated minor deviations that do not exceed 10%.

[59] G Casper, 'Apportionment and the Right to Vote: Standards of Judicial Scrutiny' (1973) *Supreme Court Review* 1; I Rubin, 'Equal Protection in Legislative Apportionment: A New Double Standard' (1974) 5 *North Carolina Central Law Journal* 308.

[60] *Evenwel v Abbott* (n 35).

to covered jurisdictions (section 4(b) VRA) and the nationwide prohibition of racially discriminatory voting procedures (section 2 VRA) have since been pivotal in racial gerrymandering adjudication.[61] The main difference between sections 2 and 5 VRA was that the latter required the absence of both discriminatory intent and effects, whereas discriminatory intent only was relevant for the operation of the former as the Constitution granted no independent constitutional claim to representation to any political group.[62]

A first concern addressed by the Supreme Court was the resort to multi-member districts for the at-large election of members of state legislatures to dilute the voting strength of racial minorities. The justices acknowledged that the use of plurality districts is not unconstitutional per se, but the burden of proof falls upon the plaintiffs.[63] Notably, the Court clarified that the combination of single and multi-member districts does not unconstitutionally discriminate racial minority groups when the redistricting plan has an ameliorative effect. This is because the preclearance mechanism encompasses a mere non-retrogression principle, which requires that the voting position of racial minorities is not diminished in respect of their previous condition.[64] The Court further held that the allegation of a non-proportional ratio between a racial group's voting potential and the legislative seats it contributed to elect was insufficient to claim invidious discrimination. What matters instead is proof that the political processes underlying the nomination and election did not guarantee their equal participation, ultimately harming their influence in the selection of representatives.[65]

The 1982 amendment of section 2 VRA updated the provision by supplementing the prohibition of discriminatory intent with a prohibition of discriminatory effects. The Court upheld the amendment by establishing a totality-of-circumstances test for voting dilution claims challenging the use of multi-member districts. This test requires that a minority group is sufficiently large and geographically compact that it could constitute a majority in a single-member district, it is politically cohesive, and that the white majority consistently votes as a bloc opposed to the preferred minority candidate.[66] Although the justices acknowledged that minority representation proportional to the group demographic size is indeed an indication of the equality of political

[61] The preclearance mechanism is currently inoperative after the Supreme Court struck down the coverage formula in *Shelby County v Holder*, 570 U.S. 529 (2013). For an insightful account of the application of the VRA provisions in electoral litigation, see RL Hasen, 'Race or Party, Race as Party, or Party All the Time: Three Uneasy Approaches to Conjoined Polarization in Redistricting and Voting Cases' (2018) 59 *William & Mary Law Review* 1837.

[62] For s 5 VRA, see *City of Rome v United States*, 446 U.S. 156 (1980); for s 2 VRA, see *City of Mobile v Bolden*, 446 U.S. 55 (1980).

[63] *Fortson v Dorsey*, 379 U.S. 433 (1965); *Whitcomb v Chavis*, 403 U.S. 124 (1971).

[64] *Beer v United States*, 425 U.S. 130 (1973).

[65] *White v Regester* (n 58).

[66] *Thornburg v Gingles*, 478 U.S. 30 (1986).

opportunities, they nonetheless declared that proportionality alone must not be considered a conclusive factor.[67]

A second prong of federal decisions addressing racial gerrymandering pertains to the applicable standard of scrutiny.[68] By relying on the Equal Protection Clause, the Supreme Court declared that the use of race in drawing district lines must be subject to strict scrutiny and an investigation of whether the plan is narrowly tailored to pursue a compelling state interest.[69] Unconstitutional gerrymanders occur when citizens are clustered in a single-member district only by reason of their race, despite other traditional districting factors such as geographical compactness, contiguity, or unity of political subdivisions. This is because it presupposes the existence of racial bloc voting and ultimately contributes to a sort of political apartheid. Therefore, when race is a predominant factor in the apportionment of electoral districts, meaning that traditional race-neutral districting principles are subordinated to racial considerations, the apportionment plan is unconstitutional. Lawmakers' intentions to remedy past violations of minorities' voting rights in pursuance of section 5 VRA or to avoid violations of section 2 VRA have been recognised as compelling state interests, provided that the plan is narrowly tailored to serve these state interests.[70] More recently, the Court clarified that, once the plaintiff has established the predominance of racial factors, states themselves bear the burden of proving that the plan was narrowly tailored to pursue the above interests.[71]

Elaborating on the relationship between sections 2 and 5 VRA, the Supreme Court held that a presumptive violation of section 2 VRA does not necessarily preclude the granting of preclearance to an apportionment plan, even when the latter has a discriminatory purpose, as long as the plan is non-retrogressive for minority voters.[72] More recently, the Court clarified that the non-retrogression obligation does not imply a duty to maintain the same percentage of minority voters in majority–minority districts, as the predominance of racial considerations amounts to a prohibited gerrymander even when the state is striving to minimise the variation of population resident in each district.[73] The *Gingles* framework, however, has been considered applicable only to districts where minority citizens form a geographically compact majority, whereas its application

[67] *Johnson v De Grandy*, 512 U.S. 997 (1994).

[68] The Supreme Court's scrutiny over the use of race in redistricting since the 1990s is discussed by MJ Pitts, 'What Has Twenty-Five Years of Racial Gerrymandering Doctrine Achieved' (2018) 9 *UC Irvine Law Review* 229.

[69] *Shaw v Reno* (n 39).

[70] *Miller v Johnson* (n 35); *Shaw v Hunt*, 517 U.S. 899 (1996); *Bush v Vera*, 517 U.S. 952 (1996).

[71] *Bethune-Hill v Virginia State Board of Elections*, 137 S. Ct. 788 (2017); *Abbott v Perez*, 138 S. Ct. 2305 (2018).

[72] *Reno v Bossier Parish School Board*, 520 U.S. 471 (1997); *Reno v Bossier Parish School Board*, 528 U.S. 320 (2000); see T Crum, 'Deregulated Redistricting' (2022) 107 *Cornell Law Review* 359.

[73] *Alabama Legislative Black Caucus v Alabama*, 575 U.S. 254 (2015).

was rejected for 'crossover districts', where minority groups would be able to elect their preferred candidate only with the votes cast by non-minority voters.[74] Notably, the creation of a larger number of 'influence districts' rather than 'safe' majority–minority districts has been considered admissible as it avoids the risk of narrowing the political influence of the minority group to a small fraction of the districts, in an effort to privilege substantial representation as opposed to mere descriptive representation.[75]

Instead, partisan gerrymandering litigation has mainly concerned the issues of justiciability in federal courts, the identification of the applicable constitutional principles, and the manageability of standards of scrutiny. The Supreme Court initially held that that a voting dilution claim raised by a political group is equally justiciable under the Equal Protection Clause as one raised by a racial group, yet it requires evidence of both intentional and actual discrimination against a political group.[76] The issue has proven particularly controversial, as demonstrated by the subsequent fragmented plurality opinion in which four justices found partisan gerrymandering always non-justiciable for the lack of any judicially discernible and manageable adjudicatory standard.[77] More recently, the Roberts Court, after discarding all assessments of partisan asymmetry built on a state-wide scale rather than district-by-district, has denied the justiciability of partisan gerrymandering challenges, holding that they present political questions which exceed the competences conferred to federal courts.[78] The justices held that the void could be filled by judicial scrutiny by state courts, which are better equipped to assess whether excessive partisan bias influenced redistricting plans, relying also on state constitutional provisions. However, this avenue appears under threat as well, despite the Supreme Court refused to endorse the 'independent state legislature' doctrine in a case adjudicated in the 2022 term.[79]

[74] *Bartlett v Strickland*, 556 U.S. 1 (2009); *Cooper v Harris*, 136 S. Ct. 2512 (2017).

[75] *Georgia v Ashcroft*, 539 U.S. 461 (2003). The decision has been considered a paramount example of the difficulties lying in the adjudication of equality claims in the domain of politics, see RH Pildes, 'The Constitutionalization of Democratic Politics' (2004) 118 *Harvard Law Review* 29, 83 ff. See also RH Pildes, 'The Decline of Legally Mandated Minority Representation' (2007) 68 *Ohio State Journal*, 1141 arguing that in *League of United Latin American Citizens (LULAC) v Perry*, 548 U.S. 399 (2006), the Court, despite finding that a redistricting plan diluted minority voting power and hence violated s 2 VRA, seemed poised 'to limit substantially the legal imperative to design safe minority election districts'.

[76] *Davis v Bandemer*, 478 U.S. 109 (1986).

[77] *Vieth v Jubelirer* (n 39). See RL Hasen, 'Looking for Standards (in All the Wrong Places): Partisan Gerrymandering Claims after Vieth' (2004) 3 *Election Law Journal: Rules, Politics, and Policy* 626.

[78] *Rucho v Common Cause*, 139 S. Ct. 2484 (2019). For what concerns standing to sue, refer to *Gill v Whitford* (n 44), where the plaintiffs proposed a so-called 'efficiency-gap' test, see NO Stephanopoulos and EM McGhee, 'Partisan gerrymandering and the efficiency gap' (2015) 82 *University of Chicago Law Review* 831.

[79] *Moore v Harper*, 600 U.S. 1 (2023). See MT Morley, 'The Independent State Legislature Doctrine, Federal Elections, and State Constitutions' (2020) 55 *Georgia Law Review* 1.

V. THE JUDICIAL REVIEW OF POLITICAL PROCESSES AND THE SUPREME COURT IDEA OF DEMOCRACY

The analysis of the wide set of decisions handed down by the Supreme Court over the six decades since *Baker v Carr* enables some consideration as to the concept of democracy advanced by the justices. In fact, the degree of intrusiveness of judicial oversight in electoral matters offers some clues of the Court's approach to the balance between political equality and political entrenchment. First, it is clear that the Court's understanding of the dynamics underlying democratic processes has been inconsistent over this extended time frame. Indeed, it has evolved over time, in consonance with the general approach of the majority of the Court that has progressively moved away from the Warren Court jurisprudence.[80]

The conceptual justification of judicial review over apportionment and redistricting processes may be traced back to a momentous occurrence in US constitutional law that has shaped post-WWII judicial interpretation for decades. The famous Footnote Four in the *Carolene Products* case gave a fairly accurate illustration of the role of the Supreme Court and the limitations to judicial review of legislation.[81] More specifically, in recognising the general deference due to social and economic legislation, which allowed it to overcome the *Lochner* jurisprudence, the Court reserved for itself a limited yet relevant niche to step into the 'political thicket'.[82] The role of the Court would be to correct the dynamics of political processes when they do not ensure the proper functioning of the popular government. It is not by mistake that the Court refers directly to restrictions to the right to vote, which are justiciable and require an intervention by the judiciary when they subject 'insular and discrete minorities' to discrimination on account of invidious prejudice. The result is that the political process is broken and useless for those minorities because they become systematically disenfranchised or deprived of any influence on the election of representatives or public policy decisions. At this point the Court is supposed to take action and redress the unfair dynamics of the political process, dynamics which if left unaddressed would contradict the idea of popular governance based on the principle of majority.[83]

Starting from the seminal work of John Hart Ely, constitutional scholarship has rooted the justiciability of reapportionment and redistricting disputes

[80] JH Choper, *Judicial Review and the National Political Process. A Functional Reconsideration of the Role of the Supreme Court* (Chicago, The University of Chicago Press, 1980) 103 ff; TM Keck, 'The Reagan Revolution to the Present' in M Tushnet, M Graber and S Levinson (eds), *Oxford Handbook of the U.S. Constitution* (New York, Oxford University Press, 2015).

[81] *United States v Carolene Products Company*, 304 U.S. 144 (1938).

[82] The *Lochner* jurisprudence took its name after the case *Lochner v New York*, 198 U.S. 45 (1905).

[83] DA Strauss, 'Is Carolene Products Obsolete?' (2010) 4 *University of Illinois Law Review* 1251.

exactly in the Footnote Four of *Carolene Products*.[84] The acknowledgment that the majority principle underlying democratic self-governance was under threat because of self-entrenchment strategies that failed to ensure the equal participation of all citizens, thereby violating the principle later codified as 'one person, one vote', justifies intrusive judicial scrutiny to ensure that the political process does not foreclose specific classes of citizens from participating in public decision-making and potentially affecting policy outcomes.[85] This phenomenon is more easily detectable with reference to malapportionment, ie, the votes of citizens weighed differently depending on the area of the jurisdiction where they resided; however, understanding its saliency for racial gerrymandering requires further effort. As illustrated earlier, although the decisions delivered by the Supreme Court in the 1970s recognised that the use of at-large systems of election curtailed the effective influence of minority voters on the choice of representatives, ultimately translating into a weak capacity to contribute to policy determinations, these decisions still fell short of effectively tackling the pernicious effects of racial gerrymandering on political equality. It was only after the shortcomings of section 2 VRA were highlighted by the Court's holding in *Mobile v Bolden* that Congress took the lead by significantly amending the provision to encompass an explicit reference to the adverse effects of voting practices on racial or ethnic minorities. The 1982 amendments internalised some of the arguments developed by Justice Thurgood Marshall in his dissent, where he criticised the dogma of reliance on the political process as a remedy by pointing at the historical disadvantage that specific minorities had experienced. This meant that the usual alternative avenues to make their voices heard were unavailable to them as the dominant political faction could regularly ignore their stances.[86]

The totality-of-circumstances test that the Court eventually enucleated in *Thornburg v Gingles* seemed to open the door for race consciousness in redistricting. However, the *Shaw* line of cases of the following decade has subjected the use of race for drawing district lines to strict scrutiny, eventually going as far as excluding the possibility that racial considerations could be the predominant factor determining redistricting choices.[87]

[84] JH Ely, *Democracy and Distrust. A Theory of Judicial Review* (Cambridge (MA), Harvard University Press, 1980). On the impact of Ely's theories on the development of election law scholarship and jurisprudence, see LP McLoughlin, 'The Elysian Foundations of Election Law' (2009) 82 *Temple Law Review* 89.

[85] PS Karlan, 'John Hart Ely and the Problem of Gerrymandering: The Lion in Winter' (2005) 114 *Yale Law Journal* 1329.

[86] *City of Mobile v Bolden*, (n 62), Marshall J, Dissenting Opinion; JH Choper and SF Ross, 'The Political Process, Equal Protection, and Substantive Due Process' (2018) 20 *Journal of Constitutional Law* 983, 1016.

[87] HA Scarrow, 'Vote Dilution, Party Dilution and the Voting Rights Act: The Search for "Fair and Effective Representation"' in DK Ryden (ed), *The U.S. Supreme Court and the Electoral Process* (Washington DC, Georgetown University Press, 2000).

Rather than settling the issue, the *Gingles* framework has instead brought about unintended consequences. The Supreme Court extended its rationale concerning redistricting beyond the original understanding, so that it applies to a plurality of groups that self-identify as minorities and revindicate representational rights.[88] It has been argued that this direct and indiscriminate application of the Equal Protection Clause to redistricting disputes contradicts the logic in Footnote Four of *Carolene Products,* as it applies a colour-blind standard of scrutiny in a subject matter historically plagued by the discrimination of specific insular minorities.[89] Ultimately, the creation of majority–minority districts to comply with the obligations of the VRA has been the object of heightened scrutiny on the assumption that race-conscious district apportionment is inherently a threat to the colour-blind society envisaged under the XIV Amendment.

The struggle to strike an adequate balance between the desire to ensure equal participation in political processes pursued through the VRA and the commitment to establish a colour-blind society, where racial considerations are eventually irrelevant, is exemplified by a case recently adjudicated by the Supreme Court. In *Allen v Milligan*, the interpretation of section 2 VRA settled in the decades since *Gingles* has been validated despite claims that it violated the Equal Protection Clause. The creation of a second majority–minority district in Alabama (which elects seven Representatives), where the Black population accounts for over 27 per cent of the resident population, was opposed on the grounds that it would be the result of race-conscious gerrymandering that would otherwise be unreasonable under any other traditional redistricting criterion.[90] The Court has discarded a claim emphasising the need to abide by racial neutrality as mandated by the Equal Protection Clause, whose endorsement would have affected the established *Gingles* standard, eventually questioning the survival of majority–minority districts in their previous form.

Against this backdrop, the assessment of the Supreme Court's understanding of the role of the federal judiciary with respect to partisan gerrymandering and the underlying conception of democracy, as may be inferred from the recent decision in *Rucho*, seems to align with a judicial interpretation that has been accused of turning the *Carolene* principles on their heads.[91] Notably, the emphasis by the majority opinion (penned by Chief Justice Roberts) on the role of Congress and state legislatures as appropriate institutions tasked with powers to effectively tackle anti-democratic practices such as partisan

[88] S Issacharoff, 'Groups and the Right to Vote' (1995) 44 *Emory Law Journal* 869, 900.

[89] SA Carlson, 'The Gerrymandering of the Reconstruction Amendments and Strict Scrutiny: The Supreme Court's Unwarranted Intrusion into the Political Thicket' (1997) 23 *Thurgood Marshall Law Review* 71, 132.

[90] *Allen v Milligan*, 599 U.S. 1 (2023).

[91] NO Stephanopoulos, 'The Anti-Carolene Court' (2019) *Supreme Court Review* 111.

gerrymandering, rather than the federal judiciary, is consistent with a general trend of the Court over the last few decades. More specifically, the Court's majority seems to have adopted a deregulatory approach towards the field of electoral legislation. However, this approach unfolds in two distinct directions that appear difficult to reasonably reconcile with one another.[92] On the one hand, the Court has retreated from the 'political thicket', deferring to the discretion of state legislatures to draw district lines according to partisan conveniences or validating voting qualifications that have an allegedly adverse impact on minorities.[93] On the other hand, the Court has interpreted deregulation as a licence to strike down federal regulations intended to foster political equality in democratic processes, thereby clearing the path for the unbridled operation of the dynamics of political processes.[94]

The key to understanding the Court's jurisprudence in the field of election law and voting rights, especially regarding apportionment disputes, lies in the *Carolene* parable. After refraining from judicial review of legislation according to the principles enunciated in *Carolene*, the justices have not only twisted its rationale of the role of judicial oversight over failures of the political process, but they are also increasingly poised to thwart efforts by other branches of government to ensure full and effective participation to democratic processes for those citizens historically denied political equality. This approach, ironically termed a 'perverse *Carolene*' interpretation, would translate into an attempt to set state legislatures free from most constraints associated with redistricting and apportionment (while adversely affecting many other features of electoral legislation).[95] If the relevant precedents in this regard appear to grant leeway to state legislative assemblies and constitutions to delegate redistricting duties to independent third parties, it appeared plausible that a Court with a reliable conservative majority accepted some version of the controversial independent state legislature doctrine, which would have made even state constitutional provisions helpless in tackling partisan gerrymandering.[96] On the other hand, the firepower of section 2 VRA, which has been the centrepiece of redistricting litigation following the neutralisation of the preclearance mechanism enshrined in section 5 in *Shelby County*, is apparently still available, as a

[92] Y Dawood, 'Election Law Originalism: The Supreme Court's Elitist Conception of Democracy' (2020) 64 *Saint Louis University Law Journal* 609, 615. See also RH Pildes, *Political Process Theory and Institutional Realism* (2020) 18 *International Journal of Constitutional Law* 1501 (arguing that 'No consistent pattern emerges regarding when courts are institutionally more formalist or more realist; even the same judge is sometimes more formalist, sometimes more realist').

[93] *Crawford v Marion County Election Board*, 553 U.S. 181 (2008).

[94] *Citizens United v FEC*, 558 U.S. 310 (2010); *Shelby County v Holder* (n 61).

[95] Stephanopoulos (n 91).

[96] The delegation of redistricting powers to an independent redistricting commission was declared constitutionally admissible under the Elections Clause in *Arizona State Legislature v Arizona Independent Redistricting Commission*, 576 U.S. 787 (2015); the issue was raised again in *Rucho v Common Cause* (n 78) 32 Slip Op.

strictly colour-blind interpretation of the Equal Protection standard for apportionment disputes has been rejected by the Court.

Rather than embracing a distinctive understanding of democracy, the US Supreme Court exercises the judicial review of electoral legislation irrespective of a predetermined theory of politics, as already noted by critics of the political process theory, who consider *Carolene*'s Footnote Four inconclusive as to the role of the judiciary in electoral disputes.[97] This indifference towards a specific theory of politics can be traced in the conceptualisation of political equality. Previously, the Court has shown an interest in conceptions of political equality concerning aggregative dynamics, as testified by the Burger Court's 'communities of interest' approach; subsequently, the Rehnquist Court embraced interpretations privileging voluntary rather than institutional political aggregation.[98] None of these conceptions are now dominant in the Court. In contrast, many of the electoral disputes seem now to depend on the intention to progressively restore state sovereignty over elections rather than on the existence of an underlying strong theory of political equality.

[97] DH Lowenstein, 'The Supreme Court Has No Theory of Politics – And Be Thankful for Small Favors' in DK Ryden (ed), *The U.S. Supreme Court and the Electoral Process* (Washington DC, Georgetown University Press, 2000).

[98] N Maveety, 'Representation Rights and the Rehnquist Years: The Viability of the "Communities of Interest" Approach' in DK Ryden (ed), *The U.S. Supreme Court and the Electoral Process* (Washington DC, Georgetown University Press, 2000).

15

Judicial Review, Electoral Laws and Democracy in India

REKHA DIWAKAR

I. INTRODUCTION

WITH A POPULATION of almost 1.4 billion, India is the world's most populous democracy, and one of the few stable ones in the developing world. Elections have been conducted regularly since 1952 by a constitutional and independent body, the Election Commission of India (ECI), and except for a brief period of emergency rule in 1975–77, India has sustained democratic rule since its independence. The size of the electorate is by far the world's largest, and voter turnout has also been rising, and in general exceeded the levels typically witnessed in western democracies.[1] The British introduced self-government to India in stages, and it was not until the end of the colonial rule in 1947 and the adoption of the Indian Constitution in 1949 that universal suffrage was proposed. According to Austin,[2] the Constituent Assembly[3] had one predominant aim when framing the Indian Constitution – to create a basis for the social and political unity of the country – and it chose to achieve this by having universal adult suffrage, and by providing for representation of voters in elected assemblies. According to the Constitution, India is a sovereign, secular, socialist, democratic republic, and a union of states with a parliamentary form of government.[4] It is a loose or quasi federation with the central government having greater power in relation to states and union territories.

India's political structure is broadly based on the Westminster style parliamentary democracy with an elected prime minister who is responsible to the

[1] In the 2019 parliamentary (*Lok Sabha*) elections, size of the electorate was about 900 million and voter turnout was 67.1%.

[2] G Austin, *The Indian Constitution: Cornerstone of a Nation* (New Delhi, Oxford University Press, 1966) 144.

[3] Most of the members of The Constituent Assembly were indirectly elected by the members of the Provincial Legislative Assemblies.

[4] The Constitution of India. www.india.gov.in.

lower house of the national Parliament (*Lok Sabha*) at the centre, and a chief minister as the head of each state government. India's electoral system to elect members of *Lok Sabha* and state legislative assemblies (*Vidhan Sabhas*) is based on single-member electoral districts (constituencies) with outcome determined by a simple plurality of votes. India also has a President who is only the symbolic head of state and is indirectly elected by an electoral college comprising members of both the houses of the national Parliament and members of state legislative assemblies. General elections are normally held every five years and involve substantial administrative arrangements staggered over weeks or even months. An independent Delimitation Commission seeks to ensure that constituencies contain roughly equal number of electors. However, due to time lag, there is some degree of mal-apportionment of seats with discrepancies in the size of population in different constituencies.

The Constitution of India is considered to be the highest law of the land and at the time of its adoption, contained 395 Articles and 8 schedules, making it the world's largest written national constitution. It draws from several sources including many other countries' constitutions and has undergone over 100 amendments since it came into force in 1950. The Constitution attempts to strike a balance between parliamentary sovereignty and judicial review. Thus, whilst the courts have been vested with the power of judicial review, the Parliament has the authority to make laws and can also amend most parts of the Constitution. The main features of the India Constitution are parliamentary form of government, federalism, weak bicameralism, Fundamental Rights, Directive principles of state policy,[5] separation of powers, amendment procedures and judicial review.[6]

The judicial system is integrated and includes the Supreme Court of India (SC) at the top, and regional High Courts and other subordinate courts. The judiciary, particularly the SC, has been entrusted with the powers to interpret the Indian Constitution and resolve disputes regarding distribution of powers between the central and the state governments. Under Article 324 of the Constitution, the ECI has been entrusted with the task of registering political parties, allotting party symbols, and planning and conducting elections. The powers of Parliament and the ECI overlap due to the coexistence of Articles 324 and 327, which make the ECI the primary body responsible for the conduct of elections, while also giving Parliament the authority to make electoral laws. Both the Parliament and the ECI are subject to judicial

[5] Fundamental Rights are provided in Arts 12–35 of the Constitution and relate to: Right to Equality; Right to Freedom; Right against Exploitation; Right to Freedom of Religion; Cultural and Education Rights; Right to Constitutional Remedies. Directive Principles of State Policy provide for certain obligations on the state to help make India a welfare state. Although these do not constitute part of Fundamental Rights, they serve as moral guide for the state while framing laws.

[6] SP Sathe 'India: From Positivism to Structuralism' in J Goldsworthy (ed), *Interpreting Constitutions. A Comparative Study* (Oxford, Oxford University Press, 2006) 216.

review in respect of adherence with the constitutional provisions and ethos. According to Article 324(2) of the Indian Constitution, the ECI shall comprise a Chief Election Commissioner (CEC) and other Election Commissioners (ECs) to be appointed by the President of India (acting on the advice of the Prime Minister) subject to any law passed by the Parliament. However, no such law has been passed by the Parliament, effectively giving the Prime Minister the power to appoint the CEC and ECs. Article 324(5) of the Constitution also provides safeguards against removal of the CEC and ECs with an aim to protect them from external influence.

India's democracy defies many political science theories, which have emphasised factors such as affluence, social homogeneity, education and industrialisation as pre-requisites for a democracy. However, India is not a rich country, is ethnically very diverse, and would probably rank low on a number of attributes of 'civic culture'.[7] Similarly, Dahl[8] cites India as a leading exception to democratic theory and mentions that in India polyarchy was established when the population was largely illiterate, agricultural and highly traditional in their beliefs. The world's most heterogeneous democracy also runs counter to Mill's proposition that democracy is close to impossible in multi-ethnic societies and not possible in linguistically divided societies.[9] The type of democracy that has been chosen in India is also radical in many ways since there is no recognition of any ethnic, religious or caste[10] basis of citizenship, no separate electorates, no religious qualification for holding office, nor a literacy test. Women are given the right to vote on the same terms as men. Election results have generally been accepted by political parties resulting in peaceful transition of power, and overall, democracy seems so deeply rooted in India that it is difficult to imagine any other form of governance in the country. To explain the sustenance of India's unlikely democracy, one needs to consider its pre-independence political history, including the effect of the British rule, the role of the Congress Party that led India's independence movement and was also the country's dominant party for many decades after independence. Further, the form of government, a multi-party system, electoral rules, and the legal and the institutional framework comprising the judiciary, the civil service and the ECI have also contributed towards strengthening India's democracy.

According to Palshikar,[11] 'India's democracy is simultaneously a subject of awe because of its scale and dogged continuity over seven decades, and also subject of some scepticism because of its many drawbacks ….' A recent criticism of India's democracy is that it is mainly an electoral democracy with

[7] A Kohli, *The success of India's Democracy* (Cambridge, Cambridge University Press, 2001).

[8] RA Dahl, *Democracy and Its Critiques* (New Haven, Connecticut, Yale University Press, 1989).

[9] JS Mill, *Considerations on Representative Government* (New York, Liberal Arts Press, 1958).

[10] The traditional caste system in India divides Hindus into four hierarchical categories – Brahmins, Kshatriyas, Vaishyas and the Shudras.

[11] S Palshikar, *Indian Democracy* (New Delhi, Oxford University Press, 2017) 11.

excessive emphasis on elections rather than empowerment and participation of citizens in governance of the country. Therefore, Palshikar[12] concludes that 'democracy in India is a somewhat inconsistent enterprise full of paradoxes and contradictory possibilities'.

II. JUDICIAL REVIEW AND THE INDIAN CONSTITUTION

Although India's Constitution conferred the power of judicial review upon the courts, the Indian political elite at the time of independence was not inclined for pro-active judicial review powers.[13] As Sathe[14] notes, at the time of independence, many Indian leaders felt that the legislature should be supreme and the courts should merely act as umpires to ensure that the parties followed the rules. Soon after independence, the judiciary and the Parliament were engaged in a struggle over the constitutionality of land reform laws. In 1950, High Courts in several Indian states nullified land reform laws as being an unconstitutional abridgment of individual property rights. To override this, the government brought in an amendment to insulate laws from judicial review by listing them on Schedule Nine of the Constitution. The constitutionality of this amendment was upheld by the SC in *Shankari Prasad Singh Deo v Union of India and State of Bihar*.[15]

During the 1950s and the early 1960s, the SC remained somewhat restrained in using its power of judicial review. In 1967, in the *Golaknath v State of Punjab*,[16] the SC held, based on a majority view, that it had the power to review constitutional amendments and that the Parliament could not curtail Fundamental Rights enshrined in the Constitution. Subsequently, in the *Kesavananda Bharati v State of Kerala*,[17] the SC ruled with a majority view that a constitutional amendment which altered the 'Basic Structure' of the Constitution would be unconstitutional. Although the justices could not agree on what this basic structure was, the following features were listed: (1) supremacy of the Constitution; (2) republican and democratic form of government. (3) secular character; (4) separation of powers between the legislature, executive and judiciary; (5) federalism. In this case, the Court also sought to differentiate between an 'amendment' and a 'replacement' of the Constitution, and noted that an amendment must leave the pre-amendment Constitution largely in place. In 1980, in *Minerva Mills v Union of India*,[18]

[12] ibid 16.

[13] SG Calabresi, 'The Union of India: Umpiring and Rights from Wrongs' in SG Calabresi (ed), *The History and Growth of Judicial Review*, Vol 1 (New York, Oxford University Press, 2021).

[14] Sathe (n 6).

[15] *Shankari Prasad Singh Deo v Union of India and State of Bihar* 1952 SCR 89.

[16] *C Golaknath v State of Punjab* 1967 SCR (2) 762.

[17] *Kesavananda Bharti v State of Kerala* 1973 4 SCC 225.

[18] *Minerva Mills Ltd v Union of India* 1981 SCR (1) 206.

the SC nullified Parliament's constitutional amendment based on the Basic Structure doctrine. It also outlined the specifics of the Basic Structure doctrine, which rendered unconstitutional amendments that impaired: (1) secularism; (2) democracy; (3) rule of law; (4) federalism; or (5) an independent judiciary (Ackerman[19]).

According to Sathe,[20] the SC '... started off as a technocratic, positivistic court in the 1950s but slowly started acquiring more power through constitutional interpretation'. This transformation over the next few decades meant that the Court re-examined the limits on the legislature to amend the Constitution and also asserted its powers to review legislative action. It also started interpreting the Constitution to give meaning to terms such as 'equality before the law', 'personal liberty' and 'freedom of speech and expression', and by the 1980s, adopted a purposive interpretation of the constitutional provisions rather than based on textual positivism.[21] The Court also acted as an umpire between the centre and states based on India's 'quasi-federal' structure that combined elements of both federal and unitary systems as also noted in *S.R. Bommai v Union of India*.[22]

Judicial review is a key characteristic of India's democracy, and its scope has been debated and clarified through various judgments of the SC. Parliament remains supreme in respect of laying down laws and amending statutes including the Constitution but its powers are subject to judicial review especially if there are concerns about adherence to the basic constitutional principles. Palshikar[23] notes that since the 1980s, there has been some criticism of the courts' broadening of the scope of their interventions including through 'public interest litigations' (PILs).[24] Although PILs have received support from many civil society groups as an effective tool to remedy the inability of governments to address issues of governance, but whether judicial interventions should be the last word on inherently political choices, including electoral laws and processes remains a moot point.[25]

III. ELECTIONS IN INDIA – KEY ISSUES AND CHALLENGES

The constitutional framework together with the Representation of the People Acts of 1950 (RPA 1950) and 1951 (RPA), represent key statutes on Indian

[19] B Ackernman, *Revolutionary Constitutions: Charismatic Leadership and the Rule of Law* (Cambridge, Massachusetts, Harvard University Press, 2019).

[20] SP Sathe, *Judicial Activism in India: Transgressing Borders and Enforcing Limits* (New Delhi, Oxford University Press, 2002) 4.

[21] Calabresi (n 13) 297.

[22] *S.R. Bommai v Union of India* (1994) SCC (3) 1.

[23] Palshikar (n 11).

[24] 'PIL' means a legal action initiated in a court for the enforcement of public or general interest in which the public have pecuniary or some interest by which their legal rights or liabilities are affected. Janata Dal v H.S. Chowdhary (1992) 4 SCC 305.

[25] Palshikar (n 11) 28.

elections. Elections in India have historically been influenced by the money and muscle power of the political parties, candidates and wealthy industrialists. Initially, after independence, parties used private donations and membership fees to finance their election campaigns and activities. Corporate contributions to parties were permitted, although these were subject to certain restrictions and disclosure requirements. The RPA introduced limits on the amount that could be spent on election campaigns, and candidates exceeding these limits could face legal action including annulment of elections.

According to Vaishnav[26] the first instances of 'booth capturing' were recorded in India in 1957, which involved the use of physical force to manipulate elections by taking over and dominating polling booths. Beginning in the 1960s, various other forms of electoral malpractices began to emerge as links between crime and politics grew that led to doubts being expressed about the legitimacy of the electoral process. Gowda and Sridharan[27] point out that by the 1960s, there were growing concerns about political funding being driven by 'black money' ie, money on which taxes had not been paid or which had been raised through illegal activities. In 1969, corporate donations to parties were made illegal, but without an alternative funding mechanism, this decision failed to sever the links between business and politics. Although corporate funding was legalised again in 1985, this problem had worsened and become entrenched in the intervening years.

Despite its wide powers, it was difficult for the ECI to address these challenges, although during the tenure of TN Seshan as the Chief Election Commissioner in the 1990s, the ECI took many robust measures through strict enforcement of its Model Code of Conduct.[28] The introduction of Electronic Voting Machines (EVMs) by the ECI and deployment of central paramilitary forces during elections also helped in mitigating blatant electoral malpractices such as booth capturing. However, Vaishnav[29] notes that as overt forms of violence and electoral malpractices receded in the 1990s and beyond, the role of money in politics grew exponentially, partly due to the changing nature of party system, increasing competitiveness of elections and an increase in election expenditure. The 1993 Vohra Committee report also revealed the nature and extent of proliferation of criminal gangs into politics (Kumar[30]).

[26] M Vaishanv, *Why Crime Pays: Money and Muscle in Indian Politics* (New Delhi, Harper Collins, 2017).

[27] MVR Gowda and E Sridharan, 'Reforming India's Party Financing and Election Expenditure Laws' (2012) 11 *Election Law Journal.*

[28] The Model Code of Conduct is a set of guidelines issued by the ECI for conduct of political parties and candidates during elections.

[29] Vaishnav (n 26).

[30] V Kumar, 'Citizen's Right to Vote: Role of the Supreme Court in Empowering Citizenry to Bring About 'a Systemic Change' Through NOTA for Cleansing our Body Politic (a Juristic Critique of Constitutional Developments)' (2014) 56(1) *Journal of the Indian Law Institute* 25–46.

According to Association of Democratic Reforms (ADR,[31] 2019) 1,500 (19%), candidates declared criminal cases against them in the 2019 *Lok Sabha* elections. Of these, 1,070 (13%) were serious criminal cases. Although these are cases and not convictions, the percentage of candidates with declared criminal cases has been increasing – see Figure 1:

Figure 1 Criminal cases declared by contesting candidates – Lok Sabha elections[32]

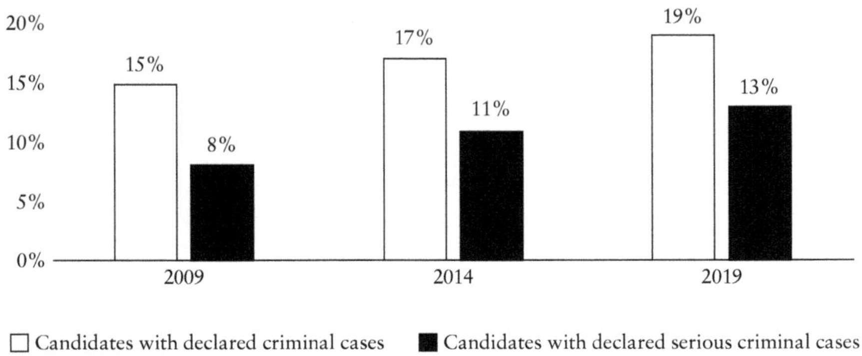

According to Vaishnav,[33] a candidate with a criminal case was, on average, almost three times as likely to win an election as a candidate who faced no cases, and notes that

> [W]hen the state is either unable or unwilling to adequately perform its most basic functions in an impartial manner, voters are often willing to turn to someone who can substitute for the state, even if that person is linked to allegations of illegal activity.

Further, social cleavages of caste and religion remain central to Indian politics and have been used by parties to select candidates and make appeals to voters sometimes in contravention to the ECI's Model Code of Conduct.

Thus, the ECI faces challenges in addressing issues such as curbing excessive election expenditure, regulating political parties, and mitigating impact of crime. According to Lateef,[34] problems faced by the ECI also 'reflect the unwillingness of political parties to subject themselves to a reform process that would better demonstrate the intent of the Constitution'. According to Diwakar,[35] 'parties in India face many challenges and issues including

[31] ADR, Lok Sabha Elections 2019 Phase 1 to 7 Analysis of Criminal Background, Financial, Education, Gender and other details of Candidates. www.adrindia.org.

[32] ibid. Source: Based on ADR.

[33] Vaishnav (n 26) 12, 291.

[34] S Lateef, 'India's Governance Challenges: Why Institutions Matter' in R Mohan (ed), *India Transformed: Twenty-Five Years of Economic Reforms* (Washington DC, Brookings Institution Press, 2018) 207.

[35] R Diwakar, *Party System in India* (New Delhi, Oxford University Press, 2017) 151.

criminality in politics, use of money and muscle power in elections, developing effective organisations and leaders, and ensuring internal democracy'. Gowda and Sridharan[36] argue that India's complex elections process, funding, and disclosure laws foster the reliance of parties on unaccounted funds for contesting elections. They suggest few remedies including partial state funding of parties' election expenditure, raising limits on corporate contributions etc although the authors admit these may have limited impact initially. Others have been sceptical about the usefulness of state funding of elections unless this is done in conjunction with measures such as candidates and parties subjecting themselves to a deeper scrutiny, more robust enforcement of electoral rules by the ECI. As Vaishnav[37] argues

> [I]n the short run, reformers must revamp how elections are funded and tackle the most egregious cases of illegality indulged in by politicians. But in the long run, there is no substitute for building up the capacity of the state to expand its writ while simultaneously taming its worst excesses.

Another important issue is about the efficacy of the electoral system. India uses the single member plurality system (SMPS) to elect members of the *Lok Sabha* and the state legislative assemblies. The SMPS has continued to be used despite various concerns including its inherent disproportionality especially in the context of achieving effective representation for India's highly heterogeneous population.[38] The Law Commission of India[39] recommended that India may retain the SMPS in the existing parliamentary constituencies but add additional 25 per cent of seats to be allocated amongst recognised political parties according to their national vote share. However, almost all parties have either shown indifference towards this issue or expressed objections to consider any change to the electoral system. Therefore, the debate about the reform of the electoral system in India remains largely academic.

Last, ensuring the independence and impartiality of the ECI is crucial for holding free and fair elections. Whilst the Constitution provides strict safeguards against arbitrary removal of the CEC and ECs, the government of the day has historically held the power to appoint them in the absence of a parliamentary law raising potential for bias.

IV. SUMMARY OF KEY JUDGMENTS ON ELECTORAL LAWS IN INDIA

This section provides an overview of the prominent judgments (mainly of the SC) on electoral laws and processes pertaining to a range of subjects including the

[36] Gowda and Sridharan (n 27).

[37] Vaishnav (n 26) xiii.

[38] R Diwakar, 'The Workings of the Single Member Plurality Electoral System in India and the Need for Reform' [2018] *Asian Journal of Comparative Politics* 1–21.

[39] Law Commission of India (2015) 255th report – Electoral reforms. www.lawcommissionofindia.nic.in.

legal status of the right to vote, powers of the ECI, use of Electronic Voting Machines (EVMs), campaign financing, voters' right to know candidates' antecedents and making election appeals based on religion, caste etc. Holding of free and fair elections is a core element of democratic functioning, and through its judgments, the SC has sought to promote India's democratic ideals and ethos.

A. The Right to Vote

Although the right to vote is not one of the Fundamental Rights provided in the Constitution, it is implicit in Article 326, which states that every citizen not less than 18 years of age and not otherwise disqualified shall be entitled to be registered as a voter. In *N P Ponnuswami v Returning Officer*,[40] the SC held that the right to vote or contest elections was a creature of statute and therefore, must be subject to the limitations imposed by it. Similarly, in *Jyoti Basu v Debi Ghosal*,[41] the SC stated that although the right to elect was fundamental to democracy, it was not a Fundamental Right. It also held that any rights or disputes related to voting or elections had to be considered within the RPA. In *PUCL v Union of India*,[42] Justice Dharmadhikari stated that the right to vote is both a constitutional and statutory right, while the other two judges held the right to be either statutory or constitutional.[43] In *Kuldip Nayar v Union of India*,[44] the SC observed that although the right to vote was a constitutional right, the manner of voting could be regulated by the statute. Thus, there has not been an unequivocal view from the SC judgments that the right to vote is a constitutional right. As Sondhi[45] notes,

> The Supreme Court has been surprisingly accepting of the incongruity that exists in a constitutional framework where democracy is part of the basic structure, elections are conducted by an independent Election Commission that enjoys constitutional status …, but the exercise of one's franchise is given secondary legal status.

B. The Powers of the ECI

In *Kanhiyalal Omar v R K Trivedi*,[46] the SC stated that the ECI's powers were to be construed liberally so that it was able to effectively discharge its functions. The SC came to similar conclusions in *Mohinder Singh Gill v The Chief*

[40] *N P Ponnuswami v Returning Officer Namakkal Constituency* (1952) SCR 218.

[41] *Jyoti Basu v Debi Ghosal* (1982) 3 SCR 318.

[42] *PUCL v Union of India* (2003) 4 SCC 399.

[43] S Dam, 'People's Union for Civil Liberties v Union of India: Is Indian Democracy Dependent on a Stature?' [2004] *Public Law* 710.

[44] *Kuldip Nayar v Union of India* AIR 2006 SC 3127.

[45] A Sondhi, 'Elections' in S Choudhry, M Khosla and PB Mehta (ed), *The Oxford Handbook of the Indian Constitution* (Oxford, Oxford University Press, 2016) 200.

[46] *Kanhiyalal Omar v R K Trivedi* (1985) SCR Supl. (3) 1.

Election Commissioner[47] and *Association for Democratic Reforms v Union of India*[48] and interpreted the ECI's powers of superintendence, direction, control and conduct of elections under Article 324 in the broadest terms. In *Common Cause v Union of India*,[49] the Court ruled that free and fair elections were a core part of democracy and that the ECI's powers included scrutinising all expenses incurred by political parties and candidates.

In exercising its functions, the ECI requires candidates and parties to observe a 'Model of Conduct' during elections and can suspend or withdraw recognition of a party for violation of the code. In *S Subramaniam Balaji v The Government of Tamil Nadu*,[50] the SC directed the ECI to frame guidelines for the content of parties' election manifestos, and thus made the ECI's model code of conduct more enforceable. In *Indrajit Barua v Commission of India*,[51] the SC held that once the electoral rolls were published and elections held on the basis of such rolls, it was not open to anyone to challenge the election on the ground that the electoral rolls were defective. According to sections 14 and 15 of the RPA, the ECI has the power to finalise the schedule of elections. In *Re Special Reference*,[52] the Court held that framing of the calendar for elections was the exclusive domain of the ECI, and that its powers were plenary in nature and could not be taken away by a law framed by the Parliament.

In *Indian National Congress (I) v Institute of Social Welfare*,[53] the SC stated that the ECI did not have powers to review its orders of registering a party under section 29A of the RPA. In *SC Agrawal v Parliament of India*,[54] political parties were brought within the ambit of the Right to Information Act 2005. However, after the Right to Information (Amendment) Bill 2013, they remain insulated from this regime. Commenting on this subject, Sondhi[55] notes that 'the peculiar position that emerges is that while the prime ombudsman and organiser of elections [the ECI] occupies an elevated, constitutional status, neither those voting nor political parties find much space within the constitutional framework'.

C. Electronic Voting Machines (EVMs)

EVMs were first introduced in 1982 state assembly elections on a limited scale. In *A.C. Jose v Sivan Pillai*,[56] the SC ruled that under the RPA, the ECI had no

[47] *Mohinder Singh Gill v The Chief Election Commissioner* (1978) SCR (3) 272.
[48] *ADR vs Union of India* (2002) 5 SCC 294.
[49] *Common Cause Registered Society vs Union of India* (1996) 2 SCC 752.
[50] *S Subramaniam Balaji v The Government of Tamil Nadu* (2013) (9) SCC 659.
[51] *Indrajit Barua v Election Commission of India* 1985 4 SCC 722.
[52] Re Special Reference No 1 of 2002, 8 SCC 237.
[53] *Indian National Congress (I) v Institute of Social Welfare* 2002 5 SCC 685.
[54] *Subhash Chandra Agrawal v Indian National Congress* CIC/SM/C/2011/001386: CIC/SM/C/2011.
[55] Sondhi (n 45).
[56] *A. C. Jose v Sivan Pillai.* (1984) SCC (2) 656.

power to use EVMs, and only ballot papers and ballot boxes were allowed. The SC reasoned that the ECI's powers were meant to supplement rather than supplant the law as provided by Article 324 of the Constitution. The SC also clarified that despite its plenary powers, the ECI could not assume new powers in areas where express provisions already existed within the statute. In 1989, the Parliament amended the RPA to add section 61A that allowed the use of EVMs in elections. In *AIADMK v Election Commission of India*,[57] the use of EVMs was challenged in the Madras High Court on the basis that Parliament had engaged in excessive delegation of powers to the ECI by allowing it to use EVMs. The High Court ruled that section 61A of the RPA was not ultra vires the Constitution and observed there were sufficient safeguards in the election rules to have the election conducted in a just, fair and proper manner. It also stated that the advantages of using EVMs outweighed those of conventional ballot boxes since no rigging was possible and results could be ascertained in a short time. The SC[58] upheld the Madras High Court decision thus allowing the use of EVMs in all elections.

In *Dr Subramanian Swamy v Election Commission of India*,[59] the matter before the SC was about the introduction of voter-verified paper audit trails (VVPAT) alongside EVMs to ensure that there was a proof that EVM had correctly registered the vote. The Court ruled that any change to the law could only be done through appropriate amendments to the statute and declined to issue any directions to the ECI. The Court cited its judgment in *Mohinder Singh v Chief Election Commissioner*[60] which had concluded that free and fair elections periodically held and based on adult franchise were at the heart of the parliamentary system. It also cited *Rameshwar Prasad v Union of India*,[61] which noted that democracy and free and fair elections were inseparable and held voters in high esteem, whose freedom to elect and vote for a candidate of their choice was paramount in ensuring free and fair elections. In *Dr Subramanian Swamy v Election Commission of India*,[62] the SC directed the ECI to introduce in a phased manner a paper trail in EVMs for the 2014 national elections. The Court noted that it was satisfied that the paper trial was an indispensable requirement for holding free and fair elections and therefore to ensure full transparency, it was necessary to set up EVMs with the VVPAT system. In *Chandrababu Naidu v Union of India*,[63] the Court provided directions to the ECI to increase the number of EVMs in respect of which VVPAT paper slips were to be subjected to physical scrutiny.

[57] *AIADMK v Election Commission of India* 2001 SCC Online Mad 1398.
[58] *AIADMK v Chief Election Commissioner* (2002) 1 UJ 387 (SC).
[59] *Dr Subramanian Swamy v Election Commission of India* (2013) 14 SCR 565–78.
[60] *Mohinder Singh v Chief Election Commissioner* AIR 1978 SC 85.
[61] *Rameshwar Prasad v Union of India* (2006) 2 SCC 1.
[62] *Dr Subramanian Swamy v Election Commission of India* (2013) 10 SCC 500.
[63] *Chandrababu Naidu v Union of India*. Writ petition. 273 of 2019.

D. Campaign Financing, Voters' Right to know Candidates' Antecedents

In *Kanwar Lal Gupta v Amar Nath Chawla*,[64] the SC examined the issue of ceiling on electoral expenditure by a candidate and noted that democracy can thrive only by limiting election expenditure so that no political party had an unfair advantage over the other. The SC ruled that parties' spending on a candidate's election should be added to the candidate's spending for evaluating if the prescribed expenditure ceiling had been breached.[65] In *Common Cause v Union of India*,[66] the SC shifted the burden of proof to the candidate to prove that the election expenditure was actually incurred by their party and not by them.

In *Dinesh Trivedi v Union of India*,[67] the petitioners requested the reports which formed the basis for findings of Vohra Committee, which had investigated the nexus between criminal elements, government functionaries and politicians. The Court recommended that a high-level committee be appointed by the President of India on the advice of the Prime Minister and after consultation with the Speaker of the *Lok Sabha*.

In *ADR v Union of India*,[68] the SC ruled that when the Act or Rules were silent on a particular subject and an authority (in this case ECI) had the power to implement it, the Court could issue directions to fill the vacuum. This ruling was given in the context of a Delhi High Court judgment[69] where it ruled that it was the function of the Parliament to make necessary amendments in the RPA and that it was not in the interest of democracy that the antecedents of contesting candidates were not disclosed to the voters. Accordingly, the High Court had directed the ECI to secure to the voters details regarding: (1) accusation for offence(s) punishable with imprisonment; (2) assets of the candidate, spouse and dependent relatives; (3) capacity and suitability including educational qualifications; and (4) information which the ECI considered necessary for judging the capacity and capability of the political party fielding the candidate. In its ruling the SC stated that a republican and democratic form of government was part of the Basic Structure of the Indian Constitution and that the citizens' right to know the antecedents of candidates was in the nature of a Fundamental Right under Article 19(1)(a). The Court also observed that a democracy could not survive without free and fair elections and without free

[64] *Kanwar Lal Gupta vs Amar Nath Chawla* (1975) SCR (2) 269.

[65] Parliament amended the RPA in 1975 to nullify the SC's decision such that party and supporter expenditures not authorised by the candidate did not count toward the calculation of a candidate's election expenses. In *Common Cause v Union of India* (1996) 2 SCC 752, the SC ruled that election expenditures by a political party would not be included with that of a candidate only if the party had submitted audited accounts of its income and expenditures.

[66] *Common Cause Registered Society vs Union of India* (1996) 2 SCC 752.

[67] *Dinesh Trivedi v Union of India* (1997) 4 SCC 306.

[68] *ADR vs Union of India* (2002) 5 SCC 294.

[69] *ADR vs Union of India* (2000). Delhi High Court writ petition No.7257 of 1999.

and fairly informed voters. The SC directed the ECI to call for information from contesting candidates on affidavit relating to criminal cases, educational qualifications and assets and liabilities of self and close family. In *Secretary, Ministry of Information and Broadcasting v Cricket Association of Bengal*,[70] the SC stated that true democracy envisaged citizens' right to participate in the affairs of the polity, and this right was meaningless unless the citizens were well informed.

In *PUCL v Union of India*,[71] the petitioner challenged the legality of section 33B of the RPA, which provided that a candidate was not bound to disclose any information apart from that required under this Act. After the *ADR*[72] judgment, the Parliament had secured the right to information to a citizen about the candidates but only to a limited extent. However, the Court ruled that the right to get information which is a corollary to the Fundamental Right to free speech and expression had no fixed connotation and could not be circumscribed. Therefore, it held that section 33B did not pass the test of constitutionality. The SC also cited *Raj Narain v State of UP*,[73] to state that the citizens had the right to obtain information on matters relating to public acts, which followed from the Fundamental Right under Article 19(1)(a). It stated that for sustenance of democratic polity it was crucial that a voter made an intelligent and rational choice about their representative.

In *Lily Thomas*,[74] the SC heard PILs that inter alia called for declaring section 8(4) of the RPA as ultra vires the Constitution. Sections 8(1), 8(2), 8(3) of the RPA provide that a person convicted of certain offences shall stand disqualified[75] from the date of conviction but according to section 8(4), this disqualification did not apply for three months, if an appeal was outstanding in a court. The SC ruled that the Parliament had powers to define disqualifications but not the date on which these would have effect. Therefore, it ruled that section 8(4) was ultra vires the Constitution.

In *Public Interest Foundation v Union of India*,[76] the SC observed that providing a representative form of government, elected freely and fairly, and comprising of a polity whose members were of high integrity and morality constituted an essential component of a constitutional democracy. Similarly, in *Manoj Narula v Union of India*,[77] the Court stated that a democratic polity was abhorrent to corruption and repulsive to the idea of criminalisation of

[70] *Secretary, Ministry of Information and Broadcasting v Cricket Association of Bengal* (2002) 5 SCC 294.

[71] *PUCL v Union of India* (2003) 2 SCR 1136.

[72] *ADR vs Union of India* (2002).

[73] *Raj Narain vs State of UP* (1975) 4 SCC 428.

[74] *Lily Thomas v Union of India* (2000) 6 SCC 224.

[75] This means disqualified for being chosen as, and for being, a member of Parliament or of the state legislature.

[76] *Public Interest Foundation v Union of India* (2019) 3 SCC 224.

[77] *Manoj Narula v Union of India* (2014) 9 SCC 1.

politics. Therefore, the SC recommended to the Parliament to bring about legislation to make it mandatory for parties to revoke membership of persons against whom charges were framed for serious offences. It also issued directions relating to disclosure requirements regarding criminal cases pending against candidates. In *Rambabu Singh Thakur v Sunil Arora*,[78] the SC heard a contempt petition regarding the alleged disregard of the directions of the Court's judgment in *Public Interest Foundation v Union of India*[79] case. The Court ruled[80] that in case of non-compliance and failure to report compliance to the ECI, political parties could be held in contempt of the SC and that the reasons for selection of candidates by the parties should be with reference to the qualifications, achievements and merit, and not on the basis of mere winnability at the polls.

E. Voters' Rights to Reject Candidates

In *PUCL v Union of India*,[81] constitutional validity of Rules 41(2)-(3) and 49-O of the Conduct of Election Rules 1961 was challenged since these were seen to violate the secrecy of voting. The petitioners argued that if a voter decided not to record their vote, a remark to this effect had to be made in Form 17-A along with a signature. The SC observed that the right to vote, if not a Fundamental Right, was certainly a constitutional right. It also stated that the Fundamental Right under Article 19(1)(a) is violated if the right not to vote is effectively denied and secrecy breached. The SC cited the decision in *Kuldip Nayar v Union of India*,[82] where it was held that parliamentary democracy and the multi-party system were inherent parts of the Basic Structure of the Constitution, and that secrecy of the vote was necessary in order to maintain the purity of the electoral system.

The SC held[83] that election rules, which treat a voter who decides not to cast their vote differently, and violate the secrecy of vote, are arbitrary, violative of Article 19 and ultra vires sections 79(d) and 128 of the RPA. The Court reiterated that democracy and free elections were part of the Basic Structure of the Constitution and cited *Indira Nehru Gandhi v Raj Narain*,[84] where it was held that democracy can function only when elections are free and fair. According to the SC,[85] not effectively allowing a voter to cast a negative vote defeated the freedom of expression and the right to liberty ensured in Article 21. Further, it

[78] *Rambabu Singh Thakur v Sunil Arora* (2020) SCC Online SC 178.
[79] *Public Interest Foundation vs Union of India* (2019) 3 SCC 224.
[80] *Rambabu Singh Thakur v Sunil Arora* (2020) SCC Online SC 178.
[81] *PUCL vs Union of India* (2013) 10 SCC 1.
[82] *Kuldip Nayar v Union of India* AIR 2006 SC 3127.
[83] *PUCL vs Union of India* (2013) 10 SCC 1.
[84] *Indira Nehru Gandhi vs. Raj Narain* (1975) Supp 1 SCC 198.
[85] *PUCL vs Union of India* (2013) 10 SCC 1.

stated that an arbitrary distinction between the voter who casts their vote and the voter who does not cast their vote was violative of Article 14. Accordingly, the SC directed the ECI to provide for a None of the Above (NOTA) button on EVMs so that the voters who decide not to vote for any of the candidates were able to do so while maintaining their right of secrecy. The Court also observed that if a large number of voters expressed their disapproval with the candidates through the use of NOTA option, it would eventually lead to the parties fielding candidates with high integrity.

F. Corrupt Electoral Practices – Use of Appeal Based on Religion, Caste, Language Etc.

In *Dr Ramesh Yeshwant Prabhoo v Prabhakar Kashinath Kunte*,[86] the SC considered setting aside the election of a candidate on the grounds of violation of sections 123(3) and 123(3A) of the RPA, which list appeals to religion and incitement of religious hatred as a corrupt electoral practice. The SC ruled that while mentioning religion during the campaign was not prohibited, it was not allowed to appeal to vote for any candidate because of their religion or to refrain from voting for any candidate because of their religion – considering the secular character of the Indian polity.

In *Abhiram Singh v CD Commachen*,[87] a reference to the SC (Bench of seven judges) arose in respect of the interpretation of section 123(3) of the RPA. Justice Lokur, while delivering the majority judgment, referred to the Court's observations in *Ziyauddin Burhanuddin Bukhari v Brijmohan Ramdass Mehra*[88] that stressed that the country's Constitution makers intended a secular democratic republic where differences (for example based on religion) should not be permitted to be exploited. Justice Lokur ruled that under the pretext of protecting one's own religion, culture, or creed one could not embark on personal attacks on others or whip up animosities or irrational fears between groups to secure electoral victories. Justice Bobde agreed with this view and stated that section 123 was intended to serve the broad purpose of checking appeals to religion, race, caste, community or language by any candidate. Chief Justice Thakur also agreed with Justice Lokur's view and added that secularism had been declared by the SC to be part of the Basic Structure of the Constitution and that religion could not be mixed with any secular activity of the state. He also stated that if the Constitution required the state to be secular, the same requirement applied to political parties as well, and that introducing religion into politics would introduce an impermissible element

[86] *Dr Ramesh Yeshwant Prabhoo v Prabhakar Kashinath Kunte* (1996) 1 SCC 130.
[87] *Abhiram Singh v CD Commachen* (2017) 2 SCC 629.
[88] *Ziyauddin Burhanuddin Bukhari v Brijmohan Ramdass Mehra* (1976) 2 SCC 17.

into body politic antithetical to Articles 14–16, 25 and the entire constitutional scheme. Chief Justice Thakur observed that sections 123(3) and 123(3A) had been incorporated to maintain the secular character of India's democracy. Further, he stated that elections were a secular exercise and that constitutional ethos forbade mixing of religions or religious considerations with the secular functions of the state.

The SC (majority view)[89] held that sub-section (3) of section 123 of the RPA must be given a broad and purposive interpretation bringing within the sweep of a corrupt practice any appeal made to an elector by a candidate or their agent or by any other person with the consent of a candidate or their election agent to vote or refrain from voting for the furtherance of the prospects of the election of that candidate or for prejudicially affecting the election of any candidate on the ground of the religion, race, caste, community or language of: (i) any candidate; or (ii) their agent; or (iii) any other person making the appeal with the consent of the candidate; or (iv) the elector.

G. Method of Appointing the Chief Election Commissioner (CEC) and Other Election Commissioners (ECs)

In a recent judgment, *Anoop Baranwal vs Union of India*,[90] which was decided on 2 March 2023, a Constitutional Bench of the SC decided that the appointment of the CEC and other ECs should be done by a committee consisting of the Prime Minister, the Leader of the Opposition (or the leader of the largest opposition party) and the Chief Justice of India. This judgment overrides the current constitutional position under Article 324(2) whereby (in absence of any parliamentary law), members of the ECI are to be appointed by the President, acting on the advice of the Prime Minister.

This case came about through a petition filed by Anoop Baranwal who argued that the prevailing system of appointing the CECs and ECs by the government of the day had the potential to create bias and compromise citizens' right to free and fair elections. Few other petitions on this matter were also combined by the SC whilst considering the matter and delivering its judgment. The SC reasoned that the intent behind Article 324 of the Constitution was to provide independence to the ECI from the political executive although the exact process of the appointment of the election commissioners was left for the Parliament to legislate on. The SC stressed that this intent had to be seen in the context of the importance of the role of holding free and fair elections in

[89] According to the minority dissenting view, since social mobilisation was an integral element of the search for authority and legitimacy, it would be far-fetched to assume Parliament intended to outlaw references to religion, caste, race, community or language in a democracy.

[90] *Anoop Baranwal v Union of India* 2023 (3) SCALE 640.

a democracy, which is part of the basic structure of the Indian Constitution.[91] Although there can be different views about the most effective method of selecting the CEC and other ECs but through this judgement, the SC intervened to fill a gap in the constitutional framework to support independent functioning of the ECI until the Parliament enacts a law on the subject, which will also be subject to judicial review.

V. DISCUSSION: JUDICIAL REVIEW OF ELECTORAL LAWS AND THE IDEA OF DEMOCRACY IN INDIA

It is commonly understood that electoral laws are inherently political and shaped by various factors including a country's history, and the nature of its party and political system. It has also been argued that 'the institutional incapacities of the courts and the unavailability of conclusive social science evidence are particularly acute in the electoral arena'.[92] Consequently, the courts can act cautiously or even 'deferentially' when reviewing the constitutionality of electoral laws and processes. In India, despite elaborate powers of judicial review provided in the Constitution, in the initial decades after independence, the courts did not routinely delve into the realm of electoral laws especially on substantive matters. Even on procedural aspects, the courts were largely content that the ECI, an independent body, had a constitutional mandate to ensure that elections held were free and fair. However, over time, judiciary in India, particularly the SC, has become more interventionist and arguably less deferential in flexing its power of judicial review including in respect of electoral laws. One should note that by the late 1970s, India's representative institutions, the legislature and the executive witnessed a decline, and the party system was no longer dominated by the Congress party. The change in judiciary's approach can also be viewed in the context of this general institutional decline and political fragmentation in India, as it repositioned itself as an institution committed to upholding the country's constitutional principles and democratic values.

Since the late 1980s and the 1990s, the ECI also expanded the scope of its powers and prescribed new rules and processes, most visibly in respect of registration of parties, disclosure requirement for candidates, enforcing model code of conduct during election campaigns etc. According to Bhat,[93] much of the regulatory expansion of the ECI has happened with the endorsement of the courts. The SC has held that the ECI's powers are plenary, and that the ECI operates in areas left unoccupied by legislation. This view is also consistent

[91] Special Reference Case 1 of 2002 AIR (2003) SC 87.

[92] Y Dawood 'Democracy and Deference: The Role of Social Science Evidence in Election Law Cases' (2014) 32 *National Journal of Constitutional Law* 179.

[93] MMA Bhat, 'Governing Democracy Outside the Law: India's Election Commission and the Challenge of Accountability' (2021) *Asian Journal of Comparative Law* 1–20.

with an increasing appreciation for the role of 'fourth branch' institutions such as the ECI in securing the vibrancy of constitutional democracies.[94]

As discussed in the previous section, the SC has also directly intervened in the review of electoral laws and processes where it has felt that there have been violations of basic democratic values and freedoms guaranteed by the Constitution. The SC has stressed the holding of free and fair elections as being the core part of Indian democracy, which it has held as being part of the 'Basic Structure' of the Constitution. Through the NOTA option, the SC aimed to provide voters with the right to express disapproval for all candidates. It has also endeavoured to enhance the transparency and accountability of the election process through its judgments requiring candidates to disclose personal information including criminal records and financial details of self and family members. The Court has observed that mere winnability cannot be the only reason for selecting candidates and directed parties to publish criminal backgrounds of candidates on their website, in local newspapers and social media. The SC has also sought to ban electoral practices related to campaign appeals made on the basis of religion, caste etc. although it is difficult to assess how this ruling will be implemented on the ground since many parties' electoral strategies are based on mobilising specific social caste and religious groups. As Khilnani[95] argues, although regional and caste politics, and Hindu nationalism embody different potentialities, they are direct products of India's four decades of independence, and it is wrong to see them as atavistic forms that attack the idea of the state and democracy; 'on the contrary, they exemplify the triumphant success of these ideas'.[96]

Thus, there are many themes and democratic principles that emerge from various judgments of the SC relating to its review of electoral laws and processes. These include: parliamentary democracy and multiparty system being part of the Basic Structure of the Constitution; right to vote being fundamental to democracy; free and fair elections being at the core of democracy; limits on election expenditure to ensure a level playing field being crucial to maintain democracy; freedom of expression and rights of voters to receive information about candidates' antecedents being in the interest of democracy and part of voters' Fundamental Rights; requirement to provide a representative form of government elected freely and fairly comprising of men and women of high integrity and morality; secular nature of Indian democracy and the elections process; corrupt electoral practices to include appeals made on the basis of religion, caste etc.

Khosla and Padmanabhan[97] argue that the SC's prominent role within the Indian democracy has been made possible through its practice of judicial review.

[94] ibid.

[95] S Khilnani, *The Idea of India* (New Delhi, Penguin Books, 2003) 58.

[96] Also see minority dissenting view of the *SC in Abhiram Singh v CD Commachen* (2017) 2 SCC 629.

[97] M Khosla, and A Padmanabhan 'The Supreme Court' in D Kapur, PB Mehta and M Vaishnav (eds), *Rethinking Public Institutions in India* (New Delhi, Oxford University Press, 2017).

Whilst doing so, it has sought to adhere to the scheme of division of powers enshrined in the Constitution and refrained to either perform the functions of the legislature or deal with the details of the implementation of its judgments. It has been argued that the SC has developed a dual identity, first as a legal institution, a court of law that has appellate and constitutional powers, and second, as a public institution that is required to engage with, respond to, and negotiate the political pressures and social expectations that surround it.[98] Even as the SC has positioned itself as the final arbiter of the Constitution, the division of powers remains a contested area; thus Parliament can pass a law, the courts can strike it down, Parliament can try to circumvent the courts by amending the Constitution, the courts can pronounce that Parliament's amendment power does not apply to the case, and so on.[99] According to the 'Substantive Thesis', it is difficult to infer whether judiciary is better than legislatures at protecting citizens' rights whereas the 'Procedural Thesis' suggests that legislatures are procedurally superior to courts because they are more legitimate, egalitarian and participatory than the courts.[100] It has also been argued that it is impossible for the courts to embody crucial democratic rights and values to the extent which can be done by the legislatures.[101] Thus, the rise of the SC may not necessarily be seen as a sign of the rise of constitutionalism, since citizens and civil society organisations have turned to the SC due a lack of other alternatives.[102]

Most of the SC's judgments on electoral laws and processes have stressed India's functioning as an effective electoral democracy with a focus on ensuring free and fair elections and empowering voters with adequate information to make an informed choice. The recent *Anoop Baranwal vs Union of India*[103] judgment is a case in point where the SC justified its intervention to create temporary regulatory processes to fill a legislative gap in respect of method of selecting ECI members although this also raises some wider constitutional questions regarding separation of powers between the legislature, executive and judiciary[104] and was 'the Court justified to disturb the constitutional machinery in place'?[105]

[98] ibid 105.

[99] PB Mehta, 'India's Unlikely Democracy: The Rise of Judicial Sovereignty' (2007) 18(2) *Journal of Democracy* 75.

[100] A Lever, 'Democracy and Judicial Review: Are They Really Incompatible?' (2009) 7(4) *Perspectives on Politics*; J Waldron, 'The Core of the Case against Judicial Review' (2006) 115(6) *The Yale Law Journal*.

[101] Lever (n 100).

[102] Lever (n 100) 110; PB Mehta, 'India's Judiciary: The Promise of Uncertainty' in D Kapur and PB Mehta (eds), *Public Institutions in India: Performance and Design* (New Delhi, Oxford University Press, 2005) 158, 171.

[103] *Anoop Baranwal v Union of India* (2023).

[104] HB Narsappa, 'Why the Supreme Court's ECI verdict is jurisprudentially unsound' (2023) *The Leaflet*. www.theleaflet.in.

[105] U Baxi, 'A Landmark, But Perplexing Portent?' (2023). www.indialegallive.com.

In general, democracy at a procedural level requires free and fair elections, separation of powers, rule of law, independent judiciary and press, before transitioning to achieve outcomes such as liberty and equality. Palshikar[106] argues that although elections have a central place in democratic practice in India and have considerable legitimacy and acceptance, 'the underside of elections makes them very unattractive and raises questions about the democratic authenticity of the state'. However, according to Saffon and Urbinati[107] 'modem democratic procedure – based on every individual's equal participation in fair and competitive elections ... is the best way of respecting equal liberty in a context of pluralism and dissent'. Further, while free and fair elections are necessary but not a sufficient condition for democracy, debates around electoral governance 'enable the crafting of democratic politics as a continuum between representation and participation', and 'the consolidation of the electoral domain has had ramifications for the deliberative and substantive dimensions of democracy in India ...'.[108]

Whilst political theorists such as Kelsen[109] have defended procedural democracy on the basis that it provides best protection for securing political freedom for all sections of society, others, for example, Rawls[110] and Habermas[111] consider that procedures on their own do not provide a normative justification of democracy. Scholars of deliberative democracy have focused on the substantive goals, procedures ought to achieve even as it is argued that normative goals of deliberative democracy may not be at odds with the one proposed by procedural democracy.[112] In *Mohinder Singh v Chief Election Commissioner*[113] the SC acknowledged that although free and free elections were at the heart of the parliamentary system, standards for social and economy democracy were higher. The SC has also invoked equality of citizens irrespective of their religion, caste etc being an important principle of India's secular democracy. Mehta[114] points out that most of the Court's judgments 'are the result of a delicate and political process of balancing competing values and political aspirations; they seek to provide a workable modus vivendi rather than to articular high values'.

[106] Palshikar (n 11) 157.

[107] MP Saffon and N Urbinati, 'Procedural Democracy, the Bulwark of Equal Liberty' (2013) 41(3) *Political Theory* 442.

[108] UK Singh and A Roy, *Election Commission of India: Institutionalising Democratic Uncertainties* (Online, Oxford University Press, 2019) 330–33.

[109] H Kelsen, 'The Essence and Value of Democracy' in N Urbinati and CI Accetti (eds), *The Essence and Value of Democracy*, trans B Graf (Lanham, Maryland Rowman & Littlefield, 2013).

[110] J Rawls, *A Theory of Justice* (Cambridge, MA, Harvard University Press, 1971).

[111] J Habermas, *Between Facts and Norms: Contributions to a Discourse Theory of Law and Democracy*, trans W Rehg (Cambridge, MIT Press, 1996).

[112] Saffon and Urbinati (n 107) 444; RA Dahl, *Polyarchy: Participation and Opposition* (New Haven, CT, Yale University Press, 1971) has also provided a normative view of procedural democracy.

[113] *Mohinder Singh Gill v The Chief Election Commissioner* (1978) SCR (3) 272.

[114] Mehta (n 99).

To this extent, the SC appears to be favouring the Kelsenian notion of the link between compromise and democracy.[115]

Based on Foucault,[116] Gordon[117] argues that '... a range of controlling mechanisms that suppress freedom, undermine plurality, and engender inequality, can legitimately function even within a "perfect" procedural democracy'. Viewed from this perspective, in India, due to various historical and sociological reasons, an individual's preferences, interests and identity may be influenced by the 'power relations' prevailing amongst different social groups. Gordon[118] concludes that if an individual is, at least partially, constituted by existing societal power relations, then the contention that procedural democracy can achieve effective participation becomes less tenable. Similarly, according to Saffon and Urbinati,[119] democracy is not merely about replacing violence, but about doing so by distributing political liberty equally although they also point out that a normative criterion based on 'equal liberty' as the ultimate goal may not be fully realisable by democracies in the real world.

Mehta[120] argues that despite Indian judiciary's interventions to safeguard democratic values, it would be stretching logic to pretend that the guardianship which the courts exercise over policy is synonymous with democracy. As Judge Hand observed 'Liberty lies in the hears of men and women, and when it dies here, no constitution, no law, no court can save it; no law, no court can even do much to help it.'[121] However, one also has to acknowledge that democracy has diverse connotations and types, with democracies displaying 'a process of differentiation rather than singularity of form'.[122] Guha[123] has argued that Indian democracy must be awarded a 'fifty percent pass mark' a view similar to that of Varshney[124] who stated that the battle of Indian democracy is 'half won'. According to Jayal,[125] India fares much better as a procedural rather than

[115] S Baume, 'What Place Should Compromise Be Given in Democracy? A Reflection on Hans Kelsen's Contribution' (2017) 1(27) *Négociations* 73–89; H Kelsen, *Allgemeine Staatslehre* (Berlin, Julius Springer, 1925).

[116] M Foucault, *Discipline and Punish* (New York, Vintage Books, 1979); M Foucault, 'The Ethics of the Care of the Self as a Practice of Freedom' in J Bernauer and D Rasmussen (eds), *The Final Foucault* (Cambridge, MA, MIT Press, 1988).

[117] N Gordon, 'Dahl's Procedural Democracy: A Foucauldian Critique' (2000) 8(4) *Democratization* 23–40, 23.

[118] ibid 8.

[119] Saffon and Urbinati (n 107) 460–63.

[120] Mehta (n 99).

[121] L Hand, 'The Spirit of Liberty' in I Dillard (ed), *The Spirit of Liberty*, 3rd edn (New York, Alfred A. Knopf, 1960) 190.

[122] PR deSouza, 'Election, Parties and Democracy in India' in P Ronald de Souza (ed), *Contemporary India: Transitions* (New Delhi, SAGE, 2000) 204–05; S Kaviraj, 'Democracy and Social Inequality' in F Frankel, Z Hasan, R Bhargava and B Arora (eds), *Transforming India* (New Delhi, Oxford University Press, 2000) 89–90.

[123] R Guha, *India After Gandhi* (New Delhi, Macmillan, 2007) 749.

[124] A Varshney, *Battles Half Won* (New Delhi, Penguin, 2013).

[125] NG Jayal, 'Introduction: Situating Democracy' in NG Jayal (ed), *Democracy in India* (Delhi, Oxford University Press, 2001) 1–49.

a substantive democracy, while Palshikar[126] argues that Indian democracy is inconsistent since different areas manifest varying degrees of democracy, and thus, 'political equality is upheld in the areas of party politics and electoral competition but not so much in the field of governance'. Overall, Palshikar[127] views Indian democracy as one that functions in an imperfect environment and remains a 'work in progress'. Therefore, one has to consider the specific context of the nature and stage of India's democratic journey and evolution when discussing and evaluating the judiciary's interventions including in the field of electoral law and processes.

VI. CONCLUSION

It is clear that the Indian judiciary, particularly the SC, has helped in sustaining Indian democracy by safeguarding the integrity of the electoral process and being a protector of citizens' rights and defender of the Constitution. The SC's status has been strengthened through many landmark rulings on electoral laws, and it has emerged as one of most powerful constitutional courts in the world. It has also strengthened the ECI's constitutional role in conducting free and fair elections although it has been argued that much of respect for ECI potentially stems from its overreach, and questions have been asked whether greater accountability and judicial oversight of the ECI's power would be more appropriate. Although there are areas where the SC could do more, for example campaign finance,[128] one has to also recognise that the SC functions within the framework of the constitutional division of powers and also has a large number of pending cases.[129] Further, the implementation of the Court's judgments on electoral laws and processes is sometimes constrained by a lack of political will and effective regulation of political parties, as well as the Court's limited resources. Overall, one can say that the judiciary, especially the SC remains one of the most trusted of India's key governance institutions and has played a progressive role in the review of electoral laws and processes to uphold constitutional principles and strengthen India's democracy.

[126] Palshikar (n 11).

[127] ibid 154.

[128] The SC recently agreed to hear a PIL of 2019, which challenges the legality of electoral bonds scheme announced by the government in 2017. These bonds are bearer instruments used to donate money anonymously to political parties and do not include any information about the buyer or payee. This means that voters will not know which individual, company, or organisation has funded which party, and to what extent. However, this crucial matter relating to campaign finance is still being considered by the Supreme Court.

[129] As on 1August 2023, there were about 70,000 pending cases in the SC. www.main.sci.gov.in.

16

The Japanese Supreme Court and the Equality of the Vote: A Careful Activism

ELISA BERTOLINI

I. INTRODUCTION

THE JAPANESE SUPREME Court (hereinafter JSC) is widely known among comparative constitutional scholarship as a passive, self-restraining, conservative and deferential court. This assessment is based on both the record of unconstitutionality decisions (11 since 1947) and the quality of the reasoning (usually disappointing). The disappointing record and reasoning are qualified as poor with respect to those of homologous foreign courts. Accordingly, judicial review in Japan has been qualified as 'a failure in more than one sense'.[1]

Several explanations – cultural, historical, organisational, institutional, strategic, constitutional positivism[2] – have been put forward. They are all plausible and persuasive; they have a point, in the sense that they may very well play a role in shaping the attitude of the Court. Nonetheless, they are not entirely satisfactory.[3] The fact that the topic is still debated proves it. It is more probable that they all exert a certain influence on both the single judge and on the JSC as a collegial body.

[1] DS Law, 'Why has Judicial Review Failed in Japan?' (2011) 88 *Washington University Law Review* 1426.

[2] S Matsui, 'Why is the Japanese Supreme Court so Conservative' (2011) 88 *Washington University Law Review* 1375 and C Martin, 'The Japanese Constitution as Law and the Legitimacy of the Supreme Court's Constitutional Decisions: A Response to Matsui' (2011) 88 *Washington University Law Review* 1527.

[3] See the articles composing the special part of (2011) 88 *Washington University Law Review* devoted to the JSC: Matsui 'Why is the Japanese Supreme Court'; Law, 'Why has Judicial Review'; JO Haley, 'Constitutional Adjudication in Japan: Context, Structures, and Values' 1467; F Upham, 'Stealth Activism: Norm Formation by Japanese Courts' 1493; Martin, 'The Japanese Constitution'; JM Ramseyer, 'Do School Cliques Dominate Japanese Bureaucracies?: Evidence from Supreme Court Appointments' 1681; H Itō, 'The Role Of Precedent At Japan's Supreme Court' 1631. Furthermore,

Moreover, scholars do not even agree on how to interpret the definition of conservative. According to Haley, the qualification of conservative should be narrowly employed, simply in the sense of sharing the same prevailing communitarian orientation and centre-right ideology of Japanese society as a whole.[4] Upham, on the contrary, rejects the idea of the overall judiciary being conservative, pointing out that, in areas such as family law and employment, judges have engage in 'stealth activism'.[5] Nonetheless, Upham himself recognises the fact that this activism cannot be applied to the judicial review.

This short premise is a requirement to verify whether the approach of the JSC on malapportionment fits this pattern.

Indeed, the JSC has ruled frequently (almost at every election claims of unconstitutional apportionment and petitions to vacate them are made) on the elections – not only at national level – reasoning on the equality of the vote (series of malapportionment cases), access to the vote (postal voting, Japanese nationals living abroad), electoral campaign (canvassing, political propaganda, and funding). Even though with respect to the latter, the JSC had a conservative attitude, upholding all the limitations, what emerges as striking is that out of the 11 unconstitutionality decisions, four are on the electoral legislation (two on malapportionment,[6] one on the overseas voters[7] and one on the law on the national review in the barring Japanese expatriates voting[8]). Malapportionment decisions clearly put under strain the boundaries of competences between the Court and the Diet, ie, the Japanese Parliament. Indeed, the JSC constantly urges the Diet to redress the imbalance and, facing the failure to act, even though it does not get as far as to nullify the elections, its irritation can be clearly perceived throughout the decisions. Nevertheless, the Court always considers that the Diet enjoys a wide discretion and seems content – as in the 2019 and 2022 decisions – a minimum attempt by the Diet to redress the imbalance. Furthermore, it is worth noting that no binding force is connected to the JSC judgments, being merely declaratory decisions. The JSC walks on the edge, when trying to mould different degrees of unconstitutionality of the elections.

Although all the profiles examined in the various decisions the JSC delivered on the electoral matter are worthy of analysis, this chapter focuses on the

see DS Law, 'The Anatomy of a Conservative Court: Judicial Review in Japan' (2009) 87 *Texas Law Review* 1545. Less recently, H Itō, 'Judicial Review and Judicial Activism in Japan' (1990) 53 *Law & Contemporary Problems* 169.

[4] Haley (n 3) 1491.

[5] Upham (n 3) 1493.

[6] *Kurokawa v Chiba Prefecture Election Commission*: Supreme Court, grand bench, 14 April 1976, 30 *Minshū* 223; and *Kanao v Hiroshima Prefecture Election Commission*: Supreme Court, grand bench, 17 July 1985, 39 *Minshū* 1100.

[7] *Kakunaga v Sekiguchi/Overseas Voters Case:* Supreme Court, grand bench, 14 September 2005, 59 *Minshū* 2087. S Matsui, 'The voting rights of Japanese citizens living abroad' (2007) 5 *ICON* 332.

[8] Supreme Court, grand bench, 25 May 2022, 76 *Minshū* 4.

equality of the vote (malapportionment issue), trying to identify whether the JSC imposes its own idea of representation, or rather upholds the margin of discretion of the Diet.

The chapter claims that on the malapportionment issue to qualify the JSC's stance as conservative would be rather shallow, risking overlooking the bigger picture. The progressive lowering of the ratio of the permissible disparity is an important point, although the careful stance of the JSC in managing the relationship with the Diet prevails.

The judgments of the JSC on the matter are structured into three steps. In the first, the JSC examines the constitutionality of the disparity of the vote and rules on it. In the second, the JSC integrates step one by considering the outcome with respect to the margin of discretion of the Diet. Based on the merging of these two steps, three outcomes on the apportionment are possible: constitutional, in a state of unconstitutionality (and the elections are valid) and unconstitutional (and the elections are invalid). Finally, the third step is the nullification of the elections (which never happened).

It is possible to fault the JSC at each one of these steps. In the first, because it fails either to identify a maximum acceptable disparity or to explain why a ratio is (un)constitutional. In the second step, the JSC seems to be too sympathetic, ie, deferent, towards the Diet, which either does not intervene or does it perfunctorily. Whilst, with respect to the third, the JSC always vacated the petition to nullify the elections. The chapter claims that steps two and three derive not by a very conservative interpretation of the equality of the vote, rather, by how the JSC interprets its role towards the Diet and as guardian of the Constitution.

After providing a general framework of the different reapportionments and electoral reforms between 1950 and 2022 and on the legal basis for the lawsuits on elections, the chapter moves to analyse the JSC case on malapportionment, outlining the more relevant and disappointing points of its reasoning. Finally, the last section discusses the claim of the chapter and thus the stance of the JSC with respect to its interpretation of the equality of the vote and on the instruments that could be employed (and not exclusively by the JSC) to enforce it.

II. A GENERAL FRAMEWORK

Malapportionment, which derives from the creation of electoral districts with divergent ratios of representatives to voters, is the most relevant issue at any Japanese election since the 1950s. Before examining the JSC case law, it seems convenient to provide some key information on the apportionment and electoral systems for the two Houses of the Diet from the one hand and on reapportionment suits legal basis from the other.

A. Apportionment and Electoral Reforms

The Constitution entrusts the Diet – composed of the House of Representatives and the House of Councillors – with apportioning and districting.[9] They are regulated under the 1950 Public Officials Election Act (POEL). The POEL did not provide for mandatory periodical reapportionment, though it deemed it as suitable; indeed, it suggested (and not dictated) to revise the apportionment every five years.

To determine the first post war apportionment, 150,000 electors (not people) were counted for the Lower House, based on the 1946 census. Therefore, when coming to districting, 117 electoral districts were drawn, each with an allocation from three to five seats, for a total number of 466.

Concerning districting and apportionment of the Upper House, the total number of Councillors was set at 250 (252 in 1972[10]). Out of the 250, 100 were elected at large, within a single national district, whereas the remaining 150 (152 in 1972) were elected at large from all the prefectures, each one of them corresponding to an electoral district. It is convenient to stress that because of the election of half the House taking place every three years, each prefecture was awarded at least two seats, disregarding from its actual population. This was not a constitutional requirement, the Constitution leaving the matter to the Diet. The Diet has interpreted the provision on the re-election every three years as if each prefecture should have a seat contested in each election. Indeed, Councillors tend to be interpreted as representatives of the prefectures. Therefore, there was already an intrinsic disparity (initial imbalance of 1:2).[11] In 1982, these 152 seats elected at large in the prefectures started to be elected by a form of proportional representation (PR). The apportionment was again based on the 1946 census and counted on 487,417 electors per councillor divided by 150.

Hence, in 1950, the disparity was 1:5.1 for the House of Representatives and 1:2.62 for the House of Councillors.

The economic development and the subsequent moving from rural to urban areas caused the increase of the imbalance, which the Diet failed to redress satisfactorily. More precisely, instead of redrawing the districts, the Diet favoured the solution to add seats (the easiest one). Furthermore, the simple increase in the number of seats proved to be just a temporary solution with respect to the continuous moving of the population.

Implementing this solution, the Diet went for the first reapportionment of the House of Representatives in 1964, by increasing the total number of 19 members. Nonetheless, the ratio remained at around 1:2. Moreover, the 1970 census revealed that the imbalance between the most populous district (Ōsaka No. 3) and the less populous (Hyōgo No. 5) was 1:4.99.

[9] Under Arts 43(2) and 47.
[10] When the Ryūkyū reverted to Japan.
[11] Haley (n 3).

Hence, a second reapportionment of the Lower House was needed. In 1975, 20 more seats were added, with the maximum imbalance being 1:3.7.[12] Rural areas continued to be overrepresented.

It is in this scenario that the first landmark decision of the JSC occurred. In 1976, in *Kurokawa v Chiba Prefecture Election Commission*, the JSC declared the maximum imbalance of 1:4.99 in the 1972 Lower House elections unconstitutional, though did not nullified them.

Again, in 1983, the JSC hinted that, after a reasonable period of time (five years) had elapsed, it would declare unconstitutional the apportionment revised based on the 1975 census, under which the maximum disparity was 1:3.94.[13]

In 1986, the third reapportionment of the Lower House took place. It did not improve the imbalance, which remained at 1:2.92. The reason was the perfunctory character of the reapportionment, defined as 'eight plus, seven minus', ie, it allocated one seat each to eight grossly disadvantaged districts while depriving seven extremely favoured of one seat each.

In this frame, 1994 is a watershed moment for the House of Representatives, with the introduction of a parallel system.[14]

The previous multi-member single districts system was replaced by a single-member districts (300 representatives elected by majority-plurality) combined with a proportional representation system (11 multi-member districts for 200, which became 180 in 2000 representatives to be elected, by the D'Hondt PR method). With respect to apportionment, the Diet increased the number of seats in the underrepresented districts and decreased the number in overrepresented ones.

In 1994, the Diet passed the Act Establishing the Boundary Commission. The Commission, established under the Cabinet Office, was entrusted with making recommendations every 10 years regarding the redrawing of boundaries of electoral districts. It is composed of seven members appointed by the Prime Minister, with the assent of the Diet, for a term of office of five years. It submits recommendations to the Prime Minister, who must then report to the Diet. It clearly emerges from the appointment procedure that the Commission is not an independent body. The Diet is expected to amend the boundaries in accordance with the commission's recommendations. As a guiding principle, the commission considered that the maximum variation should be within 1:2.[15]

[12] Chiba No. 4 and Hyōgo No. 5.

[13] *Tokyo Metropolitan Election Commission v Koshiyama*: Supreme Court, grand bench, 7 November 1983, 37 *Minshū* 1243 (reversing Tōkyō District Court, 23 December 1980, 984 *Hanrei Jihō* 26).

[14] Y Horiuchi and J Saito, 'Reapportionment and Redistribution: Consequences of Electoral Reform in Japan' (2003) 47 *American Journal of Political Science* 669.

[15] Y Hasebe, 'Cases of the Supreme Court of Japan' (2015) *IACL-AICD-BLOG*: iacl-aidc-blog.org/2015/02/17/yasuo-hasebe-cases-of-the-supreme-court-of-japan; and 'The Supreme Court of Japan: Its adjudication on electoral systems and economic freedoms' (2007) 5 *ICON* 296.

However, in the 1995 elections, the ratio was 1:2.309. The JSC, in a 1999 ruling, declared the ratio within the boundaries of the legislative discretion.[16]

In 2013, a new reapportionment of the House of Representatives following the 2012 elections decreased the total number from 480 to 475, with a decrease of five members elected in the single-seat districts (from 300 to 295).[17] The target was to set the disparity at less of 1:2.00. A further reapportionment in 2016 (Act No. 49, entered into force in December 2022) decreased the total number of representatives from 475 to 465. More precisely, the number of single-member districts decreased from 295 to 289, and the number of members elected under PR from 180 to 176. Furthermore, the same act adopted the Adams' method as a method of apportionment of seats to each prefecture in accordance with population fluctuations.

In November 2022, the Diet passed the largest-ever reform of the POEL to rebalance the Lower House districts. The new law modified both the distribution and boundaries of single-seat constituencies, aiming at narrowing the vote disparity below the two-fold level between densely and sparsely populated districts. Based on the 2020 national census, the new apportionment method would bring down the maximum imbalance from 1:2.096 to 1:1.999. Hence, the law added 10 single-seat districts to five prefectures, while cutting one each from 10 prefectures. The amendment, affecting 140 single-seat districts in 25 prefectures, also switched some seats among regional proportional representation blocks (10 less-populated prefectures, including Yamaguchi and Wakayama, will lose one seat each, while five densely populated prefectures, including Tōkyō and Kanagawa, will get between one and five extra seats). Furthermore, the boundaries of Ōsaka and other prefectures, whilst keeping their single-seat electoral districts, are to be redrawn to reduce disparities. The amendment also affected PR; more precisely, among 11 proportional representation blocks nationwide, the revised law will cut one seat each from three blocks and give them to two other blocks.

With respect to the House of Councillors, the first electoral reform took place in 1982 and the first reapportionment in 2000.

The 1982 electoral reform introduced two different types of districts: a national PR district (D'Hondt method) for 127 Councillors and prefectural districts for the 47 prefectures (each is allotted between two and eight councillors) by SNTV (single non-transferable vote). Unlike for the House of Representative (since 1994), a simultaneous dual candidacy is not allowed. However, the deviation remained at around 1:5.26.

Several reapportionments were made since 2000. In 2000, the first lowered the total number of Councillors to 242, following the elimination of six seats elected by individual constituencies and four by proportional representation.

[16] Supreme Court, grand bench, 10 November 1999, 53 *Minshū* 1441.

[17] Tokushima, Kochi, Saga, Fukui and Yamanashi were decreased from 3 to 2 representatives each.

Therefore, the 242 members are elected as follows: 146 in 45 multi-member districts (between two and 12 seats each) and 96 in one national constituency. In 2015, another reapportionment took place, merging Tottori and Shimane prefectures into a single electoral district. The same as Tokushima and Kochi, electing one councillor each. Therefore, out of the 45 multi-member districts, 43 are formed on a metropolitan or prefectural basis, while the remaining two cover two prefectures each. In 2018, even though a 2017 JSC ruling[18] declared the apportionment constitutional, the majority reformed the Upper House electoral system, adding six more seats (from 96 to 100 under PR and from 146 to 148 majority system; total number increased from 242 to 248).[19] Thus, the imbalance decreased from 1:3.08 to 1:2.985.

B. Seeking Redress: Article 204 POEL

The legal basis for reapportionment suits is Article 204 POEL. The provision entitles all voters to file a lawsuit before a high court against the validity of an election, seeking the nullification.

It is convenient to point out that Article 204 was not meant to seek redress against malapportionment. It aimed to nullify an illegally enforced election and to order a new election held for specific candidates.[20] The malapportionment suits are more concerned with the whole election, rather than of the election of a single candidate. Moreover, the aim is to prevent the application of the allocation of seats emerging from the elections. Election nullification is not always sought. However, in the last few decades, some high courts have nullified the elections in the districts falling 1964 *Koshiyama* within their jurisdiction.

Hence, the employment of this Article to malapportionment is not free of concerns.

III. THE CASE LAW

This section addresses the enforcement of the one man, one vote principle in the JSC's rulings on malapportionment issues. That is to say, whether the Court offers its own interpretation in terms of permissible deviation from the 1:1 standard and how it enforces it. With respect to the former, what emerges is that the JSC does not properly define the extent of the margin. Therefore, the Court is not able to convey a clear interpretation of the one man, one vote principle.

[18] Supreme Court, grand bench, 27 September 2017, 71 *Minshū* 7.

[19] The House of Councillors will have the full 248 seats after the 2022 half renewal.

[20] H Hata, 'Malapportionment of Representation in the National Diet' (1990) 53 *Law & Contemporary Problems* 157. W Somers Bailey, 'Reducing Malapportionment in Japan's Electoral Districts: The Supreme Court must act' (1997) 6 *Pacific Rim Law & Policy Journal* 169.

With respect to the latter point, several options are possible, such as resorting to the margin of discretion of the Diet, issuing a constitutional warning, and nullifying the elections.

The issue is of paramount importance within the Japanese experience, because out of the 17 House of Representatives elections since 1972, 15 have been challenged (exceptions are the 1976 and 1979 elections); and out of the 20 House of Councillors elections since 1962, 16 have been challenged (exceptions being the 1965, 1968, 1974 and 1989 elections).

The way the Court tries to strike a balance between the one man, one vote principle and the discretion of the Diet is relevant also with respect to the more general claim of passivism and deference as towards the Diet.

A. 1964 *Koshiyama*

The first ever decision of the JSC on malapportionment is the 1964 *Koshiyama v Chairman, Tokyo Metropolitan Election Commission* (*Koshiyama I*) case.[21]

In this judgment, the JSC adjudicated the constitutionality of the apportionment of the 1962 Upper House elections, where the disparity was of 1:4.09. The decision is significant for three main points.

First, the JSC states the justiciability of the issue. Even though apportionment belongs to the competence of the Diet as a matter of legislative policy, whenever situations of extreme inequality in the right to vote emerge, the issue is justiciable. However, on this point Justice Saitō dissented, relying on Justice Frankfurter's 1962 dissenting opinion in *Baker v Carr*.[22] According to his dissenting opinion, the JSC authority rests upon the confidence of the public; therefore, the JSC has to prove to be detached from politics and abstain from being entangled within political clashes and factionalism.

Second, strict equality must not be the only concern of the Diet when regulating apportionment. Nonetheless, the JSC recognises that it has to be most relevant. However, what must be taken into account is the historical background and the balance in the number of Councillors between administrative districts. Hence, a violation of equality must be scrutinised according to a wide range of

[21] *Koshiyama v Chairman, Tokyo Metropolitan Election Commission:* Supreme Court, grand bench, 5 February 1964, 18 *Minshū* 270. The petitioner filed a lawsuit before the Tōkyō High Court, challenging the validity of the 1962 elections. The reason was the disparity between the Tōkyō metropolitan district (four members elected out of 5,922,100 voters) and the Tottori district (one member elected out of 362,182 voters), with a ratio of 1:4.09. Accordingly, the petitioner claimed a violation of Art 14(1) – equality under the law – Art 15(3) – universal suffrage – and Art 44 – prohibiting irrational restrictions on the right to vote. Since the claim was dismissed, the petitioner appealed to the JSC.

[22] *Baker v Carr* 369 U.S. 186, 266 (1962) (Frankfurter J, dissenting).

other factors. The JSC is making the point of a sort of peculiarity of the House of Councillors, which will be more extensively discussed in future decisions.

Third, the disparity of 1:4.09 is constitutional.

Although the decision is positive, because the JSC decided not to resort to the political question doctrine in electoral matters,[23] there are some disappointing profiles.

The first is that no clear indication is provided with respect to the balance between strict equality of the vote and the other relevant factors.

The second is that when examining the disparity, the JSC does not take the chance to reason more widely, framing the specific case of the deviation as to 1:4.09 in the more general issue of malapportionment. More precisely, when does a disparity become extremely unequal and thus unconstitutional? No guiding principles are provided to the Diet on whenever it will have to proceed to a reapportionment. Besides, it clearly emerges from the reasoning that even though apportionment is a matter of the Diet's legislative policy, too great a disparity can be declared unconstitutional.

Was this an influence of *Reynolds v Sims*?[24] However, when making a comparison between the two courts, it is convenient to outline that, although the JSC was modelled after its US counterpart, Japan remained anchored to the European model. Therefore, the JSC has no equity powers as to issue injunctions or mandamus.

Koshiyama was followed when the JSC had to rule on a disparity of 1:5.08 in the 1971 Upper House elections, declared constitutional.

B. 1976 *Kurokawa*

The first decision the JSC delivered on the apportionment of the Lower House resulted in a declaration of unconstitutionality in the landmark 1976 *Kurokawa v Chiba Election Commission*.[25]

[23] H Tomatsu, 'Judicial Review in Japan: An Overview of Efforts to Introduce US Theories' in Y Higuchi (ed), *Five Decades of Constitutionalism in Japanese Society* (Tōkyō, University of Tōkyō Press, 2001) 251, 258. See K Yokota, 'Political Questions and Judicial Review: A Comparison' in DF Henderson (ed), *The Constitution of Japan: Its First Twenty Years, 1947–67* (Washington, University of Washington Press, 1968) 141.

[24] *Reynolds v Sims* 377 U.S. 533. The SC struck down state senate inequality based on the principle of one person, one vote. The majority denied the argument that states were permitted to base their apportionment structures upon the Constitution itself, which requires two senators from each state despite substantially un-equal populations among the states.

[25] The petitioner filed a lawsuit before the Tōkyō High Court challenging the validity of the 1972 elections, because of the disparity reaching 1:4.99. Again, the infringement of Arts 14(1), 15(3) and 44 was claimed.

Kurokawa's significance is not just the striking down of the apportionment (deviation of 1:4.99), rather the different stance of the JSC with respect to *Koshiyama*.

The JSC explained better the rationale of the justiciability in malapportionment suits, affirming that, even though doubts subsisted on the employment of Article 204 POEL, it was a way to challenge the violation of the principle of the equality of the vote.

The Tōkyō High Court that ruled first, abided by *Koshiyama*. Although the lawsuit dealt with the Lower House apportionment, while *Koshiyama* with the Upper House apportionment. Abiding by *Koshiyama* entailed that: apportionment and districting are under the discretion of the Diet; equality under the law is not violated just because of an existing deviation; the imbalance ratio was not constitutionally intolerable.

However, the JSC Grand Bench quashed the High Court ruling. Electoral equality is a constitutional requirement, therefore apportionment and districting of the House of Representatives in 1972 were held as unconstitutional. Furthermore, the JSC stressed that although the deviation had exceeded the permissible limit, the Diet did not redressed it within a reasonable period, as required by the Constitution.

Despite the declaration of unconstitutionality and of invalidity of the 1972 election, the JSC vacated the petition to nullify the Hight Court ruling, based on the 1963 Administrative Case Litigation Act, at Article 31, authorising the Court to preserve a defective administrative act whenever invalidating it would result in a great harm to the public interest (technique of the circumstance decision).

Two main points are to be made.

The first is the relationship between *Kurokawa* and *Koshiyama*. The JSC did not make any reference to *Koshiyama*; therefore, there is neither overruling nor distinguishing. The latter would be appropriate, considering the differences and peculiarities of the two Houses.

The second is that although the disparity of vote exceeded the constitutional tolerance – ie, the discretion of the Diet – it is not unconstitutional per se. Thus, the exceedance is not a sufficient reason to declare the apportionment unconstitutional. Indeed, what makes an exceeding disparity unconstitutional is the lack of redressing within a reasonable period, which is not set in the decision. Furthermore, with respect to the constitutional tolerance, even though the deviation was found unconstitutional, the JSC did not indicate a clear standard of constitutionality for what is a permissible variation. According to the JSC, no strict mathematical equality is needed; rather, it is the lack of a conceivable mitigating rationale that turns a deviation unconstitutional. Therefore, the JSC employs the lowest scrutiny possible, one of the rational basis.

C. 1983 *Shimizu*

The malapportionment of the House of Councillors was addressed again by the JSC in the 1983 *Shimizu et al v Ōsaka Prefecture Election Commission*.[26]

The JSC dismissed the appeal, upholding the 1979 decision of the Ōsaka High Court on the 1977 elections. The apportionment did not violate the Constitution.

The most relevant profile of the decision is the distinguishing with respect to *Kurokawa*. Since the petitioners referred to *Kurokawa*, the JSC distinguished between the House of Councillors from the House of Representatives, stating that the law provides for different election mechanisms. Furthermore, other factors than the disparity have to be taken into account with respect to the Upper House, most notably the Councillors representing local districts. Besides, the national district would favour the election of professional and experienced people, thus more suited to represent different interests. Accordingly, standards for the equality among voters necessarily differed between the two Houses. The 1:5.26 deviation, though above *Kurokawa*, is not – in the Upper House context – beyond the reasonable exercise of the discretionary power of the Diet.

However, as in *Kurokawa*, the JSC can be faulted for not providing more persuasive reasoning to justify the imbalance in the apportionment.[27]

The JSC ruled again on the disparity of the 1980 Upper House elections of 1:5.37 and of the 1983 elections of 1:5.56, with both being declared constitutional.

D. 1983 *Koshiyama II*

Prior to *Kurokawa*, in 1975 the Diet had proceeded with a reapportionment of the House of Representatives, based on the 1970 national census. However, there was already a disparity of 1:2.92. This original disparity raised concerns because by the time of the next election in 1980, it had already increased up to 1:3.94.

The JSC addressed the malapportionment again in the 1983 *Tōkyō Election Commission v Koshiyama* (*Koshiyama II*) case.[28]

[26] *Shimizu et al v Ōsaka Prefecture Election Commission:* Supreme Court, grand bench, 27 April 1983, 37 *Minshū* 345. The petitioners challenged the validity of the 1977 election, because of a deviation of 1:5.26, thus exceeding the disparity determined to be unconstitutional in *Kurokawa*. Again, the petitioners claimed an infringement of Arts 14(1), 15(3) and 44.

[27] H Tomatsu, 'Equal Protection of the Law' (1990) 53 *Law & Contemporary Problems* 109.

[28] *Tōkyō Election Commission v Koshiyama:* Supreme Court, grand bench, 27 April 1983, 37 *Minshū* 1243.

It is convenient to outline the most relevant elements of this decision in comparison with *Kurokawa*, and to look at whether clearer indications were drawn with respect to two issues: the range of permissible deviation and the reasonable period.

First, the JSC held that the inequality declared in the *Kurokawa* had not been redressed. The disparity of 1:3.94 was in a state of unconstitutionality. This is certainly the most innovative element of the decision, because the JSC introduced a new shade of (un)constitutionality. Furthermore, it proves the Court's attempt to strike a balance between the permissible deviation and the margin of discretion of the Diet. However, based on *Kurokawa*, to acknowledge the unconstitutionality inherent within the apportionment system is not enough. In addition, a second requirement has to be met, ie, the failure to redress it within a reasonable period. Therefore, the JSC concluded holding the deviation within the reasonable discretion of the Diet, because a reasonable amount of time had not elapsed since the last revision. However, critics stressed that five years was more than enough for the Diet to intervene.

Furthermore, the JSC outlined that the deviation decrease from an earlier 1:4.83 to a later 1:2.92 had eliminated the unconstitutionality. Indeed, the JSC dismissed the Tōkyō High Court's assertion that a deviation of more than 1:2 violated the equal protection principle. Accordingly, the majority seemed to imply that a deviation of 1:3 is acceptable. Opposite Justices Dando and Yokoi, dissenting, considered a disparity of 1:2 as the maximum permissible. Consequently, again relying upon Article 31 Administrative Case Litigation Act, the petition to nullify was vacated.

Finally, the JSC urged the Diet to redress the imbalance, which, in November 1983 was 1:3.94.

E. 1985 *Kanao*

In December 1983, a new election for the Lower House was held, based on the apportionment that the JSC had just declared in a state of unconstitutionality. During the 1983 election, the maximum imbalance was 1:4.40. Therefore, the election was challenged before the High Courts of Hiroshima, Ōsaka, Tōkyō and Sapporo. They all declared the apportionment unconstitutional, though, under the technique of circumstance decision, the suits were dismissed.

In July 1985, in *Kanao v Hiroshima Prefecture Election Commission*, the JSC affirmed these decisions and vacated the petition to nullify. When examining the reasoning, this decision was based upon the lines of *Kurokawa*. The 1983 deviation was in violation of the Constitution, and it had not been redressed within a reasonable period. Indeed, the most significant part of the decision was represented by dissenting opinions with respect to the employment of the circumstance technique. Four dissenting justices[29] were open to the possibility of delivering a decision invalidating prospectively an election after the lapse of a certain time (*keikoku-hanketsu* or prospective invalidation technique, consisting of declaring a warning of unconstitutionality).[30] Justice Taniguchi went further, suggesting an immediate nullification.

Globally, the JSC showed irritation for the slow action of the Diet. Therefore, before the 1986 elections, the Diet intervened in May with the third reapportionment, though very cautiously (the difference in the ratio was still 1:2.92).

F. The 1986 Combined Elections

In 1988, the JSC ruled on the combined July 1986 elections and ruled the disparity of 1:2.92 (Lower House)[31] and 1:5.85 (Upper House) constitutional.

It is convenient to mention the decision, because it was on their basis that the LDP[32] started to claim that the disparities of 1:3 and 1:6 were within the constitutional acceptable disparity.

G. Lower House Malapportionment Since 1993

This subsection provides an overview on the rulings on the Lower House elections from 1990 to 2023. The main purpose is to outline the progressive tightening of the permissible disparity, together with a more frequent resort to declare the elections in a state of unconstitutionality and thus invalid. A similar pattern can be identified with respect to the Upper House too, as will be summarised in the following subsection. However, it is convenient to stress again the fact that up to now no election, though invalid, has been nullified.

In the 1993 *Kawahara v Tokyo Prefecture Election Commission*, the JSC ruled the 1990 Lower House elections in a state of unconstitutionality, because of a disparity of 1:3.18.[33]

The JSC here clearly follows *Koshiyama II*. Although the electoral reform had reduced the disparity to 1:2.99, by the time of the elections, it had already

[29] Terada, Kinoshita, Itō and Yaguchi.

[30] Here there is a clear influence of the *Bundesverfassungsgericht* technique of constitutional warning. See BVerfG 16, 130 (1963). In this sense, see H Hata, 'Malapportionment of Representation in the National Diet' (1990) 53 *Law & Contemporary Problems* 157.

[31] *Miyakawa v Chiba Election Commission*: Supreme Court, grand bench, 21 October 1988, 42 *Minshū* 644.

[32] The Liberal Democratic Party has been the almost continuously the majority party since its establishment in 1955.

[33] *Kawahara v Tokyo Prefecture Election Commission*: Supreme Court, grand bench, 20 January 1993, 47 *Minshū* 67.

increased up to 1:3.18. Therefore, when focusing exclusively on the apportionment, it is beyond the constitutional acceptable discretion. Nonetheless, the apportionment cannot be declared unconstitutional if the Diet has acted within a reasonable time limit. Here the JSC considered that because the Diet had intervened in 1986 and the elections were held in 1990, the Diet did not fail to act.

It was an eight to five decision. Justice Kisaki, dissenting, outlined in particular that it was necessary to set the maximum disparity at 1:2. Furthermore, he was strongly opposed to the Diet taking into account non-population factors when proceeding with reapportionments. Justice Nakajima, dissenting, harshly criticised the lack of a clear acceptable ratio.

In June 1995, the JSC ruled on the 1993 Lower House elections in *Kasuga v Tōkyō Electoral Commission*.[34] The disparity was 1:2.82 and the apportionment was declared constitutional.

As previously outlined, 1994 was a pivotal year in the electoral system evolution with the introduction of the parallel voting system.

The first election testing the new system was in 1996 and the deviation was 1:2.31.

The JSC reaffirmed *Kasuga* in a 1999 ruling, applying the same standard, holding that the difference was within the Diet's discretion.

Conversely, in the 2001 *Yamaguchi v Central Election Commission*[35] case, the JSC held the 2000 Lower House elections disparity of 1:2.47 constitutional.

In 2007, the 2005 elections disparity of 1:2.17 was again declared constitutional.[36]

The trend started to be reversed partially starting from the 2011 decision on the 2009 elections. It was reversed partially for two reasons. The first is that, after several declarations of constitutionality, the JSC revived the state of unconstitutionality (the first time since 1994 when the parallel systems were introduced), entailing the invalidity of the elections. The second is that the JSC does not go as far as declaring the apportionment unconstitutional nor nullifying the elections (circumstance technique decision).

In a 2011 decision,[37] the JSC ruled that the maximum discrepancy of 1:2.30 (between the Kōchi 3 and Chiba 4 districts) in the 2009 election was in violation of the constitutionally guaranteed equality of all voters. More precisely, the seat-allocation system brought a significant deviation from the one person, one vote principle, thus lacking a rational basis. Indeed, the JSC discussed the rationale of the system, which the Diet identified as having to also reflect the opinion of people residing in less populated areas. Accordingly, the JSC pointed

[34] *Kasuga v Tōkyō Electoral Commission:* Supreme Court, 1st petty bench, 8 June 1995, 49 *Minshū* 6.

[35] *Yamaguchi v Central Election Commission:* Supreme Court, grand bench, 18 December 2001, 55 *Minshū* 1713.

[36] *Takemura v Tokyo Prefecture Election Commission*: Supreme Court, grand bench, 13 June 2007, 61 *Minshū* 1617.

[37] Supreme Court, grand bench, 23 March 2011, 65 *Minshū* 755.

out that MPs represent the nation. Therefore, the JSC reasoned, that rationale was not sufficient to deviate from the principle of one man, one vote. However, because a reasonable time had not elapsed, the elections were in a state of unconstitutionality.

The decision was replicated in a 2013 ruling[38] on the 2012 elections, where the deviation was 1:2.43. Here the JSC decided on 16 lawsuits. What is convenient to outline here is that three high courts had declared invalid the elections in three districts. Again, it is because of the last Diet's efforts to redress the malapportionment that the surviving disparity was in a state of unconstitutionality; nevertheless, the result was not unconstitutional.

The same ruling of unconstitutionality was reached in the 2015 decision[39] on the 2014 elections. In these elections, the maximum deviation was 1:2.13. However, in light of the 2013 reapportionment,

> it cannot be said that no correction had been made to these provisions within a reasonable period of time as required by the Constitution, and therefore said provisions cannot be found to be in violation of article 14, paragraph (1) or other provisions of the Constitution.

Three of the 14 justices considered that the elections were 'unconstitutional,' including two who asserted that the elections should be nullified.

Again, lawsuits seeking the nullification of the 2017 elections were brought before high courts. Just before the elections, the disparity was 1:1.98. Out of the 16 lawsuits, 13 high courts ruled the elections were constitutional. The Nagoya and the Hiroshima High Courts held the elections to be in a state of unconstitutionality. The JSC, affirming the approach that only disparities above 1:2 are constitutionally problematic, ruled the elections constitutional.[40] Furthermore, to this decision of constitutionality, as clearly stated by the Court, the assumption was that the inequality would have been rectified under the new system introduced with the 2016 POEL amendment.

The last set of lawsuits (16), filed before high courts and their branches, date back to 2021, on the elections of the same year. The disparity in the weight of a single vote had increased to 1:2.08,[41] and it had been above 1:2 in 29 constituencies. Seven of the 16 rulings handed down (including Ōsaka, Takamatsu and Akita High Courts) ruled the disparity in a state of unconstitutionality, though refusing to nullify the elections, whilst nine (including the Tōkyō High Court) dismissed the lawsuit, ruling the elections constitutional.

The JSC handed down the decision in January 2023,[42] ruling 15 to one (Justice Uga dissenting) the vote-value disparity constitutional. It is convenient to outline that this decision follows the amendment by the Diet of the law redrawing

[38] Supreme Court, grand bench, 20 November 2013, 67 *Minshū* 8.
[39] Supreme Court, grand bench, 25 November 2015, 69 *Minshū* 7.
[40] Supreme Court, grand bench, 19 December 2018, 72 *Minshū* 6.
[41] The highest disparity in the weight of votes is between Tottori No. 1 with 230,959 voters and Tōkyō No. 13 with 480,247 voters.
[42] Case number 2022 (Gyo-Tsu) 130, not yet reported.

the boundaries and distribution of electoral districts. Despite recognising the constitutional requirement of equality of the right to vote, the Court considered that this was not an absolute criterion for determining the design of an electoral system. Indeed, there is a superior constitutional need, which is the harmonisation of the equality of the vote with other policies and purposes, such as the public welfare, as long as it is reasonable to do so. The Constitution itself grants the Diet a broad discretion in the design of the electoral system. Therefore, the determination as to the constitutionality of an electoral system is to be made by examining whether or not it is justified as a reasonable exercise of the discretion vested in the Diet. Again, as in 2017, the assumption that the inequality would be rectified under the new system contributed to the constitutionality decision. However, it is clear that the JSC completely discarded its long-established goal of keeping the difference in the value of a vote to less than 1:2.0. Indeed, even though the system was in transition, the principle of equality of the vote must not be ignored. Especially because the Diet could have made adjustments for the transitory phase but did not choose to. It is the basis of the reason that would justify the vote disparity, according to Justice Uga's dissenting opinion. Furthermore, he considers that a system where the default is that there is vote disparity is not reasonable and that even in a transition period the principle of equality should not be ignored.

H. Upper House Malapportionment Since 1996

The pattern just drawn for the Lower House can be applied to the Upper House, when examining the decision from the 1992–2022 elections.

In 1996,[43] the JSC ruled the 1992 elections in state of unconstitutionality with a disparity of 1:6.59, because no mitigating rationale was conceivable for such a gross difference. The majority opinion outlined the difficulty of applying equal voting rights to the two-member districts.

Again, the JSC continued to rule the Upper House apportionment constitutional in the following elections: 1995 (disparity of 1:4.97);[44] 1998 (disparity of 1:4.98);[45] 2001 (disparity of 1:5.06);[46] 2004 (disparity of 1:5.13);[47] 2007 (disparity of 1:4.86).[48]

[43] *Ōsaka Prefecture Election Commission v Kawazoe*: Supreme Court, grand bench, 11 September 1996, 50 *Minshū* 2283.

[44] *Yamaguchi v Tōkyō Metropolitan Election Commission*: Supreme Court, grand bench, 2 September 1998, 52 *Minshū* 1373.

[45] *Yamaguchi v Tōkyō Metropolitan Election Commission*: Supreme Court, grand bench, 6 September 2000, 54 *Minshū* 1997.

[46] *Koshiyama v Tōkyō Metropolitan Election Commission*: Supreme Court, grand bench, 14 January 2004, 58 *Minshū* 56.

[47] *Koshiyama v Tōkyō Metropolitan Election Commission*: Supreme Court, grand bench, 4 October 2006, 60 *Minshū* 2696.

[48] *Yamaguchi v Tōkyō Metropolitan Election Commission*: Supreme Court, grand bench, 30 September 2009, 63 *Minshū* 1520.

It is convenient to mention briefly the 1998 *Yamaguchi v Tokyo Prefecture Election Commission* case.[49] Here the JSC seems to follow *Kurokawa*, holding again the maximum disparity unconstitutional; nonetheless, taking into account the efforts to reduce the disparity, the JSC refrained from declaring the legislative action unconstitutional.

This reasoning was employed until the 2012 decision on the 2010 elections.[50]

It is worth noting that in the 2009 *Yamaguchi v Tokyo Metropolitan Election Commission* case, which is the one immediately precedent to the 2012 decision, a majority of nine justices (five dissenting) openly admonished the legislature for its failures and, by their numbers, increasingly threatened to return to *Kurokawa* with the possibility of a more drastic declaration.

In 2012, the 2010 elections were ruled in an unconstitutional state, because of a disparity of 1:5.00, for the first time since the 1996 ruling on the 1992 elections. Again, the Diet was urged to intervene.

The same reasoning in the 2014 decision was applied to the 2013 elections.[51] Again the JSC ruled them in an unconstitutional state (the disparity was 1:4.77); and again the Diet was urged to intervene. It is important to stress that the Okayama Branch of the Hiroshima High Court decision in November 2013 vacated the elections.

Again, in September 2017 upon the 2016 elections,[52] the JSC ruled the disparity of 1:3.08 not 'in a state of extreme inequality that would generate issues of unconstitutionality'. Furthermore, the fact that in 2015 the Diet addressed the disparity issue, by reapportionment, and promised to intervene further before the next elections (which it did in 2018) led the JSC to rule the elections in a state of unconstitutionality.

The JSC ruled in 2020 upon the 2019 elections,[53] where the disparity, despite the 2018 increase of seats, was sill as high as 1:2.985. In a 10 to three decision, the JSC considered that the value of each vote was not in a state of extreme inequality, recognising efforts made by the Diet to redress the disparity.[54]

The 2022 elections have been immediately under scrutiny by high courts, because of the disparity of 1:3.03.[55] 16 lawsuits have been filled before 14 high courts and branches and they all have been adjudicated. The Sendai High Court was the only court ruling the election unconstitutional, whilst eight high courts (including the Miyazaki branch of Fukuoka, Hiroshima, Kanazawa branch of

[49] *Yamaguchi v Tokyo Prefecture Election Commission:* Supreme Court, grand bench, 2 September 1998, 52 *Minshū* 1373.

[50] Supreme Court, grand bench, 17 October 2012, 66 *Minshū* 10.

[51] Supreme Court, grand bench, 26 November 2014, 68 *Minshū* 9.

[52] Supreme Court, grand bench, 27 September 2017, 71 *Minshū* 7.

[53] Supreme Court, grand bench, 18 November 2020, 74 *Minshū* 8.

[54] Out of the 16 conflicting rulings from lower courts, 14 high courts had declared the vote weight disparity violated the Constitution's requirement for fair elections, whilst the remaining two that the election was held 'in a state of unconstitutionality.'

[55] The larger disparity was in the Kanagawa Prefecture, while the least in Fukui.

Nagoya, Ōsaka, Sapporo, Tōkyō) ruled the vote disparity, and thus the elections, in a state of unconstitutionality, though refusing to be nullifying the elections. The remaining seven (including Nagoya, the Naha branch of Fukuoka, the Matsue branch of Hiroshima, Takamatsu, and Tōkyō) ruled the elections constitutional. In the rulings declaring the poll unconstitutional or in a state of unconstitutionality, the courts considered problematic the Diet's lack of effort to redress the imbalance. The Sendai Court, in particular, stressed that the current situation where the population in constituencies with three-fold-plus vote-value disparity account for over 20 per cent of Japan's total population represents serious inequality and a serious breach of the equality of the vote as a key principle in any parliamentary democracy.

IV. CONCLUSION

This last section aims at drawing some conclusions on the JSC's attitude, on its interpretation of the one man, one vote principle, and on its relationship with the Diet, together with possible solutions.

The JSC's approach has not been a monolith. Rather, it is possible to identify four main periods, corresponding to a more or less stringent interpretation of the value of the disparity and of margin of discretion of the Diet, which are the first and the second steps in the JSC's reasoning outlined in the premise. The third step, concerning the nullification of the elections, will be examined separately.

The first period is between 1964 (*Koshiyama I*) and 1976 (*Kurokawa*). In this decade, the JSC circumvented the issue and referred to the Diet.

The second is between 1976 (*Kurokawa*) and 1985 (*Kanao*). In this decade, the JSC ruled two apportionments of the Lowe House unconstitutional. A different stance with respect to the Upper House, whose apportionment is ruled constitutional.

The third is between 1985 (*Kanao*) and 2011. In these 25 years, with the exception of the 1996 decision on the Upper House apportionment (1992 elections) and the 1993 decision on the Lower House (1990 elections), all apportionments have been declared constitutional.

The fourth period starts with the 2011 decision on the 2009 Lower House elections. From that decision onwards, the JSC has ruled the majority of the elections for both Houses in a state of unconstitutionality. The apportionment, and the consequent disparity, was unconstitutional; nonetheless, since a reasonable time had not elapsed for the Diet to act, it was not unconstitutional. Then, once the Diet had intervened (2016), despite the contrasting rulings from lower courts, the JSC considered the Diet's discretion in the choice of the redressing methods to lead to a reasonable disparity of the vote. However, there are still too few JSC decisions since 2016 to identify a new period in the case law.

Two first conclusions may be drawn.

The first is that the JSC has become more stringent when interpreting the principle of the one man, one vote. With respect to the Upper House, deviations of 1:5.00 (2010 elections) and of 1:4.77 (2013 elections) were ruled in a state of unconstitutionality, whereas in the 1980s disparities up to 1:5.85 (1986 elections) were ruled constitutional. With respect to the Lower House, the same trend can be identified, except for the two decisions that declared the legislation unconstitutional, because of no rationale of the apportionment and the Diet did not redress (1976 *Kurokawa* and 1985 *Kanao*). In the 1980s, deviations of 1:3.94 (1980 elections) and of 1:3.18 (1990 elections) were ruled in a state of unconstitutionality. Nonetheless, until the 2005 elections, disparities up to 1:2.92 were declared constitutional. Starting from the 2009 elections (2011 decision), the JSC ruled a disparity of 1:2.30 and afterwards (2012 election-2013 decision) of 1:2.43 in a state of unconstitutionality.

However, the JSC always missed the chance to explain why a certain ratio was unconstitutional and why it was not. The JSC went even further, denying that it actually had a specific ratio in mind. Even when the JSC had declared a disparity as of extreme inequality, no further argument was provided in favour of such a conclusion.

The second conclusion is that the JSC seems to endorse the speciality of the Upper House and its traditional electoral system, which was prefecture-based (even though the 2015 mergers have slightly altered this). Indeed, the JSC apparently uses the same standard of constitutionality. Nonetheless, the JSC applies it more leniently partly because the Diet is allowed to consider the fact that Councillors are elected from local districts or prefectures and therefore, are de facto representatives of their prefectures. Thus, the current electoral system, which is mainly a prefecture-based district system (although the 2015 redistricting) is still reasonable.

The more stringent approach of the JSC had the Diet proceeding with a series of reapportionments, though unable to set a constitutionally acceptable disparity. The failure can be explained by affirming that the Diet had intervened through reapportioning simply to avoid the JSC delivering an unconstitutionality decision. Because the JSC never indicated a maximum acceptable ratio, the Diet had no incentive to act and to jeopardise the seats of its members. The Diet has opted for the 'cheapest' solution, to add and to subtract seats to and from the underrepresented/overrepresented districts. However, this option may not always be viable. This makes the point when one ascertains that the Diet almost never went for a proper redistricting, which is certainly a much more delicate operation from a political standpoint. The exception has been the creation of single-member districts for Lower House elections, which for a while transformed the issue from the number of seats per district to the population of the district, ie, districting rather than apportionment. However, there are limits to how far the issue can be resolved with this method alone. Indeed, once done, in the following decades reapportionment continued to be the only adopted solution. Rural votes are more in favour of the LDP, because their voters are older and more conservative. Nevertheless, because the population continuously concentrates in big cities, the increase of the vote disparity will entail further district mergers. Hence, without a more systematic intervention from the part of the Diet, the situation will hardly improve by itself. Quite the reverse.

Therefore, the question is whether the JSC should have been more persuasive with its reasoning, in particular, in clearly setting a maximum acceptable disparity.

Indeed, the case law on electoral legislation, even though showing lately a more active and engaged JSC, confirms the usual pattern. Not necessarily in terms of passivism or deference, but of reasoning.

It emerges clearly from the overall JSC case law the perception that the role of the Court has a limited scope, in the sense that it always upholds the margin of discretion of the Diet. Usually the JSC proceeds in this direction because the starting point of its reasoning is that all rights and freedoms are inherently limited in the name of public welfare. Therefore, such an interpretation of its role in not limited to issues, having a high political connotation. Even though in the malapportionment case law the JSC does not employ this reasoning, it fails to be persuasive, because it does not set clear boundaries to the discretion of the Diet. This is on the line of its usual attitude; nonetheless, it seems that the JSC could abide by its attitude, but provide at the same time a more solid reasoning on the principle of the equality of the vote. To set a maximum constitutionally acceptable disparity would not necessarily entail a severe curtailment of the margin of discretion of the Diet. Even when the Diet tried to identify the maximum disparity for both Houses based on the decisions on the 1996 combined elections, the JSC intervened deeming the interpretation as arbitrary. It is clear evidence of the confusion on the issue. On the one hand, the government will tend to interpret the JSC's rulings at its own advantage and thus proceed with a minimum reapportionment (and not redistricting) each time. On the other hand, the JSC is continually declaring the elections in a state of unconstitutionality, thus allowing an illegitimate Diet not only to function, but also to proceed with the next reapportionment.

The situation as it is nowadays seems to be in a 'cul de sac'. The JSC fails to enforce on the Diet an interpretation of the equality of the vote, which not always clearly emerges from its decisions. This leads to the third step of the reasoning, which is the petition to nullify the elections.

What is the point in ruling elections unconstitutional (or in a state of unconstitutionality) and not nullifying them? Circumstance technique or nullify? This is the great dilemma of the JSC. Can the JSC be deemed as exceptionally conservative for not nullifying the elections? Again, it is a matter of relationship between the two branches of government as well as of the JSC interpreting its own role.

The nullification of the elections is for the JSC very problematic and seems to cause more problems rather than solving them.

The first is that nullification would undermine the legitimacy of all the decisions taken by the newly elected Diet, starting from the appointment of the PM. Therefore, it seems the only solution is to go for new elections. This solution raises many concerns, because of the significant gap existing between the election year and the year the decision is delivered. The second is related to who should pass the electoral law of the new elections. Nullifications is the last step of a declaration of unconstitutionality. Therefore, a new legislation would be needed. The new elections must be held within 40 days.[56] Furthermore, because of the unconstitutionality declaration, the Diet must amend the electoral law. Under Article 47, the Diet is the constitutional body entrusted with districting and apportionment. However, within such a short time frame this option is unrealistic. Therefore, a further question arises: who provides the new legislation? The JSC could preserve some provisions of the legislation, such as the number of seats (Article 43) and go for a single national district election and preserving the calculation method for PR. Would this result in the JSC legislating? It is a matter of interpretation. It could be said that there is no Article 41 violation, because that would not be a law but a one-time solution to a persistent unconstitutional apportionment. Besides, it is convenient also to be reminded of Article 98, enshrining the supremacy of the Constitution.

Despite all the aforementioned concerns, none could affirm that not nullifying the elections solves the problem.

The JSC could strike a balance between the discretion of the Diet and a stronger enforcement of its interpretation of the one man, one vote principle issuing a constitutional warning and go for a prospective nullification of the elections, as some dissenting opinions have suggested. It seems more and more possible that the JSC will become more stringent, not just by lowering the permissible disparity, but maybe resorting to the constitutional warning. However, the warning option too is not concern-free, because it would entail an unlawful Diet to provide the new electoral legislation. The decisions of the last decade have inaugurated a new trend. Furthermore, it emerges from each decision the growing irritation toward the Diet's failure to properly redress the disparity. Besides the phrasing of the judgments, the recent confrontation between the JSC and the LDP on that score clearly reveal this irritation.

Surely, the fact that the JSC has no power of injunction nor mandamus does not help the enforcement. That would require a constitutional amendment.

Indeed, even though the JSC usually refers to the Diet discretion and upholds any Diet intervention regardless of the effective redressing of malapportionment,

[56] Which become 22 for the Upper House and 25 for the Lower House because of Art 34(1). The reason is that under Art 34(6), the public announcement of an election must be made 18 days before an election for Councillors and 15 days before an election for Representatives.

the LDP government has been very critical of the last set of decisions. The LDP blames the JSC for having created confusion among politicians and public opinion in terms of the role that the Diet has to perform within the Japanese constitutional architecture. To declare the elections in a state of unconstitutionality, though not unconstitutional, conveys all the same the idea that the Diet's reapportionment was beyond the constitutionally acceptable disparity. Therefore, this would endanger and infringe the role of supreme body, which the Constitution bestows to the Diet. The JSC has on the contrary stressed the importance of loyal cooperation with the Diet, to finally redress the disparity and to avoid a future possible declaration of unconstitutionality (Justice Chiba concurring in the 2015 decision).

What the JSC does next will depend on whether the abiding by the margin of discretion of the Diet will prevail or not.

To conclude, it is convenient to address a solution that in recent years has periodically popped up within the political debate: the establishment of a constitutional court. It is particularly curious that the proposal comes from different sides and with different purposes. The LDP advocates the Constitutional Court as a sort of threat towards the JSC, in order to temper the recent trend. Opposite, constitutional scholars, who see in the Constitutional Court the benefits deriving from an abstract review of the electoral legislation. This could put the Court more at ease because the declaration of unconstitutionality would be completely disconnected to the electoral result and would not directly undermine the legitimacy of the Diet. Therefore, this proposal could bring the Court to better enforce its interpretation of the principle of the equality of the vote.

A quite similar solution would be to modify the JSC's interpretation of Article 81 and thus turn the JSC into a Constitutional Court. The Constitution does not deny the possibility for the JSC to rule on abstract controversies. It has been the JSC that in *Suzuki v Japan*[57] stated that it was a Court of last resort requiring a concrete legal dispute, thus refusing to be a Constitutional Court. It remains doubtful whether the JSC would ever overrule or distinguish *Suzuki*.

Although the proposal is quite appealing from some respects, it is not feasible in the short period. A constitutional amendment is per se very difficult within the Japanese context. Despite the LDP enjoying the majority in both Houses in recent years, it has pulled back from introducing the Bill in the Diet. Furthermore, even if the amendment procedure starts, it is highly probable that the LDP would focus on other sections (Article 9, the Emperor, and the Preamble), and thus ignoring the JSC.

However, what emerges clearly from the analysis is that there is no concern-free decision possible for the JSC on malapportionment.

[57] *Suzuki v Japan:* Supreme Court, grand bench, 8 October 1952, 6 *Minshū* 783. The case challenged the constitutionality of the National Police Reserve.

17

Judicial Review and Elections in Australia

JULIAN R MURPHY AND ERIKA ARBAN

NOWHERE IS THE Australian tension between legal and political constitutionalism more evident than in the judicial review cases concerning electoral law. Here, courts have grappled with the countervailing imperatives to protect individual political participation and to respect political decisions about the management of elections. For over a century, the first of these imperatives typically gave way to the second, with the courts rejecting countless challenges to electoral laws and emphasising the broad powers of Parliament to regulate the manner of elections. However, in the last two decades, the High Court of Australia has indicated an increasing willingness to intervene in electoral matters and to invalidate statutes regulating elections. This chapter will examine the significance of these recent developments against the historical background, while also placing the Australian case law within a global context.

The chapter will proceed in five parts. First, a brief summary of the constitutional text and structure and the historical (non-interventionist) approach taken by the Australian judiciary to electoral law. Second, an account of the recent case law and the discovery of what has been called an 'implied right to vote' in the Australian Constitution. Third, an explanation of the closely related line of cases on the validity of campaign finance laws. The fourth part of the chapter will be devoted to teasing out the domestic and comparative implications of this historical trajectory and positioning the Australian approach in global perspective. It will be suggested that the recent turn towards a more interventionist approach is illustrative of the Australian High Court's oscillation between legal and political theories of constitutionalism, which is partly the consequence of Australia's genealogical indebtedness to the US and the UK respectively. However, it will be suggested that the recent move to more active judicial involvement in electoral law is also explicable in light of a growing global appreciation of threats to the integrity of democratic institutions.

Before proceeding, it should be noted that this chapter does not discuss an important, but historically and conceptually distinct, aspect of the judiciary's involvement in electoral law. That distinct concept is the High Court's role as the 'Court of Disputed Returns', which is the body which determines challenges to federal candidate eligibility or electoral results either at the petition of an interested party or on a reference from Parliament.[1] Perhaps because this jurisdiction is statutory,[2] rather than constitutional, it is largely uncontroversial and widely accepted to be the most desirable way for the relevant issues to be resolved. Accordingly, it does not present the questions of constitutional principle raised by judicial review of electoral laws, which is thus the sole focus of this chapter.

I. THE FIRST CENTURY – A MODEST APPROACH

In order to understand the trajectory of judicial review of electoral laws in Australia, it is necessary first to outline the basics of constitutional text and structure that bear upon Parliament's power to make laws governing elections and the judiciary's power to review those laws.

A. Constitutional History, Influences, Text and Structure

Australia became a nation on 1 January 1901, with the coming together of the former colonies into a single federation known as the Commonwealth of Australia. The founding document was, and remains largely unaltered, the Constitution. There is considerable debate in Australia as to just how much that constitutional moment was the product of popular will and how much it was the product of an elite push for more localised power. Certainly, contemporaneous sources document a significant 'popular movement' for federation under a national Constitution.[3] This movement was comprised most relevantly of debate in popular media, drafting and revision of the constitutional document at a series of meetings of popularly elected delegates and, ultimately, popular votes in each of the colonies. Although far from truly representative, the drafting process incorporated meaningful popular elements.[4]

As is well known, the Australian Constitution was deeply influenced by the written constitution of the US and the unwritten constitutional history of the UK. Most relevantly for present purposes, the Australian Constitution adopts

[1] See, generally, K Walker, 'Disputed Returns and Parliamentary Qualifications: Is the High Court's Jurisdiction Constitutional?' (1997) 20 *University of New South Wales Law Journal* 257.

[2] See Electoral Act 1918 (Cth).

[3] WH Moore, *The Constitution of the Commonwealth of Australia*, 2nd edn (Melbourne, Maxwell, 1910) 44.

[4] H Irving, 'The People and Their Conventions' in Michael Coper and George Williams (eds), *Power, Parliament and the People* (Sydney, Federation Press, 1997) 113, 122.

the US model of a strict separation of powers but adopts the Westminster Parliament and the UK notion, albeit tempered, of parliamentary sovereignty. The 'popular movement' for federation found at least three significant expressions in the text.[5] First, the preamble describes the agreement of 'the people' as forming the basis for the Constitution.[6] Second, in language that has had a significant impact on the recent development of constitutional doctrine, both houses of Parliament are required to be 'directly chosen by the people'.[7] Third, the all-important sovereign power of constitutional amendment was secured exclusively for the people.[8] These elements of the text, combined with the drafting history described earlier, allowed contemporaries to claim the Constitution to be the 'expression of the free will of the people'.[9]

B. The Early Case Law (1901 to 1975)

The first three quarters of a century of Australian case law on the franchise is largely in the one direction, with the High Court tending to reject challenges to electoral laws and reiterate the wide (almost unlimited) power of Parliament to legislate for the governance of elections. A few examples will be sufficient to illustrate this trend.

[5] Adopting a slightly different analysis to ours, but to similar effect, Elisa Arcioni writes that 'The text recognises two main types of constitutive power – the historical involvement of "the people" in the making of the *Constitution*, and the ongoing powers of "the people" in the structures of representative government under the *Constitution*.' E Arcioni, 'The Core of the Australian Constitutional People – "The People" as "The Electors"' (2016) 39 *University of New South Wales Law Journal* 421, 424. Note that Arcioni has also drawn attention to the mention of 'the people' in s 53: E Arcioni, 'Section 53 of the Constitution: An Overlooked Reference to the Constitutional People' (2013) 87 *Australian Law Journal* 784. Moore has drawn attention to s 3: WH Moore, *The Constitution of the Commonwealth of Australia*, 2nd edn (Melbourne, Maxwell, 1910) 67 ('the emphasis of "the people", both in the preamble and sec iii, indicates the democratic origin of the Commonwealth and forever shadows the nature of its Constitution').

[6] Commonwealth of Australia Constitution Act 1900 (UK) preamble, see also s 3 of the Constitution. Note, more precisely, the preamble refers to 'the people *of the States*' (emphasis added), suggesting a notion of popular sovereignty laid over by the federal structure.

[7] Constitution, ss 7, 24. As to the mode of choice (elections) and the convergence of 'the people' and 'the electors' see *Rowe v Electoral Commissioner* (2010) 243 CLR 1, 19 [21] (French CJ).

[8] Constitution, s 128. For contemporary claims that the people's power of constitutional amendment afforded them a measure of sovereignty see RR Garran, *The Coming Commonwealth. An Australian Handbook of Federal Government* (Sydney, Angus & Robertson, 1897) 182 ('amendment of the Federal Constitution is the highest expression of the will of the sovereign people of the Nation and the sovereign peoples of the States'). See also A Twomey, 'Independence' in C Saunders and A Stone (eds), *The Oxford Handbook of the Australian Constitution* (Oxford, Oxford University Press, 2018) 96, 97 ('it is often claimed that sovereignty lies in the hands of those who make or control the amendment of the Constitution').

[9] WH Moore, *The Constitution of the Commonwealth of Australia* (London, John Murray, 1902) 61. See also J Quick and RR Garran, *The Annotated Constitution of the Australian Commonwealth* (first published 1901, Sydney, LexisNexis Butterworths, 2002) 160 (describing the Constitution as 'based upon the will of the people'); *Official Report of the National Australasian Convention Debates* (Sydney, 6 March 1891) 107 (Andrew Thynne).

In 1912 in *Smith v Oldham*,[10] the High Court was asked to strike down a law that imposed certain advertising and authorisation requirements on campaign materials. The High Court interpreted Parliament's power to regulate elections broadly, writing 'Perhaps, "regulation of elections" is an inexact term. What is really meant is regulation of the conduct of persons with regard to elections.'[11] Parliament's power to regulate elections, it was said, is a 'plenary power … incapable of restraint' other than by reference to the limits of its subject matter, ie, elections.[12] So interpreted, the High Court held that the laws under consideration were well within Parliament's constitutional sphere of competence and noted that the laws were 'to secure freedom of choice to electors'.[13]

In 1926 in *Judd v McKeon*,[14] the High Court dismissed a challenge to compulsory voting or, more precisely, held that a federal law criminalising failure to vote was within Parliament's power to make laws regulating elections. The plurality in that case emphasised again the 'plenary and unrestricted' power of Parliament to regulate elections, limited only by the requirements of the federal system that there be uniformity between the states.[15]

This line of cases emphasising the wide power of Parliament to regulate elections ran for three quarters of a century, with the High Court in 1972 in *Fabre v Ley* again emphasising that 'the legislative power of the Parliament (to enact an electoral law for the election of Parliament) is not subject to any restriction other than that which flows from s 41 of the Constitution'.[16]

C. The Seeds of Change (1975 to 2004)

The next chapter in the line of case law begins most decisively in 1975 in the case of Attorney-General (Cth); Ex rel. *McKinlay v Commonwealth*.[17] That case concerned a challenge to redistricting provisions for the lower house of federal Parliament. The challenge was made on the basis that the districts did not contain an equal number of people (or, alternatively, electors) and thus could not be described as creating a system of representation 'chosen by the people of the Commonwealth' in section 24 of the Constitution. The challenge failed, with the Court holding that the concept of choice in section 24 of the Constitution did not contain an implied requirement of equality between electoral divisions. Despite that holding, the various judgments in the case contained the beginnings of an identification of an outer limit to Parliament's

[10] *Smith v Oldham* (1912) 15 CLR 355.
[11] ibid, 358 (Griffith CJ).
[12] ibid, 363 (Isaacs J).
[13] ibid, 358 (Griffith CJ).
[14] *Judd v McKeon* (1926) 38 CLR 380.
[15] *Smith v Oldham* (n 10) 383 (Knox CJ, Gavan Duffy and Starke JJ).
[16] *Fabre v Ley* (1972) 127 CLR 665, 669.
[17] Attorney-General (Cth); Ex rel. *McKinlay v Commonwealth* (1975) 135 CLR 1.

power to regulate elections. McTiernan and Jacobs JJ, for example, held that the franchise established by law must be 'wide enough to satisfy the description "popular"'.[18] In the same breath, however, Barwick CJ asserted that the popular choice mandated by the Constitution 'is not an indirect reference to *any particular theory* of government'.[19]

In 1995 in *McGinty v Western Australia*,[20] the High Court was asked to overrule *McKinlay* and hold that section 24 of the Constitution impliedly required equality of numbers in electoral divisions for the lower house. It is important to appreciate that, in the 20 years between *McKinlay* and *McGinty*, the High Court had for the first time recognised an implied freedom of political communication in the Constitution, based in part on the representative nature of the franchise enshrined in the founding document.[21] This featured prominently in the request to revisit the issue of equality of voting power in *McGinty* just a few years later (as will be explained in section III, the implied freedom of political communication also proved significant for the validity of campaign finance laws). However, that request was ultimately rebuffed. McHugh J's remarks perhaps most pithily express the stark conclusion:

> Equality of voting power is not a fundamental feature of the Constitution. On the contrary, inequality of individual voting power is one of its striking features. … Under the Constitution, therefore, individual Australians do not have an equal share in the sovereignty of Australia.[22]

There were, however, passages in *McGinty* that provided the seeds of things to come. Dawson J recognised that the Constitution provided '*an irreducible minimum requirement* that people be "governed by representatives elected in free elections by those eligible to vote"'[23] but that 'the *form* of representative government which we are to have is left to Parliament'.[24] Here one sees the distinction between the *fact* and *form* of representative government, the former being understood as a judicially-enforceable constitutional guarantee (although not an individual right) and the latter being purely a matter for Parliament – although not without a telling suggestion that the 'fact' of representative government itself might be 'a category of indeterminate reference'.[25]

A key theme running through the case law in this area is an acknowledgement of the 'hundreds of electoral systems in existence today by which a form

[18] ibid, 35 (McTiernan and Jacobs JJ).
[19] ibid, 21 (Barwick CJ, emphasis added).
[20] McGinty v Western Australia (1995) 186 CLR 140.
[21] See Nationwide News Pty Ltd v Wills (1992) 177 CLR 1; Australian Capital Television Pty Ltd and New South Wales v The Commonwealth (1992) 177 CLR 106; Theophanous v Herald & Weekly Times Ltd (1994) 182 CLR 104.
[22] McGinty v Western Australia (n 20) 236 (McHugh J).
[23] ibid, 182 (Dawson J, emphasis added).
[24] ibid, 183 (Dawson J, emphasis added).
[25] ibid, 269 (Gummow J).

of representative government might be achieved',[26] and the unwillingness of the judiciary to be entangled in choosing between them. Dawson J called the choices between such models 'questions of a political nature about which opinions may vary considerably'.[27] Another, related, theme was the idea that constitutionalising a particular mode of representative government might stifle positive change over time, or the 'evolutionary nature of representative government'.[28] To this end, Dawson J thought it 'unwise to freeze into a constitutional requirement a particular aspect of an electoral system'.[29] Similarly, Gummow J observed that 'representative government is a dynamic rather than a static institution'[30] and noted the advantages of a limited constitutional constraints to 'allow[] for development of the institution of government by changes which may not have been foreseen a century ago'.[31]

Some of these same themes were again reiterated in 2004 in *Mulholland v Australian Electoral Commission*.[32] That case concerned a challenge to party registration requirements, and particularly a requirement (with limited exceptions) that a party seeking to register for a federal election have at least 500 members. The Court upheld the law, again emphasising the 'ample scope'[33] and 'wide range'[34] of Parliament's 'very broad power'[35] to regulate elections. In some of the judgments, however, one also sees the beginning of the Court's emphasis on the obligation on Parliament to maintain 'the constitutional idea of representative democracy'.[36] As will now be explained, this concept becomes significantly more robust in the case law of the twenty-first century.

II. THE TWENTY-FIRST CENTURY – A IMPLIED RIGHT TO VOTE?

The twenty-first century in Australia has witnessed significant developments in the judicial review of electoral laws, with the first two major[37] successful challenges to electoral laws in the cases of *Roach v Electoral Commissioner*[38] and *Rowe v Electoral Commissioner*.[39] While the force of these cases has been somewhat

[26] ibid, 183 (Dawson J).
[27] ibid, 182 (Dawson J).
[28] ibid, 279 (Gummow J).
[29] ibid, 186 (Dawson J).
[30] ibid, 280 (Gummow J).
[31] ibid, 280 (Gummow J).
[32] Mulholland v Australian Electoral Commission (2004) 220 CLR 181.
[33] ibid, 260 (Kirby J).
[34] ibid, 195 (Gleeson CJ).
[35] ibid, 296 (Callinan J).
[36] ibid, 251 (Kirby J). See also *McGinty v Western Australia* (n 20) 220 (Gaudron J); *Rowe v Electoral Commissioner* (n 7) 39 [78] (French CJ).
[37] Note that *McKinlay* also involved a successful challenge to provisions of the Representation Act 1905–1975 (Cth) regarding proportional representation.
[38] Roach v Electoral Commissioner (2007) 233 CLR 162.
[39] Rowe v Electoral Commissioner (n 7).

tempered by the later judgment in *Murphy v Electoral Commissioner*,[40] they have not been overruled and remain important landmarks in the field of judicial review of electoral law. Each of these three cases will be discussed in turn.

In 2007 in *Roach*, the High Court squarely considered the extent to which Parliament could make laws limiting the franchise in respect of criminal prisoners. The Court considered two laws. The first, enacted in 2004, limited the right to vote to prisoners serving sentences of less than three years. The second, enacted in 2006, prohibited *all* prisoners from voting. The High Court ultimately held that the former law was valid but the latter invalid. In doing so, the Court recognised 'a constitutional protection of the right to vote'.[41] As the compromise result in *Roach* makes clear, this constitutional protection was not absolute – certain people could be excluded from the franchise (such as prisoners serving sentences of three years or more). The criterion of validity was identified by Gleeson CJ to be that 'the definition of the excluded class or group would need to have a rational connection with the identification of community membership or with the capacity to exercise free choice'.[42] Similarly, Gummow, Kirby and Crennan JJ explained that a class of persons could be excluded from the franchise if that exclusion was 'reasonably appropriate and adapted to serve an end which is consistent or compatible with the maintenance of the constitutionally prescribed system of representative government'.[43]

In 2010 in *Rowe*, the Court was required to rule upon the validity of the statutory 'grace period' for voter enrolments after the announcement of a federal election. Historically, from 1983 to 2006, that grace period had been seven days but from 2006 became three days. A majority of the Court held the shorter grace period to be invalid. Central to the reasoning of key members of the Court was what might be called a one-way democratic rachet, with French CJ explaining 'The content of the constitutional concept of "chosen by the people" has evolved since 1901 … That content, being constitutional in character, although it may be subject to adjustment from time to time, *cannot now be diminished*.'[44]

The force of *Roach* and *Rowe* was tempered just a few years later, in 2016, with the High Court's judgment in *Murphy*. In that case, the plaintiffs brought a direct challenge to the seven-day grace period for voter enrolments after the announcement of an election. It was said that an exclusion period of that duration was invalid in light of the technological and administrative capacity of the government to take enrolments right up until the day of the poll. The High Court rejected that argument, and unanimously upheld the law imposing the seven-day grace period. In doing so, a number of justices cautioned against endorsing 'abstract' notions of representative government and giving them a

[40] Murphy v Electoral Commissioner (2016) 261 CLR 28.
[41] Roach v Electoral Commissioner (n 38) 174 (Gleeson CJ).
[42] ibid, 174 (Gleeson CJ).
[43] ibid, 199 (Gummow, Kirby and Crennan JJ).
[44] *Rowe v Electoral Commissioner* (n 7) 18 (French CJ, emphasis added).

hard constitutional edge.[45] While the result in *Murphy* might seem to reverse the trend in *Roach* and *Rowe*, it is important to recognise the more dramatic step the High Court was being asked to take in *Murphy*. While the former cases impugned amendments to electoral laws, *Murphy* involved a frontal attack to a law that had been in place for decades. Further, the timing of the attack in *Murphy* meant that if the High Court had ruled the law invalid there was no opportunity for Parliament to fix it ahead of the election.[46] These factors go some way to explaining the reluctance of the High Court in *Murphy* to strike down the law, which reluctance does not necessarily presage a rejection of *Roach* and *Rowe*. Indeed, neither of the former cases were expressly overruled.

III. CAMPAIGN FINANCE LAWS

Australian Parliaments – both state and federal – have long enacted laws regulating political donations and advertising. Historically, such laws were thought to fall within the competence of Parliament by reason of Parliament's general power to legislate for the regulation of the electoral process. However, the High Court's recognition in 1992 of a constitutionally implied freedom of political communication created a new forum for the judicial review of election laws, and particular laws relating to campaign finance.

The implied freedom of political communication was first recognised in *Australian Capital Television Pty Ltd v Commonwealth*.[47] In that case, the plaintiff challenged a federal law that banned the broadcast of political advertising or messaging during an election period, otherwise than by recognised political parties. The law's stated purpose was to minimise the costs of election campaigns and thus deter or otherwise protect against corruption in that process.[48] While the High Court recognised that purpose to be legitimate, the Court held that the law was invalid for disproportionality. In particular, the vice of the law was that it only selectively banned political messaging (ie, banning charities and lobbyists from broadcasting, but not political parties)[49] and, insofar as it permitted political messaging from recognised parties, it favoured incumbents.[50] Those features of the law, and others, were found by the Court to offend against a novel freedom of political communication that was implied from the Constitution, in particular from sections 7, 24 and 128 (those provisions require that the houses of Parliament be directly chosen by the people and

[45] *Murphy v Electoral Commissioner* (n 40) [177]–[179] (Keane J), [243] (Nettle J), [305] (Gordon J).

[46] See, generally, B Hord, 'Murphy v Electoral Commissioner: Between Severance and a Hard Place' (2017) 39 *Sydney Law Review* 395.

[47] Australian Capital Television Pty Ltd v Commonwealth (1992) 177 CLR 106. See also Nationwide News Pty Ltd v Wills (n 21).

[48] Australian Capital Television Pty Ltd v Commonwealth (1992) (n 47) 130–1 (Mason CJ).

[49] ibid, 145 (Mason CJ), 173 (Deane and Toohey JJ), 220 (Gaudron J).

[50] ibid, 131–2 (Mason CJ), 172 (Deane and Toohey JJ), 239 (McHugh J).

that constitutional amendments only be made with the approval of the people voting at a referendum).

It would be another two decades before the High Court again confronted the issue of political advertising and donations in *Unions NSW v New South Wales*.[51] In that case, trade unions challenged a state law that provided that only persons on the electoral roll could make political donations, the effect of which was to prohibit donations by unions, but also by corporations, associations and individuals who were not on the electoral roll. The High Court struck down the law on the basis that it infringed the implied freedom of political communication because its wide prohibition on political donations was 'inexplicable'[52] and thus not directed to the claimed anti-corruption purpose of the law. Also struck down was a provision that facilitated a cap on donations by aggregating donations between particular organisations, which aggregation provisions were found to be too selective to be proportionate.

A few years later, in *McCloy v New South Wales*,[53] a property developer challenged a different aspect of the same legislative scheme that had been challenged in *Unions NSW*. This time, the challenge was to the absolute prohibition on property developers making political donations. The Court held that the statutory prohibition was for the legitimate purpose of preventing, in the words of the statute, 'corruption and undue influence in government of the State'.[54] The Court further identified 'an ancillary purpose' which related to protecting against the *perception* of corruption and undue influence 'which may undermine public confidence in government and in the electoral system itself'.[55]

In two subsequent cases on political donations, the High Court has struck a compromise position of sorts, upholding some limits on political donations while striking down others.[56] What is worth noting in this historical trajectory is the parallel with the 'right to vote' cases. In both lines of cases, one sees almost a century of judicial non-intervention followed by a turn of the century enthusiasm for more aggressive judicial review of laws regulating elections, either to vindicate the implied right to vote or to vindicate the implied freedom of political communication. That trend turns, however, around 2010, after which time the High Court apparently became more deferential to legislative calculations about how best to protect the integrity of the democratic process. As will now be explained, at least some of those trends are explicable by reference to an initial adherence to a more US-style legal constitutionalism giving way to a more UK-style political constitutionalism.

[51] Unions NSW v New South Wales (2013) 252 CLR 530.
[52] ibid, [59] (French CJ, Hayne, Crennan, Kiefel and Bell JJ).
[53] McCloy v New South Wales (2015) 257 CLR 178.
[54] ibid, 178, [33] (French CJ, Kiefel, Bell and Keane JJ).
[55] ibid, 178, [34] (French CJ, Kiefel, Bell and Keane JJ).
[56] Spence v Queensland (2019) 268 CLR 355; Unions NSW v New South Wales (2019) 264 CLR 595.

IV. COMPARATIVE EXPLANATIONS

A. Historical Overview

As noted in section I above, the Australian Constitution enacted in 1901 drew inspiration from the US model of separated powers, but at the same time adopted a Westminster-style Parliament and a variation of the UK notion of parliamentary sovereignty, to adapt it to the federal nature of the newly formed Australian state. However, differently from the US experience (and perhaps similarly to Canada), the Australian Constitution was developed in cooperation with – rather than in opposition to – British methods of government, something that happened with the encouragement of the British government.[57] Furthermore, the Australian Constitution was not the product of a revolution or struggle against oppression, but was 'designed to give effect to an agreement for a federal union, under the Crown, of the peoples of formerly self-governing British colonies'.[58] Also, Australia followed the example of Canada in that the Australian Constitution was in fact an Act of the Imperial Parliament, albeit drafted mainly in Australia, and most of its framers 'regarded themselves as British.'[59] Finally, it is important to recall that there is no Bill of Rights in the Australian Constitution: basic human rights are largely left to be protected by the political process and the resulting Commonwealth and state laws. These observations are important since they help bring to light the close connection that existed – and to a certain extent still exists – between UK and Australian constitutional laws and practices. This close connection is one of reciprocal influence that, despite the differences between the two jurisdictions, has affected the electoral laws of each.

As the High Court explained in *Rowe* and then in *Murphy*, the electoral laws of the Australian colonies which were in place throughout the nineteenth century 'replicated important elements of the British system'[60] including its 'requirements for listing, enrolment and registration'.[61] At the same time, Australian colonies evolved faster towards democratisation than the UK, if we consider that '[u]niversal manhood suffrage was adopted in South Australia with the introduction of responsible government' followed by Victoria and New South Wales in 1857 and 1858, Queensland in 1885, Western Australia in 1893, and Tasmania in 1901.[62] Women acquired voting rights soon after federation, but they could already vote in South Australia and Western Australia.[63] The franchise is thus

[57] *Mulholland v Australian Electoral Commission* (n 32) [10] (Gleeson CJ), citing *McKinlay*.

[58] *Roach v Electoral Commissioner* (n 38) [1] (Gleeson CJ).

[59] Roach v Electoral Commissioner (n 38) [1] (Gleeson CJ).

[60] *Rowe v Electoral Commissioner* (n 7) [15] (French CJ).

[61] *Murphy v Electoral Commissioner* (n 40) [17] (French CJ and Bell J).

[62] *Rowe v Electoral Commissioner* (n 7) [14] (French CJ).

[63] ibid. It shall be noted, however, that while the Commonwealth Franchise Act 1902 provided for universal adult franchise, it excluded Indigenous people and Pacific Islanders, persons of unsound

a good example of the distance that Australians wanted to keep from Imperial laws: in fact, while admiring and respecting British institutions, the framers of the Australian Constitution departed from a British franchise based on property qualifications.[64] In fact, in the United Kingdom, 'at the beginning of the 20th century, it was possible to distinguish seven species of franchise, those identified as the property, freemen, university, occupation, household, lodger and service franchises'.[65]

With the inclusions of the election-related provisions in sections 7, 8, 9, 24, 30, 31 and 51(xxxvi), the Australian Constitution placed itself at the intersection of 'both past and future development of a democratic system of government representative of, and reflective of the wishes of, "the people"'.[66] In addition to a near-universal franchise, Australia adopted the secret ballot, something that influenced the enactment of the Ballot Act 1872 (UK), sections 4 and 20.[67] What is even more interesting is that, by the time of federation, the 'Australian ballot' as it was then known 'had been adopted in 40 of the then 45 States of the United States of America as a response to bribery and intimidation associated with *viva voce* polling methods'.[68] Finally, it should be noted that, unlike most countries, Australia has a system of compulsory voting, albeit this did not exist at federation.[69]

B. Comparative Overview: The High Court and Foreign Influence in Electoral Law

While *Bush v Gore* is perhaps the most famous case decided by a court in the ambit of election law, the judicial resolution of disputed elections or of electoral laws has in recent years become a prominent part of many constitutional and supreme courts across the world.[70] The adjudication by courts of electoral law cases, however, is delicate, since it raises questions that have a direct impact on fundamental principles like democracy, the rule of law and the separation of powers.[71] For this reason, the US Supreme Court has for a long time refused to adjudicate political questions, including on matters of electoral law, before agreeing to hear *Bush v Gore*.[72] In the UK, on the other hand, election disputes

mind, those attainted of treason and persons under sentence or subject to be sentenced for any offence punishable by one or more years of imprisonment (ibid.).

[64] *Rowe v Electoral Commissioner* (n 7) [117] (Gummow and Bell JJ).

[65] ibid.

[66] ibid.

[67] ibid, [118] (Gummow and Bell JJ).

[68] ibid.

[69] *Mulholland v Australian Electoral Commission* (n 32) [9] (Gleeson CJ).

[70] M Pal, 'Canadian Election Administration on Trial: "Robocalls", *Opitz* and Disputed Elections in the Court' (2017) 28 *King's College Law Journal* 324.

[71] ibid 324–25.

[72] *Bush v Gore* 531 U.S. 98 (2000).

have a very long history, one that dates back to the Middle Ages.[73] In this part, we look at the specific influence of US and UK, and also Canadian, case law on the Australian judicial review of electoral laws. It will be shown that comparative exchange (not necessarily influence) is fairly recent, and most obvious in cases dealing with campaign finance and related issues of freedom of speech. In particular, it will be shown that Australian electoral law cases have been sites for the contest of UK and US ideas of whether Parliament or the courts are best placed to protect the integrity of the electoral process. The following discussion will be framed around comparative analysis of: the concept of 'corruption' in electoral law; the difference between the Australian freedom of political communication and the US right to free expression; the idea of a 'level playing field'; and the notion of a 'margin of appreciation' so as to defer to Parliament in the regulation of elections.

i. Comparative Concepts of 'Corruption'

Australia's approach to the judicial review of campaign finance laws is less aggressive (and thus more deferential to Parliament) than in the US. That can be seen from a joint reading of *McCloy*, cited above, and the decision of the US Supreme Court in *Citizens United*[74] in regard to the Court's view of corruption.[75] In *McCloy*, the Australian High Court upheld certain provisions of a New South Wales law imposing caps on political donations, prohibiting indirect campaign contributions and the making of political donations by property developers, so as to prevent undue influence and corruption in government.[76] In relation to political donations, the High Court distanced itself from the US Supreme Court approach in *Citizens United*, cited by the plaintiff.[77]

Citizens United was a 2010 landmark, yet controversial, case concerning the relationship between free speech and campaign finance. The US Supreme Court held that since 'speech is an essential mechanism of democracy … political speech must prevail against laws that would suppress it by design or inadvertence. Laws burdening such speech are subject to strict scrutiny …'.[78] In *McCloy*, the plaintiffs advanced a similar idea 'that gaining access through political donations to exert persuasion is not undue influence' echoing Kennedy J saying that '[i]ngratiation and access … are not corruption.'[79] However, the High Court

[73] C Morris, 'From "arms, malice, and menacing" to the courts: disputed elections and the reform of the election petitions system' (2012) 32 *Legal Studies* 254.
[74] Citizens United v Federal Election Commission (2010) 558 US 310.
[75] A Twomey, 'McCloy v New South Wales: Out with US corruption and in with German proportionality' on AUSPUBLAW (15 October 2015) auspublaw.org/blog/2015/10/mccloy-v-new-south-wales/.
[76] ibid.
[77] ibid.
[78] Citizens United v Federal Election Commission (n 74) 3.
[79] McCloy v New South Wales (n 53) [35] (French CJ, Kiefel, Bell and Keane JJ); Citizens United v Federal Election Commission (n 74) 45.

held that 'guaranteeing the ability of a few to make large political donations in order to secure access to those in power' would be antithetical to the principle of representative government.[80]

As to corruption, the US Supreme Court has recently taken a narrow view of it, limiting it to instances where 'payment is directly made in exchange for an official act'.[81] Conversely, the High Court in *McCloy* identified different degrees of corruption.[82] A first type is 'quid pro quo' corruption, whereby '[a] candidate for office may be tempted to bargain with a wealthy donor to exercise his or her power in office for the benefit of the donor in return for financial assistance with the election campaign.'[83] A second type of corruption is defined as 'clientelism' and concerns 'the danger that officeholders will decide issues not on the merits or the desires of their constituencies, but according to the wishes of those who have made large financial contributions valued by the officeholder'.[84] Clientelism 'arises from an office-holder's dependence on the financial support of a wealthy patron to a degree that is apt to compromise the expectation, fundamental to representative democracy, that public power will be exercised in the public interest.'[85] The High Court further observed that, whilst quid pro quo and clientelistic corruption 'threaten the quality and integrity of governmental decision-making' the power of money may also threaten the electoral process though a phenomenon known as 'warchest' corruption,[86] identified as a form of corruption in other common law jurisdictions.[87]

Rather than take the more narrow approach to corruption of *Citizens United*, the High Court in *McCloy* preferred the approach of the earlier US decision of *Austin*,[88] and observed that 'the prospect that the power of money concentrated in corporate hands could distort the electoral process, by dominating the flow of political communication' and that was enough 'to justify restrictions on political campaign contributions'.[89] (However, this First Amendment jurisprudence has by now been reversed, with the prevailing view that 'an attempt by the legislature to level the playing field to ensure that all voices may be heard is, prima facie, illegitimate'.[90]) The effect of the Australian High Court's broader conception of 'corruption' in the electoral process was to permit Parliament a greater degree of latitude in the regulation of political donations. This, then, is the

[80] *McCloy v New South Wales* (n 53) [28] (French CJ, Kiefel, Bell and Keane JJ); A Twomey, 'McCloy v New South Wales: Out with US corruption and in with German proportionality' on AUSPUBLAW (15 October 2015) auspublaw.org/blog/2015/10/mccloy-v-new-south-wales/.

[81] ibid.

[82] *McCloy v New South Wales* (n 53) [36] (French CJ, Kiefel, Bell and Keane JJ).

[83] ibid.

[84] ibid.

[85] ibid.

[86] ibid, [38] (French CJ, Kiefel, Bell and Keane JJ).

[87] ibid.

[88] Austin v Michigan Chamber of Commerce 494 US 652 at 660 (1990).

[89] *McCloy v New South Wales* (n 53) [41] (French CJ, Kiefel, Bell and Keane JJ).

[90] ibid.

first example of the way in which a comparative analysis reveals the Australian judiciary to be somewhat more deferential to Parliament in the regulation of elections (and particularly campaign finance).

ii. Political Communication, Political Donations and Individual Rights

Another feature of the Australian constitutional context that gives Parliament greater scope to regulate elections is the implied freedom of political communication, which is a less severe limit than the US First Amendment freedom of speech. The differences in those constitutional constraints can again be seen in *McCloy*. There, the plaintiff submitted that 'the ability to pay money to secure access to a politician is itself an aspect of the freedom [of political communication] and therefore the subject of constitutional protection'[91] and that 'the ability to make substantial donations is part of the freedom [of political communication]'.[92] The plaintiff thus essentially identified the right to make political donations as a personal right,[93] consistent with the US law on this issue, most prominently *Buckley v Valeo*.[94]

The majority of the High Court in *McCloy*, however, explained that this was a misconception of the freedom of political communication, which differs from the First Amendment right to free speech.[95] While the First Amendment 'operates in the field of political donations and is in the nature of both a right of political expression and a right of political association',[96] the case law of the High Court considers the freedom of political communication not as a 'personal right' but as a 'constitutional restriction on legislative power'.[97] More specifically, sections 7, 24, 64 and 128 of the Constitution[98] 'imply a limitation on legislative and executive power in order to ensure that the people of the Commonwealth may "exercise a free and informed choice as electors"'.[99] Therefore, any legislative regulation of the electoral process meant to protect the integrity of the process is prima facie legitimate.[100]

This fundamental difference between the US and the Australian approach to freedom of speech was also highlighted by the High Court in *Unions NSW*, where the plaintiff resorted to some decisions of the US Supreme Court in an

[91] ibid, [20] (French CJ, Kiefel, Bell and Keane JJ).
[92] ibid, [28] (French CJ, Kiefel, Bell and Keane JJ).
[93] ibid, [29] (French CJ, Kiefel, Bell and Keane JJ).
[94] *Buckley v Valeo* 424 US 1 at 21–22 (1976).
[95] *McCloy v New South Wales* (n 53) [29] (French CJ, Kiefel, Bell and Keane JJ).
[96] ibid.
[97] ibid, [30] (French CJ, Kiefel, Bell and Keane JJ) citing *Unions NSW* (n 56) and *ACTV*.
[98] Section 7 deals with the election of senators, s 24 with the election of members of the House of Representatives, s 64 prescribes the procedures for the appointment of ministers and s 128 sets out the procedure to amend the Constitution.
[99] *McCloy v New South Wales* (n 53) [42] (French CJ, Kiefel, Bell and Keane JJ).
[100] ibid.

attempt to support the view that political donations are expressions of freedom of speech.[101] Rejecting that argument, the High Court explained that the framers of the Australian Constitution deliberately refrained from transposing in whole or in part the spirit of the First Amendment.[102]

The different, more US-orientated road, that the Australian case law could have taken is illustrated in Nettle J's dissent in *McCloy*. His Honour cited *Buckley* and argued that 'a political contribution, as opposed to its amount, serves as a "general expression of support" for a candidate ... and as a "symbolic expression of support"'.[103] He thus concluded that:

> to deny one section of donors the ability to make political donations while leaving others free to make them is both a significant restriction of the freedom of the prohibited donors to communicate their ideas about politics or government through the non-verbal means of making political donations and, logically, also a significant relative enhancement of the ability of non-prohibited donors to have their ideas about politics and government prevail. It follows that, although the implied freedom of political communication is properly conceived of as a safeguard of systemic integrity as opposed to protecting individual liberties, the prohibited donor provisions necessarily lessen the free flow of information and ideas within the system and thereby burden the freedom of political communication.[104]

iii. The 'Level Playing Field'

In *McCloy*, the High Court further engaged with UK, US and Canadian case law and legislation in regard to the concept of a 'level playing field'. The High Court resorted to *R (Animal Defenders International) v Secretary of State for Culture, Media and Sport*[105] in the part where Lord Bingham of Cornhill contended that 'in a democracy it is highly desirable that the playing field of public debate be so far as practicable level' something that is achieved where, 'in public discussion, differing views are expressed, contradicted, answered and debated' but is not achieved 'if political parties can, in proportion to their resources, buy unlimited opportunities to advertise in the most effective media, so that elections become little more than an auction'.[106]

[101] *Unions NSW* (2013) (n 51) at [98] (Keane J). Citing *Buckley* (n 94), the plaintiff explained that political donations are an expression of freedom of speech in that 'from the perspective of the donor, a political donation "serves as a general expression of support for the candidate and his views", and from the point of view of the donee, the acceptance of a donation is an expression of the willingness of a candidate to be associated with, and to accept the support of, the donor.' See *Unions NSW* (2013) (n 51), [102] (Keane J).

[102] *Unions NSW* (2013) (n 51), [102] (Keane J).

[103] *McCloy v New South Wales* (n 53) [239] (Nettle J), citing *Buckley v Valeo* (n 94) at 21–22.

[104] ibid, [241].

[105] R (Animal Defenders International) v Secretary of State for Culture, Media and Sport [2008] AC 1312, 1346 [28].

[106] ibid, [39].

The High Court then cited the Supreme Court of Canada in *Harper*,[107] where the majority upheld legislative restrictions on electoral advertising, explaining that 'the restrictions were legitimately imposed in accordance with "the egalitarian model of elections adopted by Parliament as an essential component of our democratic society"'.[108] The premise for that model was 'equal opportunity for participation' with wealth being the main obstacle to equality of participation.[109] This, the Supreme Court of Canada said, can be achieved either by providing a voice to those who cannot be heard or by restricting the voice of those who dominate.[110] Those provisions seek to 'create a "level playing field for those who wish to engage in the electoral discourse"' while at the same time enable voters to be better informed, and no voice is 'overwhelmed by another'.[111]

This idea of fairness in establishing an expenditure scheme in relation to 'level playing field' and the *Harper* decision is also replicated in the second *Unions NSW* decision. The High Court contended that, in creating 'a level playing field for those who wish to engage in the electoral discourse', the Supreme Court of Canada intended to enable voters 'to be better informed' so that 'no one voice is overwhelmed by another'.[112] As noted above, *McCloy* accepted that 'legislative purpose of promoting such substantive fairness amongst those wishing to engage in the electoral discourse' as compatible with the system of representative and responsible government.[113] This means that within the Australian constitutional system it is possible to 'restrict certain voices – those that may otherwise dominate the debate – to make room for *all* to be heard and thereby ensure that electoral choice is as fully informed as possible'.[114]

The High Court thus seemed to adhere to the Canadian understanding of equality of opportunity, contending that the Australian Constitution guarantees this equality in that it allows people 'to participate in the exercise of political sovereignty' as a facet of representative democracy.[115] The High Court thus acknowledges the legitimacy of robust legislative action to protect this conception of political sovereignty, writing '[t]he risk to equal participation posed by the uncontrolled use of wealth may warrant legislative action to ensure, or even enhance, the practical enjoyment of popular sovereignty.'[116] The High Court in *McCloy* also referred to *ACTV*, where the law was struck down as it was 'inimical to *equal participation* by all the people in the political process'.[117]

[107] *Harper v Canada (AG)* [2004] 1 SCR 827.
[108] *McCloy v New South Wales* (n 53) [44] (French CJ, Kiefel, Bell and Keane JJ).
[109] ibid, [44] (French CJ, Kiefel, Bell and Keane JJ).
[110] ibid, [44] (French CJ, Kiefel, Bell and Keane JJ) citing *Harper* (n 107).
[111] ibid.
[112] *Unions NSW v NSW* (2019) (n 56) [82] (Gageler J) citing *Harper* (n 107) at 868 [62].
[113] *Unions NSW v NSW* (2019) (n 56) [83] (Gageler J).
[114] ibid, citing the Attorney-General of the Commonwealth.
[115] *McCloy v New South Wales* (n 53) [45] (French CJ, Kiefel, Bell and Keane JJ).
[116] ibid.
[117] ibid (emphasis added).

Finally, the idea of the equal playing field can be seen to be historically informed by British influence on Australian laws. In upholding the law in *McCloy*, the High Court noted that the risks that large political donations pose for representative government have been recognised since the beginning of federated Australia and that parts of the Commonwealth Electoral Act 1902 (Cth) contained limits on expenditures in electoral campaigns that were based on an Imperial law (the Corrupt and Illegal Practices Prevention Act 1883 (UK)).[118] For this reasons, caps on political donations have been adopted by many countries having a system of representative government.[119] Against that historical and comparative background, the High Court in *McCloy* held that the provision at issue in the case was 'compatible with the system of representative government' and indeed 'preserve[d] and enhance[d] it'.[120]

iv. The 'Margin of Appreciation'

Finally, it is important to note the High Court's engagement with the Canadian case of *Harper* and the concept of a 'margin of appreciation' in its unanimous decision in *Unions NSW* of 2019. In that case, the High Court held that a state law that sets a lower cap on the allowable electoral expenditure for third party campaigners compared with expenditure allowed for political parties and candidates was unconstitutional, as it impermissibly burdened the implied freedom of political communication. In *Unions NSW*, the plaintiff maintained that 'the decision concerning the level of capping of electoral expenditure is reserved to the Parliament and not subject to scrutiny by the Court' thus implying some 'deference to Parliament' by the Court or 'margin of appreciation'.[121] The High Court accepted that *Harper* may offer some support to this claim.[122] The legislation at issue in *Harper* – as the High Court recalls – contained very restrictive provisions imposing 'caps on spending by third parties on election advertising'.[123] Both the majority and the minority upheld the legitimacy of the purposes for these restrictions, that is, 'preventing the drowning out of voices and enhancing the electoral process' as also recalled in *McCloy*.[124] However, the majority seemed to favour '"a deferential approach to Parliament" in determining whether the third-party advertising expense limits were demonstrably justified' whilst also the minority accorded '"a healthy measure of deference" to Parliament'.[125]

[118] ibid, [46] (French CJ, Kiefel, Bell and Keane JJ).
[119] ibid.
[120] ibid, [47] (French CJ, Kiefel, Bell and Keane JJ).
[121] *Unions NSW v New South Wales* (2019) (n 56) [48] (Kiefel CJ, Bell and Keane JJ).
[122] ibid, [48] (Kiefel CJ, Bell and Keane JJ).
[123] ibid, [49] (Kiefel CJ, Bell and Keane JJ).
[124] ibid, [50] (Kiefel CJ, Bell and Keane JJ).
[125] ibid, [51] (Kiefel CJ, Bell and Keane JJ) citing *Harper* (n 107) at 879 [88] and 849 [39] respectively.

Ultimately, however, the High Court continued, nothing like this can be found in Australia in regard to the implied freedom of political communication; rather, it was observed that 'deference would not seem appropriate given this Court's role in relation to the freedom and a margin of appreciation therefore cannot apply'.[126]

V. CONCLUSION

The Australian story of judicial review of electoral laws is a story of changing jurisprudential currents and competing comparative influences. For many years, the dominant force was the non-interventionist approach whereby Parliament was largely left to determine how best to manage the electoral process. However, toward the end of the twentieth century the tide began to turn to a more judicially interventionist approach, which coincided with the High Court's novel identification of the implied freedom of political communication within the Constitution. Finally, in recent times, there has been an oscillation between deference to Parliament and strict standards of judicial review, which oscillation is likely a product of Australia's mixed heritage of legal and political constitutionalism.

With regards to the influence of UK, US or Canadian laws and jurisprudence in the High Court's decisions on electoral law, we have shown how this influence is very recent, and basically coincides with the recent trend by the Court to take more cases on electoral laws. At federation, most electoral laws were drafted on the model of British laws. While much of the subsequent (and recent) comparative citation has occurred in the context of the implied freedom of political communication and the First Amendment rights in the US, the High Court has generally departed from the breath of First Amendment jurisprudence, given the different scope of freedom of speech under US and Australian law. It also seems to depart from the concept of corruption embraced by US case law, to adopt the UK and Canadian approaches.

[126] *Unions NSW v New South Wales* (2019) (n 56) [51] (Kiefel CJ, Bell and Keane JJ) citing *Unions NSW* (2013) (n 51) and *McCloy* (n 53).

18

Electoral Law, Courts, and Constitutional Law: A Complex Relationship

EDMONDO MOSTACCI, GRAZIELLA ROMEO AND CRISTINA FASONE

I. INTRODUCTION

THE VARIOUS CHAPTERS of the book describe and discuss the difficulty of subjecting electoral legislation to judicial scrutiny. Over an extended period, the court systems in many countries have demonstrated a preference for avoiding scrutinising electoral legislation, citing the inherently political nature thereof. Many courts have opted for a particularly deferential degree of scrutiny when assessing rules related to the formation and appointment of representative institutions. Good examples of this approach are the US Supreme Court's review of gerrymandering and the work of the *Bundesverfassungsgericht* in the early decades of the Federal Republic of Germany.

Traditionally, courts have refrained from rigorously scrutinising electoral legislation because of the inherently political nature of such legislation and its fundamental elements. Indeed, no electoral system can be considered politically neutral because it significantly influences the structure of the political system, the functioning of the government system, and even the preferences of citizens.[1] Additionally, electoral legislation must concretely define the principles that govern the representative relationship between institutions and the political community.[2] The strong political connotation of electoral legislation is a major theme in the literature, readily accepted as an explanation for judicial deference by scholars. However, that electoral legislation is political does not, by itself, seem to be a sufficient reason to explain the reluctance of courts to confidently adjudicate this complex subject.

[1] See M Duverger, *Les partis politiques* (Paris, A. Colin, 1951), arguing that the first effect of an electoral reform is to change not only the distribution of seats, but first and foremost the distribution of votes.

[2] M Luciani, *Il voto e la democrazia* (Roma, Editori Riuniti, 1991) 38 ff.

In particular, the 'electoral legislation is political' explanation is inadequate for two reasons. First, the rationale should apply to other politically charged issues, but this has not been the case. Numerous examples can be given of courts demonstrating 'courage' in making decisions despite dealing with politically sensitive topics. Consider, just to give a few significant examples, the decisions made in several countries in the western legal tradition concerning the voluntary termination of pregnancy during the 1970s. This is a subject that, at least at that time, was highly controversial politically and that remains contentious even today, despite social opinion becoming more favourable toward it.[3] Other prime examples include court decisions regarding social rights, public finance, and resource distribution among social groups.[4] In the US, the intense confrontation between the federal judiciary and state policymakers in the 15 years following the historic *Brown* verdict is a notable example of courts fearlessly involving themselves in a highly charged political matter.[5] Over the past 50 years, courts have consistently tackled politically sensitive issues and, in many cases, made decisions that have propelled the evolution of the law and, by extension, the modernisation of their countries.[6] Consequently, why the political nature of electoral legislation in particular has paralysed courts when other politically fraught issues have been addressed head-on demands explanation.

Second, the political explanation is unsatisfying even if we focus only on electoral matters. The political connotation of these matters has certainly not diminished over the years, yet – as highlighted in the various chapters of this volume – judicial scrutiny has become progressively more rigorous. This phenomenon requires adequate reflection. Understanding the role played by the courts may help to reveal the fundamental reason for the judiciary's discomfort in reviewing electoral laws and, in general, in intervening to a significant degree in the process linking citizens' expression – their vote – to the designation of representatives, especially in the context of parliamentary assemblies.

The central theme that emerges in the contributions of this collection is that the fundamental approach underlying western constitutionalism focuses on the individual and their position vis-à-vis the power of the state. This is, of course, a generally highly fruitful perspective; however, where the framing of political, chiefly democratic, processes is involved, such an individualistic approach fails

[3] LH Tribe, *Abortion. The Clash of Absolutes* (New York, NY, London, Norton, 1992).

[4] M Langford, 'The Justiciability of Social Rights: From Practice to Theory' in M Langford (ed), *Social Rights Jurisprudence: Emerging Trends in International and Comparative Law* (Cambridge, Cambridge University Press, 2009) 3 ff. See also KG Young, 'A Typology of Economic and Social Rights Adjudication: Exploring the Catalytic Function of Judicial Review' (2010) 8 *International Journal of Constitutional Law* 385 ff.

[5] See R Kluger, *Simple Justice. The History of Brown v Board of Education and Black America's Struggle for Equality* (New York, NY, Knopf, 1976) and AM Bickel, 'The Original Understanding and the Segregation Decision' (1969) 55 *Harvard Law Review* 1.

[6] On the concept of modernisation, see the classic work by T Parsons, *Structure and Process in Modern Societies* (New York, NY, Free Press, 1960).

to account for the dynamic interplay of individuals in the political sphere – this shift in perspective from the individual subject demands appropriate analytic approaches.

Given this context, this concluding chapter proceeds as follows. First, some constitutional texts are considered to highlight the attention given to individual rights, as opposed to the regulation of the political process (II). Then, the genealogical roots of the individualistic approach are examined (III). Subsequently, political representation is analysed as a microcosm exemplifying the discourse of political individualism (IV). Subsequently, the methodological problem is considered, as are some of the limitations associated with the individualistic approach in constitutional reasoning (V); from a comparative law perspective, examples are examined (VI). Finally, some closing remarks conclude the chapter (VII).

II. THE NORMATIVE FORMANT

Generally speaking, constitutions are terse documents. Few texts contain precise electoral instructions, with notable examples being the Constitutions of Spain (Article 68), Portugal (Article 113) and Austria (Article 26), which specify the principle of proportional representation. Rarer still is a proportional formula accompanied by more precise instructions concerning the contours of the electoral system and related legislation (such as electoral propaganda or party financing). Where constitutional provisions address political parties at all, similarly succinct language appears, with the exception of the German *Grundgesetz*, Article 21, which imposes on parties the obligation to have 'an internal system that must correspond to the fundamental principles of democracy.'

The general brevity of constitutional provisions concerning electoral matters reflects a lack of principles expressly dedicated to the precise model of political democracy that the constitution intends to uphold. In the majority of European continental constitutions, it is possible to trace various elements that exemplify the influence of the Kelsenian model of democracy, from the centrality of Parliament to skepticism toward the instruments of direct democracy. From these elements emerges a clear preference for institutional systems that favour compromise between the various political forces[7] and that, therefore, inhibit polarisation. Furthermore, the purpose of preventing political polarisation limits the reliance on institutional arrangements aimed at emphasising the decision-making capacity of the electorate. Overall, priority is given to regulation of the branches of government rather than the relationships between institutions and the political community or among social groups and intermediate bodies.

[7] See H Kelsen, *Vom Wesen und Wert der Demokratie* (Tübingen, 1929) and *Das Problem des Parlamentarismus* (Wien-Leipzig, 1924).

By contrast, provisions concerning the right to vote can be found in most constitutional texts, with formulas that are quite similar. These provisions are intended to guarantee the free participation of citizens in the electoral process and to accord equal value to each person's vote.

The special attention paid to the right to vote is reflected in the constitutional rules governing the articulation of the national territory for electoral purposes. Some constitutions stipulate the need to establish constituencies, sometimes even identifying their territorial dimension, and prescribe binding rules on the allocation to each constituency or district of a number of seats strictly proportional to the population.

An analysis of the provisions relating to electoral matters reveals that as far as the right to vote is concerned, constitutional texts are characterised by a level of detail that is comparatively much higher than the detail pertaining to the model of democracy or the fundamental contours of the electoral system.

Most constitutional texts, however, do contain detailed provisions concerning the position of members of parliament: they are called upon to represent the nation and, in general, to exercise their functions without an imperative mandate. Even here, the constitutional texts are not especially elaborated.

III. THE INDIVIDUALISTIC GENEALOGY OF LIBERAL CONSTITUTIONALISM

Constitutional texts exhibit a focus on rights pertaining to the electoral process, starting with the right to vote, but tend to neglect the regulation of the political processes that involve interaction between citizens and institutions. This feature of constitutional texts is inextricably linked to the individualistic approach that has characterised liberal constitutionalism from its origins.

The complexity of this topic does not allow for a detailed examination here. Let it suffice, therefore, to briefly describe a few considerations relevant to the present discussion. First, it is necessary to emphasise the historical influence of contractualism on modern constitutionalism, especially in common law. The proponents of liberal political philosophy played a major role in shaping the basic structures of nineteenth century society, advocating for a society characterised by individualism, with property rights as a touchstone. According to Macpherson, freedom and property are vitally linked, with the individual free insofar as they are the owner of their own person and capacities; in turn, control over one's own person and capacities is the necessary precondition for not depending on the will of others.[8] To this extent, freedom is based on what one individually possesses, and freedom is conceptualised exclusively in terms of

[8] CB MacPherson, *The Political Theory of Possessive Individualism: Hobbes to Locke* (Oxford, Clarendon Press, 1962).

natural liberty[9] – the natural human condition. The law can only recognise and protect this condition by protecting property rights as the essential and actual foundation of freedom and by limiting political power, in the sense of protecting against tyranny.[10] This perspective is inscribed in the Constitutions drafted between the end of the eighteenth century and the nineteenth century – in the North American context, the US Constitution is the example par excellence. In continental Europe, the law had to reconcile natural liberty with the need to protect public order and the stability of the legal and economic order.[11] Here, freedom is conceived of as an individual matter, and its protection is consistently vested in the form of individual rights.

The relationship between individualism and constitutionalism became more complex in the twentieth century due to the influence of two doctrines that are different but have in common the attempt to recover the social dimension in the conception of human life.[12] On the one hand, Catholic personalism aimed to recover the founding role of intermediate bodies,[13] starting with the family. On the other hand, socialist thought focused on the role played by production relationships and the division of society into classes, placing the conflict between different social groups at the centre of their reflections on society and identifying law as having a role in promoting social transformations.[14] Thus, starting with the Weimar experience, families, schools, trade unions, and business companies suddenly became the topics of constitutional provisions. However, those provisions were primarily aimed at protecting the legal positions of the individual against the constraints they might suffer at the hands of these intermediate bodies.[15] The power of intermediaries was thus checked in order to secure the rights of the individual.

[9] A Baldassarre, 'Libertà, I) Problemi generali' in *Enciclopedia giuridica* (Roma, Treccani, 1991) vol. XIX, 9–12.

[10] This approach resonates in the argument developed by B Constant, 'De la liberté des Anciens comparée à celle des Modernes. Discours prononcé à l'Athénée royal de Paris en 1819' in *Ecrits politiques* (Paris, Gallimard, 1997) 593 ff.

[11] A Padoa-Schioppa, *A History of Law in Europe From the Early Middle Ages to the Twentieth Century* (Cambridge, Cambridge University Press, 2017) 495 ff. See also CNJ Roberts, 'From the State of Emergency to the Rule of Law: The Evolution of Repressive Legality in the Nineteenth Century British Empire' (2019) 20 *Chicago Journal of International Law* 1, 7 ff.

[12] G Burdeau, *Traité de science politique – 6. La démocratie gouvernante, son assise sociale et sa Philosophie*, (Paris, LGDJ, 1956) 355.

[13] D Dewee, 'The Political Theory of Personalism: Maritain and Mounier on Personhood and Citizenship' (2013) *International Journal of Philosophy and Theology* 1, 5.

[14] M Goldoni and MA Wilkinson, 'The Tradition of the Material Constitution in Western Marxism' in M Goldoni and MA Wilkinson (eds), *The Cambridge Handbook on the Material Constitution* (Cambridge, Cambridge University Press, 2023) 25 ff. See also N Sultany, 'Marx and Critical Constitutional Theory' in P O'Connell and U Özsu (eds), *Research Handbook on Law and Marxism* (Cheltenham, Elgar, 2021) 209 ff.

[15] With reference to Italian constitutional law, see A Barbera, 'Art. 2' in A Branca (ed), *Commentario della Costituzione* (Bologna, Roma, Zanichelli-Il Foro Italiano, 1975) 50, 65 ff.

At the same time, some constitutional theories emphasised the foundational character of social dynamics.[16] The right to liberty was meant to enable the individual/citizen's participation in the life of the political community and consequently to foster the integration of the individual into society.[17] Here again, the vestiges of the individualistic approach are evident even in the twentieth century, decisively influencing the categories of constitutional thought.

Finally, in the last 30 years, the individualistic approach has been strengthened by the emergence of so-called multilevel constitutionalism. In this context, the fundamental rights of the individual take on a structural character. The role of courts as decision-making fora to respond to individually motivated judicial actions places them at the centre of the system; by contrast, supranational courts are devoid of a rootedness in a given political community and exist outside the discursive relationship with a political community, which is a relationship that generally characterises national courts – this point is highlighted by Bray and Fasone in chapter nine on the Court of Justice of the European Union and the European Court of Human Rights.[18] Finally, the technical legitimation based on legal expertise of the supranational judge results in a substantial depoliticisation of judicial decision-making and the throttling of conflict in economic and social processes.[19] All this is reflected in the focus of judicial reasoning on individuals and their legal positions rather than the social and relational context in which legal positions need to be framed.

IV. POLITICAL REPRESENTATION: BETWEEN POSITION AND RELATIONSHIP

Constitutional law's emphasis on subjective legal positions and its tendency to neglect social dynamics and processes in electoral matters can be appreciated if we consider political representation, which plays a major role in the actual functioning of democratic institutions, and the right to vote.

Political representation is animated by the interaction between representative and represented, which is particularly difficult to cognise from a legal-constitutional viewpoint.[20] From a theoretical perspective, representation can be understood

[16] R Smend, *Verfassung und Verfassungsrecht* (München-Leipzig, Duncker & Humblot, 1928).

[17] With reference to German constitutionalism, see at least E-W Böckenförde, *Staat, Verfassung, Demokratie. Studien zur Verfassungstheorie und zum Verfassungsrecht* (Frankfurt a M., Suhrkamp, 1991) and P Häberle, *Die Wesensgehaltgarantie des Art. 19 Abs. 2 Grundgesetz* (Heidelberg, Müller, 1983).

[18] On the relationship between the political community and national institutions, including the constitutional judge, see J Habermas, *Faktizität und Geltung: Beiträge zur Diskurstheorie des Rechts und des demokratischen Rechtsstaats* (Frankfurt a M., Suhrkamp, 1992).

[19] M Luciani, 'Costituzionalismo irenico e costituzionalismo polemico' (2006) 51 *Giurisprudenza costituzionale* 1643, 1658 ff.

[20] H Pitkin, *The Concept of Representation* (Berkeley, University of California Press, 1972) 8 arguing from etymology that 're-presentation' refers to 'the making present in *some sense* of something which is nevertheless *not* present literally or in fact'.

to have two distinct and complementary meanings: 'representation as a legal situation' and 'representation as a legal relationship'. The first meaning describes the capacity of a certain subject to act in the name and on behalf of another subject – this is the meaning normally used in legal discourse but is unsatisfying from the perspective of the proper functioning of constitutional regimes centred on representative democracy. Here, representation must also be understood in terms of a 'representative relationship', in which the represented person has a real possibility of directing the work of the representative.[21] Despite the centrality of 'representation as a relationship' for the proper functioning of representative democracy, the legal system is only able to directly regulate 'representation as a situation': elections are the means by which citizens identify individuals to be appointed to specific public offices,[22] and once the appointment is complete, the prohibition against imperative mandates, enshrined in most contemporary constitutions, prevents the establishment of a direct legal relationship between representatives and their constituents. It is therefore the duration of the mandate and the requirement for the representative to seek re-election that make them accountable to the demands of their constituents over the course of their term of office. The regulation of the duration of mandate also ensures that the member of Parliament (MP) or President elected is accountable for their actions to voters in the re-election campaign (ie, citizens, organised groups, party of affiliation).[23] This accountability is to be understood in a full sense, which entails the need to obtain consent and not a mere duty to report.

In this framework, the relationship of political representation has a partial legal nature: it is legal only to the extent that it is built on two legal institutions, namely the election and the temporally determined mandate, that affect its concrete instantiation. Beyond these aspects, the relationship is left to the internal dynamics of the political system. Traditionally, this dual nature of political representation is not considered problematic. The political rather than legal nature of 'representation as a relationship' imparts the relation between voters and elected representatives the flexibility necessary for the representative to consider the various competing interests of their constituents and synthesise these claims into a politically palatable outcome for all. In other words, in the scheme of representative democracy, the representative is not a mere spokesperson for the voters but is rather a subject who is called upon to interpret the various demands that emerge from the political community in order to achieve the general interest to the greatest possible extent. On this view, the prohibition

[21] E-W Böckenförde, 'Democrazia e rappresentanza' [1985] *Quaderni costituzionali* 253 f.

[22] According to Norberto Bobbio, the popular election of representatives is the 'icon' of modern democracy as an essentially representative democracy. See N Bobbio, 'La democrazia dei moderni paragonata a quella degli antichi (e a quella dei posteri)' (1987) 3 *Teoria politica* 3.

[23] On the centrality of mechanisms activating political accountability for the smooth functioning of democratic-representative systems, see L Ornaghi, 'Atrofia di un'idea. Brevi note sull'«inattualità» odierna della rappresentanza politica' (1998) 3 *Rivista di diritto costituzionale* 8, 12 ff.

against imperative mandates frees the representative from responding to specific exhortations by specific voters – this provides considerable justification for the prohibition. Being bound to respond to each individual voter's demand would impose a degree of rigidity on the voter-representative relationship that would render the whole system unworkable. Yet, more could be desired in terms of the actual structuring of political processes. Here, legal reasoning could play a more significant role and lead to the definition of a set of rules and principles capable of directing the processes of the political system that concretely shape the representative relationship.

Political representation is also directly influenced by the electoral system, and the election itself gives rise to a 'representative situation'. Electoral rules play a crucial mediating role. For example, if an election takes place in a highly charged atmosphere due to intense debate on specific issues and a candidate has clear proposals concerning these issues, the candidate's accountability if elected gives rise to a complete political community-representative relationship.[24] But if the electoral choice generally hinges on elements other than political issues, such as, for example, the personal notoriety of the candidate, the representative's behaviour will tend to become irrelevant during re-election and representation itself will be reduced to mere legal situation.

A full consideration of the political process requires an assessment of the role played by political parties, which have significantly influenced the dynamics of representation – so much so as to reverse, in some historical phases, a regime of mediated responsibility according to the deputy-party, party-voter scheme.[25] A party system firmly rooted in the 'social fabric' can accomplish the task of translating all the demands – or, at least, those with a minimum level of diffusion – expressed by the social body into political initiative. However, such a scheme seems feasible only within a sufficiently simple social body organised around a limited number of well-defined cleavages.[26] But in the present-day reality, the capacity of political parties (and politicians) to represent the community strains under the great pressure of fragmentation of contemporary societies and polarisation of political differences and ideologies;[27] at the same time, the

[24] In other words, mere consensus manifested ex post – ie, at the time of re-election – is totally unfulfilling. On the contrary, accountability plays a significant role where, at the time of the first election, a framework of priorities has been defined and agreed upon between the would-be representative and the voters. See G Pasquino, 'La filosofia politica della riforma elettorale' [1990] *Democrazia e diritto* 3, 14 f.

[25] See for instance the theorisation of the party-state (*Parteienstaat*) proposed by G Liebholz, *Strukturprobleme der Modernen Demokratie* (Karlsruhe, Müller, 1958) and Id., *Das Wesen der Repräsentation und der Gestaltwandel der Demokratie im 20. Jahrhundert* (Berlin, De Gruyter, 1960).

[26] In essence, those highlighted by S Rokkan, *Citizens, Elections, Parties* (Oslo, Scandinavian UB, 1970) and arising from the two revolutions, the national and the industrial one: the centre-periphery divide; the church-state divide; the city-country divide; and finally the industrial entrepreneur-working class divide.

[27] Summarised in the felicitous expression of 'liquid modernity' by Z Bauman, *Liquid Modernity* (Cambridge, Polity Press, 2000). However, there has been no lack of more thoughtful approaches in

proliferation of needs and demands addressed to the representative system[28] makes the work of those called upon to address society's political claims increasingly complicated.

In the field of political representation, the individual-centred approach leads to political representation being perceived merely as a positional role for the representative. By contrast, an approach attentive to the actual structure of social dynamics makes it possible to cognise and regulate representation understood in terms of a representative *relationship* rather than a position. In particular, from the point of view of electoral law, this second approach can consider the influence of the electoral system (and the rules that complement it), enabling a more robust assessment of them in properly constitutional legal terms.

V. LEGAL ANALYSIS OF ELECTORAL SYSTEMS: BETWEEN POLITICAL AND METHODOLOGICAL INDIVIDUALISM

A fuller understanding of the argument developed in the preceding sections requires further reflection, including consideration of the insights from other disciplines.

Generally speaking, the individualistic approach outlined in the preceding discussion belongs to the line of thought usually referred to as 'political individualism' and which finds its progenitors in the works of the founders of classical liberalism. This thinking has underpinned the constitutionalist discourse from the outset and, with some differences, characterises its fundamental developments throughout the twentieth century and in more recent times.

When the object of analysis shifts from constitutional texts and the constitutional discourse to the real capacity of legal norms to direct social dynamics and thereby promote social integration, the 'political individualism' approach leads to 'methodological individualism'. The latter maintains that the study of every social phenomenon must be traced back to individual actions.[29] Methodological individualism thus develops from the idea that the elementary unit of social life is individual action and that in order to explain social institutions and changes, it is necessary to demonstrate how they arise as a result of the interactions and actions of individuals.[30]

the literature, such as that offered by W Atkinson, 'Beck, Individualisation and the Death of Class: A Critique' (2007) 58 *British Journal of Sociology* 349.

[28] This is obviously reflected in the expression of votes, disrupting the classic left/right axis in favour of a polycentric preference system. On this topic see the empirical analysis by O Knutsen, 'Cleavage Dimension in Ten West European Countries: A Comparative Empirical Analysis' (1989) 21 *Comparative Political Studies* 495. See also R Rohrschneider, 'Impact of Social Movements on European Party Systems' (1993) 528 *Annals of the American Academy of Political and Social Science* 157.

[29] J Agassi, 'Methodological Individualism' (1960) 11 *The British Journal of Sociology* 244.

[30] J Elster, *The Cement of Society. A Survey of Social Order* (Cambridge, Cambridge University Press, 1989).

From a theoretical perspective, political individualism and methodological individualism are two distinct approaches with no strictly necessary correlation. However, they are linked by obvious associations: both extol the importance of the individual subject, who is placed in a position of axiological (political individualism) or epistemological (methodological individualism) pre-eminence; in this regard, they contribute to the construction of the same type of interpretation of social reality. Consequently, from a practical viewpoint, a disciplinary tradition decisively influenced by political individualism tend to attract individualistic methodological approaches.

This is not the place to address an analysis of methodological individualism in general terms nor to belittle the results that have been achieved in economic and social research by following the said approach.[31] On the contrary, we wish to highlight the partiality of such an approach, which is capable of revealing vital aspects of social interaction, but is not the only viable methodological approach.[32] Rather, the research method must be calibrated to the object of investigation and the specific aims of the research in question.

In particular, where the object of analysis is representative institutions, their functional regularities, and the concrete capacity of the political community to determine the priorities of public power, the capacity of methodological individualism to reveal social reality has been the subject of criticism and reservations.[33] In other words, understanding the institutional phenomena that lead to the creation of social reality seems to require the use of other analytic methods that adequately capture the influence of rules and institutions on the social behaviour of both individuals and mutually interacting social groups.[34] For example, the systemic effects of an electoral system, with its capacity to influence citizens' voting choices and the community's understanding of political dynamics, can hardly be ascribed to a scheme of thought centred on the individual only, their preferences, and their motivation to maximise their own utility. Similarly, scrutinising the transparency and internal consistency of an electoral law by considering almost exclusively the electoral formula on which it is constructed leads to unsatisfying results. In this regard, it might be worth

[31] Moreover, disciplinary traditions that are nowadays particularly influential, such as economics or sociology, largely follows methodological individualism. See for instance L von Mises, *Human action: a Treatise on Economics* (New Haven, CT, Yale University Press, 1949).

[32] A summing up of the criticism of methodological individualism is offered by J Heath, 'Methodological Individualism' in EN Zalta (ed), *The Stanford Encyclopedia of Philosophy* (Stanford, Stanford University Press, 2020). A critique of methodological individualism from the perspective of economics is articulated by M Blaug, *The Methodology of Economics: Or, How Economists Explain* (Cambridge, Cambridge University Press, 1992).

[33] Particularly convincing are the arguments put forward against the individualistic approach by JR Searle, *The Construction of Social Reality* (New York, NY, Simon and Schuster, 1995).

[34] Some suggestions of particular interest come from the sociology of knowledge, which shows that even individual understanding of reality is the result of social interaction. PL Berger and T Luckmann, *The Social Construction of Reality: A Treatise in the Sociology of Knowledge* (New York, NY, Anchor Books, 1966).

adopting a somewhat different perspective and developing an analysis focused on the question concerning political representation that each electoral system poses to the voter as a member of the political community. Again, investigating the ability of electoral rules to promote the accountability of representatives to their represented cohort requires an appreciation of a social dynamic that is irreducible to the subjective position of the individual voter.

In that respect, some active courts in African countries offer interesting solutions. Geyebe's chapter ten concerning a significant sample of African countries highlights how courts have interpreted their engagement with the fundamental right to vote to be crucial but unsatisfactory; thus, they have exploited their institutional role of supervising democratisation to champion voting rights in a broader context. Geyebe is particularly aware of the complexity of electoral matters and, while analysing presidential elections in a number of African countries, considers whether courts have had a role in facilitating democratisation. For Geyebe, some African courts have gone beyond an individual justice approach to act as partners with political institutions in implementing constitutional democracy.

These considerations help to elucidate two distinct phenomena that have been extensively analysed in the individual chapters of this volume, namely, first, the longstanding reluctance of the courts to subject electoral laws to thorough scrutiny and, second, the modest level of satisfaction arising from certain rulings, especially in regimes adopting a proportional electoral system. Further, the challenge of analysing the dynamics governing political representation by adopting an individualistic approach is also reflected in the judiciary's more precise examination of issues related to individual rights.

VI. INSIGHTS FROM COMPARATIVE LAW

A. Electoral Law and Courts in Majoritarian Systems

In the preceding sections we have presented an interpretative approach that may prove useful in assessing the comparative landscape discussed in the various chapters collected in this volume. The next step in developing the approach involves testing the actual explanatory potential of it and determining whether it can effectively provide a coherent framework in which to situate the legal systems under consideration. Additionally, we aim to determine whether this approach can elucidate some of the evolutionary dynamics extracted from the case law of the analysed countries.

The first area in which the interpretative approach proves to be of practical use is in examining electoral systems of a genuinely majoritarian character – whether plurality or majority – structured around uninominal constituencies. In such systems, the electoral formula is not subject to significant scrutiny by the courts: once the truly selective character of the formula is accepted, as highlighted by Pasquino in chapter two, its relative simplicity leaves little room for dispute. However, it is precisely the selective character of the electoral formula that magnifies the problem of definition of individual constituencies, which then can become the target of meaningful judicial attention.

In a majoritarian context, two aspects of the carve-out of individual constituencies may be subject to scrutiny: on the one hand, their size in numerical terms (the number of voters registered in each of them or the population residing in the relevant territory); on the other hand, the more general organisation of the constituency in territorial, demographic and socioeconomic terms.

The case law analysed in the various contributions on countries with majoritarian electoral systems reveals courts giving a significant level of attention to the size of constituencies. Leading the way on this issue was the Warren Court in the first half of the 1960s, which based its jurisprudence on both Article 1 and the Fourteenth Amendment of the US Constitution to enforce the principle of 'one person, one value, one vote'. The principle that districts must be roughly equal in electors (or in population) has also been affirmed by the French Constitutional Council and the Japanese Supreme Court. In all cases, this is not a demand for perfect equality, but rather, districts must have roughly the same number of electors (or, where appropriate, resident population), with a margin of flexibility that fluctuates depending on context; the rule may be further tempered to account for the division of territory into subfederal or substate entities.

The ability of courts to examine the numerical size of constituencies aligns seamlessly with the interpretative approach described in the preceding sections and is strongly connected to the fundamental right to vote, which would be violated if the equal opportunity for each person's vote to influence the electoral process were not guaranteed.

Conversely, the 'one person, one vote' principle does not find significant protection in those legal systems where the right to vote is weakly safeguarded by the courts. Weak protection may be attributable to several factors, such as an emphasis on parliament's authority over the electoral process – as in the case of the UK. It may also result from the absence of specific constitutional provisions concerning the right to vote or the presence of a hesitant judiciary that struggles to articulate effective doctrines to safeguard such a right, as has been the case in India.

The Australian experience is paradigmatic of the 'one person, one vote' problem: the High Court has never gone so far as to review the division of constituencies established by the political decision-makers based on such principle. However, as highlighted in Arban and Murphy's chapter seventeen, in the new millennium, the Australian courts have begun to increasingly emphasise the right to vote, as evidenced by their review of laws that restrict the franchise of criminal prisoners. Therefore, it can be argued that the difficult emergence of a constitutionally protected right to vote in the Australian context still influences the judiciary's deferential attitude toward apportionments that violate the principle of 'one person, one vote'. Relatively recent judgments in 2007 and 2010 also appear to be harbingers of significant developments in the wake of the US experience.

Canada appears to be on a similar trajectory when compared to Australia. The right to vote was affirmed by the Canadian Charter or Rights and Freedoms, adopted in the context of the Patriation in 1982. At the time, some Supreme Court rulings on the legitimacy of limitations on the right to vote for special categories of subjects, namely prisoners, provoked a strong debate. Should the development of Canadian jurisprudence led to enhanced protection of the right to vote, it is likely that this development would affect judicial scrutiny of apportionment.

Anther problematic aspect of the division of a state into constituencies is the articulation of the constituency in territorial, demographic, and socioeconomic terms. The inclusion of a voter in either constituency X or constituency Y appears to be a matter that is highly difficult to review with exclusive consideration of the right to vote or the individual's expectation of competing on an equal footing with others in the electoral process. In a majoritarian system, the citizen is guaranteed equal participation in the electoral process but certainly not the actual election of the candidate for which they voted. Hence the difficulty of assessing in legal terms – and also in moral terms, as Voyiakis convincingly argues – the practice of carving up constituencies to favour the election of candidates of a certain party or to dilute the impact of the vote of minority social groups.

Constituency carve-outs on a territorial, demographic, or socioeconomic basis contradict the requirement of equal numerical consistency and, as a consequence, detrimentally affect the full protection of the right to vote, as understood in individualistic terms. Proof of this is evident in the rule that division into constituencies must respect the articulation of the federal territory, as enshrined in Article 1 of the US Constitution, or of the state, as averred by the French Constitutional Council: this can cause significant fluctuations in the size of constituencies.

To appreciate the problem, consider the historical origin of the English majority electoral system, which developed from the conflicts between Henry III and Simon de Montfort. In this period, the practice of summoning representatives of the counties, boroughs, and towns, in the number of two for each, was established; this modus operandi was then stabilised starting with the Modern Parliament, resulting in the definition of the institutional structure that still characterises the country's political system. It was only during the nineteenth century that the English Parliament enacted a series of reforms aimed at rationalising the electoral system of the House of Commons and purging it of certain now anachronistic legacies, such as the Rotten Boroughs.[35] It was during this

[35] See EP Hennock and DC Moore, 'The Sociological Premises of the First Reform Act: A Critical Note' (1971) 14 *Victorian Studies* 321, 327 ff.

period that the original structure of the electoral system, exclusively centred on the territorial units that make up the country, gave way to a progressive redefinition of the constituencies in order to give representation to the nation as a unitary entity on the basis of constituencies made up of a more or less equal number of citizens.

The historical origins of the English electoral system reveal how the representative principle, which classically characterises it, is based on internally homogeneous constituencies, where party divisions are compensated for by common belonging to a sufficiently homogeneous territory. Hence, one party's MP can be elected and can be said to represent the entire constituency. In the contemporary context, the homogeneity of the constituency has become somewhat less significant, and the majoritarian electoral system is legitimised on the basis of the effects the electoral formula has on the political system and the certainty it confers on the electoral process. However, this does not detract from the fact that even today there is a need for a minimum level of internal homogeneity within each constituency, which is also the case outside the UK. This need is expressed primarily in the demand for territorial continuity, which in some legal systems is also asserted by the courts. Further, at least on a theoretical level, the distribution of constituencies must conform to rational population division criteria that respect the internal articulation of the political community.

Very rarely have courts been able to enforce the mandate for a rational distribution of constituencies. The difficulty has been tracing this line of argument to rights protected by the Constitution, rendering judicial review of crucial elements of electoral legislation almost entirely impracticable. The only notable exception is the jurisprudence developed by the US Supreme Court concerning racial gerrymandering and the promotion of minorities in the democratic political arena. However, this jurisprudence was made possible by the particular activism of the legislature in this area, which led to the adoption of the Voting Rights Act in 1965 and the 1982 Amendment thereof, and, in certain periods, of the courts themselves.[36] In other words, in this area, the Supreme Court played a role in rationalising the principles already established by the legislature and enforcing the need to create majority-minority constituencies designed to promote the election of minority members; in doing so, the Court's actions accorded with the fundamental need for homogeneity of constituencies discussed earlier.[37] When, in more recent times, the Court has instead wished to challenge the principles enunciated by the federal legislature,[38] it has returned to

[36] The reform of s 2 of the Voting Rights Act adopted in 1982 aims to prohibit not only intentionally discriminatory practices, but all those whose effects may result in undue restriction of the right to vote on racial grounds, in order to inhibit the dilution of racial minorities in different constituencies with the effect of preventing them from electing their representatives. See JF Blumstein, 'Defining and Proving Race Discrimination: Perspectives on the Purpose vs. Results Approach from the Voting Rights Act' (1983) 69 *Virginia Law Review* 633.

[37] *Thornburg v Gingles*, 478 U.S. 30 (1986).

[38] *Shelby County v Holder*, 570 U.S. 2 (2013).

the uncritical – or, rather, ideologically oriented – assertion of individual legal positions, to the obvious detriment of the electoral system's ability to promote the smooth functioning of the political-democratic process.

B. Electoral Law and Courts in (Predominantly) Proportional Systems

The interpretative key proposed in the chapter is also helpful in critically analysing the constitutional case law of countries with electoral systems of a predominantly proportional nature. The adverb *predominantly* is used in light of the fact that the two systems in which the most significant rulings have been made are not genuinely proportional in nature. The electoral system for the German *Bundestag* is centred on a proportional logic, which coexists with the election of 299 MPs within uninominal constituencies on a first-past-the-post basis. The operating logic of the system, which has recently been revised, remains proportional in that the remaining seats are allocated to the various parties in such a manner that the total number of seats to which each of them is entitled, including those won in single-member constituencies, is proportional. The Italian electoral system established by Law No 270 of 2005 and partially declared unconstitutional by the Constitutional Court in 2014 (ruling no. 1/2014), was instead centred on a proportional electoral formula with a majority bonus: the candidates or coalition of parties who won the elections were the recipient – either by their own strength, on the basis of the proportional distribution, or thanks to the majority prize – of 340 seats, equal to 54 per cent of the total number of seats in the Chamber of Deputies (a system animated by a similar logic was provided for the Senate). Subsequently, a new electoral system still centred on proportional representation with a majority bonus and some adjustments aimed at incorporating the Constitutional Court's criticisms of the previous system was again censured (ruling no. 35/2017), at which point the legislature finally opted for a different electoral formula.

Before devoting a few thoughts to case law in electoral matters, we believe it is useful to emphasise that a significant proportion of the countries with a predominantly proportional electoral system are either recently democratised, such as some states that once belonged to the Soviet bloc, or have experienced authoritarian interludes, at the end of which they adopted a new constitution. In all cases, these are legal systems in which the Constitution contains fairly detailed provisions on electoral matters, with explicit regulation of the right to vote and the division of territory into subnational constituencies. This latter aspect, together with the lesser importance of apportionment in proportional systems, explains why the division of territory into constituencies has not given rise to any particular controversy. On the contrary, in these countries, the courts scrutinise the mechanism for translating votes into seats.

As far as case law is concerned, a first type of experience is that of countries where the Constitution clearly mandates a proportional electoral system. Courts have intervened where the legislature designed electoral systems that clearly violated the Constitution. This was the case in the Czech Republic, as analysed by Sawicki, where the convergence of small constituencies, the d'Hondt formula, and a system of excessively high thresholds led the Constitutional Court to intervene and require the thresholds to be lowered. That, in this case, it was the constitutional framers themselves who made the fundamental decision favouring proportional representation put the constitutional judge in the position of simply having to check whether the corrections made by the legislature to the proportional character of the system were reasonable and justified; the court system could also forgo developing complex reasoning regarding the role played by the electoral system in shaping the representative relationship binding the elected assemblies to the political community.

The situation is different for countries where the Constitution does not clearly indicate a mandate or preference for a majority or proportional electoral system. In such a case, judicial activism can play a significant role. This is the case in Germany and, more recently, in Italy.

In the case of Germany, as Delledonne and Michel exhaustively discuss, the jurisprudence of the *Bundesverfassungsgericht* has undergone a particularly interesting development, from the first pronouncements on electoral matters, which were marked by a deferential attitude toward the decisions of the legislature, to those of the last 15 years, which have significantly affected the rules for the election of the *Bundestag* and of German representatives to the European Parliament.

The first significant ruling was adopted in 2008 and concerned the negative voting effect, which can occur when a party has won a significantly higher number of direct mandates in a district than the share of seats to which it would be entitled according to proportional distribution. An example may help to clarify the point. Let us imagine that party X has won all 15 direct mandates in Rheinland-Pfalz, but on the basis of the overall proportional distribution in the district in question, it is only entitled to 14. According to the law under scrutiny, the party is nevertheless allocated the 15 seats it won in the uninominal constituencies. In this context, an extra vote received in Rheinland-Pfalz might not affect the overall allocation at the national level, but it might affect the distribution of seats to which the party is entitled among the different *Länder* – for example, the extra vote might result in the loss of one seat allocated in Niedersachsen and the equal increase of those allocated in Rheinland-Pfalz (from 14 to 15). The consequence would be the loss of one seat for the party X: due to the direct mandates already allocated, the total number of seats won in Rheinland-Pfalz would remain effectively unchanged, and the extra vote would only have the effect of decreasing the seats won in Niedersachsen.

The negative voting effect is certainly a defect of the system or, to be more precise, a perverse effect of the intertwining of the election results in the two aspects of the German electoral system. In 2009, the *Bundesverfassungsgericht* scrutinised this effect on the basis of voting rights and declared it unconstitutional, giving the *Bundestag* a reasonable period of time to remedy it. However, the solution adopted did not solve the problem. Hence, in 2012, the Constitutional Court intervened again. This led to a new revision of the electoral system, which provided for an increase in the overall size of the *Bundestag* in order to ensure that the distribution of seats would be strictly proportional, with the only exception being the operation of the threshold. In this way, the possible broad affirmation of a party in single-member constituencies is compensated for by the creation of a number of additional mandates over and above the basic size of the lower house, so that direct mandates never exceed the party's share of seats on a proportional basis.

The consequence of this is a marked increase in the number of seats in the *Bundestag*, which reached 709 for the legislative session that began in 2017 and 736 in the following. So, a new electoral reform reversed the logic just explained and provided for the revocation of direct mandates exceeding the quota of seats to which a party is entitled on the basis of proportional distribution, starting with the one in which the candidate of the party won with the worst percentage of votes.

This development highlights a fundamental inconsistency in the *Bundesverfassungsgericht*'s decisions. The prioritisation of the individual right to vote has eroded the delicate balance that underlies the electoral system since the second half of the twentieth century. This balance involves combining the proportional distribution of seats with a significant proportion, approximately 50 per cent, of MPs elected through single-member constituencies. This arrangement aims to promote the territorial rootedness of elected representatives and ensure a close relationship with the political community.[39] This is a systemic aim that is particularly laudable from the point of view of the functionality of the democratic process. However, the focus on the individual's expectations ended up taking precedence, despite the relative marginality of the negative voting effect and that it was to the detriment of political formations that were already recipients of additional mandates over and above those to which they would be entitled on the basis of proportional distribution. The solutions adopted by the legislature to conform to the Constitutional Court's decisions led to an overall reduction in the weight of direct mandates because of the considerable increase in the number of MPs elected on the basis of list voting as well as the revocation, easily criticised from the point of view of respect for the will of the electorate, of direct mandates in excess of the proportional distribution of seats.

A robust debate has also been prompted by the rulings delivered between 2014 and 2016 by the Italian Constitutional Court. There is no need to retrace now the entire reasoning developed by the Court in the two rulings, as they were

[39] See R Taagepera and MS Shugart, 'Designing Electoral System' (1989) 8 *Electoral Studies* 49, 55 ff.

already highlighted in detail by Passaglia. What matters is the main argument of the Court, which mirrors the approach taken by the *Bundesverfassungsgericht*.

In essence, the reasoning developed in the 2014 judgment starts from the premise of protecting the right to vote and one of its corollaries, traditionally affirmed by Italian doctrine and the Constitutional Court's case law, namely the equal possibility of each voter to contribute to the formation of representative assemblies. Where the electoral law demands proportionality, the Court asserted, the equality of the vote is not limited merely to the theoretical possibility of equality; on the contrary, a proportional electoral system inspires in the voter the expectation that their vote *will* have a concrete effect on the electoral process equivalent to that of the vote of other citizens. Consequently, the legislature may not dictate rules that entail an excessive level of disproportionality. On this basis, only limited majority bonuses are permissible, specifically, bonuses that are sufficiently small and strictly aimed at ensuring government stability. By contrast, the bonus provided for by Law 270 of 2005 is awarded to the party, or coalition of parties, that has taken the most votes, without a minimum threshold being indicated to enjoy the benefit and with the possibility of a significant gap existing between the percentage of votes and the percentage of seats.

The Italian Constitutional Court's decision on the unconstitutionality of Law 270 of 2005 is to be welcomed. However, some of the reasoning on which this decision was based is not particularly compelling. First, a voter's expectation does not appear persuasive, as the electoral system is not purely proportional but is characterised by the bonus mechanism, which plays a major role in the law's design. The existence of the majority bonus is not only well known to the general pool of voters but has clearly affected electoral campaigns and the expectations of the political community. Yet, the idea of the equality of votes being interpreted in completely different ways depending on the electoral system adopted seems problematic. What made the 2005 electoral law constitutionally dubious concerned other aspects, starting with the absolute artificiality of the majority bonus mechanism, capable of rewarding completely heterogeneous coalitions, sometimes resulting from a mere mutual declaration by the party secretariats. At the same time, there was no mechanism to make clear to voters the actual boundaries of the several coalitions, nor the possibility of directing the vote in their favour. In other words, the electoral system required citizens to vote for a party and then treated the vote as if it had been cast in favour of a coalition, even resulting in large transfers of votes between the parties that comprised it. This made parliamentary majorities the result of alchemy and agreements between parties, without voters exercising meaningful input. Consequently, the 2005 electoral system also was deemed to lack transparency, with the bonus mechanism cited as problematic.[40]

[40] For a broader examination of the features of the 2005 electoral system see E Mostacci 'Il proporzionale con premio di maggioranza tra omissioni costituzionali e disfunzioni della rappresentanza politica' (2014) 59 *Giurisprudenza costituzionale* 4867, 4876 ff.

These considerations could have usefully served as the basis for the 2014 decision and to guide the legislature in its reform of the electoral system. However, an approach that focused on individual legal situations and paid little attention to political processes led the Constitutional Court to focus its reasoning on different and, in part, less convincing arguments.

In other experiences where the path toward democratisation has developed in complex socioeconomic conditions, courts have been tasked with supervising electoral legislation and safeguarding electoral processes more broadly. In such cases, the electoral formula is but one concern among many. Spigno, in chapter eleven, explains the role of courts in Mexico, where electoral litigation had become the means to challenge the inconsistent proliferation of electoral reforms, incomplete or contradictory regulations at the state level, and even the lack of meaningful political confrontation in the adoption of electoral legislation. Muniz da Conceição offers a similar constitutional story when he describes how Brazilian courts have played a transformative role in reshaping an electoral system characterised by heavy political manoeuvring and endemic fraud.

VII. CONCLUDING REMARKS

At the end of this journey through case law, we can state with a high degree of certainty that the evolution of case law in electoral matters over the last few decades has been positive overall, considering the very careful role courts are called on to play in this politically fraught field, and has resulted in significant innovations in many countries. At the same time, we must emphasise that in no small number of cases the court judgments appear unsatisfactory, sometimes at the level of the decision itself or, more often, because of the reasoning developed by the judges.

The interpretative approach we have proposed in this concluding chapter is far from providing an explanatory framework capable of accounting for the evolution of all countries or of fully grasping the limits revealed in the work of the courts. However, it has helped highlight a problem common to courts, a problem which is the cause of some of the weaker court decisions. The exclusive focus on individual legal positions, which has yielded promising outcomes in other areas of constitutional law,[41] has proven to be a limitation in electoral matters as well as a safety net for judges not willing to enter into the technicalities of electoral systems or remaining reluctant to interfere with political processes. The political process should enable representative institutions to channel the voice of the political community. Political representation does not

[41] From a diametrically opposed perspective, Isaiah Berlin distinguished between the negative conception of freedom (as protection from undue interference from political power) and the idea of positive freedom, in which individuals claim protection from the state. See I Berlin, 'Two Concepts of Liberty' in *Four Essays On Liberty* (Oxford, Oxford University Press, 1969) 118 ff.

end at the electoral moment when citizens choose their representatives and the political formula that will support the future government. On the contrary, the political process is validated to the extent that it ensures that individual members of parliament and, in general, representative institutions are responsive to the needs and demands of the political community, offering them a synthesis capable of effectively orienting the country's fundamental choices.

In analysing the capacity of electoral rules to contribute to this fundamental objective, focusing on the right to vote is not enough. From this perspective, comparative law is instructive insofar as it can promote the circulation between different legal systems of solutions and doctrines that have proved their worth.[42] In the case of electoral law, this means investing reasoning with a pragmatic attitude and opening up the legal discourse to contributions from other fields of knowledge. In this way, it is possible to acquire an awareness of social dynamics that is sufficiently grounded to guide the understanding of complex and articulated phenomena such as electoral processes.

This is an arduous task, which points to the difficulty of balancing law, courts and representative institutions. The latter bear the primary responsibility for the design and enforcement of electoral law, in both long-standing democracies as well as consolidating and emerging democracies, as Gebeye (chapter ten), Spigno (chapter eleven) and Muniz da Conceiçao (chapter twelve) adeptly emphasise in their respective chapters. The stability and effectiveness of democracies, particularly in the present stage of constitutional retrenchment, are precious assets, the preservation of which will, in the future, repay the effort that has been made.

[42] With this regard, see the valuable activity carried out by the Venice Commission in this field, with its opinions and with the Code of good practice in electoral matters, CDL-AD (2002) 23, Strasbourg, 30 October 2002.

Index

References to figures and tables are indicated by an italic *f* and *t* after the page number.

www.ingramcontent.com/pod-product-compliance
Ingram Content Group UK Ltd.
Pitfield, Milton Keynes, MK11 3LW, UK
UKHW020232290926
15470UKWH00002B/503

9 781509 957880